HOW TO CLIMB™ SERIES

Training for Climbing

The Definitive Guide to Improving Your Performance

Second Edition

Eric J. Hörst

FALCONGUIDES ®

GUILFORD, CONNECTICUT
HELENA, MONTANA
AN IMPRINT OF THE GLOBE PEQUOT PRESS

FALCONGUIDES®

All interior photos are by the author unless otherwise noted.
Exercise photos depicting the author are by Lisa Ann Hörst.
Text design: Casey Shain
Chart design: Mary Ballachino
Illustrations: Judy Newhouse unless otherwise noted

Library of Congress Cataloging-in-Publication Data
Hörst, Eric J.
    Training for climbing : the definitive guide to improving your performance / Eric Horst.—2nd ed.
        p. cm. — (A Falcon guide)
        ISBN: 978-0-7627-4692-7
        1. Rock climbing—Training. I. Title.
    GV200.2.H685 2008
    796.522'3—dc22   2008006490

Printed in China
10 9 8 7 6 5 4 3 2 1

Praise for *Training for Climbing*

"*Training for Climbing* is a great resource. Whether you're just starting out or already ticking 5.13, you'll find valuable information here to help you climb harder. This is the most complete and up-to-date training guide available. Better yet, it's presented in a clean and easily understandable format, with inspiring and illustrative photos."

—*Rock and Ice* magazine

"Eric Hörst has taken complex scientific training concepts and integrated these with contemporary research on climbing to produce a very readable and useful training guide. This book will lead the climber to new heights of performance."

—Phillip B. Watts, PhD, exercise physiologist
and climbing researcher, Northern Michigan University

"Hörst is uniquely positioned to bring current methods in sports psychology and exercise science to the world of climbing, and he has hit the mark in superb style! If you are passionate about climbing and getting better, *Training for Climbing* will become your dog-eared companion!"

—Richard K. Fleming, PhD, assistant professor
of psychology, University of Massachusetts Medical School

"With comprehensive textbook-like descriptions of nutrition, recovery, weight training, and structured workouts, *Training for Climbing* is a crucial addition to your climbing library. Use this book to make 5.13 a reality instead of just a dream."

—Michelle Hurni, author of *Coaching Climbing*

Reader Reviews from Around the World

"I want to tell you that *Training for Climbing* is clearly the best and most comprehensive book on climbing training methodology I have ever read. In particular, the chapters on mental training and skills/strategy training have inspired me and given me extremely valuable insights for my future workouts. Thanks for such a great work!"

—Guido (Switzerland)

"I have just read your book *Training for Climbing*, and I think it is great!"

—Sven (Croatia)

"Eric, just wanted to say thanks for writing *Training for Climbing*. Since I started reading it and training, I have improved tremendously. I am having a great time doing the strength-training exercises and just enjoying the process of climbing with a different mentality."

—Carlos (California)

"Thank you, Mr. Hörst, for helping me achieve my first 5.12a just a few days ago!"

—Hiroyasu (Japan)

"Hi Eric, I've just finished reading *Training for Climbing*—great work! Over the last 14 years I have studied climbing and to date your book is by far the most accessible to average climbers."

—Paul (Australia)

"I read a quote from your training book and consequently bought it. This book has changed my whole attitude in climbing and life due to your mental training chapter. Just wanted to say thank you!"

—Scott (Pennsylvania)

"Thanks for your great books, Eric. I have read them all—they are the best!"

—Ofer (Israel)

"What a great book! Your HIT workout definitely gave me much more strength. Thank you very much for your great work, Eric!"

—Andre (California)

"Hi Eric, I read your book *Training for Climbing*. I think it is the best book in the field."

—Roberto (Ecuador)

To two of the strongest, most innovative
and humble men ever to pull down
on rock: the *"Master of Rock"* John Gill
and the late, great Wolfgang Güllich.

*The author on **Welcome to Conditioning** (5.12d/5.13a), New River Gorge, West Virginia.*
ERIC McCALLISTER

CONTENTS

Speed climbing on the classic East Buttress of El Capitan, Yosemite, California
ERIC J. McCALLISTER

ACKNOWLEDGMENTS

Writing a book is an Everest-like undertaking. It is a team effort that takes many months or years to plan and execute, but getting to the summit still takes an immense individual effort and an indomitably singular focus.

Having completed this climb, I reflect on all that has brought me to this point—the thousands of wonderful days I've spent on the rock, the countless climbers from around the world I've had the pleasure to meet, and the dozens of partners I am grateful to have shared a rope with. Learning to climb is a long, continuous process with no end, and I thank all the people who have influenced me from my days as a wide-eyed teenage rock jock to a forty-something veteran climber. I must thank directly John Gill, the late Wolfgang Güllich, Lynn Hill, John Long, Jim McCarthy, Pat Ament, Richard Goldstone, John Bachar, Mark Robinson, the late and legendary Todd Skinner, and Tony Yaniro—all of you, knowingly or unknowingly, have inspired me and contributed to this book in some way.

Though I continue to view myself as a student of rock climbing, I enjoy more every year the role of teacher. I am humbled by all the letters and e-mails received from climbers in more than fifty countries who have read my books and articles. I appreciate all the feedback, the suggestions, and, most of all, the success stories of those who have benefited from my works. Writing climbing books is certainly not a lucrative endeavor; still, knowing that I've helped thousands of people from around the world climb better is priceless.

Creating this second edition turned out to be another massive undertaking as I tried to integrate the generous feedback and suggestions of countless climbers from around the world who read the first edition. Furthermore, I sequestered myself for days at a time to uncover and digest the latest research in sports science, nutrition, and sports medicine. And what would I do without input of my PhD'd friends Rick Fleming, Richard Schmidt, Jim Sullivan, and Phil Watts? Thanks for sharing your unique insights and knowledge!

I'd like to extend a sincere thank you to Scott Adams, John Burbidge, Jeff Serena, Shelley Wolf, Jan Cronan, Casey Shain and everyone at Falcon Press and Globe Pequot who helped bring this book to fruition. I am also very appreciative of all the climbing companies that support me and my many projects, including Nicros, La Sportiva, Verve, and Sterling. Many thanks to my close friends Eric McCallister and Jim Sullivan, my wife, Lisa Ann, and my family for their support and tolerance given my obsessive tendencies toward work and climbing. I am most grateful for the input and participation of Matt Bosley, Kyle Hörst, Charlotte Jouett, Crystal Norman, Jessica Rohm, Lorin Teres, and the gyms Earth Treks and MetroRock. Mega kudos to Thomas Ballenberger, Phil Bard, Danno Brayack, Stewart Green, Gerd Heidorn, Keith Ladzinski, Eric McCallister, Tyler Stableford, and Rich Wheater, whose photography is featured throughout the book. And I must thank my sons, Cameron and Jonathan, for joining me in my training and climbing and for teaching *me* so much—I love you both more than you can imagine.

Finally, I am sincerely thankful for my original climbing partner and real-life hero, Jeff Batzer. Despite losing five fingers and half a leg, you still possess—and show by example—the power of climbing. Jeff, you are a true inspiration—thanks, man!

INTRODUCTION

Twenty years from now you will be more disappointed by the things that you didn't do than by the ones you did do. So throw off the bowlines. Sail away from the safe harbor. Catch the trade winds in your sails. Explore. Dream. Discover.

—Mark Twain

Training for Climbing is a unique synthesis of thirty-plus years of studying, imagining, and experimenting with ways to increase climbing performance. Building on the foundation laid out in my first two books, *Flash Training* and *How to Climb 5.12*, the dozens of magazine and Internet articles that I've authored, and the first edition of *Training for Climbing*, this second edition of *TFC* establishes a new benchmark for cutting-edge, comprehensive, expert instruction on the subject of elevating climbing performance.

Training for Climbing blends leading-edge sports science, powerful practice and training techniques used by Olympic athletes (but unknown to many climbers), and potent mental-training and success strategies into a single text that will help you climb better regardless of your present ability. By faithfully applying just 50 percent of the methods contained herein, you will surely grow to outperform the mass of climbers. And if you integrate most of the material into your training, climbing, and daily ways of living, you may very well progress to levels beyond your current comprehension!

Training for Climbing is as much about developing new ways of thinking as it is about engaging in new ways of training. A common thread that weaves throughout this book is that "intelligence in climbing is not measured by IQ, but instead by the quality of your thoughts and actions." The thoughts you carry and the things you do (or don't do) are ultimately what separate you from the mass of climbers. Whether you flash or fall, become superstrong or get injured, or feel happy or frustrated, springs forth from subtle differences in the ways you think, feel, and act compared with other climbers. Therefore, the primary goal of this book is to help guide you to more deliberate and effective ways of thinking and acting in your pursuit of peak climbing performance.

Since climbing is all about an intimate dance between you and the rock, it's vital to recognize that your climbing performance evolves from the inside out, and that you only trip and fall when you blow a move. Goethe wrote, "Nature understands no jesting; she is always true, always serious, always severe; she is always right, and the errors and faults are always those of man. The man incapable of appreciating her, she despises; and only to the apt, the pure, and the true, does she resign herself and reveal her secrets." From this perspective it becomes obvious that we must always look inside ourselves to see what's holding us back. Looking outward for the reason or to place blame is a loser's game.

This book begins with a logical progression of self-analysis, goal setting, mental training, and technique training before you ever lift a weight. Chapters 1 through 4 are focused on helping you learn, most quickly, the vital mental and technical skills that separate the best from the rest in this sport. After a brief review of the history of training for climbing, you'll get started on the road to better climbing by taking a self-evaluation test that will reveal your true strengths and weaknesses as a climber. Armed with this information, you can apply more effectively the material that follows on the subjects of training your mind and developing better climbing technique and strategy.

Chapters 5 through 8 present the most in-depth look at strength training for climbing ever published. As an intensely practical person with a background in math and science, I have always felt it important to delve into the theory and application of cutting-edge sports science. Transferring this technology to training for climbing is vital to unlocking the most effective training methods and strategies. As you read these chapters, I trust you will gain new insight into the physiology of climbing performance and thus become a more physiologically effective student of training for climbing.

The concluding chapters 9 through 11 cover the often overlooked (or ignored) subjects of performance nutrition, recovery, and proper treatment and prevention of climbing injuries. Becoming a complete climber requires that you embrace these subjects with the same fervor as you would in executing your training program or plotting your next climb. Throughout the text, I have footnoted the relevant scientific literature so you can peruse the nitty-gritty details if you are so impassioned. These references and other useful information can be found in the back of the book.

To glean the greatest benefit from *Training for Climbing*, you are encouraged to employ active reading techniques such as underlining key passages, putting a star next to the most meaningful strategies, and taking notes for later review. Try lifting the most powerful phrases and posting them in places where you will see them throughout the day. Review these highlighted passages and your notes at least once a week, then reread the entire book in three months and, again, in one year. Not only will this reinforce your understanding and mastery of the concepts, but you also will gain new insight and distinctions as you become a different person at each read-through.

As you cast off into the depths of this book, I want to wish you success and happiness climbing through this world of wonder. Though we may never meet, we are connected through our shared passion for climbing. I am grateful for you taking the time to read this book, and I hope you find the material entertaining and immensely beneficial. I welcome your feedback, and look forward to hearing from you after some grand success that undoubtedly awaits you. Here's wishing you many safe and wonderful days on the rock!

Technique Photos: A User's Guide

Climbing is a vertical dance requiring precise hand and foot "steps," body positions, and movement. Unfortunately, this dance is sometimes difficult to illustrate on the static pages of a book. In *Training for Climbing* I've adopted, from college biomechanics texts, a method of labeling instructional photos with words and symbols that depict the application of force on hand- and footholds. I hope these enhanced photos will underscore the importance of body awareness and help you learn proper technique. Here are the three classes of symbols to look for:

1. Center of Gravity and Line of Gravity

The earth's gravitational pull is most concentrated at your center of gravity—the theoretical point at which gravity's pull acts on you. Standing with your arms by your sides, the center of gravity for males is about an inch above the navel, while for females it averages an inch or two below the navel. (The changing arm and leg positions of a climber in motion, however, can cause the center of gravity to shift side to side and up and down.) Center of gravity is designated here by a bullet or circle, and the earth's gravitational pull, or line of gravity, is indicated by a dashed line and arrow pointing downward.

2. Force Vectors

When you climb, you ascend by contracting your muscles to generate force—a push or pull—that is applied to the rock via the hand and foot points of contact. The direction and amount of force applied at a point of contact is called a force vector. Force vectors are represented in this book diagrammatically by arrows. Each arrow's head depicts the direction you should apply force, while the size of the arrow is scaled to the amount of force—a larger arrow means more force, a smaller one less. You'll find small, medium, and large arrows here.

3. Finesse and Dynamic Moves

Of course the purpose of climbing is to go *up*. Still, sometimes the most efficient way to do that is by twisting—or flagging, deadpointing, lunging, or other angular and dynamic movements. Such finesse movements are illustrated with a dotted line and an arrow.

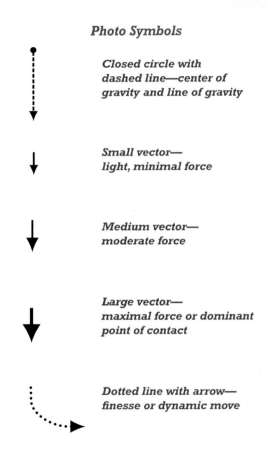

Photo Symbols

Closed circle with dashed line—center of gravity and line of gravity

Small vector—light, minimal force

Medium vector—moderate force

Large vector—maximal force or dominant point of contact

Dotted line with arrow—finesse or dynamic move

Photo Key

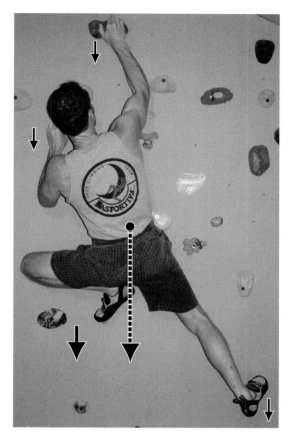

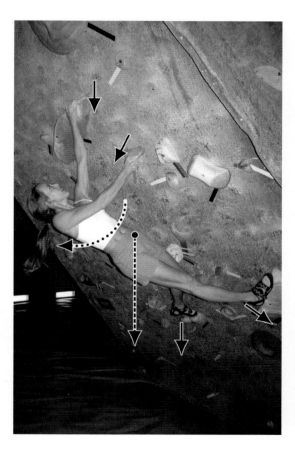

The symbols applied to this photo indicate that the climber uses both of his hands—as well as his right foot—to apply minimal force (note the small arrows, or vectors) to the hold. Meanwhile his left foot carries the bulk of his weight, applying maximal force (indicated by the large arrow, or vector). This positioning is achieved by shifting the center of gravity near—or better yet, over—the left foot.

This climber is using her hands and feet to apply nearly equal force (note the medium vectors). She twists her body (a movement represented by a dotted line) to position her left hip and center of gravity close to the overhanging wall. This shifts the line of gravity closer to her feet, putting more of her body weight onto her feet.

An Overview of Training for Climbing

A man's reach should exceed his grasp or what's a heaven for?

—*Robert Browning*

Many words can describe the wonderful activity of rock climbing—*elegant, powerful, rewarding,* and, sometimes, *frustrating.* While there may be nothing more natural and intuitive than climbing (just watch how children climb around on everything in sight!), rock climbing is indeed a complex activity with demands unique from those of living and playing in the everyday, horizontal world.

Performing in the vertical plane requires physical capabilities such as strength, power, and endurance. It also demands the development of technical skills such as balance and economic movement while gripping and stepping in an infinite variety of ways, positions, and angles. Most important, the inherent stress of climbing away from the safety of the ground requires acute control of your thoughts, focus, anxiety, and fears. In aggregate, the above factors dovetail into what may be one of the more complex sporting activities on this third rock from the sun.

The goal of this book is to explore all the topics relevant to increasing the effectiveness of your training and the quality of your climbing. As a climber of more than thirty years (who's been fortunate enough to meet and climb with many brilliant individuals), I feel the journey should begin with a

Sarah Marvez on **My 15 Minutes,**
Hueco Tanks, Texas KEITH LADZINSKI

primer on the history of training for rock climbing. Clearly, the advancements we make today are possible only because we are standing on the shoulders of the giants who preceded us. Next, we'll explore the interesting subject of genetics and the possible genetic limitations to climbing performance. This leads us into an overview of training for climbing and the things you should consider in your quest for the biggest gains in performance in the shortest possible time.

Training for Climbing: A Brief History

Compared with many other sports, the science of performance rock climbing is still quite young. Well over a hundred years of literature exists on technical aspects of the golf swing, and Olympic sports have been the subject of performance analysis for centuries. Far removed from the mainstream of organized sports and an almost countercultural pursuit just a generation ago, rock climbing was completely off the map in the emergence of sports sciences. What little information did exist on the technical aspects of climbing was mainly passed on by word of mouth in the form of tips on technique and equipment.

Nevertheless, some climbers used basic gymnastics, weight training, elementary bouldering, and buildering to either emulate actual climbing moves or gain the strength to perform at higher levels of the sport. Oscar Eckenstein, a Brit of Teutonic heritage and possibly the first documented boulderer, climbed ropes in the gym, did one-arm pull-ups, and pushed himself on small rocks during the 1890s; George Leigh Mallory was a high-bar enthusiast and one of the first to do giant swings; E. A. Baker in *Moors,*

John Gill's amazing one-arm front lever. Don't try this at home! JOHN GILL COLLECTION

Caves, and Crags (1903) tells of a colleague who "ascends the outside of an iron staircase on his fingers . . . and crosses in a sitting posture the tie-bars of a lofty roof"; Claude E. Benson in *British Mountaineering* (1909) talks of being "blessed with a basement staircase of stone . . . I am to be found hanging by my fingertips to the outside thereof." And a gymnastic exercise of the nineteenth century involved climbing the underside of an oblique ladder using arms only—a precursor of the Bachar Ladder.

Given the extreme and run-out technical climbs being done on the Elbe River sandstone near Dresden a century ago—the hardest of which are now recognized as being near 5.10 difficulty—it is reasonable to conclude that early German free climbers placed a high value on style and difficulty. It is hard to conceive of such sustained routes being climbed without some specific regime to build forearm and upper-body strength, although working routes on toprope may have been their primary method of training.

The strongest climbers of the early and mid-1900s included Oliver Perry-Smith, Albert Ellingwood, Joe and Paul Stettner, Fritz Wiessner, Jack Durrance, Hans Kraus, John Salathe, and Harold Goodro, as well as some of the early Yosemite masters such as Warren Harding, Dave Rearick, Bob Kamps, and Royal Robbins. All were natural athletes or competed in other athletic activity prior to becoming climbers. More important, they all possessed a great sense of adventure and daring—a hallmark trait of all great climbers of this era. Mike Sherrick, Robbins's companion on the first ascent of the Northwest Face of Half Dome, was an excellent gymnast who often backflipped to the ground after finishing a boulder problem, much to the chagrin of his tamer companions. Yet training as a rock climbing discipline built on vision, specificity, and intention was the innovation of a young man from Alabama who began climbing in the early 1950s.

Now one of the undisputed legends of American

climbing, John Gill is the first person known to engage in highly regimented training for climbing. Unlike the others of his day who pushed themselves on vertical crags and long rock routes in the mountains, Gill—although an alpinist and rock climber—spent more of his time on short, overhanging faces on low boulders at the base of mountains or in river valleys. Bagging summits and climbing big walls had less aesthetic appeal for Gill; he instead sought the kinesthetics of dynamic movement up overhanging rock and adroitly built a novel training program to suit.

For more than fifteen years beginning in the mid-1950s, Gill trained on a gym rope, the still rings, and with weighted, fingertip pull-ups, one-arm and one-finger pull-ups, and one-arm front levers, in preparation for his powerful bouldering ascents throughout the Midwest, Southeast, and Rocky Mountains. In the early years Gill's gymnastic moves and the extremely muscular problems they produced—even his use of gymnasts' chalk—were viewed by most climbers with bemusement, if not bewilderment. Today his legacy as an innovator, visionary, and, in fact, the father of both modern bouldering and training for climbing is the foundation that has allowed route ratings to move into 5.13 and beyond. Gill's technical ability was years ahead of everyone else, as illustrated by his very bold 1961 free-solo first ascent of The Thimble in South Dakota's Black Hills, an overhanging 30-foot inspiration now rated V4 (5.12a), and his improbable center problem (incredibly, grade V9 by modern standards!) up the Red Cross Boulder in the Tetons two years before The Thimble. Unrecognized and underappreciated at the time, Gill in establishing these standards was an early prototype of today's top-end rock gymnasts, characterized like them by precise footwork, intense focus, and awesome power.

By the mid-1960s a number of other climbers, most with a background in gymnastics, also began training specific to climbing. Pat Ament, a young gymnast from Colorado, was an early training enthusiast and went on to become a leading climber and prolific developer of hard boulder problems. In 1967 Ament and Gill began a long friendship, and these two powerful boulderers undoubtedly inspired

Pat Ament, a trained gymnast and disciple of John Gill, introduced a new level of hard bouldering—as well as chalk—to Yosemite Valley during his numerous visits in the late 1960s.
PAT AMENT COLLECTION

countless climbers throughout the Front Range and beyond.

At about the same time, famed 'Gunks hardman Richard Goldstone met Gill during a summer trip out west and was enormously impressed with Gill's one-arm pull-ups, front levers, and stiff boulder problems. Goldstone went back to the University of Chicago with an enthusiasm for training and adapted the use of surgical tubing (long utilized by gymnasts to build enough strength to do an Iron Cross) as a training aid for portions of his workouts. A few years later Goldstone returned east and became a significant presence during the rapid expansion of difficult free climbing at the Shawangunks. Goldstone discovered that Dick Williams

German climbing icon Wolfgang Güllich demonstrating his one-arm power in Yosemite's Camp 4, circa 1980. GERD HEIDORN

(another former gymnast) was already training for climbing and incorporating dynamic movements in his campaign to free climb the many steep aid routes at the 'Gunks. Other Uberfall icons of the era such as Hans Kraus, Bonnie Prudden, Jim McCarthy, and John Stannard also had great interest and long personal histories in physical fitness. Kraus went on to form the President's Council on Physical Fitness, while Bonnie Prudden became a nationally recognized fitness expert and the first female athlete to appear on the cover of *Sports Illustrated*.

Meanwhile, out west, it seemed California climbers were more and more toying with one form or another of climbing training. Dave Rearick and Mike Sherrick were specifically oriented toward gymnastics and could do presses into handstands and other gym stunts; Layton Kor was lifting weights regularly for his many outstanding ascents around Colorado and in Yosemite. Remarkably, three of the top

Yosemite free climbers of the day—Royal Robbins, Chuck Pratt, and Frank Sacherer—did very little training other than the usual regimen of pull-ups and push-ups. Jim Bridwell and Barry Bates followed in the spirit of their master-predecessors, training hard at such things as pull-ups on tree limbs in the Valley. Bates quickly developed the ability to do a one-finger pull-up with his middle finger on a sling hanging from a tree. The main thrust of their training, however, was simply to climb several days per week.

Bridwell, Bates, and others in the Camp 4 crowd were also likely influenced, directly or otherwise, by visiting climbers such as Goldstone and Ament. Rich Goldstone is believed to have installed the first pull-up bar in Camp 4 while Ament brought the toughest bouldering discipline of the time to the Valley with his first ascents of 1968. Pat Ament also brought the slack chain to Yosemite, challenging climbers to develop refined balance and focus. The revered tradition of chain and rope walking in Yosemite began with the 40 feet of slack links that Ament strung between two Camp 4 trees. (Local legend has it that Chuck Pratt one day stood on the chain and juggled three wine bottles, presumably empty!) Bridwell and others went on to develop and deploy an array of training stations around Camp 4 so impressive that Warren Harding, the Yosemite Generation's sharpest wit, soon dubbed the area the "Olympic Training Village." Harding himself preferred to build stamina for his epic multiday big-wall adventures by running to the top of Half Dome and back, a 17-mile round trip with nearly 1 mile of elevation change (and also, by his own admission, by refraining from hard liquor in the weeks before an ascent). In the years that followed, Camp 4 workout rigs introduced countless climbers from around the world to the basic elements of the future science of training for climbing.

Still, sports scientists in academia and the European mountain heartland had yet to view climbing as a subject worthy of serious and sustained study. Though ascents of the world's highest mountains were long a source of national pride in Europe, there were no Olympic medals (nor commercial sponsorships) to be won around which to build a culture of sport-specific training and achievement aimed at visible rewards. Climbing remained a rarefied pursuit, and research—where it pertained to climbing at all—was narrowly focused on the effects of long exposure to low-oxygen atmosphere. Still, the steadily growing popularity of climbing throughout the 1970s eventually gave birth to the first European studies relating to the physiological stresses and injuries associated with rock climbing.

In 1977 Pat Ament's *Master of Rock* was published. This biography of John Gill, though not focused specifically on training, served to document Gill's strength-training techniques and introduce them to a wider audience; the book quickly became not just an American classic but a kind of sacred writ for a new generation of climbers interested in pushing the absolute technical limits. *Master of Rock* opened a new door of consciousness, so to speak, of what it would take to be the best—not only in terms of physical ability but in the broader context of per-

One of the first climbers to train with weighted pull-ups, John Bachar, could pull up with nearly 140 pounds hanging from his waist! Here he trains with a "light" fifty pounds circa 1985. PHIL BARD

formance, Gill being the epitome of performance excellence in virtually all his pursuits.

From the mid-1970s through the 1980s, the worldwide growth of technical rock climbing and the first climbing competitions produced an unprecedented exchange of ideas and innovations among European, Russian and Caucasian, and American climbers. In Yosemite's Camp 4; Boulder, Colorado; and the Shawangunks of New York, small groups trained and free climbed with increasing fervor, as energetic newcomers such as John Bachar, Kevin

The author (circa 1986) on his version of the "death board," a training tool used by a handful of climbers in the pre-climbing-gym era. HÖRST COLLECTION

Bein, Jim Collins, Christian Griffith, Lynn Hill, Jim Holloway, John Long, Ron Kauk, Todd Skinner, Tobin Sorenson, Alan Watts, Tony Yaniro, and others arrived on the scene. Similarly, small groups of energetic climbers began to train in England, France, Italy, and Germany. The boulders of Fontainebleau and the ubiquitous limestone crags of the region became the proving grounds for first "sport climbers" in the early 1980s. The hard-training European climbers of the early sport-climbing era were Brits Ron Fawcett, Jerry Moffat, and Ben Moon; French icons Jibé Tribout, Antoine LeMénestral, and Patrick Edlinger; Italian's Roberto Bossi and Heinz Mariacher; and the powerful Germans Kurt Albert and Wolfgang Güllich.

In the United States no technique or aesthetic had a bigger impact on the rapid development of extreme free climbing then the import of sport-climbing tactics from Europe. Rappel-bolted routes eliminated the psychological stress and risks associated with marginal protection, and through liberal use of hangdogging, the practitioner could safely work extreme sequences and thus bring Gill-level difficulty (5.13 moves) to roped climbing. At about this time, articles on physical performance and training began to appear in American climbing magazines; academic studies, too, began to proliferate, although initially focused on the subject of injuries specific to rock climbers. Strength-training techniques remained relatively unsophisticated, although a few key innovations such as the Bachar Ladder and fingerboard jacked generic finger and pull-power training up to a higher level of intensity and specificity.

In Europe's sport-climbing culture, indoor walls had already taken hold, but it was not until 1987 that the first commercial climbing gym opened in the United States. Around the same time at the Campus Center—a weight-lifting facility at the University of Nürnberg—a strong German climber named Wolfgang Güllich developed a sport-specific form of reactive training known today simply as campus training. Between 1985 and 1991 Güllich went on to establish the world's hardest free climbs and wrote a breakthrough training book, *Sportklettern Heute* (1986), and campus training quickly became a staple of elite climbers around the world. Toward the end of the century, as at its beginning, German climbers led the way to new levels of technical difficulty and athletic achievement.

The 1990s saw climbing go mainstream with televised competitions and dozens of well-sponsored full-time climbers in training year-round. The first two books on training for climbing by American authors were published in 1993 and 1994—Dale Goddard's *Performance Rock Climbing* and *Flash Training* by this author—and articles on training became regular features of *Climbing* and *Rock and Ice* magazines. But the proliferation of indoor walls was the real wild card that allowed the average climber to practice more frequently and climb harder than ever before. All the above-mentioned factors, along with

The legendary Todd Skinner cranking hard at his beloved Hueco Tanks in 1995. ERIC J. HÖRST

improved equipment, made what was once the maximum grade, 5.10, achievable by the masses; 5.13 quickly became attainable by a handful of youngsters not even old enough to drive.

Beginning the new millennium, climbing is as popular as ever, and the limits of quantified technical difficulty have stretched to 5.15a/b and V16. The first edition of *Training for Climbing*, published in December 2002, has spread to more than fifty countries and been translated into four languages. The text introduced countless climbers to the concepts of comprehensive, climbing-specific training, and it revealed new cutting-edge strength-training strategies, such as Hypergravity Isolation Training and complex training, adapted to climbing by this author in the mid- and late 1990s. Academic researchers, alert now to the unique physiological aspects of climbing, have carried out and published the results of dozens of scientific studies in the few years since this book first appeared. The body of knowledge on the science of climbing performance has grown by

leaps and bounds since the introduction of Gill's gymnasts' chalk and Ament's slack chain; much more remains to be investigated and discovered. I trust that this new and expanded edition of *Training for Climbing* will provide a solid foundation from which the next generation of climbers and sports scientists can extend their grasp.

While the climbers of my generation trained largely in accordance with myth, anecdote, and trial and error, those entering the sport today have a significant amount of quality information on the subject, if they choose to use it. As I proclaimed at the beginning of *How to Climb 5.12*, "If you are reading this book, chances are you have what it takes to climb 5.12." As I complete this book, I maintain this same sentiment—in fact, there's a good chance you have what it takes to climb 5.13! And if you're genetically blessed, maybe even 5.15 . . .

Genetics and Climbing Performance

Excuses are like parents—everybody has them. Ironically, your parents, or more precisely the genetic material you inherited from them, might be the best excuse why you or I may never climb 5.15. Still, your genetic makeup, which substantially determines your height, flexibility, and natural strength, among other things, is a poor excuse for not being able to climb 5.10 or even 5.12. Yes, some specific 5.12 climb might require a long reach or high step that you will never be capable of making, but numerous research studies confirm my belief that the mass of climbers have the potential to succeed at the lofty grade of 5.12, regardless of genetics.

The Role of Genetics in Sports Performance

All other things being equal, genes seem to determine the differences in performance among individuals. In a sport as complex as climbing, however, you could argue that "all other things are never equal"—making the role of genetics in climbing performance hard to pin down. But let's try!

The role of genetics in what we become has been a favorite subject of scientists over the years—it's the old "nature-versus-nurture" debate. Certainly genetics would seem to play an underlying role in our natural mental climate and personality. However, it's in the physical realm of strength and motor skill that genetics *appear* to play the largest role (or at least this is where genetics seem most observable and measurable for scientists). Interestingly, a review of the research on the role of genetics on performance reveals an extremely complex subject with contradictory theories and findings among academics. One study (Ericsson 1993) suggested that hours of deliberate practice are the most important factor in determining performance, while another (Fox 1996) found that genes are responsible for half the variations in performance among individuals.

In the real, nonacademic world, it seems that neither of these studies is unequivocally correct. It appears that genetics play the greatest role in sports where the raw physical demands far outweigh the mental or technical requirements. For example, excelling at the 100-meter dash requires extreme explosive power but only basic mental and technical skill. Conversely, golf requires mastery of a wide range of technical skills and a well-cultivated mental calm, but the physical demands are much less noteworthy. Therefore, while genetics clearly play a major role in determining who makes it to the Olympics in the 100-meter dash, they should have much less influence in determining who plays in this year's PGA Championship.

Summing up: Hours of deliberate practice are a requisite for performing at a high level in complex (technical and mental) sports, whereas ideal genetics are a prerequisite for achieving greatness in the most physical pursuits, such as running and weight lifting. Rock climbing is unique among sports, however, in that it requires a near-equal balance of mental, tech-

Figure 1.1 Relative Demands of Various Sports

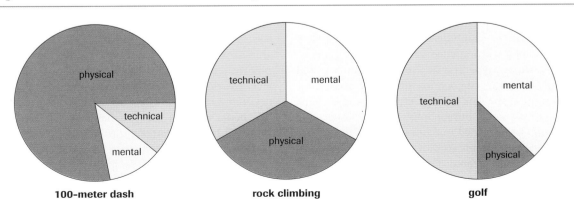

100-meter dash   rock climbing   golf

nical, and physical prowess (see figure 1.1). So you can argue that genetics do play a significant, though not primary, role in determining your level of performance in this sport.

Genetic Factors Relating to Climbing Performance

So just what genetic factors might be helping or hurting you? I bet they are different and more subtle than you think. Height and weight seem to be what most climbers consider their blessing or curse, but it's likely a number of less obvious attributes that help make possible the incredible 5.14/V14 ascents of climbers like David Graham, Chris Sharma, and the Nicole, Huber, and LeMénestral brothers.

While the aforementioned climbers exhibit a variety of body shapes and sizes, they all possess unusually high maximum grip strength, upper-body power, and/or local (forearm) endurance—beyond that which can be acquired by the average climber training "perfectly" for many years. The genetic gifts enabling these feats probably relate to hard-to-observe factors such as tendon insertions (where they originate from and insert into the bones of the hand and arms), lever length (length of bones), muscle fiber type, and hormone profiles.

With regard to tendon insertions, a slight shift in the location compared with normal provides additional leverage that gives a few lucky folks more grip strength (off the couch!) than others could achieve through years of training. Similarly, your innate ratio of fast-twitch to slow-twitch muscle fiber determines whether your natural aptitude tends toward high endurance, high strength, or neither. Finally, we each have unique hormone profiles (testosterone, cortisol, and so forth) that vary with age and sex, and this plays an underlying role in our response to training and recovery ability (Bloomfield 1994). Because of this, some people can climb hard three days in a row or respond more dramatically to training, while most of us need far more rest in order to perform well, and our training adaptations are more gradual.

If you still aren't convinced that genetics play a role in determining who will be the very best climbers, consider the three pairs of brothers men-tioned earlier. Frederic and François Nicole, Alex and Thomas Huber, and Marc and Antoine LeMénestral have all climbed at the fringe of maximum difficulty. This is not coincidence, but instead a screaming message that genetic makeup is a factor in climbing performance.

Your Genetic Potential as a Climber

If you're beginning to sense that you might lack some or all of the above genetic gifts, don't be depressed! As I stated earlier, odds are that you're "normal enough" to climb 5.12 or even 5.13. Because of the large role that mental and technical skill plays in climbing performance, you can push very high up the grade scale by maximizing your capabilities in these areas. The bell curve (see figure 1.2) shows that most of the population falls in the middle of the bell, in the area representing near-average genetic characteristics. A much smaller number of folks—call them outliers (say, one in ten)—have somewhat better or worse genetics than average. Then there are the extreme outliers (say, 1 in 1,000 or more) who have the potential to be brilliant if they discover their gift and apply themselves completely.

The fact that most of us fall somewhere in the middle of the bell curve can be uplifting or depressing, depending on your perspective. If you dream of

Figure 1.2 Genetic Potential

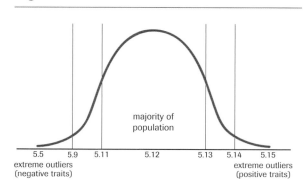

Chris Sharma and David Graham would fall into the far right portion of the curve, whereas Verne Troyer and Shaquille O'Neal would be far left.

climbing 5.15 or V15, the chart shows that even if you do everything right and dedicate your entire life to it, the odds are low that you have the genetic potential to make this dream a reality. But if you currently climb 5.5, 5.10, or what have you, you should be psyched that 5.12 is likely within your reach!

A few recent studies support this idea. One study (Barss 1997) divided a group of twenty-four recreational climbers into two groups based on climbing ability. With the exception of a straight-armed hang endurance test, there was no statistical difference in the performance of a wide variety of general and sport-specific tests between the "less skilled" group (those climbing 5.7 to 5.10a) and the "more skilled" group (those climbing 5.10b to 5.11b). Therefore, at the intermediate levels (5.7 to 5.11b), there's a poor correlation between fitness and climbing ability. The stronger climbers were not necessarily the better climbers, so mental and technical differences account for the difference in ability.

Another, more complex study (Mermier 2000) looked at a larger group of forty-four male and female climbers with a wider range of abilities (5.6 to 5.13c). The results showed that the variance in climbing performance related primarily to trainable variables, and that anthropometric variables (height, weight, arm and leg length, arm span, percent of body fat, and the like) were not a statistically significant factor. So this study also supports my sense that by optimizing technical and mental skills (the trainable variables), the average climber should be able to progress to a high level of climbing, possibly even as high as 5.13c. Note that no 5.14 climbers were included in the study, so we don't know if inclusion of these world-class individuals would have yielded similar results (I suspect not).

In fact, a third, very similar study (Watts 1993) looked only at world-class climbers (those competing in the semifinals at a World Cup event). It found that these elite individuals exhibited a higher grip-strength-to-body-mass ratio, had a lower percentage of body fat, and were of a slightly smaller stature when compared with other athletic groups. This study supports the idea that those world-class 5.14 climbers are born, not made, in that they are

extreme outliers with just the right build to be able to climb at the highest levels of difficulty.

Great Genetics Don't Guarantee You'll Be a Great Climber

Still, the premise that climbing requires equal mastery of mental, technical, and physical abilities means that good genes aren't enough to make you a rock star. Just as genetically average individuals can progress to climbing 5.12 or 5.13 by perfecting their technical and mental skill sets, genetic freaks who can crush bricks in their hands may forever remain 5.10 climbers due to poor technique or lack of mental skills.

Consider figure 1.3, which depicts the genetic potential (solid line) and real-life ability (dashed line) of a climber with average genetic makeup versus the brick-crushing genetic freak. Through dedicated, intelligent training of all the elements under her control, the average climber has pushed her ability almost the whole way out to her genetic potential. The superstrong genetic freak, on the other hand, with his poor technique and mental control, is an underachieving slacker when you compare his real-life performance with his genetic potential. Comparatively, the genetically average climber pushed the dashed line out farther and is, thus, the *real* master of rock!

Next time you go to the gym or crag, observe all the men and women, of all ages, shapes, and sizes, who are climbing 5.11, 5.12, and even 5.13. The vast majority of these folks are of average genetic makeup (located near the middle of the bell curve in figure 1.2), but through dedication and hard work on all aspects of the climbing game, they have succeeded at pushing their dashed line out toward the edge of their genetic limitations.

Limits to Climbing Performance

The top climbing grade exploded upward from 5.12d in the mid-1970s to 5.14b by the end of the 1980s. The primary reasons for this marked improvement are equipment (better shoes, stickier shoe rubber, easy-to-place active camming devices, and bolt-protected routes), better training (indoor walls, fin-

Figure 1.3 Genetic Potential

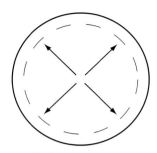

average climber performing optimally

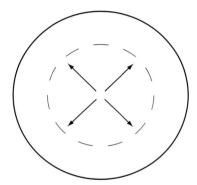

gifted climber performing poorly

Genetic potential (solid line), versus real-life ability (dashed line). Who's the peak performer?

gerboards, and so on), and more effective practice methods (hangdogging). In 1991 Wolfgang Güllich upped the ante with his ascent of *Action Directe* (5.14d). This route went unrepeated for five years and has since seen only a handful of repeats, despite attempts by many of the world's best climbers.

Now, more than fifteen years after the first ascent of *Action Directe*, the benchmark of maximum difficulty has been stretched to 5.15a/b and V16. Given the length of time required to consolidate the 5.15a grade, we have to wonder if we are approaching human limitations to free climbing. While we can never rule out another breakthrough in technology (equipment), it's highly unlikely that we will

see another grade explosion as occurred during the 1980s. Instead, slow increases will occur over the time frame of decades.

For a glimpse of what we might expect, let's look at several "mature" Olympic events. Over the last fifty years, improvements per decade have been approximately: sprinting—1 percent; distance running—1.5 percent; jumping—3 percent; pole vaulting—5 percent; swimming—5 percent; skiing—10 percent (Seiler 2000). Improved equipment surely contributed to the higher values for pole vaulting (fiberglass poles), swimming ("frictionless" speed suits), and skiing (ski technology seems to be constantly improving). Unfortunately, performance-enhancing drugs are also a very real factor in the improvements in many Olympic events.

Assuming no technological breakthroughs and no drugs, a good bet would be that the top climbing

Wolfgang Güllich on his breakthrough route
Action Directe, *the world's first 5.14d.*
THOMAS BALLENBERGER

level would increase by just a few percent per decade. I believe these gains will result from identification of more extreme outliers as participation in climbing increases and from better matching of appropriate training on a more individual basis.

Ultimately, it appears that the achievement curve, which rose rapidly in the 1970s and 1980s, is not linear ($y = kt$), but more like a logarithmic curve [$y = aLog(1 + bt)$]: increasing, but less so as time goes on. Furthermore, our current method of rating routes may be on the verge of breaking down—the difference between 5.15a and 5.15b (or V15 and V16) may be purely a function of anatomical variation in the context of a single move or sequence. This argues for an entirely different system of assessing difficulty at the top levels, such as a scale that counts the number of climbers able to do a given move or problem. Interestingly, this is the essence of John Gill's B-scale for grading bouldering problems, developed back in the late 1950s.

Gill says, "My idea was to develop a personal system that allowed basic differentiation for difficulty, but simultaneously imposed constraints on such differentiation so that an endless, open-ended stream of numbers with plusses and minuses would not result. Usually such fine differentiation would reflect merely the anatomical attributes of various climbers. B1 was to represent the highest levels of normal traditional roped climbing, and B2 was to represent a broad class of bouldering difficulty greater than B1. B3 was a (usually temporary) rating signifying a most severe route that had been done by only one person, but tried by a number of climbers. When a second climber succeeded, the route would downgrade to B2 or B1. I thought this would appeal to the competitive spirit, but avoid overcomplicating the whole process and turning it into a number-chasing game" (Escalade 2001).

Training for Climbing

As discussed earlier, there are many trainable variables to work on as part of your training for climbing program. In chapter 2 you will perform a self-assessment test to determine which of these trainable variables is most holding you back. The best training program (for you) will concentrate on the areas that can produce the greatest gain in performance output for a given training input. Of course, the goal is to train most effectively, not maximally.

A Definition of Training for Climbing

I define *training for climbing* as any practice, exercise, or discipline that increases absolute climbing performance. Clearly, this represents a broad spectrum of subjects—hence the wide range of topics covered in this book.

Through this paradigm you should recognize that training includes a wide range of activities and practices such as bouldering (to learn problem solving and develop power); climbing on a home wall or at a climbing gym (to improve technique and strength); on-sighting, hangdogging, or for that matter any climbing (to enhance your mental and physical skill sets); and traveling to experience many different types of climbing (to gain experience and a broad range of technical skills). Training also includes efforts made in ancillary areas such as stretching and antagonist-muscle training (for flexibility and injury prevention), eating properly (to enhance recovery and maintain optimal body composition), visualization and targeted thinking (to maximize mind programming and disconnect from bad habits), resting sufficiently and listening to your body (to optimize training results and to avoid injury), and evaluating yourself regularly (to determine your current strengths and weaknesses). Finally, training of course includes proper execution of various general and sport-specific exercises (to work toward your physical genetic potential).

For the sake of discriminating among these many types of training throughout the rest of the book, let's define several training subtypes—mental training, skill practice, fitness and strength training, and training support activities—as shown in figure 1.4.

Mental training involves any thought control, discipline, or mind-programming activity that will directly or indirectly impact your climbing in a positive way. The best climbers train mentally 24/7—this is one activity in which you can never overtrain—by targeting their thoughts only on things that can, in

Figure 1.4 Subtypes of Training

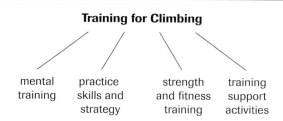

Training for Climbing

mental training | practice skills and strategy | strength and fitness training | training support activities

some way, influence their climbing and by deleting thoughts and habits that might hold them back. Unfortunately, many individuals possess mental muscle that's in an advanced stage of atrophy from underuse. Visualization is just one of the many mental exercises that can improve your climbing. Chapter 3 lays out an array of mental-training methods and on-the-rock strategies that will have a combined effect similar to unloading a heavy weight from your back (which you've unknowingly been hauling up routes). Are you ready to spread your Mental Wings?

Practice relates to time spent learning and refining actual sport skills and strategies outside of a performance setting. Just as baseball, basketball, and football players spend many hours practicing their skills outside of competition, climbers must practice by climbing a lot with the sole intention of improving climbing skill (and not worrying about an outcome such as a flash, redpoint, or on-sight ascent). It's my sense that many climbers' training programs are devoid of this vital subtype of training. We'll take an in-depth look at the subject of effective skill practice in chapter 4.

Fitness and strength training covers a wide range of activities that are performed with the primary intent of improving physiological capabilities. This includes general conditioning activities such as running, stretching, and light free-weight training as well as the more important sport-specific activities such as fingerboard, campus training, and hypergravity training. Many other activities can fall under this heading, as long as they somehow help improve your climbing performance or prevent injury. It's surprising, however, how many things done in the name of training

for climbing actually have a negative effect on climbing performance. Get ready to sort things out as we take a cutting-edge look at physical training for climbing in chapters 5, 6, and 7. Then in chapter 8, you will be guided on developing an effective and time-efficient personalized training program.

Finally, *training support activities* comprise a variety of crucial, yet often overlooked (or ignored), issues outside of your actual physical practice and training for climbing. Athletes in many other sports have known the vital role that rest, nutrition, and recovery acceleration techniques play in their ultimate level of performance. Serious climbers looking to press out their ability level toward the genetic limit must act on these issues with utmost discipline. Chapters 9 and 10 cover these important topics—applying the material may be the key to succeeding on your own "personal *Action Directe*"!

The Relationship Between Skill and Fitness

While the various subtypes of training for climbing will be discussed separately, they clearly affect one another. This is especially true when it comes to skill practice and fitness and strength training, so let's dig a little deeper.

For a beginning climber in the earliest stages of learning, a low level of fitness can slow the learning of climbing skill. A certain level of strength is necessary in order to practice enough (that is, climb) to develop the basic skills of movement, hand- and footwork, and body positioning. Conversely, too much strength enables a beginner to get by on easy to moderate routes despite inefficient movement, poor footwork, and improper body position. Obviously, this will also slow (or prevent) the development of good technique—unless, that is, the strong person makes good technique the primary goal, instead of just getting up the route no matter what.

The problem is further aggravated by the fact that people tend to develop their talents disproportionately. Strong people are most likely into strength training, flexible people probably stretch regularly, and skillful people undoubtedly climb a lot. Sure, the drudgery of working on weak points isn't fun, and at times it can be discouraging. But if you really want

Figure 1.5 Relative Gains

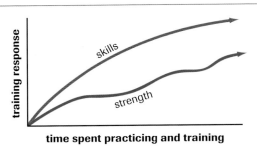

Relative gains from skill practice and strength training.

Figure 1.6 Performance Losses

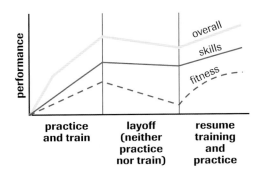

Performance losses (gains) during (and after) a layoff.

to climb harder, you must train smarter. That means knowing where to best invest your time to get the most output for your training input. For the majority of climbers, the best investment is on further development of climbing skills and strategy (see figure 1.5).

Elite climbers may have less to gain from practicing familiar forms of climbing. These expert climbers are way out on the learning curve near their ultimate skill potential, so fitness (and the mind) becomes the crucial factor in performance. Hence, we commonly see magazine articles about these rock stars that describe seemingly lethal or disastrously stressful strength-training regimes that would surely send the ordinary climber into a state of overtraining, the doctor's office, or self-defeating over-reliance on strength training as the key to improvement.

Focused fitness training is of greater importance for all climbers after a layoff, whether due to injury, winter, or some other reason (see figure 1.6). The rapid loss of strength that occurs when training or climbing ceases for a period of weeks or months is best counteracted by several weeks of dedicated fitness training (fortunately, you largely maintain climbing skill once the motor programs are well established). While this short-term training focus helps in regaining your old form, the long-term and most significant improvements in climbing ability will still result from effective skill practice until late in your career. Only at the lofty grades of 5.12 and

above does sport-specific strength become a major limiting factor.

Specific Adaptation to Imposed Demands (SAID)

Serious climbers would be wise to train and climb in accordance with the cornerstone principles of the field of exercise science. For example, knowledge of the SAID Principle (specific adaptation to imposed demands) can be leveraged to maximize the effectiveness of your training for a specific climbing goal or dream climb.

The SAID Principle explains that a certain exercise or type of training produces adaptations specific to the activity performed and only in the muscles (and energy systems) that are stressed by the activity. For instance, running produces favorable adaptations in the leg muscles and the cardiovascular system. But the muscles and systems not stressed show no adaptation, so even heroic amounts of running will produce no favorable changes in, say, the arms. Of course, the adaptations that result from running do transfer somewhat to other activities that depend on the same body parts and systems (such as mountain biking or hiking). Bottom line: The SAID Principle demands that effective training for climbing must target your body in ways very similar to climbing (body position, muscles used, energy systems trained, and so forth).

Figure 1.7   Continuum of Specific Adaptations for Various Subdisciplines of Climbing

bouldering	sport climbing	multipitch climbing	big walls	alpine

Similarly, your body adapts in a specific fashion to the specific demands you place on it while climbing. If you boulder a lot, you will adapt to the specific skill and strength demands of bouldering. If you climb mostly one-pitch sport routes, you adapt to the unique demands of zipping up, say, 30 meters of rock before muscular failure. If you favor multipitch routes or big walls, your body will adapt in accordance to the demands of these longer climbs. Or if your outings are alpine in nature, your physiological response will be specific to the very unique demands of climbing in the mountains.

The vitally important distinction here is that while all these activities fall under the headline of "climbing," they each have unique demands that produce very specific physical adaptations. Therefore, the training effect from regular bouldering will do very little to enhance your physical ability for alpine climbing. Figure 1.7 shows that the specific demands of sport climbing are much closer to those of bouldering. Consequently, the adaptations incurred from frequent bouldering will largely carry over to sport climbing (especially short sport climbs) and vice versa.

Due to the SAID Principle, your practice and training on the rocks should be spent mostly on the type of climbing in which you wish to excel. It's no mistake that the best boulderers in the world rarely tie in to a rope. Likewise, the best alpine climbers spend little time working 30-meter sport routes. Targeting your training on the specific demands of your preferred form of climbing is the essence of the SAID Principle.

In the end you must make a philosophical choice whether you want to specialize—and therefore excel—in one or two of the climbing subdisciplines, or become a moderately successful all-around climber. Certainly there is merit and reward in both approaches.

Summary of Training for Climbing

1. Training for climbing is any practice, exercise, or discipline that increases absolute climbing performance.

2. Mental training begins by increasing your commitment to all things climbing (while reducing time, energy, and thought invested in lower-value activities and hobbies) and continues with the development of uncommon self-awareness, and superior thought control and risk management skills.

3. Skill practice is paramount, since climbing skills and tactics are distinctly unique from those of other sports. Only going climbing will make you a more skilled climber.

4. Fitness training comprises both general and sport-specific exercises and activities. Novice climbers should engage in a period of general conditioning before advancing to the more stressful sport-specific exercises.

5. Training support activities are essential for all serious climbers, including scheduled rest days, proper nutrition, and use of techniques to accelerate recovery.

6. Ultimately the most effective training-for-climbing program will target limiting constraints in highly climbing-specific ways (in accordance with the SAID Principle).

Self-Assessment and Goal Setting

I know of no more encouraging fact than the unquestionable ability of man to elevate his life by conscious endeavor.

—Henry David Thoreau

The first step to improving your situation—in anything—can be expressed simply as "Know thyself." You cannot progress beyond your current state with the same thoughts and actions that brought you here. Therefore, only through constant self-evaluation will you unlock the secrets to incremental improvement. For instance, you must actively distinguish what works from what does not work, as well as be able to recognize what you need to learn versus what must be unlearned. Often the key elements are not obvious or clear, but you must accept that life is subtle; only through improving on the little things will you succeed in the big things.

In climbing, the process of improvement begins with getting to know your patterns at the crags, in the gym, and in your everyday life. You must become aware of your climbing-related strengths and weaknesses in each area of the performance triad—technical, mental, and physical—and learn to leverage your strengths and improve upon the weaknesses. Toward this end, your prime directive must be to train intelligently—that is, to engage in training activities that

*Jim Ewing on the classic **Ridicullissima (5.10d)**, Shawangunks, New York.* ERIC J. HÖRST

best address your weaknesses, while not getting drawn into the trap of training as others do.

Of course, a clear understanding of your mega goals in this sport is equally important to achieving success. Only with a clear goal in mind can you take consistent actions that keep you on route, as well as have the sense to recognize when you have wandered off route. Finally, at the very deepest level, you must closely examine your level of commitment to climbing—are you willing to make the sacrifices necessary for reaching your mega goals? This chapter will guide you through the fundamental steps of self-assessment and goal setting that, in turn, will initiate your ascent to becoming a better, more successful climber (no matter your gauge of measuring success).

Self-Assessment: The Breakfast of Champions

Identifying personal weaknesses often requires a paradigm shift—a dramatic change in the way we see things—because it's human nature to think about and practice the things at which we excel. Too many climbers (myself included) have wasted precious years practicing and training the things at which they already shine while the ball-and-chain of their weaknesses holds them back. For instance, many climbers think "more strength" is the panacea to their climbing woes; but as shown in figure 1.1, it's just one piece of the climbing performance puzzle. It requires an awakening for most climbers to recognize the thoughts and life patterns that are really holding them back and that their time and energy could be invested more productively elsewhere.

Introspection and curiosity are key attributes you must foster because, at least at the first superficial glance, your real-life experiences with failure on a climb will almost always appear to result from a lack of strength. But what about all the underlying causes that may have led to premature fatigue—poor footwork, bad body positioning, overgripping of holds, climbing too slowly, scattered focus, a missed rest, unreasonable fears, or a lack of energy due to poor diet or dehydration? As you can see, the other two-thirds of the climbing performance puzzle (technical and mental) determine how effectively you use the physical strength and energy reserves you possess. Consequently, it's my belief that the average climber wastes 50 percent (or more!) of his strength and energy due to flawed technique, inefficient movement, and poor mental control. This is analogous to having a 30-miles-per-gallon car that only gets 15 miles per gallon as the result of a horrible tune-up and a heavy foot. Therefore, the average climber can obtain a huge windfall of relative strength gains—and dramatically improve performance—by training up technique, quality of movement, and mental control.

The moral of the story, then, is that the best training program for climbing must include lots of climbing and constant self-evaluation. Spending three or four days a week on the rock (or an artificial wall) deliberately practicing skills and refining your climber's mind-set is far more beneficial than spending those days strength training in the gym. This is not to say that you can simply climb a lot and ignore all the other facets of performance. The best climbers clearly focus on putting the complete puzzle together, and this undoubtedly includes a targeted strength-training program. Still, if you can do ten fingertip pull-ups, you are probably strong enough to climb most 5.12a routes! So search vigilantly for the true but often underlying causes of failure on routes. That's the ultimate secret to optimizing your training program and establishing new personal bests on the rock.

Objective Evaluation

The best way to identify your weaknesses is to ask yourself a series of detailed questions. To identify physical and technical weaknesses, ask yourself targeted questions like: *Do I fail on a route because I'm too weak or do I overgrip and hang out too long in the midst of hard moves? Does my footwork deteriorate in the moves prior to where I fall? Do I climb too slowly through crux moves and consequently come up short on routes? Do I lack the flexibility to step onto a crucial hold or do I miss a better, easier foot placement? Am I really too short for this move or have I failed to find the body position that makes it possible for someone my height?*

Some questions for identifying mental errors are: *Do I fail to see the sequence or do I fail to try something new when the obvious doesn't work? Do I try too hard or give up too easily? Am I controlling my internal self-talk or is the critic within doing a hatchet job on me? Do I monitor and control my body tension or does my perceived pressure of the situation run the show? Do I sabotage myself before leaving the ground by doubting my ability and pondering past failures?*

In addition to investigating yourself, consider enlisting a coach to provide an even more objective view of your performance or, at the least, have a friend shoot some video of you on the rock. These detached perspectives are especially useful in identifying obvious flaws in technique, tactics, and your overall economy of effort. For example, feet skidding or popping off footholds signals lack of attention to footwork, while constant stretching for holds seemingly just out of reach is a sign you're missing critical intermediate holds or using less effective body positions. In more general terms, evaluate whether your movement looks relaxed and fluid or appears tight, mechanical, and hesitant. These outside perspectives can be a real eye-opener, and you'll probably be surprised at what you find. Still, some fundamental mistakes and weaknesses are so subtle that they are not easily observed by others or by viewing yourself on video. This is where a detailed self-assessment test comes in handy.

Taking the Self-Assessment Test

A good self-assessment test takes the white light of your climbing performance and, like a prism, disassembles it into the rainbow of colors representing specific skills. The results will reveal your true (not perceived) strengths and weaknesses—and possibly even an unknown Achilles' heel that must be addressed if you are to ever reach your potential (or break through a long-term plateau). With this knowledge, you can create the most effective training program *for you*!

In taking the assessment that follows, it's important to read each question once and then immediately answer it based on your recent experiences on the rock. Don't read anything into the questions; nor should you try to figure out their focus and shade your answers in any way. Instead of working in the book, consider making a photocopy of the test pages in order to maintain an unmarked self-assessment test with which to work (or copy again) in the future. Of course, it would be ideal to date your test and file it for future reference. Comparing successive self-assessments is a powerful way to track your long-term improvement in each area of the performance triad.

Exercise: Self-Assessment Test

Answer each question by circling the number that best characterizes your performance. To obtain the most accurate results, it's essential that you score each question according to your most recent experiences on the rock. Pause for a moment and review recent climbs to determine the correct answer for each question. Do not overanalyze the questions, however, or try to read between the lines—you will have a chance to ponder the meaning of your answers when you tally the final results.

0 = almost always

1 = often

2 = about half the time

3 = occasionally

4 = seldom

5 = never

1. My footwork (use of feet) deteriorates during the hardest part of a climb.

   0   1   2   3   4   5

2. My forearms balloon and my grip begins to fail even on routes that are easy for me.

   0   1   2   3   4   5

3. On hard sequences, I have difficulty stepping onto critical footholds.

   0   1   2   3   4   5

4. I get anxious and tight as I head into crux sequences.

   0   1   2   3   4   5

5. My biceps (upper arms) pump out before my forearms.

   0   1   2   3   4   5

6. I have difficulty hanging on small, necessary-to-use holds.

   0   1   2   3   4   5

7. I blow sequences I have wired and know by heart.

   0   1   2   3   4   5

8. I stall at the start of crux sequences. I end up having to hang on the rope and rest before I can give it a good, solid try.

   0   1   2   3   4   5

9. I climb three or four days in a row.

   0   1   2   3   4   5

10. I get sewing-machine leg ("Elvis leg").

0   1   2   3   4   5

11. I pump out on overhanging climbs no matter how big the holds.

0   1   2   3   4   5

12. I get out of breath when I climb.

0   1   2   3   4   5

13. I make excuses for why I might fail on a route before I even begin to climb.

0   1   2   3   4   5

14. I miss hidden holds on routes.

0   1   2   3   4   5

15. I have difficulty hanging on to small sloping holds or pockets.

0   1   2   3   4   5

16. I grab quick draws, the rope, or other gear instead of risking a fall trying a hard move of which I am unsure.

0   1   2   3   4   5

17. On a typical climb, I feel like much of my body weight is hanging on my arms.

0   1   2   3   4   5

18. I get very sore the day after climbing at the crags.

0   1   2   3   4   5

19. I have difficulty visualizing myself successfully climbing the route before I leave the ground.

0   1   2   3   4   5

20. I cannot reach key holds on difficult routes.

0   1   2   3   4   5

21. On overhanging routes and roofs, I have difficulty keeping my feet from cutting loose and swinging out.

0   1   2   3   4   5

22. While climbing, I get distracted by activity on the ground and/or I think about whether the belayer is paying attention.

0   1   2   3   4   5

23. I have difficulty reading sequences.

0   1   2   3   4   5

24. I get a flash pump on the first climb of the day.

0   1   2   3   4   5

25. I have more difficulty climbing when people are watching.

0   1   2   3   4   5

26. My feet unexpectedly pop off footholds.

0   1   2   3   4   5

27. I experience elbow pain when I climb on a regular basis.

0   1   2   3   4   5

28. When lead climbing a safe route, I have difficulty pushing myself to the complete limit.

0   1   2   3   4   5

29. I have difficulty finding midroute rest positions and shakeouts.

0   1   2   3   4   5

30. My first attempt on a hard route is usually better than my second or third attempts of the day.

0   1   2   3   4   5

Looking at Your Test Results

Record the scores from each question in figure 2.1 (below), and then add up each column to obtain a final score for each area of the performance triad. Compare your mental, technical, and physical scores to gain a sense of which area is your strong or weak aspect of the performance triad. If all three areas are within five points of one another, congratulate yourself for being a climber of balanced abilities. It is more common, however, to discover that one aspect of performance is much lower scoring than the other two. This area is your *major weakness,* and the most effective training program *for you* is one that targets this area for improvement.

Figure 2.1 Score Yourself

Mental	Technique and Tactics	Physical
1. _____	2. _____	3. _____
4. _____	5. _____	6. _____
7. _____	8. _____	9. _____
10. _____	11. _____	12. _____
13. _____	14. _____	15. _____
16. _____	17. _____	18. _____
19. _____	20. _____	21. _____
22. _____	23. _____	24. _____
25. _____	26. _____	27. _____
28. _____	29. _____	30. _____
_____	_____	_____
(Total)	**(Total)**	**(Total)**

Next, review each question of the self-assessment test and mark a star next to those on which you scored a 3 or less. Each of these low-scoring questions identifies a specific element of your climbing performance that is holding you back. List on a separate piece of paper or in your training log a brief description of each problem revealed. Sort and group them according to the aspects of the performance triad. As you read through the remainder of the book, keep this list of problem areas nearby and make notes of the exercises and strategies presented that address these weaknesses. Creating such a written "mind map" that displays both the problem areas and the action-oriented solutions will keep these highly powerful keys to better climbing in the forefront of your attention. Only with this awareness will your training remain on track and effective in the weeks and months to come.

As you move into the goal-setting exercises later in this chapter, refer back to the self-assessment test or your summary mind map. Focus your short- and medium-term training goals on the most dramatic weaknesses identified (the five or six lowest-scoring items). As you recognize improvement in these areas, shift your training focus onto other lower-scoring areas of the self-assessment or retake the entire test and develop a new training strategy based on the new results. For additional training tips that address each question of the self-assessment, see appendix C.

The Cycle of Improvement

Your completed self-assessment is your "boarding pass" to the Cycle of Improvement. This process cycle has three stages: Set goals, take action, and make course corrections (see figure 2.2).

A successful trip around the cycle gives birth to a new level of climbing performance—the Cycle of Improvement, in fact, becomes a Spiral of Improvement! Occasionally, reassessments are needed to update your goals relative to the "new you" and whatever new issues are now responsible for holding you back from further improvement. These new goals give birth to new actions and even more spectacular results.

Figure 2.2 Cycle of Improvement

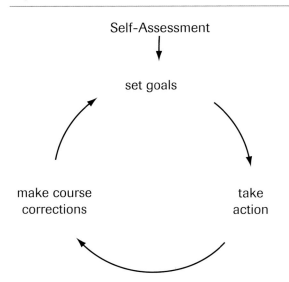

Use this three-step process to elevate your performance to the next level.

Depending on your desires, commitment, and skill level, one trip around the cycle may take anywhere from a couple of months to a year. Signs that you are ready for a reassessment and a new cycle include a plateau in performance, training that feels flat, or a drop in motivation. If you experience more than one of these signs, take a week or two off, then retake the self-assessment test and start a new cycle.

Remember that there is a big difference between employing the Cycle of Improvement and just going climbing year-round. The latter approach is unfocused and will yield slow results and frequent plateaus in performance. Conversely, a deliberate effort in all three stages—setting new goals, taking intelligent action, and making appropriate course corrections—keeps the spiral going upward toward your ultimate genetic potential.

Goal Setting

Defining specific goals enables you to perform a gap analysis of what actions you must take to bridge the gap (or possibly chasm) between where you are now and what you want to become or achieve. Effective goal setting begins with a pen or pencil and a calendar, training log, or climbing notebook. If you don't write down your goals, chances are they will remain intangible hopes and dreams that never materialize.

It's best to set goals in three time frames: short term (daily), medium term (weekly or monthly), and long term (yearly or "career" goals). Write down the goals in precise terms and with realistic deadlines. And since pictures are even more motivating than words on paper, it's crucial to create a mental picture (representing the goal) that you can recall in your mind's eye on demand. The more precise and focused your picture and written goal, the easier it will be for you to zero in on the target and take actions that will someday lead you to realize the goal.

Next, create a mission statement that summarizes the purpose of each goal-setting time frame, such as "Short term, I strive for the most effective ninety-minute workout possible" or "Medium term, I am committed to redpointing my first 5.11 by the end of the summer." Now share these goals with your climbing partner, a close friend, or significant other—someone who will hold you accountable and help remind you of the mission.

Finally, write down what one or two (or more) things you will give up in order to reach your short-, medium-, and long-term goals. This vital step is missing from most conventional goal-setting exercises, and it may be the number one reason why so many people fail to achieve their big goals in life. It's a fact that you cannot add something new and achieve the ideal outcome without sacrificing something else in its place. Ponder this powerful idea. It may explain why some of your past or present goals remain elusive.

SHORT-TERM GOALS

Short-term goals define your daily game plan. They help focus your thoughts and actions so that you are not swayed by what others are doing and don't waste precious time on less important activities (TV, partying, surfing the Net, excessive socializing). The more hectic your life, the more crucial it is that you spend a few minutes before bed or first thing in the morning doing some short-term goal setting. Folks with less difficult daily schedules may only need to set short-term goals relating to the workout du jour. Begin by writing down the primary mission of the workout, then list the specific exercises, sets, and reps as well as the approximate amount of time you will dedicate to each part of the workout (see "An Example of Short-Term Goal Setting" below). Don't forget to list what you will give up (relative to previous days or your peers) in order to fulfill these short-term commitments.

MEDIUM-TERM GOALS

Medium-term goals give shape and direction to your schedule over the course of weeks and months. This planning is best done on a calendar so you can effectively dovetail your workouts and climbing trips with your other nonclimbing activities. Try to roughly plan things out a few months in advance (see the "Setting Medium-Term Goals" exercise below).

First, block in the big events such as climbing trips, competitions, work and family obligations, and the like. Next, write in your proposed workout and climbing schedule, with special attention to maintaining enough rest days in the game plan. With the most important items now in place, you can fill in the many little, less important things in life where time allows (or this can be done on an ad hoc basis). Remember to sum up your medium-term goals with one overriding primary goal, as well as listing the activities you will forfeit in order to attain this lofty goal.

LONG-TERM GOALS

Long-term goal setting is a fun and invaluable activity in which you condense onto paper the numerous "dream" or "I wish" goals floating around in your mind. If there is to be any chance of them ever becoming reality, it's vital that they be liberated from the dreamland of your mind and put down in black and white (see the "Setting Long-Term Goals" exercise below). A magical force begins to act in your life when you write down these mega goals—your subconscious mind will go to work day and night on achieving them, and your conscious mind will suddenly find them more believable (and achievable).

An Example of Short-Term Goal Setting

TODAY'S MISSION

Focus on improving my footwork and conserving energy by practicing skills and techniques.

WHAT I WILL GIVE UP TO ACHIEVE THIS GOAL

The usual bouldering games and competitions at the gym.
For today, I'll stay off all routes that are beyond my on-site ability.
I won't rush home to watch TV.

WHAT I WILL DO

1. Warm up with fifteen minutes of light bouldering, gentle stretching, and two sets of pull-ups.

2. Perform fifteen minutes of the traverse-training drill with focus on light grip, precise footwork, and smooth movement.

3. Toprope several climbs within one number grade of my limit with the focus on practicing technique, not performance outcome (whether or not I fall).

   My practice goals are to concentrate on careful positioning and use of each foothold; to climb as briskly, smoothly, and decisively as possible between rests; to accurately read sequences before leaving the ground and while at each rest position; to remain positive, relaxed, and centered during each climb.

4. Perform three sets of ten repetitions of the one-arm lunging exercise.

5. Perform three sets of hypergravity pull-ups with ten pounds.

6. Cool down with five to ten minutes of stretching.

7. Eat a good meal within one to two hours after the workout.

8. Get seven to eight hours of sleep.

Exercise: Setting Medium-Term Goals

Your medium-term goals can include both climbing and nonclimbing items; we'll focus on the climbing-related goals here. Write down your top training goals (mental, physical, and technical) for the next three months, as well as a few climbing goals such as to-do routes or new areas to visit. Distill these goals into a single primary goal for the period, and remember to list a few things you will freely give up in order to reach these goals.

_____

_____

_____

_____

_____

_____

_____

_____

_____

_____

_____

_____

_____

_____

_____

_____

_____

Exercise: Setting Long-Term Goals

Go somewhere quiet, allow yourself to relax for a few minutes, and ponder what long-term mega goals would really energize you and make for an exceptional journey. I call these mega goals because they are the few events that you most want to achieve in your life given your current perspective. For example, you might have an ultimate grade of climbing you'd like to achieve, or possibly a specific dream climb to send or mountain to summit. Think about where you'd go if time and money were not an issue—put it down on paper and the odds increase a thousandfold that you will someday be pulling down there! By all means write down a few of your non-climbing mega goals as well, but keep the total list down to between six and eight items.

As in setting your short- and medium-term goals, it's absolutely critical that you write down a couple of major things that you will completely give up in order to reach these mega goals. Consider the activities, possessions, and people that drain your time, focus, and energy.

_____

_____

_____

_____

_____

_____

_____

_____

_____

_____

_____

_____

_____

Taking Action and Making Course Corrections

The Cycle of Improvement will spiral you upward in ability as long as the actions taken provide movement toward your goals. Sadly, taking consistent, disciplined action in the direction of worthy goals is very difficult for some people. The results of their misdirected actions always seem to leave them in an all-too-familiar situation. The phrase *same s___, different day* is born of this affliction.

If any of this sounds familiar (in climbing or life), it's important to begin taking notice of just who is directing the actions you take on a daily basis. In many cases you'll discover that outside forces are calling the shots for you—that is, you are taking the actions someone else wants you to make, not those congruent with your goals. This is what the multibillion-dollar advertising industry is all about. Large companies spend millions with the sole intent of directing your actions in their favor (to make them money and drain your wallet). So while you might have a very worthy goal of, say, "getting out of debt" or "saving for a house," advertisers cleverly divert your actions in their favor. Unless you are acutely aware of what's going on (and the power they wield over you), you will veer off your course and onto theirs—and maybe never reach your goals.

This may sound negative, but the same thing often happens when you're training at the gym or climbing at the crag. Instead of doing the precise exercises and drills you need to improve your weaknesses, you end up climbing down the blind alley of someone else's agenda. Consider how many climbing days you've spent working on someone else's dream project (one that is either over your head or just not what you had planned) when you would have gained more by getting on a different type of climb. Or ponder how often you've gone to the gym and ended up socializing and just climbing mindlessly with no goal or direction. Sure, these kinds of evenings can be relaxing and fun once in a while, but on a regular basis they will not make you a better climber.

The win–win solution is to find a partner equally motivated to taking actions that will produce the fastest possible gains in ability. With this person you can evenly split the climbing time, so that you each can work effectively toward your goals. Unfortunately, in many partnerships one person makes all the calls and gets most of the benefits of the time spent training or climbing.

In summary, strive for hour-to-hour, day-to-day awareness of the "whats" and "whys" of the actions you are taking. By formulating short-term goals, as

---

Tips for Achieving Your Goals

1. Know yourself. Live your passion. What worthy goals will drive you to excellence?

2. Regularly assess your strengths and weaknesses. What's holding you back in terms of action (or inaction) and self-defeating thoughts and habits?

3. Take the self-assessment in this chapter at least once per year, and consider getting the objective evaluation of a climbing coach.

4. Regularly evaluate the effectiveness of your actions—are you obtaining the intended results?

If not, make course corrections that will yield more effective actions.

5. Don't be afraid to step away from the crowd and pursue your own mega goals. Ally with like-minded individuals, and avoid people with bad attitudes and unproductive behavior.

6. Set mega goals that will inspire and energize you from sunrise to sunset, and make your life an amazing journey.

discussed earlier, you can best maintain your focus on the things you need to do to improve short term and advance toward your meaningful medium- and long-term goals. Finally, foster an acute awareness of the results you are getting from your actions. Peak performers are those who most rapidly recognize when they are off course, and respond with a reassessment of the situation and an appropriate course correction toward the desired goal.

If it's beginning to sound like becoming a better climber is a very mental thing, you are right! So let's dive into chapter 3, "Mental Training."

Mental Training

The wise man will be the master of his mind. A fool will be its slave.

—*Publilius Syrus*

The quickest way to enhance your performance in almost anything is to improve the quality of your thinking. This is definitely true in climbing, whether you're working a highball boulder problem, sport route, multipitch traditional line, or alpine route. All performance operates from the inside out—your beliefs, focus, fears, confidence, preparation, and problem-solving abilities form the foundation from which you will either succeed or fail.

Great performances begin with bulletproof confidence, singular focus, positive emotions, and a tough yet agile mind-set. Conversely, setbacks and failures result from the worry, doubts, tension, and uncertainties that are born from a poorly harnessed brain running wild with fearful thoughts. It's my belief that whether you (or I) will succeed or fail on a climb is often predetermined in your subconscious (or even conscious) before you ever step off the ground.

While off-season strength training and year-round technique training are paramount for progressing into the higher grades, during the climbing season your biggest breakthroughs will come from toning and flexing your *mental muscle*. Toward this

end, this chapter details two dozen powerful mental strategies and skills that will help elevate your performance and enjoyment.

Practice these skills with the same dedication and resolve as you would a new strength-training program, and you'll be pleasantly surprised with the results. Obtain the greatest payoff by applying these skills 24/7, not just when you feel like it. For some, an almost instant breakthrough will follow on the rock, while others will need to persist and let these mental skills build to a critical value before they will produce a noticeable impact on climbing. (This depends upon the current degree of tone or atrophy of your mental muscle.)

Recognize that all these mental-training skills are interlaced and can produce a powerful synergy when all are in practice. In aggregate they may produce an effect similar to unloading a ten-pound weight (or more!) from your back that you have unknowingly been hauling up climbs. I call this using your Mental Wings.

Mental Wings for Improving Performance

The late, great Wolfgang Güllich was fond of saying that "the brain is the most important muscle for climbing." What makes this statement even more provocative is the fact that Güllich was one of the strongest people to ever pull down on stone. From the mid-1980s until his death in a car accident in 1992, he opened up several new grades of maximum difficulty by leveraging the synergy of his physical and mental fortitude. I support Wolfie's sentiment not only because the mind is one-third of the climb-

Phil Hoffman deep-water soloing at Summersville Lake, West Virginia. DAN BRAYACK

ing performance triad (see figure 1.1) but also due to the fact that poor mental control can instantly sabotage your physical and technical abilities.

Below are ten strategies that you can start using today in all aspects of your life. Apply them faithfully with the knowledge that most truly successful men and women in this sport possess these skills.

1. Separate your self-image from your performance.

If you are reading this book, then climbing surely plays a major role in your life. However, if your self-image is tied too strongly or singularly to this role, it leads to an obsessive need to perform perfectly every time you touch the rock. The result is intense pressure, anxiety, and fear of failure—all of which will make performing your best difficult, if not impossible.

The fact is, you will perform best in a process-oriented frame of mind, where the outcome is accepted as unknown and allowed to unfold without anticipation. Detaching your self-image from your climbing performance is the first step to escaping an outcome-oriented mind-set. Strive to focus only on things immediate to the act of climbing—your warm-up, mental rehearsal, gear selection; when climbing, focus only on the move at hand, never projecting ahead. Accept the feedback the route gives you without frustration or judgment and liberate yourself to try new things, take chances, and—most important—*fall*. Such process orientation and self-image detachment will reduce pressure and anxiety; paradoxically, you'll climb better by not needing to!

2. Surround yourself with positive people.

There is an aura of influence that surrounds each of us, and its effects are based on our personality and attitude toward life and its events. Your thoughts and actions will affect the thoughts and actions of those around you, and vice versa. As I see it, there are three options—either climb alone, climb with upbeat and positive people, or climb with cynical and negative people. But why would you ever want to climb with the negative, excuse-making complainers of the climbing world? Their negative aura will adversely

impact your climbing and enjoyment whether you recognize it or not. The bottom line: Vow to either climb with positive individuals or climb solo. Both approaches can be hugely rewarding.

3. Stretch your comfort zone.

To improve in anything, your goals must exceed your current grasp and you must be willing to push beyond your comfort zone in your reach. In performing on the vertical plane, this means climbing onward despite mental and physical discomfort; it means challenging your fears head-on by doing what you fear; and it means attempting what looks impossible to you based on past experience. Through this process, you will stretch your abilities to a new level, redefine your belief system, and reshape your personal vision of what is possible.

4. Anticipate and proactively manage your risk.

Climbing is an activity with obvious inherent risks, and the desire to climb harder often requires taking on even more. This can come in the form of obvious physical danger such as a potentially injurious fall, or as less tangible mental risk like opening yourself up to failure, criticism, and embarrassment. It's interesting to note that for some climbers, the physical danger can feel more tolerable than the mental. As an example, consider a climber who foolishly continues upward on a horrendously dangerous route he's not prepared for because of the fear of being dissed (by those standing safely on the ground!) should he back off.

Make it your MO to carefully assess all the possible risks before starting up every climb. Determine ways that you can reduce the risk of the climb (such as rigging a belay differently than usual or getting an extra spotter or crash pad), and anticipate how you will respond to new emerging risk as you climb (for instance, discovering there are no protection placements higher up the route). As for the mental risks you might face (like the fear of failure), see Mental Strategy 1 on separating your self-image from your performance.

5. Fortify your confidence.

Your degree of self-confidence is primarily based on your self-image and the thoughts you possess minute by minute and day by day. For example, pondering past failures, allowing free rein to demeaning self-talk, or dwelling on the chance of falling will deflate self-confidence and sow the seeds of failure.

Conversely, peak performers consciously narrow their thoughts and focus onto things that will fortify and build confidence. You, too, can do this as you prepare for an ascent, by taking a mental inventory of past successes, reviewing and believing in your skills and strengths, and acknowledging your preparation and investment in training. Do all this and you will grow more energized and confident as you engage the rock, and most likely climb your very best.

6. Use visualization to foster a peak performance zone.

"The zone" is that state where everything comes together for a perfect ascent that seems almost effortless and automatic. The trick is being able to create this state on demand, despite stressful conditions such as the heat of competition or before a hard redpoint attempt. Here's how.

First, use visualization to reenact the positive feelings of a good performance in a past similar situation. Create about a sixty-second mental movie of this past event using all your senses. Make the pictures crisp and bright, and let the emotion and feeling of the success take over your body. With the positive, confident emotions of this past event now internalized for use in the present, you can begin mental rehearsal of the upcoming climb. Begin by visualizing yourself climbing the route from a detached on-TV perspective—it's in this mode of visualization that you'd develop a sequence and strategy for the ascent. Next, close your eyes and climb the route in your mind's eye—feel the moves play out successfully to create a mental blueprint for action (you'll find more detailed instruction on visualization later in this chapter). Now open your eyes and take on the route for real, one move at a time.

7. Use preclimb rituals to create an ideal performance state.

The things you think and do in the minutes and moments before you climb form the foundation onto which your performance is built. A shaky foundation generally leads to a shaky performance; a solid foundation usually gives birth to a solid performance. The nature of your foundation (sand or stone?) is influenced by the quality of your preclimb rituals. These are things you do to best prepare for the ascent, including scoping the route, visualizing the sequence, preparing your gear, warming up, and even your way of putting on your shoes. Everything down to tiny details, such as breathing rate, posture, and final thoughts, should be programmed into the rituals that lead up to the moment you step onto the rock.

Develop your rituals based on past experience. What things did you think or do before some of your best ascents in the past? What did you eat or drink, how did you warm up, and how long did you rest between climbs? Awareness of all the things (little and big) that led up to your best performances is a key to being able to reproduce similar results in the future. Once your rituals become tried and true, stick to them!

8. Control stress and tension before they control you.

This strategy is central to climbing your best, because tension kills performance. Period. Tension is often a physical manifestation of mental stress, although it can also develop in overstressed muscles or as the result of an inadequate warm-up. Either way, the outcome is the same—poor motor control (inefficient movement), unproductive emotions, and quite often failure. Here are two ways to control tension and stress on the fly. First, direct your thinking away from pressure-producing thoughts and focus only on the process of climbing. Engage the route completely and stay in the moment. Second, use rest positions to break from the process of climbing and direct your thoughts inward for a tension check. Use the six-step ANSWER sequence (described later in this chapter) to clear tension and return to center in less than one minute—perfect for use at every midroute rest position.

9. Engage in positive self-talk.

Inside our heads, each of us has a "critic" voice and a "doer" voice that gab throughout our waking hours. While the critic voice can be useful in a few situations (such as evaluating weaknesses or performance errors), it's the doer voice that compels action, keeps us positive, and, in fact, helps us perform effectively. Controlling this internal self-talk is fundamental to controlling our attitude and climbing our best.

Which voice—the critic or the doer—rules your mind? Hopefully you'll conclude that the doer's voice rules your mental roost about 95 percent of the time (or more). If not, you can surely improve your performance by eliminating the self-destructive internal dialogue. The first step is to sever your ties to negative, critical people: Their verbal and nonverbal communication will absolutely pollute your thoughts and attitude.

Next, strive to heighten your awareness of your self-talk—the goal is to think about what you are thinking about!—and allow the doer voice to run the talk show. When you notice the critic voice speaking up, determine if it is useful (for instance, to help with risk management) or just trash talk. Take the critic's non-useful comments and invert them into positive statements. For example, change *This route looks impossible* to *This route looks challenging;* replace *I feel nervous* with *I feel energized;* convert *I'll probably fall* into *I think I can do this, but if I fall it's okay because I'll get it next time.* Direct such positive self-talk on every climb and throughout every day and you will marshal psychic energy that enhances your performance in all you do.

10. Love climbing, no matter what.

A common trait of successful people is resilience to criticism and bad results, and an unwavering belief that success will come with time and effort. Developing such a mind-set takes a disciplined effort to constantly spin negative feedback into some kind of a positive—real winners never dwell on the setbacks or accept defeat.

Remember, climbing is about the journey, not the summit. Vow to love the process of climbing and

all it entails, whether it is a perfect send or a painful struggle. Sure, a perfect ascent is immensely gratifying; however, it's on the arduous journey that you actually become a better climber and grow as a person. The bottom line: Love climbing unconditionally, and you will always have a great day on the rocks!

Controlling Your Emotions

Your emotions have a direct effect on your body and mind. What you are feeling exerts an influence over the quality of your actions and your ways of thinking (see figure 3.1). Consider how nervousness before a climb can derail your concentration as well as trigger preclimb jitters throughout your body. We can then conclude that emotional control is essential for optimal performance.

Observe great climbers such as Chris Sharma and Lynn Hill at work and you will notice either positive, productive emotions or no emotion at all. Even when they fall, you sense little anger or angst—only

Figure 3.1 How Emotions Run the Show

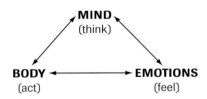

What you feel exerts an influence over how you think and what you do. Likewise, ways of thinking and acting affect how you feel.

love of the process of climbing, which occasionally includes falling. Now consider how your thoughts and emotions evolve when the going gets tough—do they sometimes become negative, fearful, or even self-defeating? If so, then your physical performance will absolutely suffer given the intimate mind-emotion-body relationship shown in figure 3.1.

The following storyline illustrates how negative emotions can sabotage performance.

1. The climber leaves the ground and moves cautiously through the initial moves. He looks apprehensive, as if he's trying not to make any mistakes.
2. As he enters more difficult moves, his breathing becomes shallow and irregular. He may even hold his breath on hard sequences.
3. Negative emotional energy rises, resulting in increased muscular tension and mental stress.
4. This building stress disrupts his coordination, balance, and footwork. Movements become tight, mechanical, and inefficient. He begins to overgrip holds.
5. He begins to hold back on hard moves, afraid to fully commit, and hangs out too long on marginal rests.
6. The fight-or-flight syndrome is triggered, adding some adrenaline to the mix. This burst of energy may help the climber thrash through a few more moves; more commonly, however, the jolt causes him to grab the rope or a quick draw, and retreat from the route.
7. The death grip sets in and flames out his muscles.
8. He falls and lets loose a few expletives.
9. Hanging on the rope, he engages in critical thinking that further raises the tide of negative emotions.

Does any part of this story sound familiar? If so, I have some good news. You can learn to rein in your emotions and thus open up a whole new level of climbing performance and enjoyment. If you have good emotional control already, I bet you can still improve your climbing by modulating your arousal level. Let's explore this murky subject of emotions and discuss how you can make some immediate positive changes.

Evaluating Your Emotional State

In evaluating your emotional state, the goal is to become aware of the "sign" of your emotions—positive or negative—and the magnitude of your arousal, high or low. Obviously, positive emotions have different effects on the mind and body than negative emotions. Similarly, the intensity of these emotions (the arousal level) plays a role in how you think and feel. To better understand this relationship, consider the Energy–Emotion Matrix (see figure 3.2).

The Energy–Emotion Matrix has four quadrants: high energy, positive emotion (upper right); low energy, positive emotion (lower right); high energy, negative emotion (upper left); and low energy, negative emotion (lower left). The matrix represents a continuum of emotion and energy across these four quadrants. Therefore, you can evaluate your present location in the matrix by grading your current energy level on a scale from 0 to 10 (low to high) and scoring your current emotional state on a scale from −5 (extremely negative) to +5 (extremely positive). Knowing where you are in the matrix and having the ability to change this location if it's not optimal in the current situation is fundamental to becoming a peak performer in any endeavor.

Obviously, your energy level and emotions fluc-

Figure 3.2 The Energy–Emotion Matrix

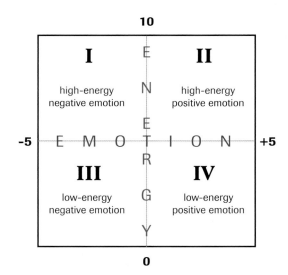

What quadrant of the matrix are you most often in?

tuate throughout the day and over the course of a climb, so your place in the matrix changes hour by hour and, maybe, minute to minute in extreme situations. I believe it's valuable to study your place in the matrix in everyday, nonclimbing situations, since your most common daily state will heavily determine your disposition when climbing (it's unlikely you can be a negative person at home and work, then become completely positive when you go climbing). Use the blank energy–emotion time line contained in appendix B to plot your changing energy–emotional state throughout the day, as shown in figure 3.3. Begin upon waking in the

morning, and score your state every thirty minutes, or when some event causes your emotion or energy to change in an instant.

After evaluating your emotional state for a few days, see if you can identify any patterns. What time(s) of the day is your energy high or low? What events seem to trigger you becoming more positive or negative? Recognizing these patterns (and effects) empowers you to make modifications, such as striving to avoid negative triggers. Likewise, you may be able to see what charges up your energy level (and when) and what type of things make it tank. If you can't avoid negative triggers, it's vital that you know

Figure 3.3 Sample Chart of Energy–Emotion Levels

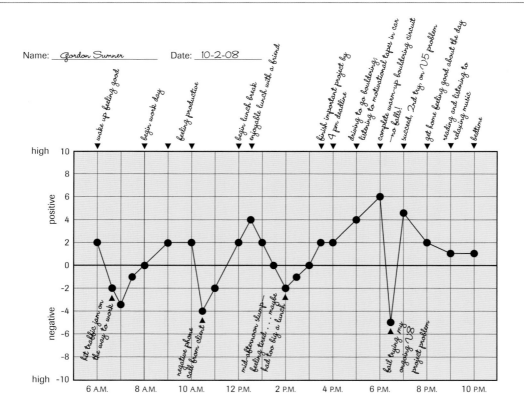

Sample chart of energy–emotion levels throughout the day, including notes of triggers or events that effected an energy–emotion change.

TRAINING for CLIMBING

how to turn your states around. Below we'll discuss ways to modify your emotional state.

It's also beneficial to track how your state changes over the course of a day at the crags, and especially during an attempt of a hard boulder problem or route. While you certainly can't write down your score while on a route, you can mentally score yourself by simply asking yourself, *What quadrant am I in?*

Before you can change your state, you must first determine the optimal state for the present moment. Of course, beginning in a positive emotional state is always ideal, but the optimal magnitude of your arousal (energy level) will vary depending on the type of task you are involved in. For instance, a low-positive (Quadrant IV) state is ideal for taking a test or meeting with your boss, while a high-positive (Quadrant II) is best for working out at the gym or playing a high-intensity sport. In climbing, it's almost always best to be in the low-energy, positive-emotion quadrant—creative thinking, learning, and fine motor skills all demand a relaxed, positive state. The exception would be when psyching up for a vicious boulder problem or a short, powerful sport route. In these cases, a high-energy, positive state is ideal.

Changing Your Emotional States

You can rapidly change your emotional state by leveraging the known relationships among the mind, emotions, and body (see figure 3.1). Just as your emotions exert an influence over your mind and body, you can use your mind and body to influence your emotions. In negative people the process tends to be reactive and runs itself, whereas happy, productive people are skilled at using their mind and body to produce positive emotions. So if you make it habit to carry your body in a positive way (good posture, head up, smiling) and think in a positive way (grateful for what you have, reliving only good memories, focusing on future goals), you will feel positive and, in fact, be a generally happy and successful person. This is one of the most powerful distinctions in this book—live it!

You should now have a good sense of the things

Tips for Optimizing Your Emotions

1. Regularly tune into your thoughts and self-talk. Evaluate what you are hearing. What quadrant are you in?
2. Supplant negative thinking with positive, productive thoughts. Direct solution-oriented thinking and dwell on your goals.
3. Use your body to change your state. Roll your shoulders back, take a few deep belly breaths, crack a big smile and laugh.
4. Leverage your emotional resources by reviewing past successes. In your mind's eye, vividly relive past great climbs and other amazing life events—feel the positive emotions charge you up in the present moment.

you can do to shift into a more positive state. Physiologically, you can take on a more extended posture and crack a smile, you can jump up and down or do anything physical, you can pump your fist in the air and exclaim "Yeah!" All these physical things will effect a rapid change in your emotions—try it now! Mentally, you can replay great events or climbs from the past, think about all you've accomplished in your life, ponder your good health or your fortune to have been born in a first-world country (where you can actually engage in a luxury activity like climbing), or visualize the medium- and long-term goals that excite you.

Hopefully you now recognize that either your emotions are controlling you or you are in control of your emotions. Happy people and peak performers (in sports and life) are those who are able to control their emotions and adjust their arousal level on demand. In our frantic society, and when participating in a potentially high-stress sport such as climbing, these emotion-modulating skills are invaluable. Strive to monitor your position in the matrix throughout the day and optimize your state when needed, and you'll discover a new quality of climbing and living!

Dealing with Fear

As I stated in *How to Climb 5.12,* "the 'no fear' mentality is for buffoons, beer-guzzling frat boys, and couch potatoes." In climbing, reasonable fears keep you alive long enough to realize your potential and to send a long lifetime's worth of stellar routes. For example, fear of taking a ground fall compels you to seek good protection on the lead and to drag a rope in the first place.

It's *unreasonable* fears that derail performance. Things such as fear of falling on a well-protected route, fear of physical discomfort, fear of failure, and fear of embarrassment must all be eliminated if you are to climb your best. There are also preclimb fears such as *I might be too tall,* or *too short,* or *too weak* to do the climb, which—left unchecked—give birth to reality.

Finally, there are subconscious, preprogrammed fears that are the root of many of the "dumb things" that seem to just happen. Have you ever fallen after the crux when the route is in the bag? Or have you slipped off a large hold or botched a wired sequence even though you felt in control? It may be that such mistakes are the result of unchallenged inner fears, not lack of ability. The key is to deal with your fears head-on (and not to run from them). Use the following exercise to identify and analyze your common fears. As the fears reveal themselves, use logic and reason to specifically counter each. If no logical counter is evident, however, the fear may be *reasonable* and worth heeding.

 Identify and Analyze Your Common Climbing Fears

Start by writing down recurrent fears that regularly hurt your performance. If you can't think of any on the spot, go for a climb and pay special attention to every preclimb thought and while-you-climb concern. List your fears down the left column, and then write an assessment of each fear in the space to the right. Use logic and reason to counter each fear. Your fraudulent fears should be easy to counter. If you identify that a fear is real and useful (for saving your neck), however, then you want to write down what action you can take to mitigate the fear.

Fear

_____

_____

_____

_____

_____

_____

_____

_____

Assessment

_____

_____

_____

_____

_____

_____

_____

_____

Dealing with fear is an ongoing process since our fears are always changing. Review each poor performance and identify what fear(s) may have contributed to your difficulties. To help you with this analysis, here's a primer on four basic climbing fears: fear of falling, fear of pain, fear of failure, and fear of embarrassment.

Fear of Falling

Fear of falling is inherent to climbing. Interestingly enough, it's not really falling that we fear but not knowing what the fall will be like. This explains why your first fall on a route is the scariest, while subsequent falls are often much less stressful. Beginners probably need some hands-on proof that falls can be safe. The best way for a would-be leader to gain trust in the system is by taking some intentional falls. Find a steep climb with bomber protection, use a good rope (and double-check your knot and buckle) and belayer, and then take a few practice falls. Start off with 2-foot falls and build up to about 12-footers (with the gear just a few feet below you). A more experienced climber fearful of falling on an upcoming on-sight climb can counter the fear during the preclimb warm-up. The tactic here is to mentally replay some past inconsequential falls and to believe fully that falls on this climb will be no different (if that is indeed the case—some falls are obviously deadly, and only a fool would ignore that possibility).

Fear of Pain

When pushing your limits, fear of pain can become a critical weakness. It causes you to give up long before your body has reached its physical limitations. The pain of climbing a continuously strenuous route is akin to that of running a mile at full speed—it freaking hurts! Fortunately, the pain is brief and perseverance pays big dividends. Decide to push yourself a bit further into the discomfort zone each time you're on a hard route. Soon your pain threshold will be redefined, as will your limits on the rock.

Fear of Failure

This deep-seated fear is often instilled during childhood when almost every action is classified by our family, teachers, and friends as either a success or a failure. We've all had childhood situations where the fear of failure was so gripping that we became immobilized and time seemed to stop. Fortunately, adults generally don't react quite this intensely, but it's still common for us to imagine all the bad things that could possibly go wrong. Once triggered, these negative thoughts can snowball and, more often than not, become self-fulfilling prophecies.

In climbing, fear of failure causes you to hold back. As your attack on a route becomes less aggressive than required, you'll find yourself second-guessing sequences in the midst of doing them, your breathing will become shallow, and you'll begin to overgrip the rock. You may even fall prey to paralysis by analysis.

Eliminate fear of failure in one of three ways. First, focus on what is *probable* instead of what is *possible*. Sure, it's human nature to always consider the worst-case scenario, but this almost never comes to pass. Counter these thoughts by considering what is probable and realistic based on past experiences.

The second way to nix this fear is to focus all your attention on the process of climbing, instead of pondering the possible outcomes. Concentrate on the things immediate to your performance—precise foot placements, relaxing your grip, moving quickly onto the next rest position, and so on. Your limited supply of energy is too valuable to waste worrying about how high you will climb or the eventual results. As William Levinson points out in his book *The Way of Strategy*, "To succeed, we must not care if we fail."

Along this same line, you must adopt the attitude that *It's okay to fall* (assuming a safe fall) and that *Falling won't bother me. I'll just get back up and give it another go*. By willingly accepting this fate (if it should even happen), you totally dissolve the fear of failure that handcuffs so many climbers. Therefore, by being okay with falling, it's less likely you will. This simple idea is one of the most powerful in this book.

Fear of Embarrassment

Finally, there is fear of embarrassment and being dissed. Get over this now or you'll never fully enjoy climbing, or reach your potential. Realize that occasional bad-performance days are inevitable. Instead of trying to avoid them, simply accept that they happen, analyze why they happened, then bury them. With this attitude you will be free to try chancy moves and risk an occasional mistake. In the long run you'll often look like a hero, but never like a zero. Surely this is better than embracing the critics and accepting mediocrity all the time.

Don't forget, your friends know how good a climber you are, and they won't think any worse of you because of a poor performance. Anyone else critical of you really doesn't matter. Work on improving your self-confidence and don't let the criticisms of others invade your thoughts.

In the end, embrace the attitude that there are no failures, only results. The results might not be ideal, but they do in fact contain important clues for improvement—do not overlook these guideposts for future success! The bottom line: By challenging your fears and doubling your exposure to fearful situations, you will double your rate of improvement and learn to excel in the most difficult and stressful situations.

Tips for Managing Fear

1. Analyze your fears to determine if they are real or imagined. Take action to mitigate the risk(s) associated with your legitimate fears.
2. Overcome imagined fears with reason— know that these phantom fears are bogus. Redirect your thinking in productive ways and resolve to dismiss all other illusionary fears that might surface.
3. Focus on the process of climbing, and detach from the possible outcomes. Let the climb unfold one move at a time.
4. Predetermine that you will accept failure should it happen. Recognize that you are not defined by your successes or failures— however, you are defined by the way you react to success and failure.

Relaxation Training and Centering

More than ever before, there are a multitude of things in our lives that can result in high levels of stress. Our jobs, relationships, possessions, even driving to the crag can trigger a stress response such as muscular tension or negative thoughts. Interestingly, it's not the events or things in our lives that actually cause the stress, but instead our reaction to them. Knowing this, you are empowered to control your reactions to everything you experience and, in turn, regulate the total amount of stress in your life.

Recognizing that an event or situation is causing you to become stressed is the first step toward controlling its effects. Foster an acute awareness of your tension levels by regularly asking yourself things like, *How do I feel?* or *Are there any growing pockets of muscular tension?* Make such tension checks a regular part of your day. For instance, do a quick check of your tension and stress levels every hour, and especially before any type of event that requires an optimal physiological state (a big meeting or hard climb). Keep an eye out for telltale signs of building tension such as a clenched jaw, overgripping a pencil or the steering wheel, or tightness and burning in the muscles of your neck, shoulders, or back.

On the rock, tension reveals itself in overgripping of holds, nervously muscling through a crux move, or a general lack of fluid motion. Again, your goal is to recognize and tone down the tension when it begins; otherwise it will rapidly snowball and sabotage your performance. This, in fact, is a common cause of blowing a sequence you thought you had wired, or falling off a route that should be well within your ability. By killing your economy of movement, building tension and stress may very well kill your performance. And it's probably been happening for so long that you don't even recognize its negative effects on your climbing.

The antidote to tension is, of course, relaxation. Following are two highly effective relaxation strategies as well as a great on-the-rock centering sequence that I call the ANSWER. Experiment with all three, and try to incorporate their use throughout your daily activities. In a short time you will become a master of stress and find yourself feeling much more relaxed—and also climbing harder, thanks to an increase in apparent strength (a result of reduced tension in the antagonist muscles and elimination of overgripping).

Progressive Relaxation

In the early 1940s American physician Edmund Jacobson developed a technique known as progressive relaxation, because he felt that by fully relaxing the muscles, you would in turn relax the mind (Garfield 1984). He found that relaxation could be best learned by deliberately tensing and relaxing specific muscle groups (see the "Progressive Relaxation Sequence" exercise that follows). This process results in a sharpened awareness of tension levels in the different parts of your body, and the ability to release the tension on demand. In time, you will be able to discern even small increases in muscular tension and act to immediately eliminate the tension before there's any degradation in performance.

 Progressive Relaxation Sequence

Perform the following procedure at least once a day. I find it most useful during a midday break, as part of a long rest period at the crag, or last thing before falling asleep. Initially, the process will take about fifteen minutes. With practice, you'll be able to move quickly through the sequence and reach a state of complete relaxation in less than five minutes. Concentrate on flexing only the muscle(s) specified in each step. This is an invaluable skill you will find very handy when using the Differential Relaxation and ANSWER Sequences that are discussed later.

1. Go to a quiet location and sit or lie in a comfortable position.
2. Close your eyes and take five deep belly breaths. Inhale slowly through your nose to a slow, silent count to five, then gradually exhale through your mouth to a slow, silent ten-count.
3. Keeping your eyes closed and maintaining slow, relaxed breathing, tense the muscles in your right lower leg for five seconds. Feel the tension in your right foot and calf muscles, then let go and relax the muscles completely. Compare the difference in

sensation between the tense and relaxed states. Repeat this process with the left lower leg. Now, with both lower leg areas relaxed, say to yourself, *My feet and lower legs feel warm and light.* Upon saying this a few times, the muscles in this area will drop into a deep state of relaxation.

4. Next, perform the same sequence in the muscles of the upper leg (one leg at a time). Tense the muscles in your upper leg for five seconds, then relax them. After doing this with both legs, finish up by thinking, *My upper legs feel warm and light.* Feel all tension dissolve as your upper legs drop into deep relaxation.
5. Repeat this process in your hands and lower arms. Tense the muscles below your right elbow by making a tight fist for five seconds; then relax these muscles completely. Repeat this with the left hand and forearm, and conclude with the mantra, *My hand and forearm muscles feel warm and light.*
6. Repeat this procedure on the muscles in the upper arm.
7. Next, shift the focus to the many muscles of the torso (including the chest, abdominal, back, and shoulder areas). Repeat the process exactly.
8. Conclude with the muscles of the face and neck.
9. You should now be in a deep state of relaxation (possibly, you will have fallen asleep). Mentally scan yourself from head to toe for any isolated pockets of remaining tension, and drain them with the *warm and light* mantra.
10. At this point you can open your eyes and return to work or climbing with a renewed sense of calm and focus. Or you can leverage this relaxed state by performing some mind programming—visualization of the process of reaching some goal or the act of climbing some project route.

Using Differential Relaxation to Enhance Performance

Differential relaxation is used in active situations where you wish to relax any muscle(s) not needed for the task at hand. I find this skill especially useful in regaining an optimal state while hanging out and chalking at rest positions on the rock. I scan for unnecessary muscular contractions or pockets of tension and, with a few deep belly breaths, visualize the tension draining from the muscle like air escaping from a balloon. Try this next time you go climbing.

Many climbers shortchange themselves and reduce their apparent strength because of undue tension in muscles not needed for upward motion or stability. Unwanted contraction of the antagonist muscles or overcontraction of the prime movers interferes with even the simplest movements and wastes a tremendous amount of energy. Observe how climbers who try too hard or get gripped on a route become extremely rigid and mechanical, maybe even while moving through an easy sequence. Instead of using their muscles optimally, they're pitting one muscle against another, resulting in stress, fatigue, and premature failure. Conversely, the best climbers actively control undue tension (it's a mainly unconscious process in top climbers), move with grace and fluidity, and maximize economy of motion and energy use. As masters of differential relaxation, they can move smooth and fast like a Porsche but still get the high "miles-per-gallon" of a Honda.

Skill in differential relaxation comes with increased sensitivity to various degrees of relaxation and tension—something you will learn quickly through daily use. Practice by releasing tension in unused muscles while in the midst of common everyday activities like driving your car, sitting at your desk, working around home, or even lying down for a quick nap. Scan your body for pockets of tension or any contracting muscles that aren't critical for the task at hand. For me, it's typically tension in the shoulders, a clenched jaw (if I'm concentrating intensely), or unnecessary fidgeting by my feet.

On the rock, strive for acute awareness of tension increases so you can nip it in the bud before it results in a drop-off in performance. It's my practice to perform these "quality assurance checks" at all rest positions. Sometimes I recognize things like general tightness in my shoulders, unnecessary tension in my legs, or a little more contraction of my arm and forearm muscles than is needed to stick the grip or body position. Differential relaxation allows me to

correct these problems almost instantly—although I find centering and the ANSWER Sequence to be beneficial in these situations as well.

 The ANSWER Sequence

Perform the ANSWER Sequence before and during each climb and in everyday situations where you need to control tension, anxiety, and focus. Initially this six-step procedure will take a few minutes to perform. With practice you'll be able to go through the sequence in about ten seconds—perfect for use at marginal rest positions where getting centered could make the difference between success and failure.

A - AWARENESS

1. Awareness of rising tension, anxiety, or negative thoughts.

Acute awareness of unfavorable mental and physical changes is fundamental to optimal performance. It takes a conscious effort to turn your thoughts away from the outer world toward your inner world. Peak performers habitually make these tension checks every few minutes, so they can nix any negative changes before they snowball out of control. Make this your goal.

N - NORMALIZE

2. Normalize breathing.

In climbing, your breathing should be as relaxed (basically involuntary or unconscious) and regular as it would be while on a fast walk. Unfortunately, many climbers breathe unevenly during hard sequences, thus creating tension and degrading performance. Your goal is smooth, even, normal breathing throughout the climb.

S - SCAN

3. Scan for specific areas of muscular tension.

In this step you perform a tension check. Scan all your muscles in a quick sweep to locate pockets of tightness. Commonly tight areas are the forearms (are you overgripping?), shoulders, upper back, chest, abdominals, and calves. The best way to relax a specific muscle is to consciously contract that muscle for a few seconds, then relax it and visualize the tension draining from it like air from a balloon (the differential relaxation technique).

W - W A V E

4. Wave of relaxation.

Upon completing the tension check above, take a single deep breath and feel a wave of relaxation wash from your head to your toes.

E - E R A S E

5. Erase thoughts of past events (or the possible future) and focus on the present.

This step involves freeing your mind from the ball-and-chain of undesirable past events. There is no benefit to pondering the last failed attempt or the heinous sequence you just barely fought through. Let go of the past and do not ponder the future—thoughts of the past and future are enemies of excellence in the present. Refocus on and engage the present moment.

R - R E S E T

6. Reset posture and flash a smile.

It's amazing how much positive energy you can generate simply by resetting your posture and flashing a smile. This final step of the ANSWER Sequence will leave you in a peak performance state and ready to climb into the zone. Trust your skills, have fun, and let the outcome take care of itself.

Getting Centered

Centering is a simple, effective means of maintaining (or regaining) complete control of your mind and body as you head up on a difficult climb or into competition. When you're centered, you feel balanced, relaxed, and confident. Conversely, being out of center is characterized by feelings of imbalance, tension, awkward movement, and sometimes even growing

stress and anxiety. And since it takes just one botched move, one piece of gear to pop out, or one burst of adrenaline to knock you way out of center, it's essential that you are aware of this dynamic and able to respond quickly with countermeasures.

The ANSWER Sequence is a powerful means for returning yourself to center in just a few seconds. The ANSWER Sequence involves deliberately redirecting your thoughts inward for a moment (usually at a rest on a climb) to modulate your breathing, level of muscle tension, posture, and mental attitude. Make its use as regular and automatic as chalking up, and you'll find yourself climbing more efficiently and consistently.

Tips for Controlling Tension and Anxiety

1. Practice progressive and differential relaxation to develop the ability to relax individual muscles on demand.
2. Strive for constant awareness of growing tension and anxiety. Take a tension check at each rest on a climb and intermittently throughout the day.
3. Target relaxation in antagonist muscles—this will improve your climbing economy and enhance flow and fluidity of movement.
4. While you climb, employ the ANSWER Sequence at each rest position to regain your center and optimal performance state.

Visualization Training

Let's start off with an example of visualization. Sit back, relax, and vividly imagine the following scene as if it were a movie playing out before your eyes.

> You are attempting to redpoint a route you have worked on before. You have just successfully climbed to the rest position that precedes the route's crux sequence. You are relaxed, calm, and confident as you shake out and rechalk. You feel a cool breeze blow across your body, and it seems to enhance the light, centered feeling you already possess. You gently grip the starting hold of the sequence, a sharp, positive fingertip edge. With steady breathing, you flash a smile and continue climbing.
>
> You match hands and pull the fingertip edge to your chest. You then high-step your right foot onto a tiny crescent-shaped flake. You've hit it just right—it feels bomber. You rock over that glued right foot, spot, and then grab a matchbook side-pull edge with your right hand. You flag your left leg across and below your high right foot to shift your center of gravity over the right foot. You then extend off the right foot with a smooth, steady motion. Your left hand reaches up to snag a two-finger pocket—it feels solid. You move your left foot up to a high smear on a small dish hold, and, with relaxed breathing, take aim on the final lunge. Then, with your mind locked on to the next hold, you throw the lunge and easily latch on to the mini bucket hold that's been so elusive. You clip the anchors and feel the rush of having ticked this personal best route.

This sequence exemplifies a fundamental and important exercise used by all the world's top athletes. Although similar to the mental rehearsals performed by some climbers, visualization goes beyond the simple task of reviewing route sequences. As in the above example, visualization involves making and playing a detailed mental movie, one with touch, sound, color, and all the kinesthetic feel of doing the moves. These mental movies enhance your climbing by helping to hardwire sequences (moves, body positions, and "feel"), increasing memory, and fortifying confidence. For this reason, use of visualization is as important to your success as your use of climbing shoes and a chalk bag. Don't leave the ground without doing it!

Many studies have shown that the brain is not always capable of distinguishing between something that actually happened and something that was vividly imagined (Kubistant 1986). (Déjà vu is such an experience—you can't always recall if the clear mental image that just surfaced is an actual memory or simply something you've thought about or dreamed.) Therefore, repeated visualization can trick the mind into thinking you've been there and done that before. Think of these mental movies as a blueprint for future actions—with this perspective, you should understand why visualization must be as detailed and accurate as possible. Any bad coding (wrong moves) or fuzzy detail (uncertain sequences) may lead to a botched sequence or fall when you climb the route for real.

Types of Visualization

There are two primary modes of visualization: disassociated and associated. Disassociated visualization provides an "on-TV" perspective, where you see yourself climbing from an observer's point of view. This mode of visualization is best for reviewing some past poor performance that you hope to improve upon. As a detached observer, you can replay the movie and objectively view the mistakes or falls without reliving the possibly unhappy emotions of the situation.

Associated visualization provides a "through-your-own-eyes" perspective and thus triggers small neurological reactions as if you were doing the climb, as well as the feel and emotion of the movie you are playing. This makes associated visualization ideal for preprogramming some future ascent. As discussed above, repeated playing of a highly detailed, positive mental movie helps trick the subconscious mind into thinking you've done the climb before. Just make sure you are using the associated, not disassociated, perspective when visualizing some future event.

DISASSOCIATED VISUALIZATION

If you are new to the practice of visualization, I suggest you begin with a simple, nonclimbing example. Go to a quiet location, sit or lie down comfortably, and relax. Using an observer's point of view (disassociated), play a mental movie of the following scene as it might appear in your apartment or home.

Visualize yourself sitting on the couch and watching TV. Note the clothes you are wearing in the scene. See yourself get up from the couch, walk over to the refrigerator, and open it. See yourself reaching in and grabbing a can of soda, then watch yourself close the fridge. See yourself opening the can as you begin to walk back toward the couch. Note the way you are walking and observe the exact instant that you see yourself open the can. Now watch yourself sit back down on the couch and take a sip of the soda.

In this disassociated example you watched the scene play out before your eyes but you did not feel or sense, in any way, what it was like to go get the soda and drink it. Reserve this perspective for reviewing negative events from the past, climbing or nonclimbing, and for route finding, imagining possible sequences, and risk management. Gather the basic information you need to improve your performance or do the climb, and then engage in associated visualization to preprogram the actual moves for a successful future event.

ASSOCIATED VISUALIZATION

Now let's reshoot the mental movie of the at-home scene from the associated point of view. This time you will live the scene through your own eyes. Feel the action play out in your imagination just as if you were acting out the scene for real. Again, sit back, relax, and picture this scene playing out in real-life detail.

As you sit on the couch, you laugh at the closing joke of a *Seinfeld* rerun. You decide to go get a soda from the fridge, so you get up and begin walking toward the kitchen. Look around the room at the various pieces of furniture (or pictures on the wall) you pass on your way to the fridge. Enter the kitchen and feel your arm tug the refrigerator door open. Feel the cool air rush out and chill your face. As you reach into the

fridge for the soda, notice the colors and design of the can, then sense the cold, damp feel of the can in your hand. Now feel your arm slam the door shut and hear the sound it makes in closing. Conclude the scene by tasting the soda as you gulp it down—what flavors do you taste?

This example reveals the explicit detail you should try to build into your associated visualization. Granted, it will take some practice to develop Steven Spielberg–like detail into your mental movies, but that's the goal. Commit to making a short "film" for all your project routes, and don't hesitate to reshoot or edit the mental movie as you gain new information or beta for the route. Quality mind programming will improve the quality of your real-life performances. Guaranteed!

Uses of Visualization

I hope you now recognize that visualization is an immensely powerful tool that can be used to enhance performance in all aspects of your life. I'm sure you use simple visualization every day, maybe without even knowing it. For example, when you think about the best way to drive across town, I'm sure you see the key turns or landmarks along the way in your mind's eye beforehand. Visualization is also used "effectively" by people who worry a lot—part of their worry ritual is wild visualization of some future event that may or may not happen to them (or some loved one). This type of negative visualization is most painful and depressing when done from an associated perspective. Such negative visualization is pathological, since you are putting yourself through the pain of some future event that may never happen.

Some climbers become consumed in the same types of negative moviemaking of future events. For instance, if you visualize yourself failing on a route or in competition, you not only preprogram this possible outcome but also destroy your self-confidence in the process. To avoid this, it's vital that you visualize only positive events and ideal outcomes when you project into the future in the associated state. Switch to the disassociated mode if you need to visualize things (from a risk management perspective) that might go wrong—say, on an on-sight lead. See from the on-TV view the possible falls you could take and what risks might be involved in the ascent. Described below are several settings where you can use visualization to improve your safety and mind-set (among other things), as well as the chances of the ideal outcome coming true.

PREPROGRAMMING A REDPOINT ASCENT

Since you've been on the route before, you could begin with disassociated visualization of your last attempt. See yourself climbing the route and note what things need to be corrected or refined for the next attempt. Now use the associated perspective to create a movie, as seen through your own eyes, of the perfect ascent you plan to make. Imagine all the important aspects of doing the route, including the crux moves, gear placements or clips, rest positions, and such. Create all the feel of doing the moves as well as the feeling of being relaxed and centered as you move into the crux. Make the movie positive and perfect in every way, and always conclude with the feeling of reaching the top.

PREPARING FOR AN ON-SIGHT ASCENT

Visualization is invaluable when applied to a climb you've never been on before. Since you have no firsthand experience, it will be very hard to create an accurate movie from the associated perspective. Therefore, you'll want to spend most of your time visualizing from a disassociated perspective.

After studying the climb from below, create images or a movie of yourself climbing the route from the on-TV perspective. See yourself dropping in gear at the obvious placements as well as hanging out at what appear to be good rest positions. As described above, you will want to visualize any hazards unique to this climb—where a lead fall might be dangerous, what you can do to minimize the risk, and so forth. Also, if you can see enough detail from the ground, consider creating two movies of possible sequences through the crux. This way, if you get up there and find that one will obviously not work, you

can call up the second movie and continue climbing without delay.

You might finish up your visualization by moving into the associated state and trying to imagine what you might feel and see as you climb the sequence you came up with from the disassociated perspective. This is not always possible but would be beneficial.

PREPARING FOR COMPETITION

In competition climbing, good visualization skills might mean the difference between winning and finishing in the middle of the pack. Depending on the competition format, you will want to employ the redpoint and on-sight visualization strategies discussed above. Since many events allow only a brief preview period, you will only be able to create a "rough-cut" movie, including the basic route path, location of the obvious rests, and whatever you can glean about the moves or sequence. Even if you can't decipher a sequence (or if you didn't get a route preview), you can still take a mental picture of the wall and project yourself climbing with grace and confidence to the top. Most important, strive to eliminate any self-defeating images that might cross your mind in the hours and minutes leading up to your ascent of the wall.

"CLIMBING" INJURED OR TIRED

If you climb for enough years, you will at some point likely find yourself laid up due to some type of injury. Whether you are out for a few weeks due to a finger injury or out for the season with a more serious problem, you can still keep climbing in your mind's eye! While this may not sound like much fun, it is an effective way to maintain your knowledge of a sequence on your project route. Vivid, associated visualization has been shown to cause low-level neuromuscular activity that helps enhance motor learning (Feltz 1983) and maintain the feel of performing some skill.

You can also use this effect to your advantage next time you pump out while working a route. Instead of thrashing around on the climb for the umpteenth time (and risking injury), call it a day and spend the time pumping a few more "mental laps" on the route. This will help solidify your knowledge of the sequence without the extra physical strain and risk of injury.

Creating Laserlike Focus

The ability to narrow and maintain focus is a crucial sports skill, especially in an activity like climbing where elements of danger exert a constant pull diverting the focus from the move at hand. Widely used, but often misunderstood in the context of a climber's lexicon, *focus* is a laserlike concentration of mental energy aimed at the most important task at any particular instant. Since every movement in climbing possesses a different most-important task, it's vital to be able to redirect your focus, in an instant, to the finger or foot placement most critical at that moment.

Think of focus as a narrowing of your concentration, much like a zoom lens on a camera. At any given moment you must zoom in on the single task most critical to your performance—toeing down on a small pocket, pulling on a manky finger jam, or

shifting your center of gravity to just the right balance point. Think about anything else and you may fail at this critical task and fall.

The most difficult part of focusing is learning to zoom in and out quickly from a pinpoint focus to a more wide-angle perspective. For example, a quarterback starts a pass play with a broad focus (when in search for an open receiver), but he instantly zooms in on a single player as he delivers the pass. In climbing, you have to do much the same thing—use a broad focus when hanging out looking for the next hold, then zoom in tight as you reach toward the hold and latch on to it. Similarly, you must zoom in tight when high-stepping on a dime edge, locking off and making a long reach, or floating a deadpoint. If you focus on anything else—your gear, your belayer, your pain, or spectators on the ground—you may as well add a ten-pound weight to your back. Poor focus makes hard moves harder, maybe even impossible.

Practicing Focus

Detailed below is a practice drill for developing focus and a preclimbing strategy for gathering focus in preparation to climb. The Singular Focus Drill is best used when you are climbing on toprope and well below your maximum grade. The Pinpointing Your Focus for a Climb exercise can be used before attempting any climb, though it's especially effective when preparing to start up a difficult route.

 Singular Focus Drill

The best time to work on your focus is when climbing a route a couple of grades below your maximum ability. Whether you're at a gym or the crag, on toprope or lead, attempt to climb a whole route by focusing solely on one aspect of movement.

For instance, try to do a route with your complete focus on just hand placements. Find the best way to grab each hold, use the minimum amount of grip strength necessary to hang on, and feel how your purchase changes as you pull on the hold. Place as little focus as is safely possible on other areas such as your feet, balance, belayer, and the like. For now, let these areas take care of themselves—allow your intuitive sense to determine where your feet go and how your balance should shift.

Chances are, you'll find this exercise quite difficult. Your thoughts will naturally wander to other tasks or even be directed to distractions on the ground. If this occurs, simply redirect your focus to the predetermined task—in this case, the handholds. It is this process of becoming aware of your lost focus and returning it to the critical task that you are after. Sharpened awareness of lost focus is tantamount to gaining control of focus.

Repeat this exercise regularly but change the focus (onto, say, foot placements or weight shifts) each time. Work on increasing the length of time you can maintain a singular focus—this helps build mental endurance. As you become more skilled, convert this singular focus drill into a dynamic focus drill where your focus constantly shifts to the most critical task at any moment. The goal is be able to shift your focus quickly among the various tasks involved in doing a route, like the flickering beams of a laser light show.

With practice, the process of directing and redirecting focus will become largely subconscious. On the rare occasions when your focus does wander away from the task of climbing, your well-trained mind will instantly recognize this loss and redirect the focus onto the climb. In this way, becoming constantly engaged and automatic on the climb helps in achieving the highly desired flow state.

 Pinpointing Your Focus for a Climb

This exercise will gather your focus into a single "beam" and quiet your mind as you get ready to cast off up a climb. Perform it after you've gone through your preclimb ritual and been put on belay.

Stand at the base of the climb, assume an extended posture (shoulders back), close your eyes, and place the fingertips of your dominant hand against the rock face. Your fingertips should be touching the wall lightly (not gripping a hold), and your hand and arm should be completely relaxed. Now take three deep belly breaths, inhaling through your nose to a count of five and exhaling through

your mouth to a count of ten. Let a wave of relaxation wash across your body, and then narrow your focus to the tips of your fingers touching the rock. Concentrate singly on the sensation of your fingertips touching the rock—you should begin to feel the thermal energy moving from your fingers to the rock (on rare occasions when the rock is hotter than your body, you will feel thermal energy conducting into your fingertips). Maintain a relaxed, singular focus on the energy exchange between your fingertips and the rock for anywhere from thirty seconds to a minute or two. If your focus ever wanders, simply redirect it to your fingertips. Soon your mind will become completely still: All your attention is pinpointed on the tips of your fingers. On reaching this state, open your eyes and begin climbing.

Using Preclimb Rituals to Create Focus

Preclimb rituals are a powerful way to narrow your focus in the hours and minutes leading up to an ascent. Like a pilot's preflight checklist, a climber's preclimb ritual should consist of every single activity, big or small, that is necessary to ensure a safe, successful journey. For example, my typical preclimb ritual begins with scoping the route to determine the best path and, hopefully, figure out the key moves and rest positions. Next, I perform a few minutes (or more) of mental rehearsal and visualization as I try to feel the moves and preprogram in the sequence. Upon gaining a sense of comfort and knowing about the route, I put on my shoes and tie in to the rope. I complete my preclimb ritual by taking a few slow, deep breaths, straightening my posture, and cracking a smile in anticipation of the great fun that awaits me. This entire ritual typically takes between five and fifteen minutes (depending on the difficulty and length of the climb), and it leaves me in an ideal state to make my best effort.

Develop your own unique rituals based on what makes you feel most prepared and psyched for a route. Think back to some of your best past performances to gain some clues as to what to include. What did you think and do in preparing for that climb? What did you eat or drink, how did you warm up, and how long did you rest between climbs? Aware-

Tips for Creating Focus

1. Train focus by using the Singular Focus Drill (page 45) while leading climbing in the gym or toproping outside.
2. Develop detailed preclimb ritual that includes warming up, scoping the route, analyzing risk, visualizing the ascent, preparing your gear, putting on your shoes, and tying in to the rope. Use this same ritual before every climb and you will consistently create a high level of focus.
3. Use the Pinpointing Your Focus exercise (page 46) as your final task before beginning up the route.
4. Strive for process-oriented thought, and avoid dwelling on past outcomes or what's ahead. Stay in the moment.
5. If you discover that your focus is scattered, simply acknowledge this and redirect your attention to the move or action at hand. Consider using the Pinpointing Your Focus exercise again.

ness of all the factors—little and big—that lead up to your best performances is a key to being able to reproduce similar results in the future.

Experiment with different rituals and analyze what seems to work best. An effective preclimb ritual doesn't need to be extravagant or long. In fact, a short, concise ritual that quickly gets you prepared and focused to climb is best. Upon developing a ritual that works, stick to it!

Mental Wings Strategies to Enhance Problem Solving and Learning

I conclude this chapter with six mental strategies to enhance your skills at problem solving and learning of a difficult sequence or complex route. Being able to quickly decipher perplexing cruxes while conserving mental and physical energy is a master skill. Learn to utilize these skills effectively and you're on your way to becoming a grand master at flashing.

1. Focus on problem solving, not performance.

One thing I love about working a hard boulder problem or project route is the challenge of studying a complex problem and gradually seeing a beautiful, unique sequence take form. Just like piecing together a puzzle when you were a kid, you can best solve a rock puzzle by remaining focused on the task and having fun regardless of how the long the puzzle takes to complete.

For instance, when working a boulder problem or crux sequence, ponder the beauty of this rock puzzle and feel the joy of being engaged in this challenging process. This disposition will shift you out of the *must-not-fail* mind-set of frustration and help turn your focus away from the problem and onto finding a solution. Remember, the brain naturally magnifies whatever you focus on. Obviously you want to magnify the possible solution, not the problem, so always be solution oriented.

2. Relax and remain positive.

Both problem solving and motor learning occur most rapidly in a stress- and anxiety-free state. Therefore, controlling tension through deep breathing, positive visualization, and remaining process-oriented is crucial for accelerating these processes.

It's also fundamental that you eliminate thoughts of *need to flash the route* or *have to redpoint the climb this attempt*—these are both positions that work against you. By entertaining such needs, you create stress and anxiety that may prevent the very thing you desire. Instead, acknowledge that falling is part of the learning process and accept each fall as providing a clue for success—so don't ignore it! Predetermine that you will accept a fall (and find the clue) if it happens and believe completely that success will come with creativity, effort, and patience. In doing so, you create the optimal state for learning and succeeding most quickly.

3. Chunk down the route.

Chunking down a long, hard route into a series of short problems makes the climb less overwhelming and easier to learn. Furthermore, these short problems or chunks can each be viewed as a short-term goal to be reached or accomplished. So, while you may fail for several days on the project as a whole, you will experience short-term success as you solve each of the individual chunks. This sense of success helps keep you energized, positive, and on track to eventually succeeding on the route.

When working through the individual chunks, avoid becoming obsessed on any one of them. Beating yourself up on, say, the second chunk of a six-chunk route is self-defeating: Even if you eventually solve this chunk, you'll be too mentally and physically wasted to put in meaningful work on the others. Therefore, it's best to move on to working the next chunk upon the onset of frustration or any judgmental self-talk, such as *I can't do this* or *I'll never figure this out*. If allowed to burrow into your subconscious, such judgments form the basis for reality. You are much better off solving the rest of the route before returning to the problem section.

Long-term achievement of a formidable goal (where short-term failures are inevitable) demands mental agility as well as the ability to trick yourself into persevering in the face of adversity. Breaking a climb into a series of more manageable chunks and setting yourself up for several small wins is a most effective strategy.

4. Engage both sides of the brain.

You may be familiar with the fact that the brain has two hemispheres—the left hemisphere, which presides over logical, practical, language, mathematical, and related matters, and the right hemisphere, which dominates in creative, artistic, intuitive, situational, and imaginary matters. The majority of people are "left-brained" and, even if you aren't, intense situations with lots of information—like climbing—tend to bring the left brain into command. The result is that many climbers leave their right brain on the ground and therefore handicap their problem-solving ability, big time! I can think of countless times I've fallen on routes because I was thinking in a linear fashion and with blinders on that prevented me from finding a key hold, sequence, or rest. (Cut me a break, I'm a scientist, not an artist!)

The right brain is best accessed when you are in a relaxed state (another reason some climbers have a tough time freeing it up). Thus, bringing it into play requires that you resist the Type A behavior of rushing up to a route and quickly going for the send, and instead get comfortable at the base of the climb, warm up slowly, and make a relaxed study of the climb before tying in to the rope. Some severely left-brained people will need to force themselves to think out of the box. Seeing the big picture and imagining all the possible approaches and sequences on a climb is a habit you may need to foster through your own initiative. Your goal should be a balanced approach to problem solving in which you can think logically and practically as well as intuitively and creatively. Being able to create (on demand) and leverage this state is one of the hallmarks of brilliant climbers such as Lynn Hill and Chris Sharma, who can perform at an exceedingly high level in a wide range of styles and settings.

5. Employ multisensory learning.

Everything we learn comes through one of our five senses, and the more senses we use in learning, the faster and easier it becomes. Climbers tend to use primarily the sense of vision before they leave the ground, and feel once they begin to climb. While the senses of smell and taste can't contribute to performance in this sport, the auditory sense can also be a powerful learning tool (Knudson 1997), particularly when faced with a tricky boulder problem or when working to memorize a difficult sequence. Climbers who give names to key holds and moves and then create verbal beta are using this trick. Remembering an obscure sequence of tiny holds by feel or vision can be enhanced with descriptive verbal beta like *high-step to the dime edge, then deadpoint to the potato chip flake*. It may sound funny, but it works.

Multisensory learning is a sign of the intelligent climber, so begin to talk yourself through sequences in addition to visualizing and feeling the moves. By talking the talk, you make it easier to climb the climb!

6. Try something ridiculous.

The biggest block to learning is judgment. Self-talk like *Others use this sequence, so that must be the best way,* or discounting a novel or improbable sequence that flashes into your mind without trying it first, is a form of self-sabotage. It's vital that you don't limit yourself this way—your brain doesn't know what you can or cannot do until you tell it. Don't prejudge sequences or your capabilities!

The best problem solvers are both creative and uninhibited. They never hesitate to try a novel solution that's entirely different from the known sequence. You can foster these skills by ignoring the obvious solution—the one that's not currently working for you—and attempting a few completely different, even ridiculous sequences.

Regardless of how improbable a given technique looks—heel hook, undercling, high step, knee bar—don't pass judgment on it until you make a few attempts with that technique. Try a variety of body positions, foot flags, lunges, and don't ignore less positive holds like Gastons, side pulls, and pinches. Eliminate the seemingly must-use hold—or at least try using it with the opposite hand. Search for unchalked holds that might unlock the sequence, and keep a constant watch for footholds that are off the main line of the route—a single missed foothold or high step can make the difference between "impossible" and "possible."

A common thread running through this chapter has been that the mental and technical aspects of climbing are intimately connected. Ahead in chapter 4 you will find an in-depth study of motor learning and performance (how you acquire skill) as well as a primer on the fundamental climbing techniques and several powerful strategies for developing superior technique. Let's climb onward.

Problem-Solving Tips and Success Strategies

1. Focus on problem solving, not performance. View each climb as a puzzle that you will enjoy and learn from, no matter what the outcome.
2. Relax and remain confident. Use the ANSWER Sequence to maintain a relaxed state, and direct positive, productive self-talk to fortify confident and sustain effective action in the face of difficult climbing.
3. Chunk down the route into manageable sections. Work the most difficult chunks first, then begin linking the sections from the top down.
4. Engage both sides of the brain. Which side is more dominant for you? Strive to bring both creative, intuitive (right brain) and analytical, practical (left brain) power to work for you.
5. Employ multisensory learning by seeing, feeling, and talking yourself through tough sequences.
6. When all else fails, try something ridiculous! Seemingly impossible cruxes often require a trick move or non-intuitive sequence, so experiment with a variety of moves and techniques no matter how improbable or inappropriate they seem to be.

CHAPTER FOUR

Training Technique and Skill

We are what we do repeatedly. Excellence, then, is not an act but a habit.

—*Aristotle*

Moving over stone is the essence of climbing and, therefore, no subject can be more central to improving your climbing than this chapter on training skill and developing technique. Despite this, the subject of strength training tends to get all the attention and hype in conversations among climbers, and getting stronger is the most popular topic of magazine articles about climbing performance. In this book mental training and improving skill and strategy come before the subject of strength training because I feel most climbers can benefit more and improve more quickly on the rock with focused training in these areas. If you want to put yourself on the fast track to the higher grades, strive to understand and apply the information contained in this chapter as much as or more than any other chapter in the book. This *will* make you a better climber.

Ironically, the majority of climbers spend little, if any, time on dedicated practice of the vast spectrum of techniques inherent to our sport. With little coaching or guidance available, most climbers unknowingly service their lust for ticking routes by constantly climbing for performance. Of course,

Ines Papert on-sights the 5.11a first pitch of the North Face of Castleton Tower, Utah.
KEITH LADZINSKI

becoming proficient (or excellent) at any sport requires focused practice of new skills and work on weaknesses that need improvement. Still, some climbers just don't want to spend time practicing on routes below their maximum grade; others avoid routes that might highlight their weaknesses. Can you imagine a baseball player who never took batting or fielding practice outside of the competition of a nine-inning game, or a quarterback who never threw a pass except on game day?

In this chapter you will learn the three stages of motor learning involved in acquiring a new climbing skill or move, as well as how the brain creates motor programs to execute specific skilled movements and generates "software" that can approximate solutions, on the fly, to unknown moves. This is powerful information if you understand it, because it will empower you to practice more effectively than the mass of climbers, rapidly develop superior technique, and grow to become a true master of rock.

Next I present a primer on the fundamental techniques of efficient climbing movement. Beginning climbers would be wise to read the unabridged coverage of climbing technique presented in my book *Learning to Climb Indoors*. Intermediate and advanced climbers can likewise benefit by reviewing—and, if needed, shoring up their use of—the key techniques detailed in this chapter.

The action portion of this chapter is a series of practice drills that you can use year-round whether you climb indoors or out. Regardless of your tenure in the sport, significant gains in your climbing technique and overall ability will result from a commitment to regularly employing some of these drills in your routine. Apply these drills to accelerate learning (or to unlearn bad habits of movement) of the fundamental techniques outlined in this chapter.

An Overview of Motor Learning and Effective Skill Practice

The importance of motor learning theory to the subject of training for climbing became apparent to me in the early 1990s as a result of conversations with Dr. Mark Robinson and thanks to ongoing input from my wife, Lisa Ann. As an LPGA golf pro (and climber) with an education in the field of kinesiology, Lisa Ann occasionally discussed the methods used by elite golfers to learn very difficult skills (for me, impossible!). At about the same time, Mark Robinson (former 'Gunks hardman and now an orthopedic surgeon in California) turned me on to an excellent text on the subject, *Motor Learning and Performance* by Dr. Richard Schmidt. Robinson then penned a breakthrough piece on the application of motor learning and performance to climbing for my first climbing book, *Flash Training* (1994). Subsequently I've studied the subject in depth, and I've even had the good fortune to engage Dr. Schmidt (the founder of schema theory) and discuss motor learning and performance (MLP) and its application to climbing. The result is a much-expanded section on MLP in this edition, along with numerous powerful practice strategies to hone your skills and technique.

Three Stages of Motor Learning

Motor learning is the process by which we acquire physical skills. Regardless of the skill—walking, driving, climbing—learning occurs in three identifiable and overlapping stages: the cognitive, motor, and autonomous stages.

COGNITIVE STAGE

This stage involves thinking about the activity, listening to explanations of it or comparisons to other familiar things, imaginative projection of what it may be like to do it, visual or kinesthetic anticipation of action, and formulation of the goals or desired results for future performance.

Early attempts in this stage are clumsy, ineffi-cient, and jerky; they expend energy and strength in wasteful ways. This is what you experience when making the first few attempts on an unfamiliar type of climbing (crack, slab, pocketed face, and such) or on a route that's especially hard for you. During practice sessions in this formative period, you examine the route from the ground in an attempt to figure out the moves and rest positions, and then attempt to climb via toprope or, perhaps, bolt to bolt on lead. Typically the results of such early attempts are rough and imperfect. With continued attempts (practice), however, the quality of performance improves as proprioceptors in the muscles, tendons, joints, and inner ear provide sensory feedback on movement and body position.

The underlying capacities involved in this stage are largely intellectual and character related and, to a lesser extent, physical. Therefore, people who enjoy early success—those who appear to have natural talent—are not necessarily the strongest, but instead the most perceptive, agile, confident, and relaxed. A real-life example of this is seen daily by climbing instructors who observe a novice female climber outperform her equally novice, but stronger, male partner during their first day on the rocks.

MOTOR STAGE

The motor stage is less a product of self-conscious effort and thought than one of automatic increases in the efficiency and organization of the activity by the nervous system and brain, as a response to continued practice. A neurological "groove" develops as multiple attempts and feedback from multiple sources (internal and external) produce more reliable and effective execution. Energy expenditure decreases, and the natural inertia of the body and limbs is used to advantage—this marked increase in economy of movement is the hallmark of the motor stage of learning.

When working a climb, this stage is represented by the attempts at redpoint when the moves and clips are known, and the goals are to develop efficiency and to preserve power and endurance for the cruxes. The underlying factors involved in this stage differ from those that lead to early success. Here, they involve the sensitivity of internal movement sensors (proprioception), the accuracy of limb movement, speed of detection and correction of minor errors, and the sensitivity of the performance to anxiety, doubt, and so on. These things are obviously less available to conscious awareness or control and are thus acquired only through dedicated practice and the chase of perfection.

In this stage the goal of action becomes more refined and demanding. The moves must be done efficiently with strength to spare, not eked out in desperation. Early, crude success should not be accepted as "good enough" since this will not lead to the best ultimate development of technique and efficiency. Having demanding goals has been shown experimentally to produce both better performance and faster gains. The goal should be to perfect movement and dominate at a certain grade (say, 5.10a or 5.12a), not just get by at it.

AUTONOMOUS STAGE

The final stage of learning is called the autonomous stage. At this point the actions are automatic and require almost no conscious attention, because movement has reached a stable and polished form. You can often do other things while in this state: For instance, you can carry on a conversation while driving a car. Or, like a chess grandmaster thinking six moves ahead, you can decipher and send a crux sequence in perfect form, on-sight. This is also the elusive flow state or zone so often touted by elite athletes. In climbing, it is reached only through dedicated, disciplined, long-term practice.

On the rock this stage can be experienced on a successful redpoint, but it more often occurs on the umpteenth repetition of a route that you have absolutely wired. You may also experience this flow state while on-sight climbing just below your maximum ability, and on rare occasions you'll feel the rapture of the zone as you send a personal-best project or float up a competition route.

Components of Skilled Performance

Despite being as intuitive and natural as walking or running, climbing can be a remarkably complex and demanding activity. Consider that the climbing gyms and crags of the world offer a playing field of infinite variation and demand for skilled performance. Compound this with the potential for adrenaline-releasing risk and the perplexing challenge of ascending a gigantic wall, and it becomes apparent that climbing is indeed a complex sporting activity.

The goal of this section, then, is to provide a primer on the theory of skill acquisition as well as introduce you to valuable practice strategies. While many climbers stumble through the maze of trial-and-error learning, you will be empowered to practice more effectively and thus obtain uncommonly good results and rate of improvement.

TYPES OF SKILLS

Motor learning scientists define *skill* as the ability to bring about an end result with maximum certainty and minimum time and energy (Schmidt 2004). In climbing, these skills possess cognitive and motor components. For example, perception and decision making precede physical execution of most on-sight climbing movements; even a well-rehearsed redpoint ascent relies on memory, focus, and sensory processes to bring about successful execution of a motor skill. Clearly, technical rock climbing will test your prowess of both mental and physical skills.

Another important distinction is that between discrete and serial skills. A discrete climbing skill is a single movement with a definite beginning and end—such as a mantle, lunge, high step, down pull, lieback, deadpoint, and the like. String many discrete skills together, however, and you now have a more complex skilled action called a serial skill. Like a gymnast performing a routine, a climber must successfully execute specific moves, but must also possess the skill to link all the moves into a complete ascent. This explains why, in preparation for a redpoint ascent, you can't just practice the individual moves—it's equally important to practice connecting the moves, since this is in itself a new skill.

MOTOR PROGRAMS

Discrete climbing skills are directed by motor programs stored in long-term memory. These motor programs, which define and shape movement, become more stable, elaborate, and long lasting as you progress through the three stages of motor learning described earlier. With consistent, quality practice, the program becomes highly precise and largely unconscious, thus freeing attention for other matters such as finding the next handhold or remembering the sequence. Conversely, climbing skills that you rarely practice or avoid will be represented by less detailed, unstable motor programs that may lead to poor execution and demand high degrees of attention.

A highly skilled climber can often look at a section of rock, see the moves, and know what skills she will need to employ. For example, she might view a short boulder problem and see a lieback move that leads to backstep move, followed by a 2-foot deadpoint move to a good hold. In ascending the boulder problem, motor programs for lieback, backstep, and deadpoint yield a sort of movement script directing essential details of movement: the muscles to be used and in what order, the force and duration of each contraction, and so on. Still, the motor programs will not specify every aspect of movement, and so the climber will make many tiny reflexive and/or conscious adjustments that modify the commands of the "movement script."

A less skilled climber may be challenged in many ways by the same boulder problem. First, he may lack the experience and cognitive skills to "see" the necessary moves. Furthermore, he may possess less refined motor programs for the lieback, drop-knee, and lunge skills that are necessary to ascend the sequence. Chances are he will need numerous attempts to feel out the moves and gather sensory feedback on body position, the muscles to be used, and the force of contraction, among other things. Repeated blocked practice attempts may eventually lead to a successful ascent of the boulder problem.

PERFORMING NOVEL SKILLS

The hallmark of an expert climber is the ability to on-sight climb at a high level on a wide variety of terrain and rock types. But how does this climber execute novel moves with a high rate of success?

After all, our playing field has infinite variability—so even the most well-traveled professional climber will fail to experience every possible motor skill and variation thereof. Understanding how novel movements are generated will empower you to practice more effectively so that you can become a master of on-sight climbing through moves you've never before experienced!

Let's use the boulder problem example above, which concluded with a deadpoint to a good hold exactly 24 inches away. Given the infinite variability of climbing moves and rock surface, it is unlikely that the climber will have previously performed a deadpoint move, from a backstep position, to a hold exactly 24 inches away. However, if the climber has thrown deadpoint moves from several different distances (say, from 15, 21, 28, and 30 inches away) and from different body positions and rock angles,

Figure 4.1 Developing Schemas

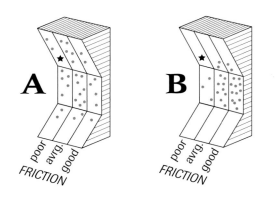

Climber A has practiced a specific skill over a wide range of conditions (dots) and thus possesses a more refined schema-rule. She will be able to closely approximate the novel move (star)—and possibly on-sight it!

Climber B has practiced the skill primary on vertical rock with good frictional properties. Therefore, he is likely to struggle in executing the novel move (star) on slick, overhanging rock.

he will likely be able to execute the novel move on-sight. This is because all the different deadpoint moves call the same deadpoint motor program into use, and this motor program is scaled to fit the novel situation according to what is known as a schema.

A schema is a set of rules developed and applied unconsciously by the central nervous system, which allows you to adjust a motor program for different environmental conditions (hold location, rock angle, friction properties, and such) by changing parameters of muscle force, body position, and speed of movement. Becoming a proficient on-sight climber, therefore, is not just a matter of learning all the different classes of skills (jamming, side pulling, down pulling, lunging, flagging, and so on); it demands that you practice these skills in a wide range of configurations and settings. Such "variable practice" (more on this below) refines the existing schema-rule for each generalized motor program, thus allowing more accurate estimation of the necessary parameters for execution of a skill in a novel situation. (see figure 4.1)

The practical application of schema theory should now be obvious: Upon learning the new climbing skill of, say, finger jamming, you want to practice finger jamming in cracks of different sizes, on different wall angles, and on rock with different frictional properties. Doing so will modify your schema-rule to expand your use of the finger-jamming motor program and effectively ascend finger cracks at almost any crag on the planet. The same goes for other climbing skills—strive to expand their use to a variety of rock types and terrain, and you will be on your way to becoming a master of rock!

Conversely, if you climb at only a few cliffs and favor a specific type of climbing, you will develop fewer motor programs and less refined schema-rules for each. These motor programs, no matter how well learned, will work only for similar situations—and they may not apply particularly well at the outer limits of difficulty at these crags. Worse yet, when you travel to new areas, your limited skills and schema-rules will leave you climbing at a much lower grade or flailing on routes of the grade you're accustomed to sending at your home area.

Transfer of Skill

In motor learning the idea of transfer relates to how practice of a skill in one activity carries over to enhance performance of another, different activity. One startling, but apparently consistent, result in this field of study is that transfer is usually either absent or small, even between seemingly similar activities (Schmidt 1991). The complexity, coordination, and integration of a skilled movement are so specific that they derive very little help from other skilled movements. Therefore, practice at climbing will improve climbing skill, coordination, and technique, while playing around on a slack chain, kicking a Hacky Sack, snowboarding, or what have you are wastes of time for the purpose of improving climbing skill (although these activities may develop mental attributes such as focus and toughness that somewhat translate to climbing).

This helps us understand why the old assumption that gymnasts, with their incredible strength and motor skills, would instantly become excellent climbers has not proven true. Although climbing and gymnastics obviously share certain physical requirements, the motor skills are very different and they are based, in part, on markedly different underlying capacities.

Rate of Improvement and Your Ultimate Skill Level

According to the Law of Practice, performance improves rapidly from its baseline level when the activity is first practiced and continues to improve in gradually decreasing amounts as ability approaches some ultimate (personal) skill level (see figure 4.2). In learning a simple task, like driving a car, it only takes a few weeks to become fairly skilled. Beyond this, all the thousands of hours you spend driving over the rest of your life will yield only a small amount of improvement.

The learning curve for complex activities, like golf or climbing, also rises rapidly upward as a result of the initial practice sessions. Because of the high complexity and wide range of skills inherent to these sports, however, you can continue to improve for many years, even decades. In fact, golf would seem

Figure 4.2 Rate of Skill Acquisition

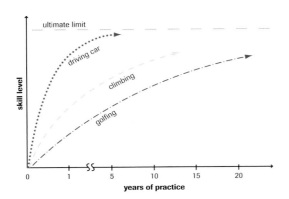

Performance improves rapidly from its baseline level when the activity is first practiced and continues to improve at a slower rate as ability approaches some ultimate personal skill level.

to be the more technically difficult sport of the two, since several gifted climbers have reached world-class status in less than five years, while the best golfer ever, Tiger Woods, took fifteen years to ascend to that level—and that was unusually fast!

As discussed in chapter 1, you can maximize your rate of improvement in a specific style of climbing by focusing your practice and training in that one area. It's increasingly common to observe climbers who quickly progress to a high level of ability in one type of climbing—say, gymnastic bouldering or overhanging crimpfest routes. Since both these endeavors require only a small subset of total climbing skills, it's possible to focus your practice on developing the small set of motor programs necessary to excel. The trade-off is that your limited motor programs will be a handicap when attempting routes outside your area of specialization—these climbs will feel hard for the grade, perhaps even "impossible."

The bottom line: Becoming a proficient, all-around climber is a long-term proposition. The most intelligent approach to training for climbing would be to emphasize learning skill over getting wickedly strong during your first few years in the sport. Devel-

oping refined schema-rules for the many different climbing skills takes you many years of climbing at wide range of areas and rock types. So while you may become a highly skilled specialist climber in just a few years, you can continue to expand the depth and breadth of your skills even after twenty or thirty years (I know that I still am!).

Practice Strategies to Accelerate Learning of Skills and Enhance Schema-Rules

If you want to maximize improvement, then you need to know how to practice optimally. Acquiring a new skill requires a progression through the three stages of motor learning before you will be able to use the new skill efficiently and intuitively. Depending on the difficulty of the skill, this process may be slow, awkward, and frustrating. Therefore, discipline and an intense belief that you will become excellent in the skill (with effort) are fundamental to the process. You must not try to get around having to learn it by relying on your strengths in other areas.

Unfortunately, many climbers do exactly this when they lunge, swing, or scum wildly through a sequence that could be done more efficiently by learning a new move, technique, or body position. Another example plays out when a competent gym or face climber first attempts to learn crack climbing. The common tendency is to avoid the awkward—and possibly painful—jams and pawl up the face on either side of the crack. In this case the climber will rapidly fatigue and likely exclaim that the route felt way harder than its grade (of course it did, since she wasn't using the proper technique for ascending the route).

The moral of the story is that you must convince yourself that no matter how hard a new move feels at first, it will become easier to execute—and perhaps even intuitive—as the result of intelligent practice. Toward this end, keep in mind that you will become most competent at a skill by practicing it on as many different rock varieties, angles, and settings as possible.

Another important principle states that learning new skills is difficult in states of fatigue, stress, fear, and urgency, whereas a fresh, relaxed, and confident approach yields rapid acquisition of new skills. Consequently, it's best to practice new skills early in your training sessions and to employ liberal hangdogging for blocked practice of crux moves. Interestingly, you can solidify skills you already possess by practicing them in a fatigued state! If all this motor learning theory is beginning to overwhelm you, worry not—following are five powerful practice strategies that distill and apply this information to produce optimal skill-learning results.

MODELING ADVANCED CLIMBERS

Modeling is a powerful technique for learning basic skills and climbing strategy. It's best used in a climbing gym where you can observe the movements, positions, techniques, and tactics of a more advanced climber, and then immediately give them a try on your own. Make a mental picture of what you want to attempt and use that vision as a starting point. Experiment, modify, and make the move your own. In practicing the new move, progress through the following four practice strategies: blocked practice, variable practice, fatigued practice, and random skill practice (described below).

You can also model what you observe at the crags. In addition to actual moves, take special note of the tactics and strategy used by high-end climbers. For example, how do they work crux sequences? Where do they find rests? At what pace do they climb? How do they go about equipping routes? Again, it's best to first experiment with your observations in the gym before testing them outdoors.

Although modeling technical skills is a powerful weapon for your arsenal, copying an elite climber's fitness training program is usually a big mistake. Remember that elite climbers have spent years conditioning their muscles and tendons to withstand extreme levels of stress. To train as they do without this long-term preparation could be disastrous.

BLOCKED PRACTICE

Blocked practice—identical repetitions of a specific move—is the most popular method of practicing a hard climbing move because it produces rapid learning of the skill in that specific situation. In learning the undercling move, for example, you would repeat the same undercling move over and over in order to refine your body position and the application of force needed to optimally perform the move.

Upon development of "feel" and early success at a new skill, however, a radical change is needed. Further blocked practice will have little value and may even result in a false sense of confidence and poor use of the skill in novel settings. Returning to our example, suppose you only practiced the one basic undercling move you first learned at the gym. Despite your expertise at that specific undercling move, you will struggle and likely fail on undercling moves on different wall angles and on the infinite playing field of outdoor climbing. The same phenomenon is seen in other sports, like a golfer who hits great wedge shots from the perfect lie of a practice range mat (blocked practice), yet on the golf course is unable to hit a solid shot from the novel lies of the fairway and rough. These examples show that, beyond the first few successful trials of a new skill, blocked practice is for blockheads! Upon achieving initial success at a new skill, you must graduate to variable and random practice.

VARIABLE PRACTICE

As explained above, learning a new skill in a specific way is just the first step in the learning process. The ultimate goal is instant and proficient use of the skill in any new situation you come upon. The tried and proven way to do this is with variable practice.

Suppose you've just learned the drop-knee move on a vertical indoor wall with large, positive holds. To incorporate variable practice you would now change the "route" conditions slightly and attempt the same drop-knee move again. After a few reps in this new setting, you'd again modify the route by changing the hold spacing and wall angle to further expand use of the skill—then continue this progression to the point that you could perform the drop-knee move in a variety of random settings. Such "variable practice" will refine schema-rules to direct effective execution of the drop-knee motor program over a wide range of conditions (angle, hold size, rock type, and frictional properties) that you may encounter in the future.

FATIGUED SKILL PRACTICE

Earlier I mentioned that you can increase your command of a skill by practicing it while in a fatigued state. In fact, beyond the initial successful trials of a skill, practice should be performed with variable conditions and levels of fatigue and never again "blocked." This may increase your rate of failure at doing certain moves—but remember, performance isn't your goal, practice is! The benefits of this practice, no matter how poor it feels, will become evident in the future. Besides, this concept actually makes good sense. If you want the ability to stick a deadpoint in the midst of a dicey lead climb while pumped, you'd better log some deadpoints in various states of fatigue during practice.

Here's the best approach. Use the first thirty minutes of your workout (while fresh) to train new skills, then move on to chalking up some mileage on a variety of routes. After an hour or so, or when you're moderately fatigued, attempt several reps of recently acquired moves and sequences. As fatigue increases, finish up with some reps of sequences or boulder problems you have more completely mastered.

In the context of a two-hour climbing gym workout, this rule emphasizes the benefit of squeezing in a greater volume of climbing "practice" ascents over doing just a few "performance" ascents with extensive rest in between. The long rests and performance climbing may make you *look* better, but the greater volume of practice will make you *climb* better!

RANDOM SKILL PRACTICE

The ability to on-sight a sequence of novel moves on "foreign" rock is the ultimate goal of your skill practice time. Toward this end, the best workout approach is a randomized free-for-all of skill types. This highly effective method is widely used in other sports and should not be overlooked by climbers as optimal training for the unknown.

There are two approaches to random training of climbing skills. First, on an indoor wall, attempt to link a sequence of very different bouldering moves. Contrive an unusual sequence of moves that will call a wide range of skills into use, and make several attempts at sending it. Alternatively, team up with your most deranged friend for a round of the Stick Game (described later in this chapter). Take turns pointing (with a broomstick) each other through an unusual sequence of widely varied skills and movements. Don't get too wrapped up in performance outcomes—if you link a random series of moves, then you are a winner in terms of developing superior climbing skill.

Another powerful method of random skill training is to climb a series of widely differing routes in rapid succession. A commercial gym with many different wall angles, a few cracks, and a roof or two is ideal. Team with a partner and toprope ten to fifteen routes of different character over the course of an hour or so. The first route may be a vertical face, the next a slab, the third a finger crack, the fourth an overhanging pumpfest, the fifth a handcrack, the sixth a roof route, and so on. This rapid recall of a wide range of motor and cognitive skills is like taking skill-fortifying steroids!

Fundamental Techniques

The essence of climbing is a dance up the wall using the four points of contact as your dance steps. Since each climb possesses a novel configuration of hand- and footholds, your challenge is to unlock the perfect sequence of moves and leverage your points of contact into this dynamic dance.

In executing any physical skill—whether it's shooting a basketball or simply running—there are fundamental techniques that represent optimal use of body position, leverage, and physical energy. While the specific techniques may be hard to observe with an untrained eye, just about any novice can spot an athlete steeped in the fundamentals: Her movements are smooth, crisp, and confident, and her demeanor reveals a poise and ease of execution, despite inherent difficulties of the situation. The bottom line: Fundamentally sound movement affords perfect economy and looks easy.

Unfortunately, becoming a highly skilled, proficient climber rarely just happens—it results from a conscious decision to develop superior technique via

Tips for Rapid Learning of Skills and Developing Good Technique

1. Engage in regular climbing "practice." That is, go climbing with the intention of learning new skills and improving quality of movement, with little regard for absolute difficulty. Climb on as many different types of rock, wall angles, and areas as possible to build diverse skills and true climbing expertise.

2. Practice new skills and techniques early in the session while you are physically and mentally fresh.

3. Use blocked practice to accelerate learning during the initial trials of a new move, skill, or sequence. After two or three successful repetitions, cease blocked practice in favor of variable and randomized practice.

4. Employ variable practice to expand command of newly acquired skills over a wide range of conditions (angle, hold size, rock type, and so forth). Vary the "route" conditions more than you expect would be the case in a real-life climbing situation.

5. Practice known skills while in varying states of fatigue to increase your mastery of them and to build long-term retention.

6. Use random practice—climb a random series of moves back-to-back—to enhance proficiency of serial skill performance. Another random practice strategy is to climb several very different routes back-to-back to mandate recall of many different motor programs.

7. Model the techniques and tactics of advanced climbers to learn new moves and climbing strategies.

8. Aspire to dominate at a climbing grade, and not just get by. Focus practice on routes at or just below your maximum difficulty and resist the urge to constantly work routes beyond your ability level.

9. When working a route, resolve to find the best way to do a move or sequence and resist the urge to just thrash up the route and deem that acceptable. As a practice method, climb a route several times to identify and learn the most effective and efficient moves and tactics.

10. Maintain a long-term perspective toward learning to climb. No matter how fast you improve or how hard you climb, realize that you can still improve technique and learn new skills—even after ten, twenty, or more years!

disciplined long-term practice. Make it your goal to learn to climb every move and every route in the optimal way, and not to be satisfied to succeed with sloppy, inefficient movement. Excellence in climbing comes only to those with knowledge of the fundamentals and a desire to make them habit. To help you on this journey, this section provides a primer on twelve fundamental techniques that you must

practice to the point of mastery. As you read through each section, ponder your current level of competency in each fundamental technique and make it an urgent part of your training-for-climbing program to improve these weak areas. For a more tangible record of your technical ability, score your command of each fundamental technique using the checklist assessment in table 4.1.

Table 4.1 Score Your Technical Ability

Evaluate yourself in each area and check the box that best represents your current ability.

Technique	Excellent	Good	So-So	Poor
Precise, quiet foot placements that carry your weight				
Handholds gripped lightly; arms in a secondary role				
Use of the Left–Right Rule for stable movement				
Economy of movement (rhythm, pace, poise)				
Use of rest positions				
Use of nonpositive handholds (side pulls, underclings, slopers)				
Use of flagging to aid stability and prevent barndooring				
Hand–foot matching and mantling				
Twist lock, backstep, and efficient movement on overhanging terrain				
Use of creative footwork (heel and toe hooks, and knee locks)				
Dynamic moves (deadpoints and lunges)				
Jam crack climbing				

Precise Foot Placements That Carry Your Weight

Given that your legs are stronger than your arms, the first fundamental of climbing is that the legs should do the majority of the work. The exceptions to this rule are overhanging routes, which demand greater use of the arms (more on this in a bit). The process of effectively using your feet begins with spotting the footholds and positioning your feet on the best part of each hold. Directing your foot placement demands attention to detail beyond that given to hand placements. Whereas handholds are easy to inspect, the greater eye-to-foot distance commonly leads to less-than-ideal foot placements. Furthermore, your feet don't provide the same degree of feel as the hands, making the quality of each foot placement more difficult to assess. For these rea-

sons, developing good footwork is an attribute that you must *make happen* via constant foot focus and practice.

The another aspect of sound footwork is proper alignment of your center of gravity directly over a foothold. Balance, stability, and application of force are optimized when your center of gravity is positioned directly over your feet, forming a line perpendicular to level ground. On a less-than-vertical wall or slab, this requires a hip position out from the wall and over the foothold. On a near-vertical climbing surface, you simply need to keep your body position straight and over your feet as much as possible. When the climbing wall overhangs, it becomes impossible to position your weight over your feet, so a new fundamental skill takes over (see "Twist Lock and Backstep" later in this chapter).

1. Keep your center of gravity over your feet so they carry most of your weight. This requires a hips-out position when climbing slabs.

2. On vertical rock, it's essential to keep your hips in near the rock to position your center of gravity over your feet.

Handholds Gripped Lightly; Arms Play a Secondary Role

In a sport where anxiety and fear often rule, it's understandable that many climbers hang on with their hands for dear life. This tendency manifests itself with overgripping of the handholds and unnecessary muscling of moves with the arms. The end result is rapid fatigue, pumped forearms, and an eventual need to hang on the rope to rest and recover. You can avoid this outcome by practicing—

and making habit—the fundamentals of proper hand and arm use. These critical skills include gripping each handhold with the minimum force required, using the arms mainly for balance and not as a primary source of locomotion, and pushing with the feet in unison with modest arm pull.

Begin by making each hand contact a conscious process. Whereas many climbers just grab a hold with little thought and continue with the process of climbing, you must make each hand placement a

Conserve energy by gripping the rock lightly and maintaining straight arms, especially when you're climbing on overhanging terrain.

each handhold takes but a split second, yet it's a master skill that separates the best from the rest.

Beyond gripping the rock, you need to decide just how much you need to pull down on a given handhold. As discussed earlier, it is imperative that you push with your feet and let the leg muscles carry the load. Think of your arms as points of contact that simply prevent you from falling backward off the wall. In climbing a ladder, for example, your feet do all the work while the arms mainly provide balance. While rock climbing is far more complex, hold this model in your mind as the ultimate goal—the arms maintain balance while the legs drive movement. Still, there will be occasions on which your arms will need to briefly carry much of your weight. In these situations it's imperative that you maintain straight arms. This way the bulk of your weight is supported by the skeletal system of your upper body and not by your muscles.

The Left–Right Rule for Stable Movement

The magic of efficient climbing movement comes from the synergistic interaction of the arms and legs and a constant transfer of force and torque through your body. To this end, the Left–Right Rule states that maximum stability and ease of movement comes from the pairing of a left hand and right foot (or a left foot and right hand) in harmonious action. Let's again use climbing a ladder as our model. Ascending a ladder with opposing hand–foot combinations (say, the left hand pulling and right foot pushing at the same time) is so intuitive that it's almost impossible to climb a ladder any other way. Suppose you tried to climb a ladder with nonopposing hand–foot combinations, such as a right hand and right foot working together; you'd immediately begin to barndoor or rotate sideways off the ladder. Thus, the Left–Right Rule is a fundamental for balanced, stable movement.

While you don't need to even consider the Left–Right Rule in ascending a ladder, formulating movement up a climbing wall is much more complex: The position and shape of the hand- and footholds wreak havoc with your intuitive sense of movement. Thus, in seeking to reposition your hands and feet on the

thoughtful act. First, consider where the best place is to grab the hold. It's not always on the top, and it often relates to the location of your last foot placement. Now as you grab the hold, focus on using a light touch that yields soft forearms. Sure, certain holds will demand that you bear down hard on them, but most don't. Your goal must be to try to use each hold with a light touch, and then increase the gripping force only as much as is required for the move at hand. This process of minimally gripping

wall, it's helpful to ponder which holds will provide the best opportunity for a left–right combination. Easy climbs will often provide a pulling right hand that can combine with a pushing left foot (or vice versa). More difficult climbs tend to be more devious because the holds are smaller, farther apart, or displaced off to the side of the route line. Advanced climbers will often be able to intuit the best way to proceed; however, beginners must be willing to try difficult sequences multiple ways to discover and learn the best solution.

Move with Perfect Economy

The technical paramount is to climb with perfect economy. Make those two words, *perfect economy,* your mantra every time you touch the rock. Perfect economy means discovering the way to do each move—an entire route, for that matter—with minimal energy expenditure. If you have a cat, you can observe highly economic movement firsthand. Most of the time a cat moves in a slow, smooth, deliberate way; sometimes, however, a situation demands a powerful, dynamic leap to maintain perfect economy. Catlike movement should be your technical model for efficient climbing: smooth, quiet, leg-driven movements, but with an unhesitating shift to an arm-pulling, dynamic movement when it is required to most efficiently execute a difficult move. Here are five attributes of economic movement that you should aspire to.

QUIET FEET

Quiet foot movements are one of the hallmarks of a climber with great technique. Conversely, feet that regularly pop off footholds or skid on the wall surface are typical of an individual possessing lackluster footwork and poor economy. For many climbers, noisy footwork is just the way they climb—it's a habit that developed over a long period of time, as well as a flaw in their technique that will prevent them from ever reaching their true potential. Your goal, of course, is to learn to climb with good foot technique even in the toughest times. This means concentrating on each foot placement, keeping your foot steady and firm to the hold, and standing up on

the foot with confidence as you proceed smoothly to the next hand- or foothold.

RHYTHM AND MOMENTUM

Like any dance, climbing should have a natural rhythm that utilizes momentum and inertia. Climbing in a ladderlike motion yields the rhythm *step, reach, step, reach.* However, a better rhythm for effective movement is often *step, step, reach, reach,* since it allows the legs to direct and drive the movement. There are obviously many other rhythms, and every unique sequence possesses a *best* rhythm of movement and, more important, a best use of forward momentum to help propel successive moves. This is especially important on difficult climbs with large spacing between holds. Consider how you use momentum in moving hand-over-hand across monkey bars at a playground, with each movement blending into the next in a perfect continuity of motion. Make this "monkey bar" model of smooth, continuous motion your goal when climbing through strenuous sequences. (Ironically, many climbers do just the opposite, engaging crux sequences in a slow, hesitant way.)

SMOOTH MOVES AND RELAXED BODY

Smooth, fluid movement is another hallmark of high economy, while stiff, mechanical movement is a sign of poor technique and a high burn rate of energy. One of the keys to smooth, efficient climbing movement is learning to contract only the muscles necessary for engaging the rock and directing movement (usually these will be the muscles of your forearms, shoulders, abdomen, thighs, and calves). The easiest way to achieve this is to periodically switch your focus to the antagonist muscles and scan for unnecessary tension (in the upper arms, hips and legs, torso, neck, and face) that is making the agonist muscle work harder and burn more energy than necessary. Take a few slow, deep belly breaths and visualize the tension escaping the antagonist muscle like air from a balloon—such mental imagery really helps the process. Now return your focus to executing the next climbing movement, but continue alternating your focus back and forth between *directing movement* and *directing relaxation.*

PACE

Pace is another aspect of climbing economy that becomes increasingly important as a route gains in steepness and difficulty. While an easy climb with large holds allows you to ascend at a leisurely pace, a crux sequence or overhanging terrain will demand that you kick into high gear and surmount the difficulty in short order. When climbing near your limit, it must be your intention to move as briskly as possible without any drop-off in technique (skidding feet, botching sequences, and such). Reduce the pace at the first sign that your technique is suffering. It helps to identify obvious rest positions ahead of time, and then make it a goal to move from one to the next as fast as possible. Ultimately, knowing just the right pace on a given route is a sense you will develop with experience. Practice climbing at different speeds and on different types of routes, and you'll quickly foster the subtle skill of proper pace.

STEADY BREATHING

A steady flow of oxygen to the muscles is important for energy production and recovery, and it's the slow, deep, steady belly breaths that best get the job done. Many climbers, however, have a tendency to shift into shallow, rapid breathing as fatigue and mental anxiety grow. Worse yet, some climbers unknowingly hold their breath at times of high stress. These are two tendencies that you must be aware of and proactively counteract if you are to climb your best.

Before every climb, pause to close your eyes and take several slow, deep breaths. Feel your belly expand outward as you slowly inhale, and then allow the air to escape sparingly through pursed lips in a slow ten-second count (count in your mind). As you commence climbing, strive to maintain the same slow, steady breathing that you initiated on the ground. This is, of course, often difficult, since a dicey sequence or strenuous move can trigger irregular breathing patterns. Consequently, it is critical that you use every rest position as an opportunity to reset your breathing cycle with a few slow, deep belly breaths. Such proactive breath control is like topping off your gas tank—do it frequently, and you'll rarely hit empty.

Optimize Use of Rest Positions

Finding efficient rest positions is as important as finding the best way to do a crux sequence. If you miss a good rest stance, you miss an opportunity to physically recover as well as mentally "read" and prepare for the next section of the climb. Consequently, locating rest positions on a climb should be viewed with the same sense of importance as locating all the key holds—make this part of your pre-climb visualization routine.

Upon reaching a rest step, assume a body position that will allow the most fatigued muscles to rest (usually the forearms, biceps, and calves). An optimal rest position consists of your feet in the rest-step position, legs straight, and hips over the legs or in a position midway between the feet (should they be on holds more than shoulder width apart). Unfortunately, rest positions on vertical to overhanging climbs make complete weighting of the feet more difficult—often impossible. While you still want to place as much weight as possible on the footholds, a significant amount of weight will remain on your arms. In this case it's absolutely vital that you hang with straight arms, so that the bones are providing the support, not the muscles of the upper arm. Still, your forearm muscles will need to contract in order to maintain a grip on the handhold. The best strategy, then, is to attain a stable stance and shake out alternate arms every ten to twenty seconds. Use the G-Tox method described in chapter 10.

Clever Use of Opposing Forces

You have already learned the importance of the Left–Right Rule for enabling stable movement. On easy climbs this left-right combination is usually a pulling right hand along with a pushing left foot (or vice versa). More difficult climbs tend to be more devious, however, so you'll need to consider all the other possible arm positions—side pull, Gaston, and undercling—and figure out how to match one of these with an opposing foot placement. Detailed below are a few of the most common left–right combinations called into use on difficult climbs. You should practice each of these on the bouldering wall in order to develop its unique motor skills. Vary your hand and foot placements as much as possible to acquire a broad range of use for each hand–foot combination.

SIDE-PULL ARM AND OUTSIDE EDGE OF OPPOSITE FOOT

Side-pulling arms are a staple move on almost every moderate to advanced climb, but it's your foothold selection that often determines the effectiveness of this move. In most cases it's best to use the outside edge of the opposing foot, not the inside edge. Doing this may feel awkward at first, but you'll find a nat-

Pairing a side-pulling hand with the outside edge of the opposite foot (and a hip turn) provides great stability and reach. LISA ANN HÖRST

ural sense of stability once you learn to appropriately set your hips over the outside-edging foot. The key is to concentrate on rotating your hips so that the hip opposite the pulling hand is turned into the wall— that is, your face and chest will rotate toward the side pulling hand. This very stable position will allow you to step up your free (nonopposing) leg and quite possibly your free (nonopposing) hand as well. Occasionally a move will dictate that a side-pulling hand must be combined with use of the inside edge of the opposing foot. While this, too, is a fairly stable body position, it provides less reach upward with the free hand. Therefore, anytime you are struggling to reach a handhold, try using the outside edge of your shoe and a hip turn to maximize reach.

GASTON AND INSIDE EDGE OF OPPOSITE FOOT

The Gaston (aka reverse side pull) is the most unnatural and weak arm position, yet it's a fairly common move needed to unlock many crux sequences. Use of the Gaston is best opposed by the inside edge of the opposite foot. Combining a Gaston with an outside-edging foot is strenuous but doable if absolutely needed. Practice this move in a variety of ways to gain comfort and strength in its use. As with all these advanced moves, the bouldering area is the ideal proving ground to experiment with and learn the skills.

UNDERCLING AND INSIDE OR OUTSIDE EDGE OF OPPOSITE FOOT

Frequently overlooked by inexperienced climbers, undercling hand positions are often essential for unlocking difficult sequences on steep terrain. What's more, an underclinging hand helps maximize your reach with the free hand, and it positions your arm and body in a naturally strong position. Typically you will undercling a hold somewhere near your torso while you press with an opposing foot. This foot can edge with either the inside, outside, or toe portion of the shoe, although use of the outside edge is best for maximizing your reach. Remember that in edging with the outside of your foot, it's best to turn the hip opposite the pulling hand to the wall.

The undercling move can save the day on a reachy move lacking a positive down-pull hold. Use a hip turn and the outside edge of your opposite foot to maximize reach, stability, and power.
ERIC McCALLISTER

In extreme situations you may even need to use a foot smear to oppose the underclinging hand. This is a very powerful but important move that you should train on a bouldering or system wall.

SIDE-PULLING LEFT AND RIGHT HANDS

Use of opposing handholds is a key move for unlocking a sequence that lacks any usable down-pull or undercling handholds. Most common are two opposing side pulls that you'll draw inward to create tension through your arms, shoulders, and upper body. While you will be unable to create much upward movement, this opposition will allow you to upgrade one or both feet. Ideally, you'll want to upgrade the foot that opposes the better of the two side pulls, so that it sets up a stable left–right combination. This will enable you to release the other side-pulling hand so as to upgrade it to the next hold. Another possibility is opposing Gaston holds. Though strenuous, you may occasionally need to grab two Gastons at or just above head height and pull outward in order to support your weight while upgrading a foot position. This is a most advanced move that requires a high level of base strength.

Use Foot Flagging to Enhance Stability

Flagging is the alternative technique for maintaining stability when a left–right hand–foot combination is not possible. Suppose you are attempting to use a right-hand and right-foot combination to propel upward movement. Upon releasing your left hand to make a reach upward, you will immediately begin to barndoor. This sideways rotation is hard to fight and often results in a fall. However, a simple flagging of the free leg (in this case the left) significantly improves stability and balance by shifting your center of gravity more directly over the supporting (right) foot and under the supporting (right) hand. Practice using these flagging techniques on a vertical wall and then expand their use onto overhanging terrain. You will soon discover that foot flagging is an indispensable technique for steep, thin, balancy move.

Mantling and Hand–Foot Matching

The mantle move is often called upon to overcome a long reach between holds. Depending on the size of the hold to be mantled, you may be able to press your entire palm onto the hold or, possibly, just your fingertips. The left–right combination of pushing and pulling hands provides great stability, so you will be able to upgrade one or, possibly, both feet. In many cases you will match a foot (the same side as the mantling hand) on the same hold that you are mantling; it is then often possible to shift your center of gravity over that foot and stand up.

Severe climbs frequently demand that you

Unstable moves and a tendency to barndoor can often be overcome by a flagging foot—which shifts your center of gravity closer to the weight-bearing foot.

twist lock and backstep together helps draw your body in toward the surface of the overhanging wall. This changes the force vector on the handholds, making them feel more positive and secure. More important, this drawing-in of the body places more weight onto the footholds. Proper execution of these moves, however, requires practice and a significant amount of strength through the core muscles of the torso. See chapter 6 to learn exercises for strengthening these core muscles.

The twist lock is typically used to ease the upgrading of a hand on an overhanging section of wall. For example, consider the situation in which your left hand is on a good hold and you'd like to reach up high with your right. While you could attempt this move straight-on—chest facing toward the wall in a neutral position—it's far less strenuous to turn your right hip to the wall before making the upward reach. Proper positioning of the feet is critical for making this move work. Since the right hip is turning to the wall, you'll need to use the outside edge of your right foot on a hold somewhere below or in back of your body (hence the term *backstep*). Usually you'll find a complementary left foothold to help maintain the twist-lock body position. The feet then press in unison while the left arm pulls down and in toward your torso, creating the twist lock. Finding just the right body position is the key to providing a secure twist lock; when you do, you'll notice that a surprising lack of effort is needed to reach up and acquire the next handhold. This amazingly efficient locomotion over steep terrain is the magic of the twist-lock technique. *See photos on next page.*

Use Creative Footwork with Heel and Toe Hooks, and Knee Locks

Heel hooks, toe hooks, and knee locks are real difference makers when it comes to moving over steep terrain and surmounting overhangs. Given the strength of the leg muscles, a good heel hook is often better than a handhold in helping turn the lip of a difficult roof. Similarly, toe hooks and knee locks provide terrific support when you're cranking a serious move on overhang rock. Let's take a brief look at each.

adroitly match your foot onto a tiny crimp or finger pocket hold. Quick, precise execution is essential to maintain forward inertia as you progress through such tenuous sequences.

Twist Lock and Backstep on Steep Terrain

The twist lock and backstep are the bread-and-butter moves of a steep-wall connoisseur. As a climbing wall tilts back past vertical, it becomes increasingly difficult to place a high percentage of weight on your legs. Consequently, a greater portion of body weight must be supported by your arms—which, of course, possess less absolute strength than the legs. Use of the

1. Without the twist lock, the climber's neutral, straight-on body position places the center of gravity way out from the wall. This makes for strenuous, inefficient movement.

2. The twist lock with its hallmark hip turn draws the center of gravity in closer to the wall, thus placing more body weight onto the feet, increasing reach and enhancing grip on handholds (thanks to the changing force vector of the arm pull).

HEEL HOOK

Heel hooks are the major go-to move when you're turning the lip of a roof, topping out on a boulder problem, or copping a quick shakeout while on steep terrain. In these cases you'll likely have your hands on holds at or above face level and intend to place one of your heels on a hold off to the side near shoulder level. Which heel you choose to hook with depends on two factors: the availability of a decent-size hold on which to place your heel, and the location of the next handhold that you hope to acquire. This next reach up is best made with the hand on the same side as the heel hook. So if it looks like the next

attainable hold is set up for the right hand, it would be best to use a right heel hook. Once set, pull with the heel hook as if it were a third arm and, of course, pull with both arms as well. Often it helps to think about *pulling your heel toward your rear end;* this will maximize use of the leg muscles and help shift your center of gravity toward the heel hook. Meanwhile, the other foot should inside-edge or smear on the wall to help contribute to the upward motion. As you gain elevation, make a quick reach to the next handhold and then switch your heel hook into a standard step-down foot placement.

Heel hooks can make a huge difference in pulling a tough roof or copping a shakeout on steep rock.

TOE HOOK

The toe hook is a foot move used mostly in pulling overhangs or in navigating roofs. This technique involves simply hooking as much of the top-laces side of your shoe as possible on a large protruding hold. Sometimes you will toe hook onto a hold with a bent leg, and then straighten that leg as your hands move out the roof. Ideally you'll have one foot toe hooking while the other foot pushes off a nearby hold. This opposing push–pull combination enhances the foot purchase on the holds and lowers the chance that your feet will come swinging off the roof (a common problem). Strive to keep your arms and legs in the straight position as much as possible so that your body weight is being supported more by bone than by muscles. Done properly, you can navigate a surprisingly large roof, with the limiting factor being forearm endurance. Experiment with this foot

technique in the bouldering area and you'll gradually gain skill and confidence in climbing with your back to the ground!

KNEE LOCK

Knee locks are a boon on overhanging walls and roofs with large protruding holds—that is, if you know the technique and can find a position to exploit this "thank-God" move. On a severely overhanging climb with no obvious rest positions, finding a knee lock may be your only hope for a rest. Look for a place where you can step your toe onto a hold and then lock in your knee against a larger opposing hold. Such a knee lock provides surprising purchase; it will allow you to drop one hand at a time to shake out and chalk up. Occasionally you will come upon a knee lock that's so solid, you'll be able to cop a rare no-hands inverted rest! Of course, miss the knee lock and you have no choice but to sprint up the climb in the hope of reaching the anchors before the pump clock runs out.

Use Dynamic Moves When They Offer Greater Economy

Throughout this chapter I've stressed the importance of climbing with maximum economy—the goal being to climb a move, a sequence, and an entire route in a way that requires minimal energy. In most cases the hallmark of economical climbing is smooth, relaxed movement that utilizes the feet and legs over the muscles of the upper body. Such controlled, fluid movement is often referred to as static climbing. The opposite of static style is dynamic or explosive movement, and there are certain moves and sequences that demand dynamic movement to achieve maximum economy. In particular, vertical routes with tiny handholds and overhanging routes with long reaches often require dynamic movements.

The key is to know which moves are best attempted dynamically versus statically, and this is a recognition skill that takes years to fully develop. When working a route, it's best to attempt a crux in both a static and dynamic way to determine which style yields the most economical passage; otherwise you'll never know if there was a more effective method, and you'll miss out on an important learning opportunity. Let's examine the two primary forms of dynamic movement: deadpoints and lunges.

DEADPOINTS

Consider a situation in which both hands cling to poor holds, and you would fall off the wall if either hand let go for more than an instant. It's in just such a predicament that the deadpoint move will save the day, because it allows you to make a rapid hand upgrade despite the fact you can't hang on to the wall statically with a single-hand contact point. How's this possible? It's the magic of the deadpoint!

Envision a basketball player making a jump shot. He jumps straight up and shoots the ball at the peak of his flight, a moment of apparent weightlessness before gravity returns him to the floor. This instant of weightlessness and stillness is the deadpoint. Climbers can similarly exploit the apparent weightlessness of the deadpoint to upgrade a hand position as in the desperate situation described above. But instead of jumping like our basketball player, the climber needs to use a smaller, more controlled motion to facilitate the delicate upgrading of a hand from one small hold to another.

For example, imagine a tenuous move on a vertical or slightly overhanging wall in which you want to upgrade your right hand, but you can't make a static reach for the hold. Initiate the deadpoint movement with a small droop downward (or a release outward in the case of an overhanging wall) immediately followed by a firm drawing-inward of the handholds toward your torso. This drawing-in of your body is akin to—but less dramatic than—the basketball player's jump, and there will be an instant when the motion peaks and you'll be able to flash your hand up to snag the next hold. A well-executed deadpoint is calculated and controlled such that it flows naturally in perfect economy. In extreme cases you may need to execute several deadpoint moves in a row in order to climb through a series of small handholds that you could never hang on to for a static movement.

LUNGES

Unlike the careful, controlled movement of a deadpoint, the lunge (or dyno, as it's often called) is a full-on leap for an out-of-reach hold. In lunging, the arms and legs explode in unison to propel your body upward toward the next good hold. Lunges typically end in one of two ways: Ideally you latch on to a hold and regain control of your body; however, it's also possible that you will fail to catch the target hold

All all-out lunge move should be reserved for situations in which a static move would be more difficult or impossible. Here Matt Bosley lunges to crimp pay dirt at Earth Treks.

and end up falling on the rope or the bouldering crash pad.

Lunging is like any other skill in that it takes practice and a high level of confidence before you will be able to exploit the move in severe situations. It's also a strenuous and stressful move that has led to many shoulder injuries. Consequently, it's best to view lunging as a last-resort move that you only pull out of the bag when nothing else appears possible. In the heat of a crux sequence, though, it often comes down to a gut feeling as to whether you should try to throw a lunge or attempt a static sequence. Ideally it would be best to lunge only when climbing statically would require more energy. In fact, a perfectly executed lunge in just the right situation is a classic example of climbing with high economy, despite the apparent burly nature of the move.

Executing a lunge is very physical, but also requires good timing and a belief that you can reach the next hold. Much like a gymnast attempting her hardest move, throwing and sticking the perfect lunge requires laserlike focus and an intense belief in a successful outcome. Begin by locking your eyes on the target hold and visualize exactly how your hand will hit—and stick!—the hold. Next, look down and concentrate on maximizing an explosive launch off your four points of contact. In many cases it helps to "cock" your lunge by drooping or bouncing before you catapult upward. As you go airborne, your eyes will naturally return to a pinpoint focus on the target hold. Now stick it!

Jam Crack Climbing

Crack climbing involves techniques and tactics far different from the skills outlined above, and therefore you need to develop completely novel motor programs and schema-rules. I advise novice climbers to consult John Long's *How to Rock Climb!* for more comprehensive instruction than I offer here.

FINGER- AND HAND-JAMMING TECHNIQUES

Just how your hands engage a crack depends on the size of the fissure. The narrowest cracks will accept little more than the tips of your fingers. Most often you'll place this jam with your index finger on the bottom and your elbow out to the side. This way, when you pull on that arm, the elbow will rotate downward and produce a twisting of the fingers that further anchors them into the crack. One thing you will notice in larger finger cracks (around an inch wide) is that your fingers tend to slide down instead of jamming solidly. In these situations it's vital to look for constrictions or bottlenecks along the crack and attempt to place your jams in or just above these narrower spots.

Cracks ranging from 1 to 3 inches wide are the domain of hand jams. You can execute a hand jam in the thumb-up or thumb-down position. Vertical cracks are often better climbed thumb-down, whereas cracks that slant to the side may be more easily climbed with the lower hand jamming thumb-up and the high hand jamming thumb-down. As in finger jamming, scan hand cracks for constrictions or bottlenecks that will provide the most bombproof jams imaginable. Cracks with little variance are more challenging, as they require a bit more effort to create a solid jam. The key is to cup your hand inside the crack to generate outward pressure and friction on the inside of the crack. Furthermore, jamming thumb-down exerts a twisting force on the jammed hand as you pull down, and this tends to increase the security of the jam.

Fist jamming is the optimal technique for cracks about 4 inches wide. The technique here is simply to insert your hand with the palm facing into the crack and then make a fist. In closing your hand tightly, the width of your fist increases, making it stick like an oversize cork stuck in the top of a wine bottle. Cracks larger than 4 inches require a difficult off-width technique in which your arm and leg are jammed to gain purchase.

FOOT TECHNIQUES

There are two primary foot techniques used in crack climbing: feet inside the crack and feet on the rock face. In climbing thin finger cracks, you have little choice but to search for edges on the rock surface on

Crack climbing is vastly different from face climbing, yet one fundamental remains the same: Let the leg do most of the work.
ERIC McCALLISTER

which you can edge or smear (as in face climbing). The exceptions are offset cracks (where one edge of the crack is set out from the opposite edge of the crack) and larger finger cracks, which occasionally afford a foot smear on the exposed edge of the crack.

Look for stems, high steps, outside edges, and even backsteps in attempting to use your feet optimally. Cracks wider than about 1 inch provide exceedingly solid foot placements by means of foot jamming. The simple technique involves turning your foot side-the foot. In climbing a continuous hand or fist crack, you will simply need to leapfrog one foot above the other in a series of foot jams about 1 foot apart.

LIEBACK TECHNIQUE

Finally, there's liebacking, a unique method of climbing cracks that are located in the vertex of a dihedral or corner. The lieback technique is fairly strenuous since it places your body in a sort of rowing position with your arms pulling and your legs pushing in a powerful opposition. Feet smear on one wall of the corner while your fingers cling to the edge of the crack and arms remain as straight as possible. Move upward by simply walking your feet up the wall and sliding (or leapfrogging) your hands up the crack. With practice you'll learn to position your hands and feet to provide the greatest leverage at the lowest possible energy expenditure. Of course, as in all kind of strenuous climbing, moving quickly is fundamental to maximizing performance.

CRACK-CLIMBING STRATEGY

Effective crack-climbing strategy is nearly identical to optimal face-climbing strategy—climb briskly and efficiently, utilize your legs as much as possible in generating locomotion, and pause for long periods only at definitive rest stances. Just as in your clumsy first days attempting any new climbing technique, expect your initial forays at crack climbing to feel awkward and frustratingly difficult. Trust that you will rapidly acquire the unique motor skills and that crack climbing will soon become less strenuous and a heck of a lot of fun.

In your formative days of crack climbing, use the security of a toprope to experiment with different techniques and subtle variations of the basic jamming skills described above. Don't be satisfied with just thrashing up a crack to the top; instead strive to learn the best way to do each move with the goal of climbing each crack in good style and with minimal energy burn. As a practice method, climb single-pitch crack routes a few times in a row to refine your skills and learn the subtle finesse moves that will eventually make you a master crack climber!

Finger- and hand-jamming skills are subtle and require practice to perfect. Here crack master John Bachar pumps laps on his "crack machine," circa 1985. PHIL BARD

ways—so that the sole of the shoe is facing inward and your knee is bent outward—and inserting as much of your foot as possible into the crack. Depending on the crack's size, you may be limited to jamming just the toe portion of the shoe (narrow hand cracks) or its entire front half (fist cracks). Once you're secured in the crack, your knee will naturally rotate back to center as you stand up on

Smart Training Drills for Enhanced Learning of Motor Skills and Strategy

Having performed the technical evaluation in table 4.1 and the self-assessment in chapter 2, you should now have a clear picture of your technical weaknesses. But knowledge is not enough; to improve you must act! Dedicate a portion of two climbing sessions per week to improving your weaknesses and you will become a better climber.

Regardless of whether you plan to climb in a gym or at the crag, it's important that you make the distinction between time spent *practicing* versus *performing*. Unfortunately, many climbers handicap themselves by constantly focusing on performance as they succumb to the natural tendency to climb as close to their limit as possible. We've all seen climbers with horrible footwork flailing repeatedly on a steep route so that they can eventually tick some impressively difficult route. While they may ultimately succeed at sending their "5.hard" climbs, they gain little in technical ability from this exercise—and in fact they further groove their bad habits and poor technique. I call such practices "stupid training."

Conversely, intelligent climbers will dedicate a block of practice time early in the workout when they're mentally and physically fresh. During this practice period or day (if at the crags), the goal is to seek out routes that will target their technical weaknesses. Since performance is not a goal, there is no hesitation to hang on the rope and experiment with moves, body positions, and sequences that feel awkward or difficult.

For example, if backstep and drop-knee moves are a weakness, you'll want to dedicate some time during each workout to getting onto steep routes that demand these moves. No matter your weaknesses, it's likely that the type of routes you must get on will be intimidating, since up to this point it's probably been your tendency to climb routes that favor your strengths. If you are poor at drop-knee moves, for instance, I'll bet you avoid steep routes because they feel especially hard and look overly intimidating to you. The same goes for any style of

climbing—slab, thin face, cracks, roofs, what have you. You must partake in regular practice on the terrain and type of routes that target your top technical weaknesses as identified in the self-assessment and table 4.1. Excellence comes no other way.

Following are a few practice drills and games that will enhance your rate of learning new skills and correcting weaknesses, as well as making the process a little more fun. More examples of such speed learning practices can be found in my book *How to Climb 5.12*.

 Bouldering

Bouldering is often touted as the supreme method for developing sport-specific strength, but it's even more effective for learning climbing skills and acquiring new schemas. For proof of this, consider a recent bouldering session in which you worked a difficult problem a few times before eventually succeeding. Did you ultimately succeed because your strength increased after each attempt, or did each successive attempt result in learning of the body positioning, feel, and hand- and footwork necessary to do the moves most efficiently and successfully? I think the answer is obvious.

With all the restraints of roped climbing removed, bouldering allows you to narrow your focus and partake in relaxed, repeated attempts at learning a specific skill or sequence of moves. Sports scientists call this blocked practice, because the fixed moves can be practiced over and over again until they are successfully acquired. Once a skill is perfected, however, there is little benefit to additional blocked practice of that skill. Further learning demands that you either move on to practicing a new skill via blocked practice (say, a new boulder problem with new moves and positions) or modify the original problem so that some element of it has changed (say, angle, hold size, hold position or spacing, or the like). This latter strategy is known as variable practice, and it's the gold standard for learning a skill that must be performed in a variety of positions or settings: hitting a golf ball from an infinite variety of lies, shooting a basketball from anywhere on the court, floating a deadpoint from any one of a million different body positions.

Indoor walls and home gyms are the ideal setting for variable practice. Supposed you want to gain skill at, say, using undercling holds and hip turns on overhanging cliffs. To begin, set a problem with a relatively easy sequence of underclings and hip turns. Practice the sequence several times until you feel it's 100 percent wired. Now redesign the problem with slight changes in the hold positions and locations, and repeat the practice drill until this, too, is wired. Next, reduce the hand- and foothold size and repeat the drill. Keep repeating this process until you've exhausted the possibilities.

Completion of this variable practice drill might take anywhere from a single evening to a couple of weeks. Regardless, the end result is comprehensive schemas surrounding this type of movement, and rapid recall and execution of the skill in some future performance setting. So, while bouldering outdoors on a wide range of move types and angles is best for building a diverse library of climbing skills, using the variable practice strategy on an artificial wall enables comprehensive learning of a new type of movement in a wide range of configurations. Clearly, there is great value in both formats, so get busy!

 ### Traverse Training

Like bouldering, traverse training is a no-frills activity that affords focused practice on numerous technical aspects of the climbing game. Although some people find ad-lib traversing along a cliff base or at a climbing gym boring, this drill does have some major benefits when compared with working a known, graded boulder problem. When working the graded boulder problem, it's natural to want to succeed at any cost, even if your technique is sloppy and inefficient. As discussed earlier, it's difficult to develop new skills in such a performance setting.

Conversely, traversing for the sake of practicing technique and movement eliminates the pressure to perform. You can experiment with new grip posi-

tions, gentle and precise foot placements, and various body positions with no concern about whether or not you step off the wall. Maximize the benefit of this drill by carefully spotting each foot placement, concentrating on shifting your center of gravity over the leading foot, relaxing your grip as much as possible, and learning to move quickly and confidently through thin, tenuous sequences. Finally, strive to remain calm and relaxed at all times, and refocus on your feet anytime you sense you're losing control.

To mix things up and increase the intensity and benefit of traverse training, you can also play around with various elimination or focus drills. For example, try doing a complete traverse using only two fingers (the index and middle fingers, for example, or middle and ring fingers) of each hand. This drill forces you to maximize the weighting of your feet (a good thing); it's also an excellent way to increase your finger strength. As another variation, challenge yourself to do a complete traverse using only open-hand finger positions. (This will be especially difficult and beneficial if you naturally favor the crimp grip.) Be creative and make up other drills, such as "side-pull only," "undercling only," or "cross-through only" elimination traverses. Beginner and intermediate climbers have much to gain from performing these drills on a regular basis.

 ### Toproping and Hangdogging

Toproping and hangdogging are the ideal formats for practicing difficult moves near your limit or when diving into unfamiliar terrain like pocket or crack climbing. As discussed earlier, a relaxed, low-stress environment is critical to rapid learning of new skills. Obviously, climbing on toprope or on lead, bolt-to-bolt, represents a low-stress setting where you can experiment with tricky, awkward moves without the risk of a serious fall and injury.

When attempting a route that is continuously hard or with multiple cruxes, it's best to break it down into smaller sections or chunks. This reduces the mental burden by allowing you to view and solve the route in parts. Much like working a boulder problem, you can employ blocked practice to work a sequence repeatedly. Once a problem is solved and programmed to a high likelihood of success, you can move on and begin work on the next chunk. Upon solving all the chunks (and after a good rest), your next goal should be to combine chunks. For example, on a route that you had broken down into four hard sections, you would try to link the top two chunks, and then move down and link the top three chunks. Such incremental learning will wire you for a successful redpoint or toprope ascent after another rest or on your next outing or day at that area. (*Note:* See chapter 5 of *How to Climb 5.12* to learn many more strategies for working and sending project routes.)

The Stick Game (aka Send Me)

This popular game is great for learning to quickly assess and execute a novel, unknown move on-sight—a vital skill when you're on-sight climbing at the crag or in competition. Best played on an indoor wall, the drill requires at least two players who take turns pointing out (with a broomstick) impromptu boulder problems for the other to ascend. Begin by identifying the starting hand- and footholds for the climber; then, as she pulls up on them, the course setter points to the next hold to be used. Continue in this fashion until the climber falls or the problem is done. Commonly, the game is played with open feet—that is, the climber can use any foothold she likes.

First Touch

First Touch is a great practice drill for would-be competition and on-sight climbers—though anyone can benefit from its use. An indoor facility with a wide range of toprope routes is the ideal setting for this drill. As the name implies, you must climb a route by using each handhold in the exact way that you first grab it—no readjusting or changing your grip after you first touch it. By climbing many routes in this fashion (and, of course, obeying the guidelines completely), you will learn to examine holds more closely—both from the ground and while climbing—and thus increase the likelihood you'll use them optimally from the first touch. On lead, this skill saves you time and energy, both of which increase your odds of on-sighting a route.

Tracking and Elimination

This drill can be used indoors when you're bouldering or on toprope. The goal is simply to climb a route by tracking your feet on the exact same holds used by your hands. It's kind of like climbing a ladder, where you press down on a rung with your right hand and make room to step on that same rung with your right foot. As a type of elimination drill, this will make a climb much harder than it would be if climbed with all the holds on route. Therefore, if you normally practice skill by climbing 5.10 or 5.11 routes, you'll want to do this drill on routes in the range of 5.7 to 5.9.

If you climb indoors a lot, exercise your creativity and develop other elimination drills that might improve your skill, strategy, and strength. For instance, begin eliminating certain hand- and footholds from the routes you have ruthlessly wired. There's little to be gained from blocked practice of the same tired routes over and over again. So challenge yourself by eliminating the five biggest holds from the route, or by limiting yourself to grabbing the holds only as side pulls or underclings, or with only two fingers, or what have you. Not only can this make for some good fun for you and your friends, but it's also an excellent way to enhance your skill practice and overall ability.

Downclimbing Routes

When I'm leading or toproping indoors, it's rare that I climb a route to the top and lower off without trying to downclimb as much of the route as possible. There are many benefits to this practice beyond the obvious one of doubling the pump. If you know you are going to downclimb a route, you become a more observant and focused climber on the way up. What's more, since poor footwork is a leading handicap for many climbers, there's a lot to be gained from this practice, which demands intense concentration on footwork!

At first you will find downclimbing to be difficult, awkward, and very pumpy. But that's the MO when first attempting anything new that's worthwhile (read *challenging*). As your hold recognition improves, however, and as you learn to relax and fluidly reverse the route, you'll find that downclimbing a route often feels easier than sending it in the first place. This is because your eccentric (lowering) strength is greater than your concentric (pulling) strength, and due to the fact that by leading with the feet while downclimbing you learn to maximally weight them and conserve energy. All of the above make downclimbing a killer drill—one not to be overlooked by any serious climber!

Speed Training

When the rock gets steep and the moves hard, there's no more important weapon to have in your arsenal than being able to climb fast and precisely.

Climbing quickly is primarily a function of skill, not strength or power (I'm not talking about lunging wildly up a route). In fact, the less strength and endurance you possess, the more important this skill becomes.

To begin with, it's important to note that there is no benefit to climbing faster if you begin to botch sequences or if your technique degrades. Therefore, you want to practice speed climbing on routes you have completely wired and, likely, at a number grade or two below your personal best. Climb several laps on the route (rest between attempts), each incrementally faster than the previous. Attempt to climb about 10 percent faster on each successive lap, but back off the accelerator at the first sign that your technique is suffering.

Perform this drill a few times a week for several months, and you'll find yourself naturally moving faster when climbing on-sight or redpoint at the crags. This new skill alone could push your redpoint ability a full grade higher over the course of a single season—a much greater gain than you'd achieve from strength training alone!

Theory and Methodology of Strength Training

Man is in a position to act because he has the ability to discover causal relations which determine change and becoming in the Universe.

—*Ludwig von Mises*

Perhaps no sport can match rock climbing for the dramatic increase in the mean level of performance of its participants in recent years. Today's average climber is capable of a standard that few climbers dreamed of achieving when I began climbing in the mid-1970s. Furthermore, many weekend warriors are able to progress to the lofty levels of 5.12 and 5.13—grades that hardly existed three decades ago. The reasons for these incredible improvements include sticky-soled shoes, sport-climbing tactics, and, more than anything else, the advent of climbing gyms and a growing focus on sport-specific strength training.

Still, there are many arguments among climbers about the best way to train, and people frequently tell me that they are confused by the often conflicting training information that has been published. Surely an article or book describing the training practices of some 5.14 climber is of little help for average climbers—it might even get them injured. Alternatively, joining a health club and performing the typical weight-lifting workout would be of little

Stephen Meinhold on **Mango Tango (5.13d),** *New River Gorge, West Virginia.* D A N   B R A Y A C K

benefit for most climbers; in fact, it may even hurt their climbing performance!

As a result of all the confusion, numerous climbers have quipped to me that they have decided to "just climb" as training for climbing. While this is an excellent strategy for novices, intermediate and advanced climbers definitely need to partake in some sport-specific strength training if they want to continue to improve and, hopefully, someday reach their genetic potential.

The goal of this chapter (as with this whole book) is to help you avoid—or step out of—the muck and mire of confusion that surrounds so much information on training for climbing. Toward this end, I will arm you with a basic understanding of the theory and science of strength training. I have always felt that the theoretical person is a practical person. Therefore, gaining knowledge of training theory will enable you to act and train more practically and effectively. Furthermore, you will be able to evaluate more critically and effectively what you read elsewhere.

Overview of Strength and Fitness Training for Climbing

Just for the record let me state that simply going climbing is *not* the best method of strength training for climbers. This is because the ultimate goals of these two activities are very different. Consider that when rock climbing, it is your goal to avoid muscular failure at all costs—you want to reach the top of a boulder problem or climb before the muscles of your arms and forearms pump out. Conversely, when training for climbing you purposely fatigue the muscles and in some cases even target-train a muscle for failure. Simply put: When climbing, you avoid failure; when strength training for climbing, you pursue failure.

Another example that underscores the difference between climbing and training for climbing is the way in which you grip the rock. In climbing, the rock dictates a random use of many different grip positions; at times you may even deliberately vary the way you grip the rock. As a result it's unlikely that any single grip position will ever get worked maximally, and therefore the individual grip positions (crimp, open hand, pinch, and so forth) are slow to increase strength. This should help you understand why a full season of climbing will indeed improve your local forearm endurance (anaerobic endurance) but do little to increase your absolute maximum grip strength. Therefore, varying grip positions is a great strategy for maximizing endurance when climbing for performance, but it stinks for training maximum grip strength. Effective finger-strength training demands you target a specific grip position and work it until failure.

On the following pages, we'll delve into the science of strength training and reveal some of the other secrets to highly effective training for climbing.

A Primer on Exercise Physiology

While there is no need to get into an advanced-level discussion of exercise physiology, I feel it's beneficial to have a basic understanding of some functions involved in strength training. For instance, understanding how different types of muscle fiber become "recruited" into action and how the muscles adapt to training stress offers key distinctions in how to best train your upper-body muscles for strength and power. Furthermore, knowledge of the body's energy systems and why muscles fail can give clues as to how you might modify your climbing to maximize power and local endurance.

Muscle Movements and Roles

The production of movement involves three different muscular actions, as well as three basic roles the muscles can play during an athletic performance.

- **Concentric contraction:** Muscle action in which the tension developed produces a shortening of the musculature, as in the biceps during the upward phase of a pull-up.
- **Eccentric contraction:** Muscle action in which the muscle resists as it's forced to lengthen, as in the biceps during the lowering phase of a pull-up.
- **Isometric contraction:** Muscle action resulting in no shortening of the muscle (no movement), as in musculature of the forearm while gripping a handhold.
- **Agonist:** The muscle or muscle groups causing an action to occur. For instance, the biceps and the latissimus muscles of the back are some of the prime movers in the pulling motions common to climbing.
- **Antagonist:** The muscle or muscles providing an opposing force to the primary muscles in action. For example, the muscles on the back of your forearm oppose the action of the forearm flexor muscles when gripping the rock.
- **Stabilizer:** The muscle or muscle groups that help stabilize the skeletal structures so that tension of the agonist (prime movers) can produce smooth, effective movement. In climbing, there are many small and large stabilizers (including the antagonist muscles) that come into play, from the arms to the core muscles of the torso and down through the legs.

Muscle Fiber Types

There are two distinct types of muscle fiber: slow twitch and fast twitch. Fast-twitch fibers are further subdivided into two main subcategories: Type IIa and Type IIb. A third subcategory of Type IIc fibers has been identified, though they exist in only very small numbers.

- **Slow twitch (ST):** These Type I fibers make up approximately 50 percent of the total skeletal muscle, though genetic variation can range from about 20 percent to 80 percent (Bloomfield, et al., 1992). They are recruited primarily during low-intensity, aerobic endurance activities.

- **Fast twitch (FT):** These fibers are recruited during high-intensity movements or activities. Type IIa (FTa) fibers are energized through both aerobic and anaerobic processes and are, therefore, fatigue-resistant. These fibers excel at longer-duration high-intensity activity, and they would be most active when climbing long, hard routes. Type IIb (FTb) fibers have the fastest contraction time and generate energy almost entirely through the anaerobic system. These fibers are recruited during brief, maximum movements such as a difficult boulder problem or a powerful crux move.

Your relative percentage of FT and ST muscle fibers is genetically determined and varies little in response to training. Naturally strong climbers are likely gifted with a higher-than-normal percentage of FT fibers (among other things), whereas gifted mountaineers, who can keep on going like the Energizer Bunny, likely have a higher percentage of ST fibers. Fortunately, ST fibers can be taught to act like FT fibers through use of certain training protocols (Chu 1996), which I will introduce later.

RECRUITMENT

Muscle fibers of the same type are organized into motor units. ST motor units innervate between 10 and 180 fibers, while FT motor units innervate up to 800 fibers (Bloomfield, et al., 1994). When a muscular contraction is triggered, motor units are recruited on an as-needed basis beginning with the smaller ST motor units. As muscular tension increases, a greater number of ST motor units will join in, and if the tension grows further, the larger FT motor units will begin to fire. Maximum muscular force is eventually achieved if all motor units (ST and FT) are recruited into action (see figure 5.1).

Knowing this physiological process should help you understand why it's important to train with high intensity and with maximum weight (resistance) if you want to recruit, and make stronger, the FT fibers. Compare this with "just climbing a lot of routes" for training: That way you would recruit primarily ST fibers on the many moderate moves and only occasionally recruit the FTa fibers when you

Figure 5.1   Muscular Force Production

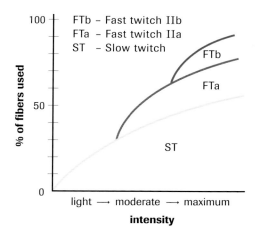

Maximum muscular force eventually can be achieved if all motor units (ST and FT) are recruited into action.

encountered hard moves. The high-threshold FTb fibers would seldom be called into action—only when a move or sequence required explosive power or application of maximum strength.

Muscular Adaptations to Strength Training

Two primary adaptations occur in response to strength training—adaptation of the neural system and adaptation of the muscular system.

ADAPTATION OF THE NEURAL SYSTEM

The nervous system adapts to strength training in three ways: motor learning, motor unit synchronization, and disinhibition.

- **Motor learning:** The first neural adaptation, motor learning, should sound familiar after reading chapter 4. During the initial work at a new exercise (say, uneven-grip pull-ups or even campus training), your primary limitation will be a lack of coordination and feel for the exercise. The first few weeks should yield rapid improvement as a result of motor learning and improved coordination among the prime mover, stabilizer, and antagonist muscles. Beyond this point, further strength gains will depend on other adaptations taking place.

- **Motor unit synchronization:** Motor unit synchronization is the second neural adaptation that increases strength. Suppose you have acquired the coordination and motor skills needed for performing a given exercise—or perhaps you're adding a new exercise that requires no learning (such as hanging on a fingerboard). Initial training triggers motor units to fire in a rather random, asynchronous manner. Continued training, however, enhances motor unit synchronization; eventually most of the motor units will fire in unison, resulting in more strength and power.

- **Disinhibition:** The final neural adaptation, disinhibition, is most important (and exciting) for intermediate to advanced climbers in search of gains in maximum strength and power. The neuromuscular system has a built-in feedback mechanism that acts as a safeguard during times of increasing force production. The Golgi tendon organ, located in the musculotendinous junction, is sensitive to the level of tension in the muscle, and in situations of high force it sends inhibitory signals that prevent further motor units from firing. In most individuals this protective response limits force production to some amount far below your absolute maximum-force-producing potential. It's like putting a restrictor plate on the engine of a race car to limit its top speed to 150 miles per hour, even though it's capable of 225. Fortunately, regular high-intensity training reduces the sensitivity of the Golgi tendon organ (disinhibition) and thus opens up a new level of maximum strength.

The difference between your maximum voluntary force and the absolute maximum capacity is called the strength deficit. Research has shown that significant gains in strength are possible by training to reduce these neural inhibitions. One study (Tidow 1990) showed that untrained individuals possessed strength deficits of up to 45 per-cent; that is, neural inhibition was reducing their maximum strength to almost half of their absolute capacity. The study also revealed that targeted training by elite athletes reduced strength deficits to only 5 percent. Therefore, large gains in strength are possible without ever growing a larger, heavier muscle!

As a final note, the best type of training to produce disinhibition depends on the magnitude of your strength deficit. Intermediate climbers, who likely have larger strength deficits, would benefit most by training with heavy loads (heavy pull-downs, hypergravity training on a fingerboard or HIT system, and so forth). Elite climbers with smaller strength deficits might realize further improvements only through a combination of high resistance (hypergravity) and high-speed (reactive/plyometric) training.

ADAPTATION OF THE MUSCULAR SYSTEM

Long-term gains in muscular strength result from increases in the size of the individual muscle fibers (see figure 5.2). This process of growing larger muscles is known as hypertrophy. Since there is a strong relationship between the size and the strength of muscles, your ability to grow stronger over the long term depends to some degree on hypertrophy.

Certainly large muscles in the wrong place (such as legs, chest, and shoulders) are a liability to climbers. Even overdevelopment of the all-important pull muscles can be a bad thing if it's the result of exercising in a nonspecific way (such as heavy free-weight or circuit training). For example, baseball-size biceps that result from doing heavy biceps curls will not only underperform on the rock but also get in the way and prevent you from locking off effectively while you are climbing.

Still, any muscular hypertrophy occurring in the forearms, arms, and back resulting from sport-specific training should be viewed as a good thing. In fact, an experienced climber who has been training for a long time and doesn't realize a little hypertrophy probably isn't training effectively or eating right. Since most hypertrophy occurs in response to high-

Figure 5.2 Muscular Adaptations to Strength

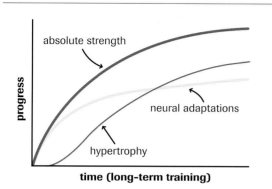

Initial gains in strength result mostly from neural adaptations, whereas long-term gains will somewhat depend on hypertrophy.

intensity, heavy-load training, you would want to train with higher resistances (hypergravity training) to trigger this adaptation.

It's interesting to note that a highly trained neuromuscular system is not absolutely necessary for being a strong climber. As mentioned in chapter 1, a small number of individuals possess tendon insertion points at a larger distance from the joint (axis of rotation) than the rest of us with average genetics. These gifted people will exhibit what seems to be amazing strength given their modest body builds. Other genetic factors, such as having a slight build or an unusually high percentage of fast-twitch fibers, may further enhance their physical prowess. With this in mind, you can see why these rare climbers will be incredibly strong regardless of the type of training, if any, in which they engage. Hence it would be a mistake to copy their training methods, and you should question the advice of anyone who instructs you to train like such-and-such a 5.14 climber does.

Energy Systems

In climbing, energy production in the crucial pull muscles most often comes from the ATP-CP system and the lactic acid system. The lactic acid system can function both in the presence (aerobic) or absence (anaerobic) of oxygen.

ATP-CP

The ATP-CP system provides rapid energy for brief, intense movements such as a vigorous boulder problem or a few maximal crux moves. In training, the ATP-CP system is the primary fuel source for brief, intense exercise lasting less than fifteen seconds—for example, campus training or doing a one-arm pull-up. ATP and CP are high-energy phosphate compounds resident in all muscle cells in small amounts; intense exercise, however, will exhaust the supply in a matter of seconds.

LACTIC ACID

Consistent, moderate- to high-intensity exercise lasting between ten seconds and about three minutes calls the lactic acid energy system into play. This is the primary energy system that fuels your climbing up a long boulder problem or a sustained crux section of route. Carbohydrates, in the form of glycogen, fuel the lactic acid system, which can operate in either the presence or absence of oxygen.

- **Anaerobic:** High-intensity exercise forces the muscles to create energy in the absence of oxygen (anaerobic) and at the expense of lactic acid production. The resulting accumulation of lactic acid leads to fatigue, muscular pain, and, eventually, muscular failure. This limitation of anaerobic energy production helps explain why sustained climbing on maximally difficult moves is limited to about three minutes or less (if there are no rests). Consequently, climbing as quickly as possible from rest to rest is the best strategy on hard, sustained routes.

  The *anaerobic threshold* is defined as the workload or oxygen consumption level at which lactate production by the working muscle exceeds the body's ability to remove lactate. Therefore, once you cross this threshold level, the net amount of lactic acid increases, and muscular failure soon follows (see figure 5.3). Depending on your level of conditioning, the anaerobic threshold may be crossed at an exercise intensity of anywhere between 50 percent and 80 percent of maximum. Becoming winded (oxygen debt) and burning muscles are two signs you have crossed the anaerobic threshold.

Figure 5.3 Supercompensation Cycle

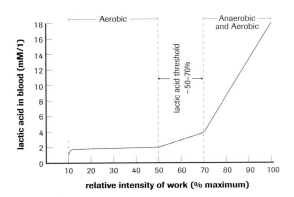

Once the anaerobic threshold level is crossed, the net amount of lactic acid increases, and muscular failure soon follows

The above knowledge underscores the importance of using an interval approach to high-intensity climbing. In sending a hard route, you want to avoid crossing the anaerobic threshold for as long as possible and, once you do cross it, climb as quickly as possible to a rest or easier terrain. Only then will you get back down below the anaerobic threshold and allow your body to begin lowering blood lactate concentration. Depending on the amount of lactic acid in your system, it could take twenty minutes or more to return to a baseline level of blood lactate (Watts 1996).

- **Aerobic:** Muscular action lasting longer than three minutes demands use of oxygen to produce energy. With ATP-CP reserves depleted and high muscle and blood lactate levels (from anaerobic energy production), exercise can continue only if the intensity of movement is reduced (see figure 5.4). Anaerobic energy production is limited to an

amount proportionate to the liver's ability to remove lactic acid (and convert back to glucose) from the blood. Therefore, aerobic energy production takes over and powers most of the muscle action by means of a breakdown of carbohydrates, fats, and (if exercise continues long enough) protein in the presence of oxygen. Since aerobic energy production does not produce lactic acid, low-intensity movements may continue for several hours without cessation (as in hiking or climbing over easy terrain).

Figure 5.4 Supercompensation Cycle

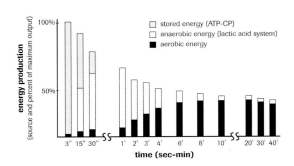

Brief, maximal muscular action is fueled by ATP-CP. After about fifteen seconds, anaerobic energy production becomes the primary energy source. Exercise lasting longer than three minutes depends mostly on aerobic energy production, though muscular output is only a fraction of maximal.

Training Principles

Possessing a basic understanding of relevant training principles empowers you to make the most of your time investment in training. Without getting too deeply into sports science, let's examine the important principles of specificity, individualization, progressive overload, variation, rest, and detraining.

Specificity

The principle of specificity of training may be the most important of all. It simply states that the more specific a training activity is to a given sport—in velocity of movement, pattern of movement, body posture, range of motion, and type of contraction—the more it will contribute to increasing performance in that sport. Therefore, for an exercise to be effective at producing usable strength gains for climbing (such as grip strength, lock-off strength, or lunging power), it must be markedly similar to climbing in many ways. The more specific the training activity or exercise, the greater the benefit to your climbing performance. Let's look at a few examples of how this rule applies to training for climbing.

Circuit training or pumping iron does not train the muscles in the slightest way similar to their use in rock climbing. Consequently, health-club-style weight training is largely a waste of time for climbers, except for those possessing unusually poor levels of general fitness. Some intermediate climbers have disputed me on this, since they have noticed improvement on the rock while participating in weight-training regimens. Since gains in climbing skill and strategy produce most of the increase in overall ability during the first few years in the sport, however, these folks would have improved regardless of the type of training they participated in. They probably would have improved as much with a training regimen outside of climbing itself consisting of ice skating and poker playing.

Squeezing a rubber hand doughnut (or other similar spring-loaded device) is likewise unproductive for improving your finger strength for climbing. Grip strength shows a remarkable amount of specificity depending on the grip position (crimp, open hand, pinch), the positions of the wrist and elbow, the intensity of the contraction, and even the type of contraction (isometric, concentric). Furthermore, since your grip tends to fail while you are pulling down on it with near-maximum load, it must be trained in much this same way. Consequently, squeezing a rubber doughnut is basically useless as climbing training, though it does have some value as a warm-up exercise and in injury rehabilitation.

What about the basic pull-up (palms away), a most popular exercise among climbers? Obviously the motion is similar to climbing, but your posture, your degree of body tension, and the exact positions of your hands and arms do not vary randomly as they do on rock. What's more, the ability to stop or lock off your arm in some novel position is often more vital in climbing than is the simple act of pulling. Therefore, to produce the most transfer of your pull-up training to the rocks, you want to alter the pull-up in a variety of ways with every set. For example, you might change the distance between your hands, stagger one hand lower than the other (use a webbing loop), and include some lock-offs or stops in the motion at a variety of arm angles. This approach would be much more advantageous than just doing pull-ups in the same fixed position.

Finally, let's consider the concept of cross-training as some individuals try to apply it to climbing. Clearly, the idea that performing any other sports activity might improve climbing performance is in blatant conflict with the principle of specificity. In fact, the only sports in which cross-training seems to be practical are the aerobic endurance sports, as popularized by the triathlon phenomenon.

Individualization

No climber on this planet is quite like you; therefore the most effective training program for you will be different from that of any other climber. This might sound obvious, but many climbers copy the training program of their peers or, worse yet, imitate what some elite climber does. I consider this a rather stupid approach to training.

The most intelligent training program (for you) would take into account your strengths, weaknesses, and previous injuries, as well as your goals and the amount of time you have available to work out. Furthermore, since you may recover from training at a faster or slower rate than others, your optimal amount of rest may dictate a different workout frequency. Consequently, it would be wise to develop and execute what seems to be the best program for you and ignore how others train.

Progressive Overload

This granddaddy of training principles states that in order to increase physical capability, it is necessary to expose your body to a level of stress beyond that to which it is accustomed. You can achieve this overload by increasing the intensity (greater resistance), volume, or speed of training, or by decreasing the rest interval between successive sets. Depending on the exercise and which of these exercise parameters you choose to vary, the overload will result in adaptations resulting in more strength, power, anaerobic endurance, or stamina. For example, increasing exercise resistance and speed will produce gains in maximum strength and power, whereas decreasing rest intervals and increasing volume will improve muscular (anaerobic) endurance.

While it's probably a good idea to vary the method of overload from time to time, the best method of overload for you depends on your climbing preference. If bouldering is your favorite type of climbing, then you'd want to favor training that builds strength and power (and create overload by increasing resistance and speed of exercise). In training for roped climbing, however, it would be best to increase volume and decrease rest intervals to improve muscular endurance. Finally, big-wall and alpine climbers looking for greater stamina should create overload by increasing total volume of exercise.

Variation

One of the most common training errors among all athletes is the failure to regularly change their training program. This principle states that the body becomes accustomed to training stimuli that are repeatedly applied in the same way. Therefore, if you go to the climbing gym and engage in the same basic routine every time, your strength and climbing gains will eventually plateau despite what feel like good workouts. Strive to vary your training by manipulating the type of overload (per above) as well as mixing up the type and order of climbs and exercises performed.

Periodization, another form of variation, involves alternating the overall workout intensity and volume from session to session. For example, with indoor training you might alternate workouts among "high volume" (doing many moderate routes), "high intensity" (hard, powerful bouldering), and "high, high" (climbing as many hard routes as possible). You could also vary your workouts every few weeks as in the 4-3-2-1 Training Cycle described in chapter 7. Bottom line: Make the principle of variation a cornerstone of your training for climbing program and you will get uncommonly good results!

Rest

The muscular adaptations discussed earlier occur between, not during, workouts. Sufficient rest and healthy lifestyle habits (including proper nutrition and adequate sleep) are fundamental to maximizing the strength gains that result from training stimuli. As a rough guideline, complete recovery (supercompensation) takes anywhere from twenty-four to seventy-two hours depending on the intensity and volume of the stimulus (see figure 5.5). For example, it might only take one day to recover from a high volume of low-intensity activity like climbing a bunch of really

Figure 5.5 Supercompensation Cycle

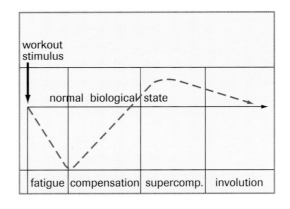

Complete recovery (supercompensation) takes anywhere from twenty-four to seventy-two hours, depending on the intensity and volume of the training stimulus.

easy routes or just hiking, whereas it will likely take two or three days to recover completely from a high volume of high-intensity exercise, such as climbing a bunch of routes near your limit, or performing hypergravity and campus training in a single workout.

The importance of this principle cannot be overstated, since training too often (or resting too little) will eventually lead to a decline in performance and/or injury (see figure 5.6). This is known as the overtraining syndrome, and it's surprisingly common among serious climbers. Observe how many climbers out there are whining about their nagging injuries or complaining that they are "not getting stronger" despite their dedication to hard training. You now know why: overtraining.

Another factor leading to overtraining or unusually long workout recovery is the mistake of placing too much training stimulus on the neuromuscular system. As shown in the Supercompensation Cycle (figure 5.5), the workout stimulus results in neuromuscular fatigue and a temporary degradation in functional ability. With adequate rest, the system regenerates to a level higher than before the workout. Interestingly, working out beyond a certain point provides no additional stimulus for growth, though it does make further inroads (muscular

breakdown) from which you must recover. This is an important concept to keep in mind when performing high-intensity training. Doing twelve sets of campus training probably provides no more stimulus for growth than six sets, but by doing twelve sets you dig yourself a deeper hole from which it will take longer to recover. The same argument could be made against doing twenty sets of pull-ups or spending sixty minutes hypergravity training on a fingerboard. Summing up: In high-intensity training, less is usually more.

Detraining

Upon cessation of strength training (or frequent climbing), recent gains in strength begin to erode slightly in just ten to fourteen days. A more significant decrease in strength will occur in the weeks that follow if training or climbing does not resume. While some downtime is a good thing each year (mentally and in the case of nagging injuries), frequent breaks in training make it very difficult to acquire long-term gains in strength.

If you are someone who travels a lot on business, or for some other reason frequently misses a week or two of training, you can temporarily delay the detraining by leveraging your knowledge of the lengthened supercompensation period after high-intensity workouts. Since we know that it can take several days to recover from a long, intense workout, performing such a workout the day before the beginning of your break would delay the beginning of detraining by a few more days. Therefore, you might return from the break and be at peak strength even after ten days off. This long period of supercompensation after extremely strenuous training or climbing also explains why the many enthusiastic climbers who are unknowingly overtraining discover a new level of strength after taking a week off from training and climbing.

Figure 5.6 Long-Term Training Response

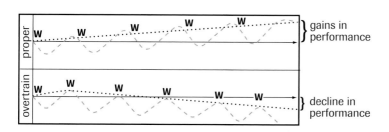

Adequate rest between workouts allows full supercompensation and long-term gains in performance. Conversely, workouts too close together result in a long-term decline in performance.

Tips for Effective Physical Training

1. **Specificity:** For an exercise to produce usable strength gains for climbing, it must be markedly similar to the physical action of climbing, including velocity and pattern of movement, body position, range of motion, and type of contraction.

2. **Individualization:** There are no other climbers quite like you; therefore, your optimal training program will be different from those of all other climbers!

3. **Overload:** To increase physical capability, it is necessary to expose your body to a level of training stress beyond that to which it is accustomed. This can be achieved by increasing training intensity, speed, volume, or by decreasing the rest interval between sets or climbs.

4. **Variation:** Since the body adapts to training stimuli, it's essential to regularly vary training activities and workouts every few days or weeks.

5. **Rest:** Neuromuscular adaptations occur during periods of rest and sleep, not during workouts. Therefore, sufficient rest and a healthy lifestyle are essential for making the most of your training investment.

6. **Detraining:** Skipped workouts or frequent breaks in a training cycle will make strength gains unlikely and may lead to a loss of climbing fitness.

Training Methods

Detailed below are the concepts and methods central to effective strength training for climbing. Since the pull muscles are most often the limiting physical factor in climbing, examples of how this information applies to climbing will focus on training these body parts.

Strength Training Versus Local Endurance Training

Strength training results in neural and muscular adaptations that eventually enable muscle action at higher loads. Meanwhile, training local muscular endurance (aka anaerobic endurance) produces different adaptations—such as increased density of capillaries and mitochondria (the little ATP "factories" inside cells)—that will help sustain longer periods of vigorous muscle action (see figure 5.7). Certainly all climbers would benefit from enhancement in both areas; the form of training you emphasize, however, should match the demands of your preference climbing subdiscipline (per the SAID Principle explained in chapter 1).

Climbing icon Tony Yaniro long ago pointed out that "if you cannot pull through a single hard move, then you have nothing to endure." From this perspective, strength training could be viewed as more important for all climbers, save big-wall and alpine enthusiasts. This notion is supported by the fact that strengthening a muscle also improves its endurance, because a stronger muscle can use a smaller percentage of maximum strength to execute a sequence of nonmaximum moves. What's more, a stronger muscle will have a higher absolute anaerobic threshold than a weaker muscle with higher endurance capabilities. Conversely, endurance training will not increase maximum strength one iota.

Muscular Strength Versus Muscular Power

Strength is defined as the force a muscle group can exert in one maximum effort. Your ability to pull a single hard movement or grip a small, difficult handhold is a function of your maximum strength. Muscular power is more complex, because it is the product of force and the distance through which the force acts. Therefore, power is the result of strength and speed. This would be expressed as: power = strength x speed (where speed = distance/time).

So while strength and power are clearly related, they differ in the rate at which a force is applied.

Figure 5.7   Physiological Adaptations to Training

Structure, System, or Energy Source	Adaptations from Strength Training	Adaptations from Endurance Training
Muscle fiber size	Increase	No change or decrease
Capillary density	No change or decrease	Increase
Neural disinhibition	Increase	No change
Mitochondrial density	No change or decrease	Increase
Muscle glycogen	Increase	Increase
ATP-CP	Increase	No change

Adaptations from strength versus endurance training.

Figure 5.8   Rate of Force Production

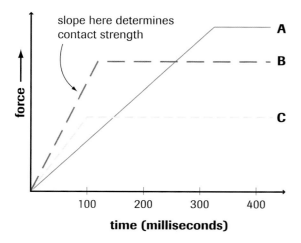

Hypothetical grip strength of three climbers. Climber A has the greatest absolute grip strength, while Climber B has the best contact strength.

A real-life example that helps clarify this distinction relates to your ability to grip a tiny hold versus your ability to quickly stick (draw in) a small handhold at the end of a lunge. Figure 5.8 shows hypothetical force–time curves for three climbers. Climber A possesses the strongest grip strength and can hang on the smallest holds, but he is not very powerful. Climber B has less absolute strength than Climber A, but she is more powerful. Consequently, she can summon her strength more quickly (that is, she has greater contact strength), and she will be more successful at catching dynos and quickly latching on to tiny holds. Climber C is neither strong nor powerful—he'd better stick to climbing slabs.

Obviously, it's ideal to maximize your strength and power, much like Climber B. This can be achieved by partaking in a variety of exercises that train both strength and power.

Training for Strength

Rate of strength gains, as a result of training, decreases as a function of your current level of strength. Therefore, initial increases in strength will result from even a poorly conceived and executed training regimen. Adaptations in stronger, more advanced climbers occur more slowly—and possibly not at all unless they are using the best training methods. This helps explain why so many intermediate to advanced climbers feel they are no longer getting stronger: For them, further gains require advanced training techniques and the discipline to apply them precisely over a long period of time.

In terms of training maximum strength—your ability to pull a single maximum move or grip a small edge or pocket under full body weight—it is widely accepted by sports scientists that exercising at high intensity and heavy loads is the most important factor. Furthermore, the muscles must be progressively loaded beyond the point to which they are accustomed. In the weight-lifting world, this is achieved by performing three to ten repetitions at some high load, which is increased over time. Unfortunately, this is a difficult protocol to create for the purpose of developing finger strength for climbing. For instance, what do you do to create progressive overload of the fingers (forearm muscles) once you are strong enough to handle your own body weight over steep terrain? The obvious answer is to "climb longer," which is exactly what many climbers do. This strategy, however, develops endurance of strength (anaerobic endurance), not maximum strength.

BOULDERING AS STRENGTH TRAINING

A better strategy is to seek out progressively more strenuous boulder problems that seem to require near-maximum strength. The drawback here relates to the fact that it's very difficult to say if you fell off a move because of muscular failure or because you performed the movement poorly (bad technique). Further diluting the training effect is the randomness of handholds in size and shape, which dictates the use of different grip positions—we now know that varying grip position is a good endurance strategy, but it's poor for building maximum grip strength. Consequently, while you may notice some gains in strength and power from bouldering, you can assume that it's not providing you with the greatest strength gains possible. There are just too many variables involved.

Bouldering on a steep artificial wall represents a better format for upper-body strength training, because you can control the size and distance between holds and minimize the technical aspects that might spit you off before muscular failure. Still, there are practical limits to how far you can increase hold spacing and decrease the size of the handholds—beyond a certain point the moves will become overly technical or the tiny holds too painful to climb on. As described above, it's necessary to perform three to ten maximum repetitions before reaching muscular failure (for the purpose of developing maximum strength); in the case of climbing with both hands, you would need to perform six to twenty total hand movements before failure.

HYPERGRAVITY TRAINING

Once the above strategies have been exhausted for the purpose of developing further gains in maximum grip strength, you need to up the ante by employing hypergravity training. At advanced levels of training for climbing, the importance of training at progressively higher intensity and with heavier loads cannot be overstated. This is best achieved by adding extra weight to your body while performing certain controlled, sport-specific movements. As a result, your fingers (and other upper-body pull muscles) are exposed to a load and intensity not previously experienced at normal body weight. The extra weight simulates a greater-than-normal gravitational pull (hence the name *hypergravity*). After a period of hypergravity training, you will return to the rock and feel like you are climbing on the moon!

The dramatic gains in strength produced by hypergravity training are the result of neural and muscular adaptations (discussed earlier). In particular, it likely triggers a higher degree of disinhibition and hypertrophy that may never result from climbing at the lower resistances of body weight. I also suspect that hypergravity training may trick ST muscle fibers into acting like FT fiber—more on this later.

As a disclaimer, it must be pointed out that hypergravity training is an advanced strength-training method to be used only by well-conditioned and advanced climbers with no recent history of injury. Chapter 7 discusses the four best applications of hypergravity: weighted pull-ups, weighted fingerboard hangs, weighted bouldering, and Hypergravity Isolation Training (HIT).

FUNCTIONAL ISOMETRICS

Functional isometrics involve superimposing one or more isometric contractions within the concentric or eccentric phase of an exercise motion. This strategy has been shown to provide significantly greater strength gains (16 percent more in one study) than those achieved by doing the same exercise without intermittent isometric contractions (O'Shea 1989). Greater overload during the isometric contractions is what stimulates the muscle for enhanced strength gains. The overload is created by removing the load-lightening effects of momentum and use of stored potential energy (a benefit of the elastic properties of muscle and tendon).

You can best leverage this method when training to strengthen your pull-up and lock-off strength. Superimposing numerous lock-offs (isometric contractions) within a set of pull-ups will produce surprising gains in absolute strength. And unlike hypergravity training, even novice climbers can safely incorporate this strategy into their training regimen.

Tips for Training Maximum Strength

1. Train with high-intensity exercises that produce muscular failure in three to ten repetitions. With body exercises, add weight as needed (hypergravity training) to meet this training criteria.
2. Isolate movements and grip positions to maximize specificity and best target your training.
3. Seek out (or set) burly, nontechnical boulder problems that will test you physically.
4. Rest at least three to five minutes between exercises. Quality maximum-strength training requires fresh, full-on efforts.
5. Regularly vary your workouts and cycle your training focus every two or three weeks. Occasionally employ functional isometrics and hypergravity training to mix things up and generate progressive overload.

Power Training

When climbers talk about "power," they are typically referring to the need to make quick, strenuous reaches or handhold grasps on steep terrain. This type of movement is the stuff of steep sport climbs and V-hard boulder problems. As I explained earlier, power is the product of strength and speed as expressed by the equation: power = strength x speed (where speed = distance/time). Since you have just learned several leading-edge methods for increasing strength, we now need to consider ways to effectively train the other factor in the power equation, speed.

First, you must recognize that there is an inverse relationship between force and velocity—creating maximum force, as in high-load strength training, can only be done at relatively slow speeds (see figure 5.9). Conversely, performing an exercise at high speed demands use of relatively light weights (low force production). The problem is, in climbing (and training for climbing) we are usually dealing with the weight of our body and exercising with movements that are difficult or impossible to do at a high rate of speed (compared with, say, a sprinter training on the track). The most effective and practical approach, then, is to try to train at the highest speed possible at less than body weight, or with moderately fast speed at body weight.

BOULDERING TO TRAIN POWER

In climbing a steep, strenuous boulder problem, chances are you are performing some movements that meet the power-training criteria above. Assuming you are using your feet, then your arms are carrying less than body weight; and undoubtedly you are moving quickly—perhaps lunging—on the very hardest moves, so your upper-body muscles are working at a relatively high speed. Consequently, sending hard, steep boulder problems is a good method of power training (duh!). The training limitations relate to the fact that the typical boulder problem might only include one or two high-speed power moves, and as such it lacks the repeated movement needed for optimal training stimuli. This is, again, where indoor walls are preferable to out-

Figure 5.9 Force Versus Velocity Curve

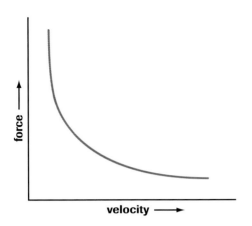

Creating maximum force, as in high-load strength training, can be done only at relatively slow speeds.

door bouldering, since you can design a problem up a steep wall that requires several moderately fast power moves (ideally five to ten movements that can be performed in ten seconds or less). If climbing on medium to large handholds, power gains will come primarily to the larger pull muscles of the upper arm and back, whereas an advanced climber able to swing powerfully up a problem of small holds will be training both the forearm (grip) muscles and the large pull muscles.

PULL-MUSCLE SPRINTS

Another good power-training strategy for the large pull muscles is to perform pull-ups, Bachar Ladder, or some other form of pull training at a rate faster than is normal for training. In doing such pull-muscle sprints, your goal is to fire the pulling muscles as fast as possible for five to ten seconds. In doing Power Pull-Ups, for instance, it's important *not* to lower to a straight arm position at the bottom of the range of motion in order to facilitate the most rapid turnover rate possible. Of course, doing a set of Power Pull-Ups will be difficult if you lack base strength at the pull-up motion. In this case you should try to simulate

hypogravity (reduced gravitational force) so that you are executing the correct number of pull-ups at a resistance less than body weight. You can achieve this by standing in a few loops of thick elastic cord or surgical tubing, or by training on a lat pull-down machine. Regardless of the exercise used, do two or three sets, with a three- to five-minute rest between sets, toward the end of your workout when your muscles are well warmed up.

REACTIVE TRAINING

The National Academy of Sports Medicine defines reactive training as a quick, powerful exercise that couples a forceful eccentric contraction, followed immediately by an explosive concentric contraction. This advanced training technique (often referred to as plyometric training) holds great potential for advanced climbers looking to increase their contact strength and power—it's also rife with risk for those who misuse or overuse reactive training exercises such as campus training, lunging exercises, and other explosive movements.

When used properly, however, reactive training will actually strengthen tendons and ligaments—and, of course, the muscles too—and, thus, increase your resistance to injury when out climbing a physically stressful move or sequence. Consequently, I advocate a limited amount of reactive training for intermediate climbers, with an increase in volume and intensity of reactive training as one enters the elite category. One qualifying rule that no climber should overlook is that reactive training will be more harmful than beneficial if performed while injured. In particular, any finger, elbow or shoulder problems must be rehabilitated (rest and antagonist-muscle training) before engaging in reactive training of any type.

First used by Russian athletes in the 1960s, reactive training was originally applied to climbing by the late Wolfgang Güllich with the advent of campus training. Before we get into this and other types of reactive training, let's first look at the unique stimulus (and adaptations) created by these powerful movements. Given that reactive training involves fast, dynamic movements, the resistance used (training load) must be significantly less than in the maximum-

Tips for Training Power

1. Exercise at faster-than-normal speeds with exercises such as Power Pull-ups, Uneven Grip Pull-Ups, and Lat Pull-Downs.
2. Set a nontechnical boulder problem with several long, powerful moves. Send it several times.
3. Employ reactive training techniques such as One-Arm Lunging and campus training to maximize neural excitement.
4. Leverage Complex Training strategies for elite-level power training.
5. Rest three to five minutes (or more) between sets so that you can make a high-quality effort each time.
6. Cycle on and off power-training exercises every two to three weeks.

strength training exercises above. For many climbers, the resistance will need to be less than body weight in order to allow for the rapid movement and turnover that's essential for effective reactive training. The resultant adaptations of such speed training are primarily neural, so reactive training alone will produce little in the way of hypertrophy. Still, the numerous neural adaptations of properly executed reactive training will result in highly practical—and often surprisingly noticeable!—gains in lunging ability and contact strength (like Climber B in Figure 5.8).

In chapter 7 I will detail several reactive training exercises of varying difficulty and injury risk. The safest, and therefore the most appropriate for non-elite climbers, are reactive exercises performed at less than body weight and with some measure of control. For example, One-Arm Lunging and Campus Touches are two reactive exercises that most healthy intermediate climbers can incorporate into their training with little risk. By contrast, reactive exercises that involve full body weight and double-handed, drop-and-catch movements are extremely

stressful and appropriate only in small doses for injury-free, elite climbers. The impact forces inherent to drop-and-catch exercises like campus training Double Dynos are dangerously large and injury may result from improper execution or overuse.

Anaerobic Endurance (A-E) Training

Anaerobic endurance training is of high importance if your goal is sending difficult rope-length routes or long, sustained boulder problems. Think of A-E as your ability to maintain a high level of strength output over a relatively long period of time. As shown in figure 5.4, true maximum strength output (near 100 percent intensity) can only be sustained for a few fleeting moments. Anaerobic endurance relates to how long the muscle can function above the anaerobic threshold—that is, at a level not far below the absolute maximum. Of course, muscle action above this threshold generates lactic acid faster than the liver can metabolize it. Inevitably, blood lactate concentrations become so high that the working muscle fails or functions only at a much lower aerobic intensity (below the anaerobic threshold).

The goal of A-E training is to produce muscular adaptations that will enable you to climb above the anaerobic threshold for as long as possible. Through repeated exposure, the muscles adapt by developing a higher tolerance to elevated blood lactate, enhanced lactate removal (due to increased capillary density) and metabolism, increased mitochondrial density, and other increases in cardiovascular efficiency. If you frequently climb to the point of getting a Hindenburgian forearm pump, then you have already acquired some of these adaptations. Let's look at three methods of training anaerobic endurance.

HIGH-REPETITION TRAINING

High-repetition training involves performing a high enough number of consecutive exercise movements that the muscles shift from burning ATP-CP for fuel to breaking down glycogen (and creating lactic acid) to sustain exercise into the anaerobic training zone. Exercise resistance and intensity should be high enough to bring the muscles to near failure in, at most, two or three minutes. However, the weight should not be so great as to cause failure in less than about thirty seconds (or fifteen reps).

Since climbers are interested in increasing anaerobic endurance in the pull muscles and forearm, let's consider a few training methods using a simple pull-up bar or fingerboard. Remember, the primary training requirements are that the exercise must last for between thirty seconds and three minutes *and* it should pump you up! For training forearm endurance, you could do a series of one- to two-minute straight-arm hangs on a pull-up bar. As you near muscular failure, step down and rest for one to two minutes, and repeat. For the large pull muscles or the arms and back, you could train on a lat pulldown machine or with Frenchies or high-rep pull-ups on a fingerboard. Many climbers will need to stand in loops of latex tubing or bungee cord to reduce the resistance so as to meet the thirty-seconds-to-three-minutes training requirement.

CLIMBING INTERVALS

Climbing intervals are the gold standard for training anaerobic endurance, because the exercise routine is tremendously specific to how we have to climb on hard routes. Consider that most long boulder problems or roped routes possess a couple (or more) hard sections as well as intermittent sections of easier terrain or rest stances. Such stop-and-go climbing likely pushes you in and out of the anaerobic threshold—you get pumped and start breathing harder on the hard section, and then you recover somewhat when you reach easier moves or a rest position. Climbing intervals simulate this exact scenario by alternating one to four minutes of strenuous climbing with an equal or longer period of easy climbing or rest (1:1 to 1:2 work-to-rest ratio). This, in fact, mirrors the way serious runners (and other athletes) perform interval training—runners commonly alternate fast and slow intervals in 100-, 200-, or 400-meter increments. Interval climbing is just another one of the ways we can successfully transfer to climbing the training methodology used in other sports (though more often than not this isn't possible). You will learn several applications of interval training in chapter 7.

THE TABATA PROTOCOL

The Tabata Protocol is a highly specific method of interval training that is popular among elite speed skaters, cyclists, middle-distance runners, and swimmers; but serious climbers can benefit from this training strategy too. Developed by Dr. Izumi Tabata at the National Institute of Fitness and Sports in Japan, the Tabata interval is twenty seconds of high-intensity exercise followed by ten seconds of rest (a 2:1 work-to-rest ratio). This interval is repeated eight times to create four minutes of the most grueling training you can imagine.

The Tabata Protocol differs from traditional interval training in three ways. First, the twenty-second work interval is much shorter than traditional intervals. The second difference, then, is that this shorter work interval must be performed with 100 percent exertion. Third, the rest interval is just ten seconds, which is so brief that very little recovery can occur before the next work interval begins. Research has

Tips for Training Muscular Endurance

1. Use high-repetition exercises that allow fifteen to fifty repetitions before you approach muscular failure.
2. Climb or traverse thirty to one hundred total hand movements on a moderately difficult route (for you) without stopping for a rest.
3. Train or climb to the point of getting pumped, but always stop before reaching the point of muscle failure.
4. Engage in climbing interval training comprising roughly equal-length climbing and rest periods.
5. Notch up training overload by increasing repetitions or reducing the rest intervals (between sets), not by increasing resistance. Give the grueling Tabata Protocol a try.
6. Cycle on and off anaerobic endurance training every two to three weeks.

shown this protocol to be uniquely effective in producing gains in both anaerobic and aerobic capacity (Tabata 1997), although longer rest intervals are superior for training anaerobic recovery (removal of lactic acid and other metabolic by-products). Consequently, climbers can benefit from use of both the Tabata Protocol and the traditional interval training methods described above.

You can leverage the Tabata Protocol in several ways to enhance your climbing performance. The most obvious is to alternate twenty seconds of sprinting and ten seconds of walking for a total of eight run–walk intervals—likely the most insane four minutes of exercise you'll ever engage in!—to increase your total anaerobic and aerobic capacity (VO_2 max). Applied to climbing-specific exercises, you could use the Tabata Protocol to train pull-muscle endurance (Lat Pull-Down Tabata) and forearm endurance (HIT Strip Tabata). However, it's highly questionable whether it would be beneficial to utilize the Tabata Protocol with less specific free-weight exercises, as commonly done by bodybuilders and other athletes. It's my belief that your limited reserve of mental and physical energy is better invested in climbing-specific training activities.

Stamina Training

Stamina training and strength training are at opposite ends of the exercise spectrum. Therefore, you cannot optimally train for both maximum strength and maximum stamina—nor can you expect to become excellent at both. Just as no one has ever won an Olympic gold medal in both the 100-meter dash and the marathon, it's highly unlikely we'll ever see a climber who boulders V15 and summits Mount Everest without oxygen. The mental and physiological requirements are just too different.

Chapter 1 introduced the SAID Principle, which explains that training time should be invested in a way most specific to your primary focus in climbing. If your focus is bouldering, sport climbing, or multipitch free climbing, then training maximum strength and anaerobic endurance must be at the center of your fitness-training program. Conversely, big-wall and alpine climbers would most benefit from stamina training, in addition to some anaerobic endurance training.

It's well known that the best method for developing stamina is long, slow distance aerobic training. Applying this method to climbing involves performing a high volume of low- to moderate-intensity exercise lasting several hours or more. Putting in frequent long days of climbing is undoubtedly the best stamina-training method for rock climbers—training doesn't get any more specific than this! For the average weekend warrior, however, putting in ten to twenty full-length climbing days per month is improbable. Engaging in regular aerobic activity is the best training alternative for triggering the numerous adaptations within the cardiovascular system, such as increased heart stroke volume, lung capacity, and intramuscular capillary density. In the

Tips for Training Stamina

1. Perform a high volume of moderate-intensity exercise. The total duration of exercise session should be measured in hours, not minutes.
2. Log frequent all-day climbing adventures with a goal of twelve to twenty-five pitches of total climbing.
3. Engage in one to two hours of sustained aerobic activity (running, biking, or brisk hiking with a light pack on) as a substitute for all-day climbing workouts.
4. Strive for a total of ten to twenty stamina-training days (all-day climbing and aerobic workout days) per month.
5. When training time is limited, use aerobic interval training and the Tabata Protocol—both will improve aerobic capacity.
6. Take a full week of rest every two months or prior to the beginning of a climbing trip or expedition.

aggregate these adaptations will improve stamina as well as the ability to function at altitude.

In the final analysis, the average rock climber will not benefit from large amounts of stamina training. With the exception of the overweight climber (wanting to lower percentage of body fat), any aerobic activity beyond a few twenty-minute sessions per week would not be advantageous. As stated above, stamina and strength training are opposites, so excessive aerobic training should be viewed as an enemy of anyone pursuing maximum strength.

Complex Training

I'll conclude this section on training methodology by introducing you to the exciting concept of complex training. Complex training represents the leading edge of strength and power training, and it's now in use by elite athletes in numerous sports. Applied to climbing, the complex training protocol described below may represent the most powerful training concept known to climbers at this time.

Complex training involves coupling a high-force, low-speed exercise (such as hypergravity training) with a higher-speed, reactive-training exercise. Of this pair, the first exercise caters to developing maximum strength, while the second targets power. Research has shown that performing these two very different exercises back-to-back (and in the order of strength first, power second) produces gains in strength and power beyond that achieved by performing either exercise alone. While no studies have been done with climbers, there is compelling research in the use of complex training to increase vertical jump that shows phenomenal gains in absolute ability (Adams, 1992). In this study six weeks of strength training produced a 3.3-centimeter increase in the vertical jump, compared with a 3.8-centimeter increase after six weeks of reactive (power) training. The group performing complex training (strength and reactive) for six weeks experienced an incredible 10.7-centimeter increase in jumping ability.

To understand why a coupling of these two exercises produces such a synergistic gain in strength and power, we must examine the unique ways in which the neuromuscular system is stressed. This two-step process begins with high-intensity strength training that excites the muscle to near-maximum motor unit recruitment. The second step takes the already excited muscle and challenges it to function at higher speed. In this way complex training stimulates the muscle fibers in conjunction with the nervous system in such a way that slow-twitch fibers are taught to behave like fast-twitch fibers (Chu 1996). Consequently, complex training could be viewed as the magic-bullet exercise for the average climber born with an average percentage of fast-twitch fibers (approximately 50 percent).

Incorporating the complex training method into your program could be done in several ways. Remember, the key is a back-to-back coupling of a maximum-strength exercise and a power exercise with no rest (only as long as it takes to chalk up) in between the two exercises. Intermediate climbers might couple Hypergravity Pull-Ups with One-Arm Lunging. Or they could perform a maximum boulder problem that is really fingery followed by a set of Campus Touches. Rest for three to five minutes between coupled sets.

A more advanced protocol would couple a set of heavy Hypergravity Isolation Training (HIT) with a set of Double Dynos on a campus board. This latter strategy of combining HIT and drop-and-catch reactive training should be a staple technique of elite climbers: It may represent the single best training protocol for fulfilling genetic potential in finger strength and upper-body power.

Obviously, complex training is an advanced technique that produces both high passive and active stresses—it should be used only by well-conditioned, intermediate to elite climbers with no recent history of injury. Furthermore, its use should be limited to once or twice per week, and it should be cycled on and off about every two weeks. Finally, complete recovery from a complex workout could take as long as three to five days. Any other strenuous training or climbing during the supercompensation period would tend to negate its benefits.

Summary of Complex Training

1. Complex training is the most advanced method for developing maximum strength and power.

2. Only well-conditioned, injury-free advanced intermediate and elite climbers should engage in complex training.

3. Couple a maximum-strength exercise and a power-training exercise back-to-back with no rest in between.

4. Rest for at least five minutes between sets so that each training couplet is a high-quality effort. Do only three to ten coupled strength-power sets. Never more.

5. Engage in complex training once or twice (elite climbers only) per week. Use complex training as part of the maximum-strength and power phase of a training mesocycle.

C H A P T E R   S I X

General Conditioning Exercises

What lies behind us and what lies before us are tiny matters compared to what lies within us.

—*Oliver Wendell Holmes*

The previous chapter provided an overview of the principles and methods of strength and fitness training for climbing. With this understanding, we can now take a more purposeful look at the dozens of conditioning exercises that are of value to climbers. In this chapter you'll learn a variety of basic, yet important, warm-up and general conditioning exercises; chapter 7 will then provide a detailed look at the many climbing-specific exercises for the pull muscles of the upper torso and arms.

Since failure while climbing often seems to center on lack of arm and finger strength, you may be tempted to skip this chapter in favor of total immersion into the climbing-specific exercises. Please don't! No matter if you are a beginner or elite climber, the content of this chapter is essential for building a balanced body that can best learn climbing skills, maintain coordinated movement despite growing fatigue, and tolerate high amounts of climbing with minimal injury risk. By regularly using the general conditioning exercise described herein, you will develop and maintain a solid physical foundation from which you can train and climb hard for many years to come.

Rachel Melville on **Table of Colors (5.13a), Red River Gorge, Kentucky.** DAN BRAYACK

Divided into five parts, this chapter will delve into optimizing body composition, improving flexibility, core conditioning, antagonist-muscle training, and aerobic training to improve stamina. The first section on optimizing body condition is especially important since strength-to-weight ratio correlates well to climbing performance. While most climbers obsess on improving the strength side of the equation, it's equally important to achieve a reasonable climbing body weight.

In the next section you will learn about flexibility training. While warm-up and stretching is a common least-favorite activity among climbers, it is actually indispensable if you want to refine your movement skills, best prepare your joints and muscles for climbing, and lower injury risk.

Following this you will learn a dozen must-do exercises for your core and antagonist muscles. The core muscles of your torso are called into play for every climbing movement, and they are especially important when climbing on overhanging terrain. Regardless of wall angle, however, a stronger core will enable you to step higher, move your hips better to optimize center-of-gravity placement, and create torso tension and torque for hard, powerful movements. The antagonist muscles play a similarly vital role in facilitating smooth, balanced movement and protecting the joints. Twice-weekly use of the upcoming antagonist exercises will strengthen and stabilize your elbows and shoulders—important if you want to climb hard and say off the disabled list.

The chapter concludes with a primer on stamina training. While lack of stamina may rarely be a limiting constraint in bouldering or sport climbing, improved stamina can help speed recovery between attempts and ascents. Of course, possessing a high level of stamina is an essential for all-day, pedal-to-the-metal wall ascents and alpine climbing endeavors. Thus, engaging in some stamina-training activities can elevate performance, regardless of your climbing preference.

Optimizing Body Composition

As explained earlier, climbers with less-than-ideal body composition can increase their strength-to-weight ratio most quickly by decreasing weight, not by increasing strength. Every serious climber should ponder whether or not body composition represents a significant limiting constraint. Obtaining a measurement of your percentage of body fat is the best way to determine if you need to work on this area. Given this data, you can decide how much training time should be spent on improving body composition versus other climbing-specific exercises.

Measuring Your Percentage of Body Fat

Most health clubs and some universities have the equipment necessary to measure your percentage of body fat, so getting your body fat measured may be just a phone call and a few miles away. A study of athletes in a variety of sports reported that males possessed body fat ranging from 4 percent in wrestlers to 8–12 percent in runners and 16 percent in football players, with an elite average of below 12 percent (Wilmore 1983). The same study showed that female athletes possessed body fat between 8 and 25 percent, with an elite average of 15 percent. Therefore, a percentage of body fat near these elite average levels (12 percent men, 15 percent women) is a good initial target for most climbers. Given that climbing performance is directly correlated to strength-to-weight ratio, however, your ultimate goal should be a few percentage points lower—perhaps 6 to 8 percent for men and 10 to 12 percent for women. One study (Watts 1993) revealed that some elite male and female climbers possess body fat as low as 4 percent and 9 percent, respectively. However, extremely low body fat is neither desirable nor advised, since it will adversely affect your energy levels and recovery ability, as well as cause numerous health problems (especially among women).

If you are unable to get a professional body fat measurement, you can always employ the highly economical, at-home method—that is, pinch a fold of skin just above your hip. If you can pinch an inch or more (thickness of the fold), you definitely need to drop some body fat. A fold between 0.5 and 1 inch thick indicates you may be slightly overweight for a climber. If you pinch less than 0.5 inch of fat, then your body fat is likely at or below the target averages stated above.

In addition to optimizing your percentage of body fat, you should consider the size and location of the muscles you carry. For instance, it is indisputable that possessing hulking leg muscles is as bad or worse for a climber than carrying a spare tire around the waist (especially since muscle weighs more than fat per unit volume). Since the legs muscles are never the weakest link while climbing, you should limit or eliminate any training practices that might increase the size of your legs. The same goes for any weight-lifting exercise or practice that produces a bulking-up effect in any other part of the body. This subject was covered in chapter 5, but it's worth pointing out again that strength training must be extremely specific in order to transfer to climbing. Heavy squats, maximal bench presses, and other traditional body-building exercises such as biceps curls are of little benefit for many high-level athletes since they lack absolute specificity (Bell 1989). And for climbers, these exercises are surely counterproductive since they will result in hypertrophy and weight gain.

Strategies for Optimizing Body Composition

Certainly there are genetic limitations to how much you can change your body composition through training and diet. Some people are naturally going to carry a little more body fat; others naturally have a larger frame and bulkier muscles. Still, many novice climbers can improve their body composition significantly in a way that will benefit their climbing. The two key strategies are improved dietary surveillance and increased aerobic training.

Performance nutrition will be discussed in depth in chapter 9, but for now let me state the obvious—reducing body fat is possible only if you create a net calorie deficit over the course of many days and weeks. Simply put, burning more calories than you consume causes the body to tap into and burn fat reserves. Crash dieting is unhealthy and dangerous, especially for a serious athlete. Instead strive for, at most, a 500-calorie deficit per day. Over the course of a week, this would add up to a 3,500-calorie deficit and equal the loss of one pound of body fat. Surely the bathroom scales will indicate that you've lost more weight, but this additional weight loss is all in the form of water and glycogen. This nonfat weight loss will return next time you eat a surplus of calories that can replenish the muscle glycogen stores.

Your daily calorie deficit is best created by a combination of reduced calorie intake and increased calorie expenditure. For burning fat, nothing beats aerobic activities such as running, biking, and swimming. Given a healthy back and knees, select running as your choice activity since it will not result in muscle hypertrophy (growth in size) in the legs. Moderate-intensity swimming and biking on relatively flat terrain are the next best alternatives. Unfortunately, mountain biking over rugged terrain is a leg-muscle builder. No matter what you choose, make it your goal to perform a minimum of thirty minutes of sustained moderate-intensity aerobic activity at least four days per week.

If your schedule is too busy to accommodate this two-plus hours of aerobics per week, recent research indicates you can get a similar (and possibly better) fat-burning effect from shorter, high-intensity interval training (King 2001). For instance, after a three-minute slow warm-up jog, alternate a minute of sprinting with a minute of jogging for an additional twelve minutes. This vigorous fifteen minutes of interval training may burn less fat during the actual training than the slow thirty-minute run, but its metabolism-elevating effect will have you burning more calories for the rest of the day. Regardless of your chosen mode of aerobic training, you can max-

Tips for Optimizing Body Composition

1. Use a combination of dietary surveillance and exercise to lower your percentage of body fat.
2. Strive for four, thirty-minute (or more) aerobic workouts per week.
3. Adjust calorie intake to produce approximately a 500-calorie-per-day deficit. See chapter 9 for more nutritional tips.
4. Reduce aerobic training activities (and reinvest the training time in climbing-specific exercises) as you approach your optimal percentage of body fat.
5. Do not obsess over body composition—do the best you can given your genetics, and remember that climbing is two-thirds mental and technical. You can climb at a high level despite less-than-ideal body composition.

imize the fat-burning effect by doing it first thing in the morning and before eating breakfast.

Upon reaching your desired percentage of body fat, cut back somewhat on the aerobic training and refocus your efforts elsewhere. Slowly reintroduce more calories incrementally and watch your waistline and body weight. The goal is to find a level of calorie consumption equal to your daily energy use and thus maintain a steady body weight.

In summary, I want to emphasis that while optimizing body composition is an important aspect of training for climbing, it is not *everything*. Sadly, some climbers obsess over minimizing their body fat to the point of starving themselves—this is obviously a flawed training strategy and not a fun way to live. Sure, there are a few anorexic climbers who climb at a very high level thanks to their finely tuned mental and technical skills; however, their malnutrition is indeed limiting them (imagine how good they'd be if they ate right!) and may eventually lead to hardships such as injury and illness.

Flexibility Training

While there is rarely a need for extraordinary flexibility in climbing, regular flexibility training will have a positive influence on your training and performance. Considering that movement is the very essence of the vertical dance we call climbing, anything you can do to help facilitate smooth, efficient movements will enhance your performance. Flexible agonist muscles and tendons will function better—and are more resilient—when exposed to the high dynamic force loads common to climbing. What's more, flexible antagonist muscles will levy a lower inherent resistance to the opposing agonist muscles, enabling smoother, more economical movement. Given all these benefits, why would any climber not engage in some flexibility training as part of every workout?

Stretching exercises have, of course, been long used by athletes as part of a warm-up routine before training and competition. Such pre-performance stretching is useful as long as it is preceded by a warm-up activity to increase joint and muscle temperatures. Static stretching alone can injure a cold muscle (Shrier 1999, 2000)! Engage in five to fifteen minutes of low-intensity exercise such as jogging, cycling, or easy climbing (vertical walls with good holds) before beginning your flexibility training or pre-performance stretching. When climbing outdoors, the hike to the cliff base often provides the perfect lead-in to your preclimb stretching as long as it's lengthy enough to increase your breathing rate and cause a light sweat.

Detailed below are seventeen stretches that are ideal for fulfilling the above-stated goals. Certainly there's no need to spend an hour stretching each day; in fact, that could be viewed as a poor use of your training time. Instead commit to ten minutes of gentle stretching as part of your warm-up for climbing and training. Some additional stretching on climbing rest days is useful for maintaining range of motion in tight muscles (always warm up first) and as lower-body flexibility training to improve hip turnout, stemming, and high-stepping ability. Consult the muscular anatomy photos in appendix A if you are uncertain of the location of the muscles specified in each stretching exercise below.

Upper-Body Stretches

Perform each of the following stretches as part of your warm-up routine before any hard training or difficult climbing. As stressed above, it's essential to perform five to fifteen minutes of general exercise before stretching. At the very least, do fifty jumping jacks followed by twenty arm circles and twenty finger flexors. Complete the pre-stretching warm-up with a few minutes of self-massage to the finger tendons, the palm of your hand, and the forearm muscles and biceps.

ARM CIRCLES

Arm circles provide a nice dynamic stretch that warms up your shoulder joints and increases circulation to your shoulders, arms, and fingers. Do this before you engage in any of the upper-body static stretches that follow. Stand with your arms out to the side and parallel to the floor, and begin moving your arms in small circles. Gradually increase the size of the circle until you feel slight tension in the shoulders—go no larger with the circles beyond this point and do *not* wildly whip your arms or perform a rapid windmill-like motion! Complete twenty slow, smooth arm circles and then proceed to the Finger Curls.

FINGER CURLS AND MASSAGE

This is a must-do warm-up movement for climbers, because it increases circulation to the forearm muscles and spreads lubricating synovial fluid in the joints of the fingers. Stand with your arms relaxed by your sides. Close your hands to make relaxed fists, and then quickly open your hands and fan out the fingers as if you're trying to flick water off your fingertips. Continue for thirty to forty repetitions. Use a pace that allows about two repetitions per second. Now perform a minute or two of massage to the palmar side of your fingers and hand—this will encourage blood flow and help warm the tendons and tendon pulleys.

FINGER FLEXOR STRETCH AND MASSAGE

This rudimentary stretch targets the forearm muscles that enable finger flexion and your grip on the rock.

1. Palm down.

2. Palm out.

Be sure to perform this stretch in the two-handed positions shown above. In a standing position, bring your arms together in front of your waist. Straighten the arm to be stretched and lay the fingertips into the palm of your other hand. Position the hand of your stretch arm so that the palm is facing down with the thumb pointing inward. Pull back on the fingers of your straight arm until a mild stretch begins in the forearm muscles. Hold this stretch for about twenty seconds. Release the stretch and turn the hand 180 degrees so that your stretch arm is now positioned with the palm facing outward and the thumb pointing out to the side. Using your other hand, pull your fingers back until a stretch begins in the forearm muscles. Hold for ten seconds. Repeat this stretch, in

both positions, with your other arm. Finish up with a minute of self-massage to the forearm flexor muscles using deep cross-fiber friction (see page 215).

FINGER EXTENSORS STRETCH

This important stretch is unfortunately overlooked by many climbers. It stretches and warms up the numerous extensor muscles and the often tight brachioradialis muscle of the back of the forearm; when used daily, it will help your prevent tendinosis of the outer elbow (often called lateral epicondylitis). In a standing position, bring your arms together in front of your waist. Straighten the arm to be stretched and then make a tight fist; place the fist in the palm of your other hand. With your fist hand in the thumb-

1. Thumb up.

2. Thumb down.

up position, gently pull the fist inward to create a mild stretch along the back of the forearm. Hold this stretch for twenty seconds. Now release the stretch and rotate the fist until it's in the awkward thumb-down position. Again, use your free hand to flex the fist and hold for twenty seconds—hold a solid fist and keep your arm straight to best work this strange yet important stretch. Repeat with your other hand.

FINGER ISOLATION STRETCH

This isolation stretch, along with massage of the fingers and hands, is very effective for warming up your precious digits. Work through this sequence one finger at a time. Either sitting or standing, bend one arm at the elbow to position your hand palm-up

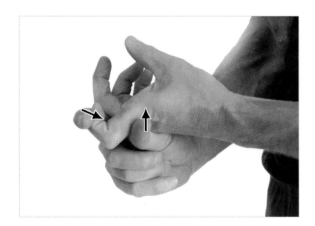

Finger isolation stretch.

at chest level. Curl your fingers about three-quarters of the way, but do not close your hand or make a fist. Extend your hand fully into a hand-back position. Place the index finger of the other hand across the last digit of finger to be stretched and position the thumb under the finger near the hand knuckle. Gradually apply pressure with the index finger to further close the bent finger and to push it back in the direction opposite that to which it flexes. Stop when you feel mild tension in the joints. Hold this stretch for ten seconds. Release the finger for a few seconds and repeat the stretch for another ten seconds. Repeat this process with all eight fingers. Stop immediately if you experience any pain.

SHOULDER, CHEST, AND BICEPS STRETCH

Sit on the floor with your feet flat and knees bent about halfway. Position your arms just behind your hips with the elbows straight, palms flat, and fingers pointing back. Slowly walk your hands away from your hips until you feel mild tension in your biceps. Hold this position for twenty seconds. Walk your fingers back a few inches farther to increase the tension a bit more. You may also feel some mild stretching in your shoulders and chest. Hold this position for twenty to thirty seconds before releasing the stretch.

RHOMBOIDS AND TRAPEZIUS STRETCH

This is a great stretch for the shoulder and upper-back muscles that are so heavily used in climbing vertical and overhanging walls. From a standing position, bring one arm across your chest until the hand rests on the opposite shoulder. Maintain the bent elbow at chest level so that your arm is parallel to the floor. With the other hand, grasp behind the bent elbow from below. Pull on the bent elbow until you feel tension in your shoulder and upper back. Hold the stretch for ten seconds. Release the stretch for a few seconds before repeating for twenty seconds more. You can stretch the shoulder muscles more completely by slowly working your bent elbow

Shoulder, chest, and biceps stretch.

Rhomboids and trapezius stretch.

Triceps, shoulders, and latissimus stretch.

up and down a few inches from the horizontal position. Repeat this stretch with the other arm.

TRICEPS, SHOULDERS, AND LATISSIMUS STRETCH

Stand erect with arms overhead and bent at the elbows. Grab one elbow and gently pull it toward the back of your head until you feel a stretch in the back of your upper arm. Hold the stretch for ten seconds. Release the stretch for a few seconds, and then perform a secondary stretch for about twenty seconds. You can extend this stretch down through the shoulder and the side of your back by leaning sideways slightly in the direction the elbow is being pulled. Repeat this stretch with your other arm.

SHOULDERS AND UPPER-TORSO STRETCH

This is a great climbers' stretch because it works many of the shoulder and upper-back muscles that are so used and abused in climbing. Stand erect and

Shoulders and upper-torso stretch.

extend your arms overhead. Cross your wrists, place your palms together, and interlace your fingers. Now reach your fingertips toward the sky and feel the stretch through your shoulders and upper back. Hold this extended position for ten seconds and then lower your hands to release the tension. Repeat the stretch a second time, but this time reach for the sky and then move your hands backward a few inches to enhance the stretch.

Lower-Torso and Leg Stretches

The legs, hips, and lower back are areas where many climbers benefit from improved flexibility. Greater hip turnout, stemming, and high-stepping ability in particular will markedly improve your center-of-gravity placement on vertical routes and quality of movement on all routes. While your ultimate degree of flexibility is largely a function of genetics, dedicated daily stretching will produce some gains in functional flexibility. You will need to decide if targeted flexibility training of your lower body is a good use of training-for-climbing time. Is lack of flexibility holding you back on the rock? Quite often it's hard to tell, since inadequate lower-back, hip, and leg flexibility will sabotage efficient movement and climbing technique in very subtle ways. It would thus be wise for all climbers to engage in a modest amount of lower-body stretching, both as part of a pre-performance warm-up and as a rest-day flexibility-training activity. Here are eight stretches to put to use beginning today.

BUTTOCKS AND LOWER-BACK STRETCH

This stretch will improve hip flexion and help facilitate high-stepping. Lie flat on your back with both legs straight. Bend one leg and grasp it behind the thigh or over the top of the knee, and pull it toward your chest. Hold the stretch for ten seconds, then release for a few seconds. Pull the bent leg toward your chest again for a secondary stretch of about twenty seconds. Repeat with the other leg.

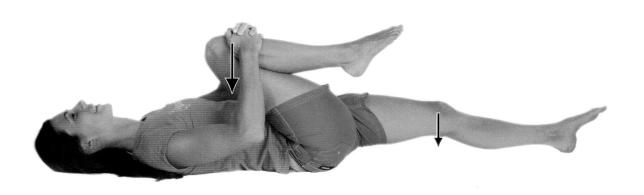

Buttocks and lower-back stretch.

Hamstrings stretch.　　　　　　　　　　　　*Adductor stretch.*

HAMSTRINGS STRETCH

The muscles along the back of the thigh are chronically tight in many climbers, thus restricting stem and high-step movements. Lie flat on your back with one leg straight and the other bent, with the sole of that foot flat on the floor next to your opposite knee. Lift the straight leg upward, grab it behind the thigh or calf, and pull gently forward until you feel the stretch down the back of the leg. Hold this stretch for ten seconds, and then release it slightly for a few seconds. Pull the leg once again for another twenty- to thirty-second stretch. Be sure to maintain a straight leg all the while. Repeat with your other leg. You can also work this stretch by looping a fitness band over your foot and regulating the stretch by pulling on the band, or by having a partner apply pressure on your leg using the PNF stretching technique described below under "Tips for Safe and Effective Flexibility Training."

ADDUCTOR STRETCH

This wall stretch is one of the very best lower-body stretches for climbers. Lying on the floor eliminates strain on the lower back and allows you to relax and let gravity do the work. Wearing socks will reduce friction between your heels and the wall, helping maximize the range of the stretch. Lie on the floor

with your buttocks about 6 inches from a wall and your legs extending straight up it with about a ninety-degree bend at your hips. Slowly separate your legs by sliding your heels out to the sides. Concentrate on relaxing throughout your body and allow gravity to extend the split until you feel mild tension in your legs and groin. Hold this position for ten to twenty seconds. Try to split your legs farther apart; if needed, grab your thighs to apply some downward pressure to extend the stretch. Hold this position for thirty to sixty seconds.

GROIN STRETCH

This is an excellent stretch for improving hip turnout. Flexibility gains from this stretch will allow you to move your center of gravity in closer to the wall—more over your feet—on near-vertical climbs. Sit upright with your legs flexed and knees out to the sides so that you can bring the soles of your feet together. Grasp your ankles and rest your elbows on the inside of the thighs. Press down with your elbows to apply light pressure on the thigh until you feel mild tension in your groin and inner thigh. Hold this stretch for ten seconds, and then release it for a few seconds. Apply pressure for a secondary stretch of twenty to thirty seconds. Next, lie down flat on your back while keeping your feet together. Relax

1. Stretch while sitting.

2. Stretch on your back.

and allow gravity to pull your knees toward the floor for another thirty seconds to one minute.

QUADRICEPS AND HIP FLEXORS

This is a common wall stretch, often used by runners, that provides a nice stretch of the quadriceps and psoas (hip flexor) muscle. Stand near a wall or other object that you can hold on to with one hand for balance. Now flex the leg on the supporting hand's side and bring the heel up to near your buttocks. Reach behind your back with the free hand and grasp the foot of your bent leg. Slowly pull upward on the foot to induce a stretch in the quadriceps and hip flexors. Hold this for ten seconds, then release the stretch slightly for a few seconds. Pull upward again for another twenty to thirty seconds of stretching. Repeat this stretch with the other leg; remember to switch the supporting hand so that you are holding the bent leg with the opposite hand.

CALF STRETCH

The gastrocnemius and soleus muscles of the calf are the unsung heroes of climbing performance. Stretch mthese muscles before and after every day of climb-

ing! Stand with one foot about 3 to 4 feet ahead of the other. Bend the front leg and shift your hips forward while keeping your rear leg straight and the heel in contact with the floor. Rest your hands on your forward knee or lean against a wall or other solid object to maintain balance as you shift your hips far enough forward to produce a stretch in the calf muscles. Hold this stretch for twenty seconds, and then shift your hips back to the starting position to release the stretch for a few seconds. Move your hips forward to produce a secondary stretch for thirty to sixty seconds. Maintain heel contact with the floor throughout. Repeat with the other leg.

UPPER- AND LOWER- ABDOMINAL STRETCH

Lie flat on the floor with your arms bent and palms flat next to your shoulders. Slowly press your shoulders away from the floor until you feel mild tension in your abdominals. Keep your legs and pelvis in contact with the floor for the duration of this stretch—it helps to contract your buttocks in order to maintain the position and reduce stress on your lower back. Hold the stretch for ten seconds, then

Quadriceps and hip flexors.

Calf stretch.

return to the starting position for a few seconds. Press up for a secondary stretch of twenty to thirty seconds. Relax and allow the curve of your spine to extend up through your upper back and neck. Look forward, but not up toward the ceiling. Do not be overly aggressive with this stretch—proceed with caution, especially if you have a history of back problems. Stop immediately if you experience any pain in the lower back.

OBLIQUES AND BACK STRETCH

This final stretch will help prepare your body for the torso-twisting, hip-turning, drop-kneeing movements that are so common on steep sport climbs and boulder problems. Sit erect on the floor with one leg straight and the other bent and crossing over the opposite knee. Slowly turn your body toward the side of the bent leg until you feel mild tension in your lower back, hips, and the side of your torso. Maintain

Upper- and lower-abdominal stretch.

Obliques and back stretch.

a level head position and fix your eyes on the wall to the side of the bent leg. Hold the stretch for ten to twenty seconds, then return to the starting position for a few seconds. Perform a secondary stretch for twenty to thirty seconds. If needed, you can increase the stretch by levering your elbow against the thigh of the bent leg. Repeat the stretch in the other direction. Be sure to switch leg positions.

Tips for Safe and Effective Flexibility Training

1. Always engage in five to fifteen minutes of jogging, jumping jacks, or easy climbing before beginning flexibility training. Stretching a cold muscle can lead to injury.
2. Stretch in a slow, gradually progressive manner. Stretching should produce mild discomfort, but never sharp pain.
3. Perform a primary stretch of ten to twenty seconds. Release the stretch for a few seconds before performing a secondary stretch for twenty to thirty seconds.
4. Direct slow, deep breathing throughout the stretch. Inhale through your nose and exhale through your mouth.
5. Maintain a neutral back position—neither rounded nor hyperextended—to maximize the stretch and avoid injury.
6. Limit "gain" stretching to the lower body; excessive upper-body stretching is counterproductive and could lead to injury. Perform only light stretching of your shoulders—a small degree of tightness is good and needed to protect the shoulder joint.
7. Refrain from excessive stretching of the forearm flexors prior to climbing, since this will reduce your maximum strength and power for up to one hour. Favor light stretching and sports massage prior to maximal climbing.
8. An alternative stretch method, known as PNF, replaces the period of relaxation between the primary and secondary stretches with a period of muscular contraction. For most of the stretches described, this will require a partner to create an immovable resistance against which you can contract for six seconds. After this isometric contraction, relax completely and allow the stretch to lengthen the muscle. This is especially useful technique for individuals trying to overcome uncommon lack of flexibility in the legs and hips.

1. Start with legs bent and hands behind head.

2. Crunch upward and repeat.

Training the Core Muscles

In climbing vertical to overhanging rock, the core muscles of your torso play a key role in enabling your arms and legs to maximize leverage and transfer torque from hand to foot and vice versa. Many beginner and intermediate climbers making their initial forays on steep terrain find good-looking holds more difficult and pumpy to use and modest-length reaches feeling surprisingly long. The root of these difficulties is probably a complex blend of poor technique and insufficient strength in both the arms (obviously, they are the ones getting pumped up!) and, less noticeably, the torso.

As you might expect, one good way to strengthen these core stabilizer muscles is by climbing frequently on steep terrain. If your specialty is climbing overhanging routes or if you regularly boulder on steep cavelike routes, chances are you've already developed a high degree of strength in these muscles (though you could probably still benefit from additional conditioning). If you are new to climbing, however, or if you have previously climbed mainly vertical to less-than-vertical routes, you would likely benefit significantly from some targeted training of these core muscles.

Two "strength tricks" first popularized in climbing by John Gill are the gold standard of core-muscle strength. The front lever and straight-arm flag both require steely torso muscles. If you can do these two tricks, then your training time is better spent on areas other than the stabilizing muscles of the torso. Otherwise, employ a blend of bouldering and traversing on steep walls and executing the eight exercises described below.

ABDOMINAL CRUNCH

Lie on the floor with your legs bent at about ninety degrees and your feet flat on the floor or hovering in the air about knee height above the floor (better isolates the upper abs). Cross your arms over your chest or place your hands behind your head (harder), but do not interlace your fingers behind your neck. Now lift your shoulder blades off the floor and exhale as you "crunch" upward. The range of motion is small—the goal is to lift your upper back off the floor, but *not* to ascend all the way as you would in doing old-school sit-ups. Continue up and down at a brisk pace that takes just over one second per repetition—but don't go so fast that you are bouncing off the floor. Perform as many crunches as possible. Your long-term goal should be fifty to seventy-five repetitions. As your conditioning improves, you can perform a second set after a three-minute rest.

HANGING KNEE LIFT

This strenuous exercise targets the lower-abdominal muscles in a very climbing-specific way—much like lifting your legs on an overhanging route. Do these hanging from a pull-up bar, the bucket holds of a fingerboard, or a set of Pump Rocks with your palms facing away. Briskly lift your knees up to your chest level, allowing your legs to bend naturally with the motion. Pause for a moment, then lower your legs slowly until they return to a slightly bent position. Immediately begin the next upward repetition, and continue these knee-lift movements at a steady pace until you can no longer perform the full range of motion. Your long-range goal is twenty-five to thirty repetitions. Rest for three minutes before performing a second set or moving on to the next abdominal exercise.

SIDE HIP RAISE

This surprisingly difficult exercise works the oblique muscles along the side of your torso. Lie on your side on the floor and press up with the floor-side arm straight and supporting your weight so that your body forms a triangle with the floor. Rest the free arm along the other side of your body. Keeping the supporting arm straight, lower your hip until it touches the floor and then immediately raise it back up to the starting position. Repeat this lowering and raising of the hip in a slow, controlled manner for ten to twenty (hard) repetitions. Rest for one minute and then switch sides to perform another set.

AQUAMAN

The Aquaman is a great core exercise that particularly homes in on strengthening the commonly

1. Lift knees.

2. Pause and repeat.

weak muscles of the lower back. Lie facedown on the floor with your arms extended overhead, your legs straight with pointed toes, and your head in a neutral position. Begin by simultaneously raising one arm and the opposite leg as high as comfortably possible. Hold the top position for one second, then return to the starting position. Repeat by raising the opposite arm and leg off the floor simultaneously. Again, hold for a second in the top position before returning to the floor. Continue this alternating exercise motion for a total of twenty repetitions or until you can no longer perform a slow, controlled movement. Rest for three minutes before performing another set.

ONE-ARM, ONE-LEG BRIDGE

This strenuous exercise calls into play almost every muscle from your hands to your feet, and as a result it's remarkably hard and tiring! Assume a push-up position with your torso straight and in line with your feet. Spread your feet shoulder width apart, with your toes in contact with the floor. Keeping your arms, back, and legs straight, lift one foot and the opposite hand off the floor for approximately five seconds. Contract the muscles of your arms, shoulders, core, and legs as needed to maintain balance. Switch foot and arm positions so that your other arm and leg are now supporting your weight. Hold this position for about five seconds. Continue

1. Keep arm straight.

2. Lower hip to floor, then return to start position.

1. Raise one arm and leg.

2. Then the other.

1. Lift one hand and foot.

2. Then the other.

Front lever.

alternating the supporting arm and leg every five seconds. To make the exercise harder, occasionally use the arm and leg on the same side. End the exercise after one minute, or earlier if you cannot maintain balance on the single arm and leg. Rest for three minutes and perform a second set.

FRONT LEVER

Introduced to climbing by the legendary boulderer John Gill, the Front Lever is the gold standard of core-muscle strength. It is a very difficult gymnastics move, so expect this exercise to feel hard—or even impossible! Fortunately, you can make it a bit easier by simply bending one leg or having a spotter hold your feet. Begin by hanging straight-arm from a bar or a set of rock rings (ideal). Pull up halfway, then push your hands forward, drop your head backward, and lift your legs. Do all this in a single quick motion while attempting to position your entire body—head to toe—parallel to the ground. Squeeze tightly throughout your shoulders, torso, buttocks, and legs to hold this position for three seconds (if you can). It helps to think about *pushing your hands toward your hips,* even though you'll be in a stationary position. The goal is to hold the lever for three seconds before lowering yourself slowly to the starting position.

Immediately pull up into a Front Lever again and hold for three seconds. Perform three to five (hard) total Front Levers. Rest for three to five minutes before performing a second set.

Safety note: The Front Lever places a great deal of stress on your shoulders and elbows (just like steep climbing), so it is inappropriate for novice or out-of-shape climbers or anyone with ongoing elbow or shoulder problems.

STEEP-WALL TRAVERSING

Climbing overhanging walls is the ultimate core-training exercise, and it's obviously the most specific. The best training strategy is to traverse sideways across a long overhanging wall, or back and forth across a shorter wall. The only drawback to this exercise is that lack of finger strength and climbing ability will prevent some climbers from traversing long enough to adequately work the core muscles. Here's how to do it.

Select a section of wall that overhangs between thirty and fifty degrees past vertical. Using medium-size handholds and small footholds, traverse across the wall at a steady pace. Avoid extremely technical or strenuous moves. Try to make long sideways reaches with your hands and feet—the longer the

Single-Leg Squat

1. Feet a bit more than shoulder width apart.

2. Lower yourself over one foot and press up.

horizontal reach, the more your core muscles will need to work to maintain balance and stability. Allow your body to twist and turn as needed to execute the moves, and concentrate on contracting your core muscles to prevent body sag, sway, or swing. Continue traversing for at least one minute, and alternate leading with your hands and feet. Rest for three to five minutes before performing a second or third set. Adjust the difficulty of the traverse by using holds that are closer (easier) or farther apart.

SINGLE-LEG SQUATS

This final exercise isn't strictly a core exercise, but it does train the leg and core muscles in a very specific way that mimics the process of pressing out a high-step move and maintaining a balanced center of gravity throughout. It's actually quite difficult. I suggest you use this exercise at least twice per week—it will provide payoffs on the rock!

Stand erect with your feet a bit more than shoulder width apart—the farther apart they are, the harder this exercise—and your hands gathered behind your hips. Slowly bend your left leg and begin shifting your center of gravity to the left as you lower yourself over your left foot until the bottom of your thigh is about parallel to the floor. Now press back up with your left leg to return to the starting position. Maintain a nearly straight right leg throughout this down-and-up motion. Immediately begin another repetition with the same leg. Continue for ten to thirty (hard) repetitions, or stop when you can no longer control your downward motion. After a brief rest, perform a set with your right leg doing the squatting motion.

Training the Antagonist Muscles

The muscles that are antagonist in most climbing movements include the pectorals (chest), deltoids and trapezius (shoulders and upper back), triceps (back of the upper arm), and the finger extensors (outside of the forearm). Consult the anatomy photos in appendix A if you are unfamiliar with these muscle groups. Strength and flexibility in these mus-

cles is fundamental to controlled, precise movement and for maintaining joint stability. Unfortunately, few climbers regularly engage in training of these antagonist muscles; the agonist pull muscles get all the attention. Growing imbalance subsequently develops around the elbow and shoulder joints, thus increasing instability and risk of injury. Outside of the fingers, the most common injuries among climbers are elbow tendinosis and shoulder impingement and subluxation. You now know why.

As common as injuries are in this sport, it surprises me that so few climbers commit to regular training of the antagonist muscles. The time commitment is minimal, and the exercises themselves are not that difficult. On average it would take only about twenty minutes, twice per week, to gain all of the benefits of antagonist training. Any more than this is

Reverse Wrist Curl

1. Maintain neutral wrist.

2. Curl dumbbell up.

TRAINING for CLIMBING

unnecessary and undesirable, since excessive antagonist training and use of extremely heavy weights would gradually build heavier, more bulky muscles.

Upcoming are several exercises for strengthening the antagonist muscles that help support optimal function of the elbow and shoulder joints. Healthy climbers can begin using all of these exercises, whereas anyone with ongoing elbow tendinosis or a shoulder injury of any kind should follow a prescribed rehabilitation program (which may include some of these exercises).

Hand and Forearm Muscles

The musculature of the forearms is some of the most complex in the body. Climbing works these muscles in a very specific way that, over time, can result in tendinosis on either the inside or outside of your elbow (more on these injuries in chapter 11). Use the following two exercises to strengthen the finger extensor and pronator muscle groups—two small but highly important muscle sets. If there are two exercises in this book that every climber *must* do, they are these.

REVERSE WRIST CURLS

Use this in conjunction with the forearm stretches provided earlier in this chapter as an insurance policy against lateral epicondylitis. Consider doing one set of Reverse Wrist Curls during your warm-up for climbing and two more sets as part of your cooldown.

Sitting on a chair or bench, rest your forearm on the far end of your thigh so that your hand faces palm down and overhangs the knee by several

Pronator

1. Palm up.

2. Lift hammer to vertical.

inches. Firmly grip a five- to fifteen-pound (much harder) dumbbell, and begin with a neutral (straight) wrist position. Curl the dumbbell upward until the hand is fully extended. Hold this top position for one second, then lower the dumbbell back to the starting position. Avoid lowering the dumbbell below a horizontal hand position. Continue with slow, controlled reverse curls for fifteen to twenty repetitions. Perform two sets with each hand, with a two- to three-minute rest between sets. Use a heavier dumbbell if you can easily execute twenty repetitions. Well-conditioned individuals may need as much as a twenty-five- or thirty-pound dumbbell.

An alternative exercise, though perhaps less beneficial, involves opening your fingers against the resistance of a strong rubber band. This method is best used as a preclimbing warm-up. Store a thick rubber band in your car or climbing pack, and do a set of finger extensions before you perform your warm-up stretching.

PRONATOR

Arm-pulling movements naturally result in supination of the hand. If you perform a pull-up on a free-hanging set of Pump Rocks, you'll discover that your hands naturally turn outward or supinate as your biceps contract. Consequently, training forearm pronation is an important antagonist exercise for climbers to maintain muscle balance across the forearms. There are several different ways to train forearm pronation, but the easiest is with an ordinary three-pound sledgehammer.

Sit on a chair or bench with your forearm resting on your thigh, hand in the palm-up position. Firmly grip a sledgehammer with the heavy end extending to the side and the handle parallel to the floor. Turn your hand inward (pronation) to lift the hammer to the vertical position. Stop here. Now slowly lower the hammer back to the starting position. Stop at the horizontal position for one second before beginning the next repetition. Continue lifting the hammer in this way for fifteen to twenty repetitions. Choke up on the hammer if this feels overly difficult. Perform two sets with each hand.

Alternatively, you can cut a 14-inch length of 1-inch-diameter dowel (or purchase a blank dumbbell bar) and mount a few one-pound weights on one end. A total resistance of only two or three pounds is all you need.

Training the Large Push Muscles

These exercises are equally vital for maintaining balance in the stabilizing muscles of the shoulders and upper torso. The three exercises described below will go a long way toward maintaining the necessary balance and, hopefully, the health of your shoulders through many years of rigorous climbing. If you have an existing shoulder problem, these exercises may help mitigate the pain and prevent further injury. Still, it's essential that you to see a doctor or physical therapist for guidance specific to your affliction.

While the three following exercises can all be performed on standard health equipment (Cybex, free weights, and so forth), I would not advise that you buy a club membership just to gain access to the necessary machinery. Instead a onetime investment in a few dumbbells (less than $50) is all you need. Alternatively, you might ask the climbing gym you patronize to purchase a few dumbbells for the purpose of training the antagonist muscles of the forearms and upper torso.

SHOULDER PRESS

The shoulder-press motion involves a motion that is almost exactly opposite that of pulling up while climbing—thus no exercise is more central to antagonist-muscle training. Although you can execute this exercise with a common health club shoulder-press machine, performing dumbbell shoulder presses provides a more complete workout of the many small stabilizing muscles of the shoulders. Here's how to do it.

Sit on a bench with good upright posture and feet flat on the floor. Begin with bent arms, palms facing forward, and the dumbbells positioned just outside your shoulders. Press straight upward with your palms maintaining a forward-facing position. As your arms become straight, squeeze your hands slightly inward until the dumbbells touch end-to-end. Lower the dumbbells to the starting position.

1. Palms face forward.

2. Touch dumbbells end-to-end.

The complete repetition should take about two seconds. Continue this motion for twenty to twenty-five repetitions. Strive for smooth, consistent motion throughout the entire set. Rest for three minutes and perform a second set.

Women should start with five-pound dumbbells and advance to ten- or fifteen-pounders when they can do twenty-five reps. Most men can begin training with fifteen- or twenty-pound dumbbells and then progress to twenty-five and thirty pounds as they are able to achieve twenty-five repetitions. Over the long term it's best not to progress beyond 40 percent of your body weight (total weight lifted): Heavier weight may build undesirable muscle bulk.

BENCH PRESS (OR PUSH-UPS)

The bench press is a staple exercise of power lifters and bodybuilders, but it's also useful to climbers striving to maintain stable, healthy shoulders. The key is to use only moderate weight—begin with a total equal to about 25 percent of your body weight and progress up to 50 percent (never more). For example, a 160-pound climber would begin training with two 20-pound dumbbells (40 pounds total) and progress up to training with, at most, 40-pound dumbbells or 80 pounds with an Olympic bar.

Lie flat on a bench with bent legs and your feet flat on the floor. Using an Olympic bar or two dumbbells, begin the exercise with your hands just above chest level and palms facing your feet. If you're using a bar, your hands should be a few inches wider than your shoulders. Press straight up with a slow, steady motion. If using dumbbells, squeeze your hands together to touch the ends of the dumbbells together upon reaching the top position. Return to the starting position, pause for a moment and then begin the next repetition. With a bar, be careful not to bounce the bar off your chest. The goal is slow, controlled movement that takes about two seconds per repetition. Continue for twenty to twenty-five repetitions. Rest for three minutes before performing a second set.

As an alternative, push-ups provide a workout similar to the bench press. Begin with your hands shoulder width apart and build up to doing two sets of twenty-five repetitions. If necessary, move your hands closer together to increase training resistance. Conversely, beginners should do the push-ups with their knees on the floor until they are able to progress to the normal feet-on-floor position.

DIPS

Dips are an excellent exercise for strengthening the many muscles of the upper arms, shoulders, chest, and back. What's more, the dip motion is quite similar to the mantle move in climbing and thus provides a very sport-specific benefit! Some health clubs and gyms possess a parallel-bar setup ideal for performing dips. Alternatively, you can use the incut ninety-degree corner of a kitchen counter, or set two heavy chairs in a parallel position. A set of free-floating Pump Rocks or gymnastics rings are my personal favorite, as they provide a more dynamic (and difficult) workout.

Position yourself between the parallel bars, Pump Rocks, or other apparatus. Jump up into the straight-arm starting position with your hands drawn in near your hips. Slowly lower until your arm is bent ninety degrees—do not lower beyond this point! Immediately press back up to the starting position. Continue this up-and-down motion, with each repetition taking about two seconds. Strive to complete ten to twenty (hard) repetitions. Perform two or three sets with a three-minute rest between each. Don't rush or bounce through this exercise, and never lower beyond a ninety-degree arm bend.

If you are unable to do at least ten dips, enlist a spotter to reduce the resistance as needed so that you can reach this goal. The spotter should stand behind you and lift around your waist or, more easily, pull up on your ankles (bend your legs and cross them at the ankles to facilitate this).

Antagonist-Muscle Training Tips

1. Regular training of the antagonist muscles will make you a more biomechanically sound climber and vastly reduce your risk of elbow and shoulder injuries.

2. Perform all of the antagonist exercises described in this section at least twice per week. Use relatively light weights that enable you to perform fifteen to thirty (better) reps with each exercise.

3. Dips are most beneficial, but for many people they are difficult to perform at full body weight. If needed, engage a training partner to help you perform at least fifteen dips per set.

4. Most important, perform Reverse Wrist Curls and Forearm Pronators before and after every climbing workout. These exercises provide a valuable dynamic warm-up before climbing, and may help you avoid the elbow tendinosis that can result from muscular imbalance.

1. Press straight up.

2. Slow, controlled movement.

1. Straight-arm start.

2. Bend to 90 degrees, then press to starting position!

An Overview of Stamina Training for Climbing

Stamina is the ability to resist fatigue while engaging in sustained or intermittent physical activity for an extended period of time. Some people refer to this attribute as endurance, since it is largely a function of one's aerobic and anaerobic endurance. Depending on your preferred type of climbing, the impor-

tance of stamina can range from minor to paramount. In bouldering, for example, the need for strength and power far exceeds that for stamina. Conversely, stamina supersedes strength and power for alpine and big-wall climbing. In the middle of this continuum are multipitch climbing and all-day sport climbing, which require strength and power, as well as significant stamina.

As in other types of conditioning, there are sport-specific and general ways of stamina training. The most specific—and therefore effective—approach would be to train as you perform. That is, to develop stamina for long days of cragging, you would train by logging many long days at the crags. Obviously, this approach is not an option for many recreational climbers with commitments to job, school, and family. A more practical training alternative, then, is to engage in general stamina training such as running and biking coupled as often as possible with high volumes of climbing at the gym or crags.

Stamina Training for Boulder, Sport, and Multipitch Climbers

Excellence at bouldering and sport climbing requires abundant strength and power, precise technique and efficient movement, and a killer instinct, but very little in the way of stamina. The exception are long boulder problems and sport and multipitch routes that do test anaerobic endurance (local to your forearm and upper-body pull muscles) and your body's ability to sustain exercise near or beyond its lactate threshold. So, while stamina training will have no real impact on your maximum-move ability, it will enhance recovery between climbs, as well as increase your anaerobic threshold and ability to persevere through long, sustained boulder problems or sport routes.

But before you set out to run five miles per day, remember that high-volume stamina training could be viewed as the enemy of strength and power train-

Indoor lead walls are the ideal platform for interval training. Here Lorin Teres pulls down at Metro Rock, Boston. ERIC McCALLISTER

ing of the upper body. Not only would it divert time you could invest more effectively—say, in bouldering—but regular high-mileage aerobic activity results in systemic fatigue that may prevent you from training and climbing up to your potential. Furthermore, excessive aerobic training has a catabolic effect on the muscles of the upper body: That is, the body begins to metabolize muscle during long training sessions.

Let's examine two popular stamina training strategies: climbing intervals and running intervals.

CLIMBING INTERVALS

Climbing through a timed bouldering circuit or doing timed laps on a route is the most specific form of stamina training for boulderers and crag climbers. This is analogous to a weight-lifting circuit-training program, which research has shown to yield gains in cardiovascular (aerobic) conditioning. In bouldering, the goal is to climb a series of moderately difficult problems with only brief rest intervals in between. Select problems that are a few grades below your maximum ability—the right grade problem should make you work, yet not test you maximally or cause you to fall off repeatedly. When climbing with a rope, the training goal is to climb five laps on a moderately hard route, each comprising three to six minutes of climbing followed by three to six minutes of rest. This is basically the same workout strategy as in training local forearm endurance, so by engaging in climbing intervals you are training both anaerobic endurance and stamina.

Although this drill can be performed at an outdoor crag, it's ideal for use at a commercial gym with friendly holds and nontechnical overhanging terrain. The goal is to train the body, not climbing skills or technique—so regardless of whether you are interval training on a boulder problem or route, the moves should not be so hard that you fall off.

The goal in stamina training is to develop the capacity to sustain moderately difficult climbing activity while avoiding complete muscular failure. If you develop a deep muscular pump, immediately decrease the climbing difficulty so that you don't shift into training anaerobic endurance. It's important to have a training plan and stick to it, whether it's to climb a few laps on a route or send a circuit of ten boulder problems. Decide how long you will rest between each ascent, then stick to a prescribed schedule. Purchase a stopwatch (less than $10 at most sports stores) to time precise rests between climbs. This is a great thirty- to sixty-minute stamina workout!

Whether you are climbing route intervals or a bouldering circuit, ask your belayer or spotter to join in on the session. It's of great benefit to have a partner who's vested in the training—this will enhance motivation and create a training synergy that is mutually beneficial. Take turns timing each other with the stopwatch, and have fun!

RUNNING INTERVALS

Competitive runners view interval training as the gold standard for increasing one's capacity to sustain moderate- to high-intensity running and race-day pace. These benefits come as a result of an increase in aerobic capacity (VO_2 max) and lactate threshold. The long-term benefits of this training methodology are so profound that all serious medium- to long-distance runners incorporate some form of interval training into their monthly training cycle.

The physiological adaptations of interval training can also be a boon for serious rock climbers. While the act of running intervals is hardly specific to climbing, its effects on the cardiovascular system are not far different from a long, multicrux route. If you engage in any form of long, strenuous climbing, you can be sure that running intervals will improve your performance, in terms of both improved total stamina and accelerating recovery between efforts.

The most common interval-training program is to run alternating fast and slow laps on a track. Although you can also run intervals on a road or trail, the ease of setting a goal and gauging distances makes running on a track preferable. For initial training sessions, set out to run 2 miles—that's an aggregate distance of fast and slow laps. As a rough gauge, your fast laps should feel like 80 to 90 percent of your maximum speed and result in your getting significantly winded. Try to hold the fast pace for a complete lap, and then pull back to a jog for the "slow" lap. Continue alternating fast and slow laps (or half laps) for a total of eight.

Stamina Training for Big-Wall and Alpine Climbers

Big-wall and alpine climbing are obviously more about all-day or multiday stamina than possessing fingers of steel. If such stamina climbing is your cup of tea, your training should be specific to these demands. The two best training strategies here are high-volume climbing and high-volume aerobic exercise.

ALL-DAY CLIMBING

This is a classic train-as-you-climb strategy. If you have the resources nearby, then no training could be more specific than chalking up many long days on the rock. You could do this in the form of climbing as many routes as possible from sunrise to sunset at a cragging area or by racing up a Grade IV or V big-wall route in a day. Ideally the goal would be to engage in two or three all-day climbing workouts per week—do this for a few months and you'll develop amazing climbing stamina! For many climbers, however, it may only be possible to train this way a few days per month. In this case, you will need to engage in some high-volume aerobic training as an adjunct for all-day climbing.

HIGH-VOLUME AEROBIC TRAINING

The goal here is to engage in four, forty-five- to ninety-minute aerobic workouts per week with a focus on mileage over speed. This could be any combination of running, swimming, cycling, brisk hiking, and trail running.

As your conditioning improves, consider increasing the number of workouts to six or eight per week. To do this—and to help make these workouts fit with your other life activities—you will need to double up on some of your workouts. For example, you might go for a long run in the morning then an hour-long bike ride in the evening, or vice versa. If you engage in such two-a-day workouts, it is best to take at least a six-hour break between the two. This is clearly an advanced aerobic training program, but it might be just the ticket in the weeks leading up to a long wall climb or high-altitude expedition.

Stamina-Training Tips

1. All climbers can benefit from some stamina training. Boulderers and crag climbers will enhance recovery rate between climbs, whereas big-wall and alpine climbers will gain valuable general endurance for ultralong days and ascents at elevation.

2. Boulderers and sport climbers will benefit the most from brief interval training (Tabatas) and running 2 to 3 miles of track intervals.

3. The most effective stamina training for big-wall and alpine climbers is climbing for mileage—that is, putting in frequent long days on the rock. Alternatively, regular long-distance aerobic activities (running, cycling, hiking, and such) lasting forty-five to ninety minutes or longer will yield substantial gains in aerobic capacity.

4. Two-a-day stamina workouts are especially effective in preparation for single-day wall ascents and high-altitude expeditions.

Climbing-Specific Exercises

Training means not only knowledge of the things which will build the body, but also knowledge of the things which will tear down or injure the body.

—*Bruce Lee*

More than any other, this chapter details the exercises that most climbers associate with training for climbing. Given what you've learned in the first half of this book, however, you know that climbing-specific exercises are just one piece of the climbing performance puzzle. That said, great physical gains await if you regularly and properly use the exercises that follow. The key, of course, is to identify and execute the exercises holding the most value for you—that is, those that target the specific physical weaknesses you identified in chapter 2's self-assessment test and from your on-the-rock experience. Chapter 8 will then guide you in crafting a maximally effective training program given your current ability level and experience.

Exercises in this chapter are divided into two main sections: exercises that target the forearm muscles controlling your finger strength and endurance, and exercises that target the large pull muscles of

Emily Harrington sending Lulu (5.14a), Rifle, Colorado. KEITH LADZINSKI

your upper arms and back. Each section has three subdivisions that classify exercises according to what physical capacity they most train: maximum strength, power, or local (anaerobic) endurance. The exercises in each subdivision are organized according to relative difficulty for the average climber, beginning with the easiest exercises and ending with the most severe, advanced-level exercises. Exercise difficulty and the appropriateness of an exercise for a given ability level is a most vital distinction. A novice climber could be injured in attempting an advanced-level exercise, whereas an advanced climber would gain little outside a warm-up by performing a beginner-level exercise. To help you in appropriate exercise selection, tables 7.1 and 7.5 classify the exercises according to difficulty.

Before we dive into the details of thirty-three must-know exercises, I want to provide you with a deeper understanding of how your fingers and arms are used in climbing. Your levels of strength and endurance on various climbing movements are very specific to the grip and arm position used. Awareness of all the grip and arm positions is therefore an essential precursor to effective training in the most climbing-specific and effective ways.

An Overview of Sport-Specific Strength Training

According to the Principle of Specificity, training gains in strength, power, and local endurance will transfer favorably to climbing only if the exercise is extremely similar in motion, body position, and functional use. It must therefore be a primary goal of climbing-specific training to train the fingers and arms in ways that are most similar to their use in climbing. Moreover, the most high-value training is that which targets your weaker finger and arm positions. While it's natural to favor certain finger and arm positions—usually the strongest—as you climb, the greatest training payoffs come from targeting your weakest links. In doing so, neuromuscular adaptations gradually make you stronger and more confident in using every grip and arm position. It's this kind of attention to subtle training details that differentiates average from extraordinary in training outcomes and future climbing performance.

Finger Positions

The basic finger-grip positions are full crimp, half crimp, open hand, and pinch. Of course, there are many variations of the above positions—for instance, a one-, two-, or three-finger pocket can be gripped with a half-crimp or an open-hand position.

FULL CRIMP

The full crimp is favored by many climbers since it provides what feels like the most secure lock onto small handholds. The hallmark of the full crimp is the hyperextension of the first joint of each finger and the sharp flexion of the second finger joint. The full-crimp grip is then secured by locking your thumb over the end of the index finger. Unfortunately, this grip position places the highest force load on the joints and tendons, and overuse can result in nagging finger injuries; excessive use of this grip is also hard on the lateral aspect of the elbow and may lead to injury. While it is absolutely necessary to use and train the crimp grip, the best approach would be to limit to holds that cannot effectively be gripped any other way. The full-crimp grip excels on small, square-cut edges, shallow flakes, and any hold that possess a small incut or recessed edge.

HALF CRIMP

The half-crimp grip is just a variation on the full crimp in which you do not thumb-lock over the index finger. This reduces slightly the aggressive angles on the first and second joints of the finger, thus making the grip a bit more ergonomic. The trade-off is that the half crimp often feels less secure than the full, although you can develop strength and comfort in the half crimp through regular use and training. The half-crimp grip is most often used on small edges and shallow, incut pockets.

OPEN HAND

The open-hand grip has distinct advantages over the crimp grip. First, the open-hand position is kinder to the finger tendons and joints, since it softens the joint angles and may allow the rock to provide some tendon support (your fingers wrap naturally over a curved hold). Furthermore, despite its frequently less secure feel, the open-hand position can be trained to become your strongest grip position on all but smallest crimp and incut holds (which require a crimp grip). This grip is most effective on rounded or sloping holds, and particularly when pulling on pockets. If you're unfamiliar with the open-hand grip, it will feel quite awkward and unlikely at first. But rest assured that your open-hand grip strength will improve quickly with targeted training.

PINCH GRIP

The pinch grip is vital for latching on to protruding holds such as pebbles, tuffas, and opposing edges. Due to the protruding nature of indoor climbing holds, use of the pinch grip is far more common indoors than on natural rock faces. Fortunately, our hands are designed to excel at pinching. Difficulties in using the pinch grip in climbing tend to relate more to the size, smoothness, and positiveness (or lack thereof) of the pinch. Like all the other grips, however, you can improve your use of this grip through targeted training at pinching holds of different shapes, widths, and depths.

Arm Positions and Movements

Regardless of how you grip the rock, it's the arms that utilize this point of contact to create torque, leverage, and upward movement. Therefore, it's vital to distinguish between grip position—the point of contact—and the arm position that connects this point of contact to your torso.

Finger Positions

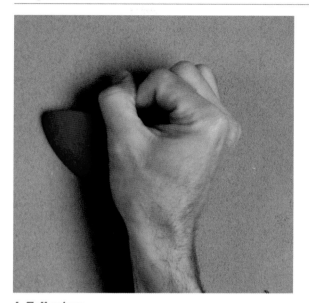

1. *Full crimp.*

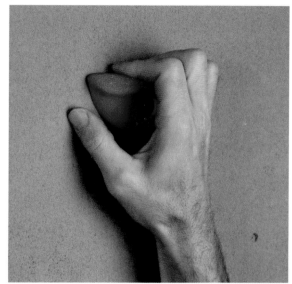

2. *Half crimp.*

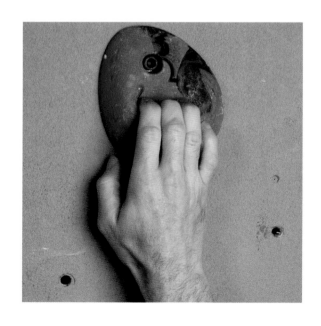

3. *Open hand.*

4. *Pinch grip.*

The five primary positions are the down pull, the undercling, the side pull, the reverse side pull or Gaston, and the mantle or press down. As in training the finger positions described above, it's essential that you incorporate all five arm positions into your training. Later on you'll learn about System Wall Training, the best method of targeted strength and endurance training for the various arm positions.

DOWN PULL

The down pull is by far the most common arm position used in climbing, as it's the arm position you would use to ascend a ladder hand-over-hand. With each grip on the rock, the arm begins in a position above your head with the palm facing downward. From this starting position you can either hang straight-arm in a static rest position or pull downward to aid in upward movement. When used to aid in locomotion, the down-pulling arm often concludes its work in the lock-off position typified by the arm bent at an acute angle with the elbow pointing downward and your hand pulled in tight against the side of your chest. This range of motion from the above-the-head, straight-arm position to hand-against-chest lock-off is the single most fundamental arm movement in climbing. Consequently, your strength and endurance at this pulling motion will increase if you simply climb a few days per week. Still, targeted pull-down and lock-off training is useful to accelerate the development of strength and endurance.

UNDERCLING

An inverted, downward-facing handhold demands gripping the usable surface palm-up while contracting the arm muscles with the arm bent in an elbow-down or elbow-back position. In a fashion opposite to executing a down-pull movement, the undercling pull is usually released slowly in an eccentric contraction as you move up the rock. Although many of the muscles used are the same as in down-pulling, strength gains at underclinging largely require training that isolates the arm in this invert position.

SIDE PULL

As the name implies, this arm position involves pulling inward on a hold that's out to your side and facing away from your body. This position places your arm in a naturally strong position, and thus difficulties in using side pulls often relate to poor body position and foot placement (bad technique) rather than lack of strength. Consequently, the most effective methods of training the side-pull position are those that involve actual climbing. For example, System Wall Training (described later in this chapter) provides highly specific training that fosters improvements in body position and use of the feet while side pulling. Similarly, climbing a gym route using only side-pull arm positions and the associated body and foot techniques is a highly effective form of isolation training.

REVERSE SIDE PULL (AKA GASTON)

The more difficult reverse side pull is called into play in using side-facing edges that are located in front of your body or just above your head. For instance,

Arm Positions and Movements

1. Down pull.

2. Undercling.

3. Side pull.

4. Reverse side pull.

5. Mantle.

imagine a left-facing vertical edge in front of your face. The best use of this hold would often be to grab it with your right hand (thumb down) and pull outward to the right. This is the classic Gaston move, and this shoulder-wrenching move requires targeted training. In addition to training the Gaston position while bouldering or on a System Wall, it's imperative that you engage in the antagonist-muscle training described in chapter 6. The Gaston position places the shoulder joint at risk of subluxation; only through regular push-muscle training will you be able to fortify your shoulder joints and lower injury risk.

MANTLE

Mantling is the exact opposite of down pulling: Your arm begins in a bent position near your torso and then pushes downward. An ordinary life use of mantling is the simple act of pushing yourself out of water at the edge of a swimming pull—both hands contact the edge of the pool palms-downward as they push down from near your chest to below your waist. In climbing, the mantle move is significantly more difficult since there's no water to provide the lightening effect of buoyancy. Furthermore, it is rare in climbing to come upon a large, flat surface on which to mantle (except at the top of a boulder problem). Instead you will often need to mantle with your fingertips on a shallow edge or pocket, and in extreme cases even press down with only your thumb resting on the top edge of a hold. Regardless of the amount of finger or hand contact with the rock, however, the mantle arm position requires targeted training if you are to become a master of throwdowns!

Finger and Forearm Training

The following pages on finger and forearm training will likely be the most referred to in this entire book. This is completely understandable given that many failed attempts on a boulder problem or climb are accompanied by pumped forearm muscles. Of course, the intelligent climber will always analyze whether failure was actually the result of an underlying problem in sequencing, technique and tactics, or mental control. This is a crucial distinction that all

climbers must consider in evaluating their performance and training-for-climbing focus. This being said, more finger strength and forearm endurance certainly can't hurt—and if you are looking to increase your capabilities in these areas, well, you've come to the right place!

Before we move on to the exercise details, I must proclaim the number one rule in finger training: *Don't get injured!* While this rule is presumably self-evident, a surprising number of enthusiastic climbers get injured by training too much or in attempting advanced exercises for which they are not ready. You can best reduce your risk of injury by employing a prudent approach to finger training and by following these basic guidelines.

- Always perform a progressive warm-up that gradually builds from easy full-body activity to difficult, sport-specific exercises.
- Make a conscious effort to avoid the most painful and stressful holds (such as sharp, small-radius edges and pockets that feel tweaky).
- Eliminate redundancy by using a few different exercises each session. Don't just train for an hour on a single apparatus (such as the fingerboard or campus board) or keep attempting the same heinous boulder problem over and over again.
- Immediately stop training at the first sign you may be injuring yourself. Break for a few minutes—or days—to assess the cause of the pang and severity of the potential injury.
- Rest more than you think you need to—your muscles and precious digits will thank you! Consider three or four days of aggregate training and climbing per week to be the limit. Any more than this tempts injury and certainly doesn't allow enough recovery time to maximally benefit from your training.

Maximum-Strength Exercises

According to the principle of specificity, efficacy of training to improve grip strength for climbing is proportionate to how well it targets the neuromuscular system in ways similar to its use in climbing. For example, squeezing a tennis ball or rubber doughnut works some of the same muscles used in gripping a

Table 7.1 Classification of Finger- and Forearm-Training Exercises

		Beginner	Intermediate	Advanced
Maximum Strength	Bouldering	✓	✓	✓
	Hypergravity Bouldering		✓	✓
	Fingerboard Pull-Ups		✓	✓
	Fingerboard Repeaters		✓	✓
	Fingerboard Pyramids		✓	✓
	Heavy Finger Rolls		✓	✓
	Hypergravity Isolation Training (HIT)		✓	✓
Contact Strength and Power	One-Arm Traversing		✓	✓
	One-Arm Lunging		✓	✓
	Campus Laddering		✓	✓
	Campus Lock-Offs		✓	✓
	Campus Double Dynos			✓
Anaerobic Local Endurance	Bouldering Traverses	✓	✓	✓
	Straight-Armed Hangs	✓	✓	✓
	Fingerboard Moving Hangs		✓	✓
	Bouldering and Route Interval Training		✓	✓
	HIT and System Interval Training		✓	✓
	Tabata Protocol		✓	✓

climbing handhold; however, the muscle force, hand and finger positions, and energy system used are very different. Therefore, squeezing a rubber doughnut is ineffective for increasing functional grip strength for climbing. Conversely, hanging on a fingerboard or bouldering on small, strenuous-to-grip handholds is very specific and, thus, highly effective training.

The degree to which a given exercise will produce gains in functional grip strength for climbing can be estimated by considering the following requirements. The more of these requirements an exercise meets, the more effective it will be at producing gains in usable grip strength.

1. **The exercise must be high intensity throughout the entire set.** In climbing, higher intensity is created by increasing wall angle, decreasing hold size, or increasing hold spacing. Unfortunately, there's a definite limit to how far you can go with each of these. Beyond a certain point, it's more effective to increase intensity by adding weight to your body. Adding just ten pounds can make a huge difference in training intensity on overhanging walls and can yield a leap in finger strength in just a couple of weeks. Interestingly, very few climbers are aware of this fact!

2. **The exercise must produce rapid muscular failure, not failure due to technique.** In the weight-lifting world, muscular failure in three to ten reps is considered ideal (though different texts prescribe slightly different values). This is also valid for climbing, but translates to strenuous climbing with failure in six to twenty total hand movements (three to ten moves per hand). In climbing, however, there's always the lingering

Table 7.2   Determining Specificity and Effectiveness
of Common Finger-Strength-Training Exercises

Exercises	High Intensity?	Rapid Failure?	Specific Movement?	Isolate Grips?
Bouldering	yes	maybe	yes	maybe
Fingerboard	maybe	yes	no	yes
Heavy Finger Rolls	yes	yes	no	no
One-Arm Lunging and Campus Training	yes	yes	sometimes	no
Hypergravity Isolation Training (HIT)	yes	yes	yes	yes

question of whether failure resulted from muscle failure or failure of technique. Thus, the best exercise for training grip strength would reduce the technical requirements as much as possible and eliminate training of footwork or arm positions.

3. **The exercise must be specific to climbing positions and movements.** The principle of specificity instructs us that strength gains resulting from a certain exercise are specific to situations involving similar position and movement. The greater the difference between the exercise and sport use, the less the strength will transfer. Thus, the best grip-strength-training exercises involve actual climbing movements, whereas an exercise performed while standing or hanging would transfer less.

4. **The exercise must focus on a specific grip position for an entire set.** In climbing, the rock dictates a random use of varying grip positions. Since strength is specific to each grip position, such cycling of grips allows you to climb much longer than you could if you used the same grip repeatedly. That's great if you are climbing for performance; however, it's not ideal for training finger strength. That's why a full season of climbing builds local forearm endurance but may leave you with about the same maximum grip strength as

last year. Effective grip-strength training must hammer a specific grip position until failure. Due to the limited transfer of strength among grip positions, you'll need to train several, including open hand, half crimp, full crimp, pinch, and the three two-finger pocket combinations or "teams."

Let's examine seven exercises that will produce beneficial gains in finger strength. They are listed in order, from the most basic exercises appropriate for all climbers to the most highly targeted advanced exercises.

BOULDERING

Bouldering is the most straightforward way to train grip strength. Without the constraints of a rope and gear, bouldering allows you to focus on climbing the hardest moves possible. Inherent to hard bouldering, however, are some limiting factors that diminish the potential to build maximum grip strength. Consider that technical difficulties may prevent you from climbing up to the point of muscular failure. Furthermore, the rock dictates the use of many different grip positions, thus, making it difficult to isolate a single grip position and work it to failure.

Despite these limitations, bouldering should be a staple of your training program. It will build some functional strength while at the same time developing mental and technical skills. Consequently it's a good training strategy to couple bouldering with one of the other finger-strength-training exercises described in this section. Use the following training strategy to best stimulate gains in finger strength via bouldering.

Select a boulder problem that appears to be strenuous, but not technically difficult. Favor overhanging problems, which will place more weight on your hands and maximize the training effect. When bouldering indoors, try to locate—or consider setting—problems that isolate a specific grip position. For example, a problem that possesses a lot of crimp holds will be best for training crimp strength. Attempt to climb the problem two or three times with sufficient rest between each ascent to allow a good effort. As a guideline, rest for at least three minutes between attempts of short bouldering problems and five minutes or more between longer problems.

Move on to another strenuous-looking problem that appears to target a different grip position, such as pinch, two finger pockets, open hand, and such. Ascend this problem two or three times, with adequate rest between attempts. Continue bouldering for thirty to ninety minutes, and then finish your finger training with one of the isolation exercises described below.

HYPERGRAVITY BOULDERING

Advanced climbers with several years of bouldering under their belt eventually reach a point where they no longer achieve significant gains in finger strength despite regular, hard bouldering. Fortunately, hypergravity bouldering and the HIT workout (described later in this chapter) are powerful training strategies that will

yield further gains in high-end finger strength. To do this, you'll need to invest in a ten-pound weight belt (a five-pound belt for climbers weighing less than one hundred pounds) or fill a fanny pack with five or ten pounds of scuba diver's weights (check TrainingForClimbing.com for a current weight belt retailer). Here is the best strategy for engaging in hypergravity bouldering—this is an indoor training strategy only!

Hypergravity bouldering with a twenty-pound weight belt.

Overview of Fingerboard Training

Since its advent in the mid-1980s, the fingerboard has become the standard apparatus for performing pull-ups and straight-armed hangs. What's more, the fingerboard is economical (less than $100) and can mount in just about any apartment or home. So if you don't have the space or resources for a home climbing wall, consider a fingerboard mandatory. In fact, even those with home walls find the fingerboard an excellent tool for warm-ups and the many pull-muscle exercises to be discussed later.

The obvious strengths of fingerboard training are its ease of access and the ability to isolate a wide variety of grip positions. Advanced climbers progressively add weight to their body (hypergravity) to train maximum grip strength with a series of brief, high-intensity hangs. The strategy for training endurance requires a lighter load (less than body weight), best achieved by placing your feet on a chair (or footholds on the wall) so that you can circulate your grip around the board for several minutes in a manner similar to climbing.

To maximize effectiveness of fingerboard training, it is important to know about the grip–relax repeating sequence (GRRS) and to try to mimic this action in your training. Consider that it's a good climbing tactic to move quickly through cruxes and to get on and off difficult holds (the grip–relax) as fast as possible. This conserves energy reserves and even allows for brief, but invaluable steps in recovery between each grip. The physiology behind this process relates to the fact that blood flow is occluded (closed off) during peak contractions and resumes only when the muscle relaxes. Inevitably, if you have to grip a hold maximally to stick it, then the blood flow in your forearms is occluded and your grip will ultimately fail in a matter of fifteen seconds or less. Given a brief "relax" period between each maximum grip (the few seconds while your other hand grips), however, you can climb on for a surprisingly long time. Top climbers use the GRRS to keep them going and going up the most improbable-looking routes.

Of course, a complete warm-up is imperative before any fingerboard training. Ideally, perform some light general exercise to elevate your heart rate and muscle temperature. Proceed to crank out a few sets of pull-ups along with gentle stretching of your fingers and upper body. Complete your warm-up with some self-massage of the fingers, forearms, and arms, and consider reinforcing the tendons at the base of your fingers with a few tight turns of tape (especially if you plan to train with added weight). Limit your use of the fingerboard to a maximum of three days per week—any more than that and injury risk skyrockets! Furthermore, stop training at the first sign of pain in joints or tendons, and consider taking a few days or more rest from training.

Complete a general and specific warm-up. That is, work through various basic warm-up and stretching exercises, and then move on to some general climbing and bouldering lasting at least thirty minutes. Now clip on your weight belt and predetermine a target number of "burns" (attempts and ascents) that you will perform at hypergravity. As a guideline, limit yourself to about five burns on your initial session, then build to fifteen to twenty burns as you gain confidence and strength.

Select nontechnical, overhanging boulder problems that possess small- to medium-size holds, but no tiny and tweaky features. Since you are climbing with a weight belt, favor problems that are a couple of grades or more below your limit. It's important to avoid taking an out-of-control fall while climbing with the extra weight on your body. Climb the problem two or three times with a rest for three to five minutes between ascents.

Move on to another strenuous-looking problem that appears to target a different grip position. Consider taking the time to set "theme problems" that possess only holds of a certain shape and size—this is the best way to target and train a weak grip position. Ascend this problem two or three times, with adequate rest between attempts.

It's important to remember that hypergravity bouldering is stressful on the fingers, elbows, and shoulders, and it's critical that you stop training at the first sign of pain in any of these areas. Gradually work into hypergravity bouldering over the course of a few weeks. Begin with five burns, one day per week, and work toward the advanced program of fifteen to twenty burns, twice per week.

FINGERBOARD PULL-UPS

When I first began climbing in the mid-1970s, fingertip pull-ups on a doorjamb were the main form of home training for climbers! All these years later, performing these crimpy pull-ups on a 0.75-inch-deep fingerboard edge is still good for a quick training fix if you have no access to a climbing gym or other equipment. Perform one to two sets of pull-ups using each of the three primary grip positions—full crimp, half crimp, and open hand—and perhaps a

couple more sets using the finger pocket holds if you are accustomed to this grip. Always perform the finger warm-up and stretching exercises detailed on page 102 before training.

FINGERBOARD REPEATERS

Repeaters are the best fingerboard exercise for developing maximum grip strength, since they target specific grip positions with repeated high-intensity contractions. Before you get started, however, it's imperative that you perform a complete warm-up—otherwise your fingerboard may become the "injury board." Don't take chances; use the upper-body warm-up and stretching exercises detailed in Chapter 6. Consider reinforcing the tendons at the base of your fingers with a few tight turns of tape (see Prophylactic Taping Methods in chapter 11).

Begin by surveying your fingerboard to identify pairs of grips that you can use—both hands must engage identical holds! Select five to ten grip positions to be trained: for example, open hand, pinch, crimp, sloper, three-finger pocket, and various two-finger pocket combinations. Begin by training your weakest grip position—the one that is most difficult to use when climbing—and end with your strongest.

Execute one set of ten Repeaters. Each hang should last just three to five seconds with a rest between hangs of less than five seconds. To be effective, the hangs must be high intensity and require that you bear down hard to maintain the grip for a three- to five-second count (count *one thousand one, one thousand two,* and so on). You may need to add anywhere from five to twenty pounds of weight around your waist (hypergravity training) to make the task this difficult. It may take you a few sessions to determine the exact amount of weight needed for a specific grip position. Use a smaller fingerboard feature if you need more than twenty pounds to make this exercise difficult (see table 7.3).

After completing a full set of Repeaters, take a three- to five-minute rest. Perform light stretching or self-message during this recovery period. Select a different pair of holds and begin a second set of Repeaters. You may need a different amount of weight around your waist for this new grip position.

Table 7.3 Sample Fingerboard Repeater Workout

Grip Position	Reps/Hangs	Weight Added (lbs.)	Rest Before Next Set or Grip (mins.)
Pinch	10	0	3
Open hand	10	0	3
Two-finger pocket (pinkie/ring)	10	0	3
Two-finger pocket (index/middle)	10	10	3
Two-finger pocket (middle/ring)	10	10	3
Small crimp	10	10	3
Three-finger pocket (all but pinkie)	10	20	3
Medium crimp	10	20	3

Figure 7.1 Fingerboard Pyramid Training

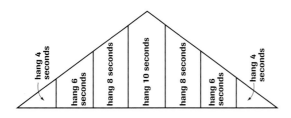

Using the same pair of holds, follow each step precisely with just a five-second rest between each step. That is, hang four seconds, rest five seconds, hang six seconds, rest five seconds, hang eight seconds, and so on.

Rest again for three to five minutes, and then begin a third set of Repeaters using a different set of holds. Continue alternating sets of Repeaters with rest periods for a total of five to ten sets.

FINGERBOARD PYRAMIDS

According to the Principle of Variation, it's beneficial to regularly vary your fingerboard training. The pyramid method is a good alternative for training maximum grip strength. Using the same pair of holds, progress through the full seven-step pyramid shown in figure 7.1. After a three-minute rest, perform another pyramid on a different set of holds. Ideally, you want to work all the primary grip positions (as in doing repeaters) over the course of seven to fifteen full pyramid sets. Limit yourself to only a three-minute rest between sets. Use smaller holds or add weight to your body if this regimen seems less than maximum (the last few steps of each pyramid should be difficult to execute).

HEAVY FINGER ROLLS

Todd Skinner turned me on to this exercise back in 1990, and I've since become a true believer. Muscular gains from this exercise are reasonably quick and obvious, and they seem to translate fairly well to climbing despite the obvious lack of specificity to climbing. Todd credited these finger rolls for some of his most significant gains in finger strength since he first picked up on this exercise from a couple of Soviet climbers he met on the World Cup circuit in 1987.

The Soviet climbers claimed that heavy finger rolls produce measurable gains in forearm circumference (a sign of muscle hypertrophy), whereas strength gains from fingerboard or campus training are primarily the result of neurological adaptations. This statement seems reasonable, because the heavy finger rolls cause repeated, high-intensity eccentric and concentric contractions of the forearm muscles. Therefore, pairing up heavy finger rolls with a reactive training exercise may produce the synergistic gains that have been shown to result from such complex training (see page 92).

Performing these heavy finger rolls is quite simple and requires twenty to thirty minutes. You will need access to a set of free weights and a bench-press bar with ball-bearing sleeves—maybe the only good reason for a climber to join a health club. A squat rack is also essential as your "spotter."

The body position for this exercise is critical to reduce strain on the lower back, elbows, and wrists. Stand with good posture and hold the bar (palms away) in front of your thighs. Focus on keeping a slight bend at your knees, elbows, and hips. The motion of the finger curl is only the few inches from the open-hand position to the closed-hand position. Ideally you want to lower the bar as far as possible without it falling from your hand—perform the exercise over a squat rack so that it will catch the weight should it slip from your fingers.

As far as weight is concerned, it must be heavy! Maximum-strength training demands the use of an appropriately heavy weight that only allows you three to ten very intense repetitions. While finger rolls with a "light" weight (such as thirty- or forty-pound dumbbells) may pump you up, they are ineffective for developing maximum finger strength. After a warm-up set with the bar weighted to about 50 percent of your body weight, the goal is three to six heavy sets with a rest of at least three minutes between sets. A

weight about equal to your body weight is a good first guess for a working weight. Add more weight if you can do more than six reps; remove it if you can't do at least three repetitions per set. With practice, you should be able to build to 150 percent of body weight.

A few other suggestions: Never train the heavy finger rolls more than twice a week and, in accordance with the Principle of Variation, cycle on and off this exercise every few weeks. Also, tape the base of your fingers and consider placing a few turns of 1.5-inch tape around your wrist when your working weight is greater than your body weight. Focus on keeping your wrists nearly straight throughout—you

Performing heavy finger rolls with squat rack as "spotter."

are not doing wrist curls! Finally, take a week or two off at the first sign of any pain in your finger tendons or wrists.

HYPERGRAVITY ISOLATION TRAINING

Hypergravity Isolation Training is unquestionably the best method of developing climbing-specific grip strength. Use the HIT workout as part of a training cycle or an off-season program during which time you can dedicate yourself to performing the exact protocol described below. Given its stressful nature, it's best to cycle on and off HIT every couple of weeks. For instance, as part of an off-season (winter) program, you might do four HIT workouts over the course of two weeks of maximum-strength training, and then spend two weeks training anaerobic endurance by climbing for volume (bouldering intervals or laps on routes). Another popular schedule is to incorporate HIT into the three-week maximum-strength phase of the 4-3-2-1 Cycle described in chapter 8.

Always perform a thirty-minute warm-up comprised of gentle stretching and bouldering of increasing difficulty. The HIT workout trains six basic grip positions, beginning with your weakest grip position and concluding with your strongest. For most people the training order will be: pinch grip, two-finger third team (pinkie and ring finger), two-finger second team (index and middle finger), two-finger first team (middle and ring finger), full crimp, and half crimp. Here's how you do it.

1. Sit on the floor below the first HIT Strip, and then grab onto the lowest pair of pinch holds. Pull up and grab the next higher left-hand pinch hold. Adjust your feet as needed and then upgrade your right hand to the next higher pinch hold. Continue up the pinch holds until both hands are grasping the top pair of pinches (four total hand moves).
2. Immediately begin reversing the sequence by alternating left and right pinch holds to descend the wall. Again, your feet can use any holds and your body can turn naturally to provide optimal body position and tension for each hand move.
3. Upon reaching the starting pinch holds, immediately start back up the wall using only alternating

pinch handholds. Continue up and down the wall until your pinch grip fails.
4. Upon stepping off the wall, use a stopwatch to time a rest of exactly three minutes before beginning the next set. Meanwhile, record the total number of hand movements (or reps) into your training notebook.
5. If you were able to do twenty or more hand moves, then you must add weight when training the pinch grip in the future. Add five pounds if you just barely succeeded at climbing twenty hand movements; and ten pounds if the twenty movements felt easy. Note that doing more than twenty reps (ten movements per hand) will train anaerobic endurance, while adding weight to produce failure in ten or fewer reps per hand trains maximum grip strength, which is of course the goal here.
6. After your three-minute rest, proceed immediately with your next set on the HIT Strips. Advanced climbers with experience at HIT should perform a second set of the pinch grip, while those new to HIT should move onto the next grip position.
7. Continue alternating training burns with rests of exactly three minutes, until you have worked through all the grip positions. Always record the number of hand movements performed as well as the amount of weight added for each grip position. This information will be helpful in doing future HIT workouts and it will quantify—finally—that your finger strength is indeed increasing!
8. Safety note: Tape your middle and ring fingers using the X method shown on page 228. This is imperative when training with twenty or more pounds added to your body. End your HIT workout early if you experience any pain in the joints or tendons of your fingers or arms.

This completes your HIT workout, though you may wish to do a few sets of hypergravity pull-ups or some lock-off exercises to complete strength training of your upper body. As a cool-down, do ten minutes of light bouldering. Take two or three rest days before engaging in another workout or going climbing—although you can do antagonist or aerobic training on these rest days.

The History of Hypergravity Isolation Training

In the mid-1990s I set out to develop the most targeted training method for developing maximum finger strength. Much experimentation with equipment designs and training protocols led to what I call Hypergravity Isolation Training (HIT). While similar to the System Wall Training described later in this chapter, HIT is more highly refined and better targets the forearm muscles. By removing the training of arm positions (as in System Training) and through the progressive addition of weight, HIT is the ultimate maximum grip-strength-training method for climbers. Since I first promoted this exciting training method in my book *How to Climb 5.12* in 1997, HIT has been adopted by thousands of climbers around the world as their top choice for training finger strength. (*Note:* This HIT workout is not to be confused with the popular bodybuilders' "HIT program.")

In the adjacent photo you see me training on third-generation HIT Strips (available from Nicros, Inc.), a unique platform I develop for optimal HIT workouts. Each HIT Strip possesses identical crimp edges and two-finger pockets that

The author (plus twenty pounds) on a HIT wall.

are ideal for laddering up and down until failure. Weight added around the waist is increased or decreased to produce grip failure in twenty or fewer total hand movements (ten or fewer per hand). Feet simply step on resident holds on the wall, and the body should twist and move just as it would in climbing a steep route. This is obviously an extremely specific exercise that targets—and indeed hammers!—all the major grip positions used in climbing. For intermediate and advanced climbers, there is simply no better way to train grip strength.

The effectiveness of HIT is a result of its fulfillment of the four fundamental requisites for training maximum grip strength explained on page 137. While the other finger-training exercises meet one, two, or three of these requirements, only HIT meets all four. Visit the Nicros.com Training Center for more information on the HIT Strip System and how to build a HIT wall.

Table 7.4 Sample HIT Workouts

Grip Position and Set	HIT Novice— Weight to Add (lbs.)	HIT Expert— Weight to Add (lbs.)	Reps per Set	Rest Between Sets (minutes)
Pinch	0	20	<=20	3
Two-finger third team	0	20	<=20	3
Two-finger second team	10	40	<=20	3
Two-finger first team	10	40	<=20	3
Full crimp	10	40	<=20	3
Half crimp	10	40	<=20	3

Note: *Weights are approximations for a 160-pound climber. Use similar percentages of your own body weight if it's much different. After a few cycles of HIT, you may want to execute two sets using each grip position.*

HIT Workout Tips

1. **Always engage in an extended period of warm-up activities** and bouldering before beginning a HIT workout.

2. **Limit your total hand moves** per set to twenty or fewer (ten or fewer per hand) by adding weight around your waist. Purchase one or more ten-pound weight belts or, alternatively, place several scuba divers' weights into a fanny pack. Do not use a weighted backpack—this weight would be cumbersome and unnatural due to its displacement from your center of gravity.

3. **Climb briskly and without hesitation**—do not stop or pause midset to rest or chalk up. Consider using a spotter so that you can climb confidently up to the point of failure.

4. **Try to climb through the reps with normal foot movements and body turns.** Smaller footholds (about an inch deep) are better, yet giving too much thought to footwork will slow you down—the goal is to train your fingers, not footwork and technique.

5. **Limit rests between sets to exactly three minutes.** Use a stopwatch and stick to the planned order and schedule of exercises. Only this way will you be able to quantify and track your gains in finger strength! If you're sloppy about the length of rests, the numbers become meaningless.

6. **Keep a training book** in which you log the weight added and reps performed for each set. Then you'll always know what weight you need for a given set and can easily track your gains (weight and rep increases) from workout to workout.

7. **Always do your HIT workout in the same order,** and never perform more than two sets per grip position! Performing a third set will provide few added stimuli, but it will dig a deeper hole for you to recover from (requiring more rest days) and add to your risk of injury.

8. **Tape your fingers** (X method) to help protect your tendons and increase skin comfort.

9. **Sand down the HIT Strips** slightly if the texture causes pain that prevents you from completing each set to muscular failure.

10. **Increase rest days** if you find your HIT reps and weights decreasing. If you ever feel weak on the rock after a HIT workout, it's due to insufficient rest—it can take up to three or four days to recover from a HIT workout. Expect initial workouts to require a longer recovery period, whereas your future adaptations will speed recovery to just two or three days.

11. **Cycle on and off HIT every two weeks,** or employ HIT workouts during the three-week maximum-strength phase of the 4-3-2-1 or 3-2-1 Training Cycles (see chapter 8).

Contact Strength Exercises

Contact strength is your ability to quickly grab a hold and stick it. This capacity is directly related to the speed at which you can recruit the forearm's muscular motor units and summon peak strength. While the maximum-strength-training exercises described earlier will yield some improvement in contact strength, reactive training exercises that emphasize speed and shock loading is the optimal method for increasing contact strength. Since fast, dynamic movements are fundamental to effective reactive training, the resistance used (training load) must be significantly less than in the maximum-strength training exercises. For many climbers, the resistance will need to be less than body weight to allow for the rapid movement and turnover (change in direction) that's essential for effective reactive training.

As explained in chapter 5, reactive training is appropriate for only intermediate and advanced climbers with no recent history of finger, elbow, or shoulder injury. Begin with the tamer feet-on exercises (less than body weight) and progress gradually to the feet-off exercises over the course of months or years. A few sets of reactive training will impart all the stimuli that are necessary for favorable adaptations—resist the urge to perform additional sets. Remind yourself that such neural training does not produce extreme fatigue, so if you train to the point of high fatigue, you are doing far too much and tempting injury.

Following are five reactive training exercises listed in order from least stressful (lowest force load and injury risk) to most severe (highest force and injury risk). Controlled One-Arm Traversing and One-Arm Lunging are ideal icebreaker exercises for climbers wishing to add some reactive training to their routines. Both exercises are to be executed on a vertical to slightly overhanging (harder) modular wall, so that each one-arm movement results in a dynamic catch that "shocks" the forearm muscles. Contact strength gains achieved through this form of feet-on "reactive light" training are limited, however—beyond a certain point you will need to graduate to feet-off campus training to stimulate further gains.

ONE-ARM TRAVERSING

One-Arm Traversing is a simple exercise with two big payoffs: increased grip strength and speed of contraction (contact strength). Use this exercise twice per week as a complement to maximum-strength-training exercises such as hypergravity bouldering, heavy finger rolls, and such.

Select a vertical section of an indoor wall with enough room to traverse ten to twenty feet on medium-size handholds and small- to medium-size footholds. Climb up onto the wall so that your feet are just a foot or two off the floor. Now remove one hand from the wall and hold it behind your back. Begin traversing with small, quick lunges from one handhold to the next. Optimal technique is to draw in your body toward the wall and lunge to the next handhold, doing so all in one smooth motion. This drawing-in of the body facilitates a quick grab at the next hold while upward momentum briefly reduces your load—this is commonly called a deadpoint move. Advance your feet onto new footholds as needed to keep your center of gravity over your feet and maintain balance. Continue traversing in this way for eight to twelve total hand moves, and then step off the wall. After a brief rest, step back up on to the wall and traverse the opposite direct using the other hand. Perform two or three One-Arm Traverses with each hand.

As a final note, it's important to perform only small, controlled lunges that allow you to catch the next hold with a slight bend in your elbow. Shoulder and elbow injuries could result from consistently catching lunges with a fully extended arm. Stop using this exercise if you feel pain in your fingers, elbows, or shoulders.

ONE-ARM LUNGING

Once you are proficient at One-Arm Traversing on vertical walls, you can proceed to one-arm up-and-down lunges on a slightly overhanging wall. This exercise is also done feet-on, although the up-and-down motion creates greater dynamic force, especially on the downward catch. This extra stress will trigger further neuromuscular adaptations, and it's a good icebreaker before graduating to campus training.

Select a section of indoor wall that overhangs anywhere from five to twenty-five degrees past vertical—the steeper the wall, the more difficult the exercise—and possesses numerous medium- to large-size hand- and footholds. Ideally you can set a few modular holds specifically for performing this exercise. Set two footholds about a foot off the ground, and then set two nontweaky medium- to large-size handholds, one in front of your face and the other about 2 feet above that.

Climb onto the wall and balance your weight evenly on the two footholds (on a steeper wall it's best to simply stand on the floor, as shown in the photos). Grip the higher of the two handholds with one hand, then let go with the other hand and hold it behind your back. Now drop down, catch the lower handhold, and immediately lunge back up to the higher starting handhold. Continue lunging up and down for eight to twelve total hand movements, then step down off the wall.

After a brief rest, step back up on the wall and perform a set of One-Arm Lunges with the other hand. Perform two or three total sets with each hand. One cautionary note: This exercise dynamically loads all components of the fingers and arms. Proceed with caution, and cease using this exercise if you experience any joint or tendon pain.

One-Arm Lunging

1. Grip the higher handhold.   *2. Drop down to the lower.*   *3. Lunge back to the higher.*

CAMPUS LADDERING

As the name implies, this exercise involves climbing in a hand-over-hand, ladderlike motion up the campus board with no aid from the feet. Unlike Double Dynos (described later), this laddering exercise uses controlled dynamic movements that are less likely to result in injury. Consequently, this is a better staple exercise for regular use, and it is the perfect ice-breaker exercise for climbers new to campus training.

Hang with nearly straight arms from the bottom rung of the campus board. Your hands should be about shoulder width or slightly less apart. Striving for brisk, fluid motion, climb hand-over-hand up the campus board using alternating rungs for your left and right hands. Your goal is to ascend the board as

Overview of Campus Board Training

Campus board training is an invaluable exercise for advanced climbers specializing in bouldering or sport climbing. No matter how naturally strong you are or how hard or often you climb, I speculate that you can quickly add another 10 percent (or more) to your contact strength and power with just a few weeks of campus training. Unfortunately, the dynamic nature of campus training exposes the tendons and joints to potentially dangerous force loads—your fingers, elbows, and shoulders are all at risk. Engage in too much campus training, or experiment with this technique before you are ready, and you will get injured. Here are some important guidelines that will help reduce your risk.

- Engage in campus training only if you are an advanced intermediate to elite climber (leading 5.11 or bouldering V5) with at least three years of climbing experience and no recent history of finger or arm injury. The most stressful Double Dynos exercise must be reserved for only highly conditioned, elite climbers (leading solid 5.12 or bouldering V8).
- Warm up thoroughly. Spend at least an hour performing various warm-up activities and bouldering on increasingly more difficult problems before beginning your campus training.
- Reinforce your finger tendons with a few tight turns of athletic tape. See page 228 for instructions.
- Emphasize speed over volume. Three high-speed, explosive sets are far more beneficial than six sloppy, poorly executed sets with frequent pauses between hand moves.

- Do not campus train while in a state of high fatigue or if you have any doubts about the health of your fingers, arms, or shoulders.
- Immediately terminate your campus training at the first sensation of pain in your joint or tendons.
- Rest a minimum of two days after a campus training workout. Limit yourself to two modest-length sessions per week, and cycle two weeks on and two weeks off.

You will need to build a campus board separate from your home climbing wall, or talk the owner of your local gym into building a campus board if there isn't one already. At home you'll likely be able to only build a modest-size board if you have standard-height ceilings. Since the bottom of the board needs to be around 4 feet off the floor, you'll be limited in the number of rungs you can mount. The plywood board onto which you mount the rungs should be angled at precisely fifteen degrees past vertical. Make or purchase rungs that range in depth from 0.75 inch to 1.5 inches. Mount small rungs about 6 to 8 inches apart; the largest rungs are best spaced about 8 to 12 inches apart. I'd advise you purchase campus rungs from one of the indoor training companies—these rungs are quite affordable, and some companies provide detailed construction plans.

The three primary campus training exercises are Laddering, Lock-Offs, and Double Dynos. Gradually introduce yourself to this new training method over the course of a few months. Begin with laddering during the initial sessions and progress to Lock-Offs and Double Dynos as your strength and confidence allow.

fast as possible. Match hands on the top rung, and then descend carefully by dropping hand-under-hand down alternating rungs to the bottom position.

Perform a total of six to twelve hand moves, never more. To increase difficulty, skip rungs as you hand-over-hand up the board or, if available, use smaller-size rungs. (Laddering on small rungs tends to train contact strength more than upper-body power, whereas longer reaches on larger rungs better isolates one-arm power and lock-off strength.) Rest for three to five minutes before you engage in a second set. Limit yourself to a total of three sets during your initial campus workouts. As you gain conditioning, you can do up to six sets or begin a gradual shift to training with the Double Dynos.

CAMPUS LOCK-OFFS

Campus Lock-Offs, also known as Campus Touches, train contact strength and the one-arm lock-off ability that's often called on for making a long reach on steep climbing terrain.

Begin by hanging with both hands from the bot-

Campus Lock-Offs

1. Hang from a lower rung.

2. Lunge up to grab a high rung.

tom (or second to bottom) rung of the board. Pull up forcefully with both hands, and then in a fast, continuous motion lunge up with one hand to grab the highest rung possible (usually the third, fourth, or fifth rung, depending on the spacing). Engage the high rung for an instant, and then drop back down to the starting hold and lower to the starting (hanging) position. Immediately, pull back up and lunge with the opposite hand to grab a high rung. Again, engage the high rung for a moment, before dropping down to the starting hold and lowering to the starting position. Continue in this alternating fashion for up to twelve total touches (six per hand).

Rest for three to five minutes before you perform another set. Do two to four sets. You can make this exercise much harder by touching, but not grabbing onto, the high hold at the top of each lunge. The goal is to hold the one-arm lock-off position for one second before dropping back down to the bottom position. Hard!

3. Drop back to the lower rung.

4. Lunge up with your other hand.

CAMPUS DOUBLE DYNOS

This dynamic up-and-down, fully airborne exercise is most recognized as true campus training, and it's the most effective at producing neural disinhibition and building maximum contact strength and pulling power. This is also the most stressful and potentially injurious exercise that climbers engage in, since the dynamic double-handed drops generate a force several times your body weight. Are your fingers and tendons ready for this level of stress? It's my belief that the answer is no for over 95 percent of climbers. If you think you are ready for this exercise—are you an elite climber with no recent finger, elbow, or shoulder injuries?—then introduce it gradually and cautiously.

Begin by hanging from the third or fourth rung on the campus board. (It's good to number your rungs beginning with the bottom rung as "number one.") Simultaneously let go with both hands and drop to catch the second rung. Immediately explode upward with both hands to catch the third or fourth (harder) rung. This is one full repetition, but don't stop! Without hesitation, drop down to and again catch the second rung. Explode back up to the third

Campus Double Dynos

1. Hang from the third or fourth rung.

2. Drop down two-handed to the second rung.

or fourth rung. Continue this double-handed, drop-down-and-explode-up sequence for up to six repetitions (up–down couplets). Stop prematurely instead of risking a failed downward catch—and have a bouldering crash pad in place just in case.

Rest for three to five minutes before you engage in a second set. Perform a total of just two or three sets during your formative workouts; however, you can build up to six or eight sets as you gain conditioning and confidence. Limit yourself to just one or two sessions per week, and cycle on and off campus training every two weeks.

A few important training tips: Execute Double Dynos only on rungs that are 0.75 inch or more in depth. In terms of training stimulus, speed of repetitions is more important than the number of reps, distance traveled, or size of rungs. Specifically, strive to turn around the catch on the lower rung and lunge upward in about a quarter of one second (hard, but ideal). And, as stated earlier, it's wise to firmly tape the base of your fingers (use A2 ring method in this case, depicted on page 228). Finally, terminate your campus training at the first sign of pain in your fingers, arms, or shoulders.

3. Immediately explode upward.

4. Catch starting rung and repeat.

Forearm Endurance Exercises

Endurance local to the forearm muscles, physiologically known as anaerobic endurance, is what enables you to hang on and pull through many hard moves in a row. Your ability to persevere through a long sequence of strenuous moves, despite a growing forearm pump, is a function of several attributes including your limit strength, your body's ability to remove blood lactate, and the mind and body's tolerance to the fatiguing effects of lactic acid. Central to the removal of lactic acid is the density of the capillary network that innervates the forearm muscles—the more capillaries are present and the larger their diameter, the faster lactic acid can be cleared from the muscle.

Simply climbing a few days per week is moderately effective for building local endurance. A few of the more popular strategies are climbing laps on routes, interval training on boulder problems, and performing long traverses. As long as your climbing activities produce a muscular burn and pump, you can rest assured that your body will adapt favorably to your endurance training. Following is a full breakdown of the exercises you can use to increase your forearm endurance.

TRAVERSE TRAINING

Traverse training is an effective endurance-building strategy that dates back to John Gill's training in the 1950s. Select a section of cliff base or indoor wall that will allow you to traverse for at least two to four minutes without reaching muscular failure or falling off because of technical difficulties. The ideal traverse will be hard enough to elicit a forearm pump, but not so severe that you pump out and fall off—you actually want to end your traverse before your muscles give out. Upon stepping off the wall, take a rest of about equal length to the time you spent traversing. Do three to five total traverses.

STRAIGHT-ARM FINGERBOARD HANGS

Though it's a very basic exercise, novice climbers can find it quite challenging to attempt to hang from a fingerboard or pull-up bar for a minute or two. An untrained forearm muscle will typically begin to burn from lactic acid accumulation after the first minute, making the second minute an exercise in stretching both the physical and mental boundaries. While you would rarely have to hang out on a single hold this long on a route, this exercise does seem to benefit beginner climbers by increasing forearm endurance and through the developed sense of just how long the forearm will perform while in the burning mode. Persistent hanging in a single position can cause injury in a small number of individuals with loose shoulders as well as in those who are significantly overweight. Cease doing these straight-

Traversing is a popular method for training forearm endurance. Here Front Range icon Christian Griffith gets a pump on at Morrison, Colorado, circa 1998. ERIC J. HÖRST

arm hangs at the first sign of any shoulder pain.

There are two possible training strategies. Many people simply time how long they can hang until muscular failure, then rest for five minutes and repeat for a total of five sets. A better approach would be to employ an interval-training strategy in which you end each interval before reaching muscular failure while decreasing the rest interval. In effect, this will increase the total amount of time you will be hanging and likely produce a better training effect. A true novice would want to do brief intervals—say, hang for twenty seconds then rest for forty seconds, and repeat ten to twenty times. As endurance improves, graduate to using the Tabata Protocol (see page 94) in which you hang for 20 seconds and then rest for just 10 seconds. Repeat this hang-rest interval for a total of six to eight sets before taking an extended rest of two to five minutes. You can then repeat the Tabata with two to five other gripping positions—a heck of a forearm endurance workout!

One important safety tip for Straight-Arm Hangs: Maintain tension in your shoulders by consciously contracting the muscles surrounding the joint—this will help protect the shoulder from injury.

FINGERBOARD MOVING HANGS

This exercise allows you to work the board continuously for several minutes, much like climbing a long sustained sequence on the rock. Doing this requires somewhere to place your feet while your hands circulate around the board using the grip–relax repeating sequence (GRRS). The best way to do this is to mount your fingerboard so that it's set a foot or two out from a wall onto which you have mounted a few small footholds. Another possibility is to hang the board above a doorway, then position a chair or stool a couple of feet behind the board. Either way, you will be able to use your toes for support as you circulate your hands around the fingerboard.

Perform a twenty- to thirty-minute warm-up comprising some aerobic activity, stretching, and some pull-ups and easy hangs on the fingerboard. You should break a light sweat and feel a slight pump in your arms.

Fingerboard moving hang with feet on wall.

Mount the board and then place your feet on footholds or on the edge of a chair. Begin moving your hands around the fingerboard, changing hand positions every three to five seconds. After a minute or two, you will begin to develop a pump in your forearms. Move both hands on to the largest handholds on the board, and shake out each arm for about thirty seconds in an attempt to recovery a little. After this brief shakeout, continue moving your hands around the board for another minute or two. Once again, move to the large holds if you need to shake out and rest your muscles a little. Continue in this fashion with the goal of staying on the board for a total of five to ten minutes. Dismount the board, and take a rest of about ten minutes before proceeding with a second and third set.

BOULDERING AND ROUTE CLIMBING INTERVALS

This is one of the most effective exercises for building forearm endurance, and it should be a staple of every serious climber's workout program. As the name implies, climbing intervals involves repeating laps on a moderately difficult boulder problem or climb. The training protocol is to alternate climbing burns with rest intervals, much like the interval training performed by runners. The rest phase should be roughly proportionate to the length of the climbing phase. Therefore, if your climbing phase involves sending a ten-move boulder problem (which might take about thirty seconds), you'd want to take a rest of only thirty seconds to, at most, one minute between burns. A longer climbing phase, such as lapping a steep sport climb or moving around your home wall for four minutes, should be followed by a similarly long rest. The climbing-to-rest ratio should be between 1:1 and 1:2.

Select a boulder problem or route that will be strenuous, yet at a level of difficulty that you will be able to successfully ascend several times. It's also important that the route is void of tweaky holds or severe moves that might be injurious when climbed repeatedly and in an increasing state of fatigue.

Climb the route, and then begin a rest period that's about equal to the length of time you were climbing. Resting any more than double the length of the climbing phase will diminish the training effect. Use a stopwatch so you stay within these guidelines.

After the rest period, begin your next interval. Climb the boulder problem or route and then take the prescribed rest break. Continue with these climbing intervals until you can no longer complete the boulder problem or climb. If you can successfully perform more than five intervals, then select a slightly more strenuous climb for your next workout.

A most important training aid is a climbing partner to join you in this workout—your partner will climb during your rest breaks, and vice versa. The camaraderie and encouragement will help you hang on through the increasing pump and pain of interval training.

HIT OR SYSTEM WALL INTERVAL TRAINING

The HIT Strip platform or a specialized System Wall can also be used to train anaerobic endurance via an interval-training strategy. This requires an approach that's completely different from the HIT maximum-strength workout described earlier. The goal now is to climb thirty to sixty total hand moves with only brief rest periods and no weight added to your body. For most climbers, it will be impossible to climb enough hand movements using the weaker pinch and two-finger pocket third team on the HIT system. Therefore, I suggest you train two different general finger positions: the two-finger pocket (in which you cycle through all three two-finger teams) and crimp (in which you alternate full- and half-crimp as you climb). Perform a comprehensive warm-up of moderate climbing and stretching before engaging in this form of isolation training. Moreover, it's important to tape your middle and rings fingers (use the X method shown on page 228) so that you won't have to stop prematurely due to skin pain.

Train two-finger pocket endurance first. Sit on the floor below the first HIT Strip or pair of System Holds, and then grab onto the lowest pair of pocket holds using the two-finger third team. Begin laddering upward by grabbing alternating strips with the left and right hand. Upon reaching the top strip, immediately reverse the sequence back down the wall. Climb with open feet (use any footholds you like) and allow your body to naturally twist and turn to provide optimal position. Use the two-finger pocket third team for as many hand moves as possible, then switch to the second team and finally the first team. Continue laddering up and down for thirty to sixty total hand moves.

Rest for two or three minutes, and then commence with a high-rep set using just the full- and half-crimp grips. Again, strive for a total of thirty to sixty repetitions. Upon completing the two sets, take a five-minute rest. Consider repeating the above sequence one or two more times. This should result in a deep pump and lactic acid burn—a highly specific and effective local endurance workout!

THE TABATA PROTOCOL

As introduced in chapter 5, the Tabata Protocol is not an exercise per se, but instead a highly specific method of interval training that can be applied to a wide variety of exercises and activities. Research has shown this protocol to be uncommonly effective in training both the anaerobic and aerobic pathways, despite what is a small time investment in training (Tabata 1997). In the context of training forearm endurance, the Tabata couples twenty seconds of maximum-intensity climbing with a ten-second rest interval. This climb–rest couplet is repeated up to eight times before any addition rest is taken. The result is four minutes of forearm-pumping, finger-cramping exercise!

Following is one application of the Tabata Protocol for training anaerobic endurance of the forearm muscles on the HIT System. You can also apply this same training strategy to other climbing exercises such as Heavy Finger Rolls, Straight-Arm Fingerboard Hangs, and Lat Pull-Downs.

Sit on the floor below the first HIT Strip, and then grab onto the lowest HIT Strip using either the two-finger pocket or crimp-grip holds. Begin the first twenty-second work interval by briskly laddering up and down using alternating HIT Strips. Most climbers achieve about fifteen hand moves (1.5 laps on the strips) in twenty seconds, but you'll need to determine exactly how many hand moves you can do in twenty seconds. Rest for exactly ten seconds, and then resume climbing up and down the HIT Strips for another twenty seconds. Climb with open feet (use any footholds you like) and allow your body to naturally twist and turn to provide optimal position. Rest again for exactly ten seconds, and then begin your third twenty-second climbing interval. Continue for six to eight total intervals, which will take three or four minutes, respectively. Rest for five minutes before you ponder a second HIT System Tabata!

Remember, the efficacy of the Tabata Protocol depends on precise work and rest intervals and maximum exertion. Stick to the schedule exactly—the ten-second rest is barely enough to quickly rechalk your hands and reposition below the first HIT Strip. Similarly, the climbing intervals should be intense and exactly twenty seconds in length. If you aren't exhausted and gasping for breath by the seventh and eighth intervals, then you need to add a ten- or twenty-pound weight belt to simulate hypergravity for future sessions. Finally, vary the grip position you use every set to help you persevere through the Tabata, and consider taping your fingers to limit skin wear and pain. Do no more than two Tabata sequences per workout, and limit use of Tabata to just two days per week.

Enlist a partner to time (use a stopwatch) exact work–rest intervals of twenty and ten seconds, respectively. Have your partner call out the "start" and "stop" points for each interval over the four-minute Tabata. Upon completing your four minutes of training, switch roles and direct your partner through the arduous four minutes—it's payback time!

Pull-Muscle Training

In this section you will learn how to train for maximum strength, power, and anaerobic endurance in the large pulling muscles that help propel you upward and enable static lock-off positions. While the standard pull-up has long been a staple exercise for climbers, its effectiveness is greatly limited for anyone beyond novice ability. Upon reaching a modest level of pull-up strength—can you do fifteen to twenty pull-ups?—it becomes more important to train lock-off ability, one-arm strength, and raw power. Following are details on sixteen exercises for training the large pulling muscles of the upper arms, shoulders, and back.

Maximum-Strength Exercises

As in building maximum finger strength, training to increase pulling and lock-off strength requires high-intensity stimulus that will produce rapid muscular failure. This is a vastly different workout strategy from that described for building anaerobic endurance (in which you want to *avoid* muscular failure). Revisit the training methodology described in chapter 5 if you need clarification of the ideal protocols for training maximum strength, power, and endurance. Described below are six exercises for training maximum strength.

Table 7.5 Classification of Pull-Muscle Exercises

		Beginner	Intermediate	Advanced
Maximum Strength	Pull-Ups (or lat pull-down machine)	✓	✓	✓
	Aided Pull-Ups	✓		
	Hypergravity Pull-Ups		✓	✓
	Uneven-Grip Pull-Ups		✓	✓
	Steep-Wall Lock-Offs		✓	✓
	One-Arm Lock-Offs			✓
Power	Power Pull-Up		✓	✓
	Big-Move Bouldering		✓	✓
	Inverted Ladder Climbing		✓	✓
	Campus Training		✓	✓
	Feet-Off Bouldering			✓
Anaerobic Endurance	Slow-Motion Pull-ups	✓	✓	✓
	Pull-Up Intervals	✓	✓	✓
	Frenchies		✓	✓
	Enduro Steep-Wall Lock-Offs		✓	✓
	System Wall Training		✓	✓

PULL-UPS AND LAT PULL-DOWNS

As mentioned above, pull-ups are the most obvious exercise for climbers, and they are highly effective for beginner-level climbers. If you are unable to do a single set of fifteen pull-ups, then you should make pull-ups a staple exercise that you engage in three days per week. Perform your pull-ups on a bar, the bucket hold of a fingerboard, or a set of free-hanging Pump Rocks. Use the Aided Pull-Up method described below if you are unable to do at least eight pull-ups.

Mount the bar or board with your hands in a palms-away position (the way you usually grip the rock) and about shoulder width apart. Pull up at a relatively fast rate in order to reach the top position in one second or less. Pause at the top position for just a moment, and then lower yourself to a two-second count. Subvocalize *one thousand one, one thousand two*. Upon reaching the bottom position, imme-

diately begin your next pull-up. Continue in this fashion until you can no longer perform a complete pull-up.

Do three to five sets with a rest interval of at least three minutes between sets. As your pull-up strength improves, begin to vary the distance between your hands to better simulate the wide range of hand positions you'll encounter in climbing. Switch to Hypergravity Pull-Ups (described below) when you are able to do three sets of fifteen or more pull-ups.

AIDED PULL-UPS

Use the Aided Pull-Up if you can not do at least three sets of eight pull-ups. The strategy is simply to have a spotter hold you around your waist and lift a portion of your body weight so that you can do eight to twelve less-than-body-weight pull-ups. Use this exercise three days per week, and soon you'll be doing pull-ups on your own!

Mount the bar or hangboard with your hands in a palms-away position and about shoulder width apart. With the spotter standing behind you and holding lightly around your waist, begin doing pull-ups with the spotter providing help only on the upward phase. Pause for a moment at the top position, and then lower yourself to a slow two-second count. The spotter should let go during the down phase so that you are lowering your full body weight. Continue doing pull-ups in this manner until you reach eight to twelve total repetitions. Rest for five minutes and then perform two more sets.

Eventually you'll find that doing the same pull-up training becomes monotonous and provides little additional gain in climbing strength. At this point it's best to employ one of the following variations on the pull-up, or even to cut back on pull-ups, replacing them with other pull-muscle exercises on the pages that follow.

HYPERGRAVITY PULL-UPS

As your pull-up ability improves, you will need to add resistance to continue training maximum strength. Remember, pull-ups in sets of more than about ten reps will train muscular endurance more than strength. Fortunately you can employ the hypergravity training technique described earlier to train for higher levels of pull-ups strength. Weighted pull-ups are a simple yet highly effective way to notch up your training and strength gains! Wearing a ten-pound weight belt (or more) while doing your pull-up training will trigger the neuromuscular system to adapt to your higher apparent body weight. Upon returning to the rock to climb at body weight, you will feel noticeably lighter and climb stronger given this newfound überstrength. Here's how to do it.

Attach a ten-pound weight belt around your waist. Extremely fit individuals may need to use a twenty-pound belt or a heavy weight vest. Grip a pull-up bar in the palms-away position or use the largest holds on a fingerboard. Your hands should be about shoulder width apart. Pull up at a relatively fast rate in order to reach the top position in one sec-

Hypergravity pull-up with a sixty-pound vest.

ond or less. Pause at the top position for just a moment, and then lower to a two-second count. Subvocalize *one one thousand, two one thousand.* Upon reaching the bottom position immediately begin your next pull-up. Continue in this fashion until you can no longer perform a complete pull-up.

Perform two to four sets with a rest interval of at least three minutes between sets. Increase the weight added by ten pounds when you are able to do three sets of twelve repetitions. One important safety note: Do not hang in the straight-arm position to rest between repetitions—this is extremely stressful on the shoulders. Stop using weighted pull-ups if you sense any unusual pain in your shoulders or elbow.

UNEVEN-GRIP PULL-UPS

This is an excellent exercise for developing one-arm strength and lock-off ability. Train with Uneven Grip Pull-Ups long enough and you'll eventually develop the rare ability to do a One-Arm Pull-Up. This exercise requires a setup that offsets one hand 12 to 24 inches lower than the other. You can loop a sling over a pull-up bar or extend one of a pair of free-floating Pump Rocks.

Begin with your hands offset vertically by about 18 inches. Pull up with a focus on pulling hardest with the high hand. As you ascend to the height of your lower hand, begin pushing downward (think

mantle) with it to continue in aiding further upward motion. Continue to pull up with your high hand until it is drawn in tight against the front of your shoulder. Lower to a two-second count in returning to the start position, then immediately begin the next repetition. Continue in this manner until you can no longer pull up the whole way with your high hand. Rest for a minute or two, and then switch hands to train the opposite side. Perform two or three sets on each side with the goal of five to ten repetitions per set. Increase the vertical distance between hands if you can do more than ten reps; decrease the distance if you cannot do at least five repetitions.

Uneven Grip Pull-Up

1. Pull mostly with your higher hand.

2. Lock off on higher hand, lower, repeat.

This exercise is highly functional in that the strength gains will transfer completely to the rock. Although you will perform this exercise on an overhanging bouldering wall, the goal is not to actually climb a problem. Instead, you will be performing repeated One-Arm Lock-Offs while using the same hand- and footholds. This is very similar to the lock-off exercise described above in the campus training section, although it's less dynamic and allows for use of your feet on the wall. This way, you can turn and tense your body as needed to facilitate a solid, efficient lock-off position. Such extreme specificity is what

makes for the high level of transfer to the rock.

Execute this exercise on an overhanging wall that's between thirty and fifty degrees past vertical. Begin in a sit-down position below the wall so that you can grip onto two similar starting holds. A deep, positive hold or an incut HIT Strip or System Hold is best, since the goal of this exercise is to train lock-off endurance, not your grip. Place your feet on any two holds on the kickboard at the base of the wall and lift your rear end off the floor. This is your starting position.

Now pull up on the handholds and lock off one arm, so that you can reach up with the other hand

Steep-Wall Lock-Off

1. Reach upward while locking off one arm.

2. Hold, then drop back down.

Climbing-Specific Exercises

to touch—not grab onto—a hold at full arm reach. Allow your body to twist and tense as needed to make the lock-off solid. Hold this lock-off position for two seconds, before dropping back to the starting position. Immediately pull back up and lock off on the same arm. Hold this lock-off for two seconds, then return to the starting position. Continue this lock-off-and-reach motion with the same arm locking off for a total of six to twelve repetitions. Use large hand- and foot-holds if you cannot do at least six lock-offs, whereas you will need to add weight (ten-pound weight belt) if you can do more than twelve lock-offs.

Rest for a minute or two, then perform a set with the other arm locking off. After training each arm you'll want to take a five-minute rest before performing a second set with each arm.

ONE-ARM LOCK-OFFS

The ability to hold a steady one-arm lock-off is vital for hard bouldering and roped climbing. This exercise is obviously very specific to this need—but it does demand a high level of base strength for proper execution. If you cannot hold a solid one-arm lock-off, it would be best to train with Hypergravity Pull-Ups or Uneven-Grip Pull-Ups instead of this exercise.

Begin with both hands grasping the top of a single Pump Rock. If you plan to lock off on your left arm, for example, place your right hand on top of your left—but with your right hand grabbing from the opposite side of the Pump Rock. Using a pull-up bar, grip the bar with your hands side by side and the palms facing each other. Pull up into the lock-off position, and then immediately let go with the top hand (in this case the right). Hold the static lock-off position as long as possible, ideally for between five and fifteen seconds (hard). It helps to think about pulling the Pump Rock toward your armpit. When you begin to lose the lock-off, either grab back on with the other hand or lower yourself slowly to the straight-arm position. Take caution not to drop yourself rapidly into the straight-arm position!

Dismount and rest for one minute before executing a one-arm lock-off in the same fashion with the other arm. After executing one lock-off with each

One-arm lock-off.

arm, take a three-minute rest before performing another one-arm lock with each arm. Do a total of two to four lock-offs with each hand.

Power-Training Exercises

When climbers talk about power, they are typically referring to the need to make quick, strenuous reaches or handhold grasps on steep terrain. This type of movement is the stuff of steep sport climbs and V-hard boulder problems.

Physiologically, your ability to move powerfully is a function of how fast muscular motor units can be called into play and how well they are trained to fire in unison. Effective power-training exercises must then target the nervous system with fast, dynamic motions that are far different from the strength- and endurance-training exercises covered in this chapter. Inherent to power training are high dynamic force loads, which provide beneficial training stimuli but also threaten the joints and tendons of the fingers, arms, and shoulders. For this reason, the following power-training exercises are inappropriate for beginner or recently injured climbers, as well as anyone lacking the maturity and discipline to follow the training and rest guidelines.

Adequate rest between power exercises and workout sessions is also crucial. As a rule you should not engage in more than two power workouts per week. Furthermore, individual workouts should be relatively brief: Training intensity and speed are more important than training volume. In fact, performing a high volume of power exercises (or training power more than twice per week) is a prescription for injury. Constantly remind yourself that in training power, *less is more.*

POWER PULL-UPS

This simple power-building exercise can be performed on any pull-up bar or fingerboard. Initially, you may train power exclusively by doing a few sets with this exercise; or you could just do a single set as a sort of power warm-up before executing one of the other exercises described below.

Grip a pull-up bar or the largest holds on a fingerboard in the palms-away position. Your hands should be about shoulder width apart. Now explode upward with the goal of doing the upward phase of the pull-up as fast as possible. Pause at the top position for an instant, and then lower to the starting position at a slightly slower rate. Upon reaching the bottom position, immediately explode upward with the next pull-up. Strive to rapidly change directions slightly before your arms reach full extension—this rapid turnover is essential to optimal training. Never drop forcefully onto straight arms and cease using this exercise if you experience any elbow or shoulder pain. Continue with these explosive pull-ups for a total of five to ten repetitions. Do not do more than ten reps, regardless of the feeling that you could continue on with the exercise. Rest for three minutes before doing a second and third set.

BIG-MOVE BOULDER PROBLEMS

If you are an avid boulderer, then you are likely already using this training strategy. The goal is to climb several powerful six- to ten-move boulder problems that demand full effort in throwing and sticking several big moves. The ideal route will feature mostly positive, medium-size holds that will not test your grip strength—the goal here is long, powerful movements that fully call into play the pulling and lock-off muscles. Moreover, the climbing movements do not need to be all-out lunges, but instead controlled, powerful reaches between reasonably good holds. When you find the right route (or set it), try to send it five times with about a three-minute rest between sends.

INVERTED LADDER AND ROPE CLIMBING

Rope or ladder climbing is one of the very best ways to develop awesome upper-body power. Legendary boulderer John Gill used rope climbing as a staple training exercise, and years later John Bachar popularized inverted ladder training among climbers. The Bachar Ladder, as it became known, was a popular training exercise of high-end climbers throughout the 1980s. Since the advent of indoor climbing walls, however, rope and ladder climbing have fallen largely out of use. Still, serious climbers would be wise to incorporate some rope or ladder climbing into their training program. Both apparati provide for feet-off, campuslike movements, thus requiring a high level of base strength to execute. The equipment needs are either a 1.5-inch manila gym rope or a homemade inverted rope ladder.

After a lengthy warm-up of pull-ups and mild upper-body stretching, begin from either a standing or sit-down (harder) position. Grip either the rope or ladder rung with both arms at near-full extension. With an explosive two-arm pull, begin climbing up the rope or ladder in a fast, smooth, yet dynamic motion. The goal is to maintain steady upward motion for the duration of the ascent, although it will likely take some time to develop this ability. Upon reaching the top, slowly lower yourself down arm-over-arm in a smooth, controlled motion; do not drop down in a fast, jerky manner that will shock-load the elbows and shoulders. Dismount the rope or ladder—do not climb additional distance without a rest.

Rest for three to five minutes before you make your next climb. Perform three to five total laps on the rope or ladder, always taking an adequate rest so that you can make a quality effort. Highly conditioned individuals should strive to increase the speed of ascent instead of doing additional sets. As with all high-intensity exercises, it's best to cycle on and off this exercise every few weeks. Only use Bachar Ladders constructed with static rope. Stop rope or ladder training if you feel any pain in your elbows or shoulders.

CAMPUS TRAINING

As described in the contact strength section earlier in this chapter, campus training is a highly effective reactive training method for developing raw power. Use of the campus training exercises described on pages 149–53 will build power in your large pull muscles as well as your fingers. So in using these exercises, you are getting a training two-for-one—that is, training contact strength and pulling power! Still, campus training is appropriate only for fit, healthy intermediate to advanced climbers. Proceed with caution!

FEET-OFF BOULDERING

Often called campusing, this is another popular indoor training exercise among advanced boulderers. The goal is simply to ascend a section of overhanging wall by climbing hand-over-hand with no use of the feet. Such no-feet climbing is extremely difficult and certainly an elite-only training method. As in the big-move bouldering described above, select six to ten move problems with medium to large holds that are void of sharp, tweaky features. An appropriate training goal is to do five feet-off ascents with a three- to five-minute rest between ascents.

The author on his Bachar ladder, circa 1990. HÖRST COLLECTION

Endurance-Training Exercises

Detailed in this section are five of the more grueling exercises in the book. Training anaerobic endurance requires repeated, sustained bouts of exercise of a length and intensity that will elicit a significant release of lactic acid. These exercises are designed to do just that, and the result of doing each will be a wicked muscular pump and the hallmark burn of lactic acid. Of course, the payoff is that your body will respond to this stimulus in ways that will gradually improve anaerobic endurance and, thus, your ability to climb at a high intensity for an extended period.

SLOW-MOTION PULL-UPS

These are, as the name implies, regular pull-ups performed in slow motion. Take five seconds to go up, and come down to a slow count of ten. Your goal is to perform between four and eight pull-ups, which will take between one and two minutes. Terminate the exercise, however, before you reach failure. Attempt to do three sets with only a three-minute rest between sets.

PULL-UP INTERVALS

This is a great exercise that trains the pull muscles to persevere during periods of elevated blood lactate. The goal here is to complete twenty Pull-Up Intervals that each comprise a set number of pull-ups and a rest period for a total of exactly one minute (aggregate). Use a stopwatch or clock with a second hand so that you can stay on an exact training schedule.

Start the stopwatch, mount the pull-up bar or fingerboard (use the bucket holds), and immediately commence doing five pull-ups. Strive for a smooth, steady pace that takes about

two seconds for each complete repetition. After five pull-ups, dismount and rest for the remainder of the one-minute interval.

At the one-minute mark, begin your next set of five pull-ups. Upon completion of the fifth pull-up, dismount and rest for the remainder of the second

Feet-off bouldering is an advanced method for training power.

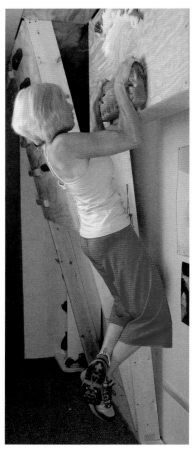

1. Lock off at top position.   *2. Lock off at ninety degrees.*   *3. Lock off at 120 degrees.*

one-minute-long pull-up interval. Continue performing these five-repetition, one-minute intervals for a total of ten to twenty minutes. If you make it to ten minutes, you will have completed fifty pull-ups in aggregate—a pretty good intermediate-level pull-up workout. If you make it the full twenty minutes, add one more pull-up per set next time. If you cannot make it to at least the ten-minute mark, however, reduce the number of pull-ups per set to just three or four.

FRENCHIES

These babies may be the best anaerobic endurance pull-muscle exercise on the planet! Not only will they fry your muscles with a wicked lactic acid burn, but you will notice a marked improvement in your pull-up and lock-off ability after just a few weeks of training. The efficacy of this exercise results from the unique combination of isometric contractions superimposed over the pull-up motion.

Begin with a single pull-up (palms away, hands

shoulder width apart) and lock off in the top position for a five-second count. Now lower to the bottom and pull up to the top again, but this time immediately lower yourself halfway down to an arm angle of ninety degrees. Hold a solid lock-off here for a five-second count, then lower yourself to the bottom. Immediately crank another pull-up, but this time lower to a lock-off with an arm angle of about 120 degrees. Again hold for five seconds, then lower to the bottom position. This sequence of three lock-offs constitutes a single cycle, but you should continue on with another cycle (or more) until you can no longer pull up. Record the number of cycles (or partial cycles) in your training notebook as you take a five-minute rest. Do a total of two or three sets.

Use bungee cords or a spotter to remove some body weight if you cannot do at least two full cycles per set. Conversely, you should add a ten- or twenty-pound weight belt once you are able to do five full cycles in any given set.

ENDURO STEEP-WALL LOCK-OFFS

This exercise is identical to the Steep-Wall Lock-Offs described on page 161, except that you will alternate arms with each lock-off you make. This way the muscles on each side get a brief rest while the other side is performing a lock-off. This training strategy will allow you to train much longer (compared with performing the lock-off on the same side, as in the strength-training strategy earlier) and therefore train anaerobic endurance in the crucial lock-off muscles. Your training goal is a total of twenty to fifty lock-offs, which will result in between one to two minutes of exhaustive exercise. Use larger hand- and footholds or a less overhanging wall if you cannot do at least twenty total lock-offs.

Take a rest break, and then perform a second and third set. The length of rest to take will depend on your level of conditioning. For initial training sessions, take up to a five-minute rest between sets. As your conditioning improves, reduce your rest to as little as one minute—an elite-level anaerobic endurance workout!

SYSTEM WALL TRAINING

System Wall Training is one of the best comprehensive training methods available to climbers. While it's not the best method of training absolute finger strength, it does provide a highly specific workout of the entire body—from the fingers to the toes—that will develop functional strength in the crucial muscles of the arms, upper body, and core. The efficacy of System Training results from its ability to fatigue a specific combination of grip and arm position while you perform actual climbing movements up a steep wall. For instance, you can lap a System Wall using only the undercling arm position and the open-hand grip position, or you could climb the wall using identical side-pull arm positions and half-crimp grip positions. On a well-built System Wall, there are many other possibilities.

The base wall for System Training should be at least 6 feet wide, 8 to 10 feet in length, and at an angle of between twenty and thirty degrees past vertical. Still, it's the type and arrangement of holds that make System Training work. You need to obtain (or make) a large number of identical holds that can be mounted symmetrically to enable training of all the different finger and arm positions (introduced earlier in this chapter). The best bet would be to purchase eight to twelve system holds that can be mounted in pairs side by side and at shoulder width going up the wall. You could also use matching modular holds or cut different-size blocks of wood to create a variety of routes up your wall. Regardless of the hold type, space the identical pairs of holds about 15 to 20 inches apart so you can move up and down them in a ladderlike sequence. Complete the wall with a variety of small footholds scattered about—again, the ideal setup would possess perfect symmetry of both hand- and footholds.

There are many creative ways to train on a System Wall, but the most fundamental is to climb the wall while isolating a specific combination of grip and arm positions. As shown in figure 7.2, there are many possible permutations of grip and arm positions to train. One training strategy would be to do a single set (one up-and-down lap) using each grip–arm couplet. Another strategy would be to do sev-

Figure 7.2 System Training Permutations

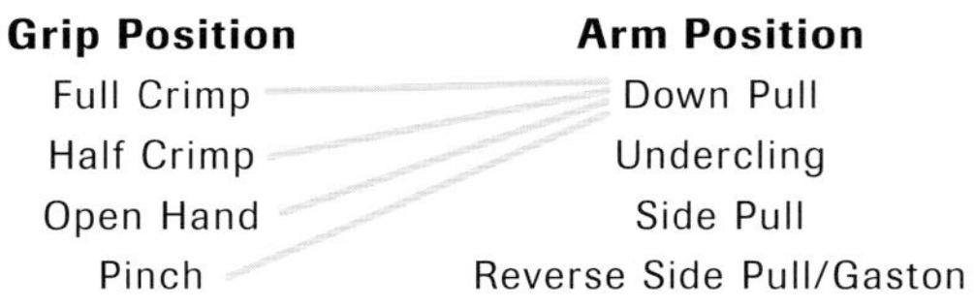

Grip Position	Arm Position
Full Crimp	Down Pull
Half Crimp	Undercling
Open Hand	Side Pull
Pinch	Reverse Side Pull/Gaston

Work up to sixteen permutations of grip and arm positions.

eral sets that train a specific grip–arm pair that's either a known weakness or common feature on some project you are working.

In System Training it's important to leverage the knowledge you gained in reading chapter 5. If you lack anaerobic endurance, for instance, use larger hand- and footholds that will allow you to lap the System Wall a few times (in other words, shoot for twenty to fifty total hand movements). To train pure strength, however, you would want to climb on smaller holds and with more difficult arm positions that produce failure in ten to twenty hand moves (five to ten per arm). Rest between sets for at least two to three minutes. Finally, keep a training log in which you detail the exact positions and holds used, the number of reps and sets, and the amount of rest between sets. This will help maintain motivation as well as quantify your strength gains.

Complex Training

Complex training is a cutting-edge training method used by elite athletes in many sports, including most power-oriented Olympic events. Applied to climbing, the complex training protocol described below is one of the most advanced strength-training concepts available. Since introducing complex training in the first edition of *Training for Climbing* in 2002, I have heard from countless climbers around the world who have leveraged this technique to increase their grip strength and upper-body power. You can, too, as long as you are a relatively advanced climber (solidly 5.11 or V5) with no recent history of finger, elbow, or shoulder injuries.

Complex training involves a coupling of a high-resistance, maximum-strength exercise with a power-oriented, high-speed exercise. Research has shown that performing these two very different exercises back-to-back—and in the order of strength first, power second—produces gains in strength and power beyond those achieved by performing either exercise alone.

Incorporating complex training into your program can be done several different ways; the key is the back-to-back coupling of a maximum-strength exercise and a power exercise (see table 7.6). To get started, you might climb a very fingery near-maximal boulder problem and then immediately do a set of One-Arm Lunges with each hand. Taking things up a notch, you could send a hard boulder problem with a ten-pound weight belt around your waist and then immediately ladder hand-over-hand up a campus board (sans weight belt). To up the ante further, you could do a Hypergravity Isolation Training set (with ten to forty pounds around the waist), then immediately perform a set of Double Dynos on the campus board (at body weight). This later strategy of combining HIT and a reactive-training exercise like campus training should be a staple technique of elite climbers, and it may represent the single best training protocol for pursuing absolute genetic potential for finger strength and upper-body power. Begin by doing just three coupled sets; increase to a maximum of six to eight coupled sets over the course of a few months. Rest for five minutes between sets.

Obviously, complex training is an advanced technique that produces both high passive stress and high dynamic stress. It should thus be utilized only by well-conditioned climbers with no recent history of injury. Furthermore, its use should be limited to once every three or four days, and it should be cycled on and off about every two weeks. Finally, complete recovery from a complex workout could take as long as three to five days. Any other strenuous training or climbing during the supercompensation period would slow recovery and may limit the benefits of complex training.

Table 7.6 Complex Training Combinations
(pick one exercise from each column and perform back-to-back)

Maximum-Strength Exercise	Power Exercise
• Heavy Finger Rolls (p. 142)	• One-Arm Lunging (p. 147)
• Hypergravity Pull-Ups (p. 159)	• Campus Laddering (p. 149)
• Hypergravity Bouldering (p. 139)	• Campus Lock-Offs (p. 150)
• HIT Strip Training (p. 144)	• Feet-Off Bouldering (p. 164)
	• Campus Double Dynos (p. 152)

Designing Your Training Program

Action without thought is a form of insanity; thought without action is a crime.

—*Albert Einstein*

For much of the twentieth century, the American climbing scene was dominated by eccentric, alternative types who, as a rule, rejected conventional styles of living and recreation. While this renegade bunch pushed the limits of difficulty and boldness on the rock, they were hardly of a mind-set that would consider doing any supplemental training (other than drinking!). In fact, the handful of individuals who did train, outside of climbing itself, were viewed with amusement and even called "cheaters" by a few traditionalists.

This all changed in the 1980s and 1990s as climbing went mainstream. Supplemental training just seemed natural to the large number of individuals entering climbing with backgrounds in other sports. At the same time, a growing number of elite climbers trained fervently while pushing the envelope of difficulty on the rocks. Suddenly the masses of climbers "got it"—there was indeed a causal connection between sport-specific training and climbing ability! Of course, John Gill exemplified this way back in the 1950s.

Today most serious climbers perform supplemental training, and tens of thousands of beginner and

*Andy Raether on the first ascent of **Gutless Wonder** (5.14b), Puoux, Colorado.* KEITH LADZINSKI

intermediate climbers are enamored of the idea of training to climb harder. Commercial climbing gyms have opened in almost every major city, and home training walls are now viewed as a necessity among serious climbers. Consequently, there is a growing need for information on how to structure a training program and effectively integrate it with indoor and outdoor climbing activities. This, of course, is the purpose of this chapter—to help you craft a safe and effective training program given your current fitness level and climbing ability.

Before getting started, we'll take a look at the keys to designing an effective program. You will learn the value in premeditating your workout, the importance of targeting your weaknesses, and the ways to sustain motivation and provide a peaking effect. Next up, you will learn how to structure your program to include microcycles, mesocycles, and an annual macrocycle—this form of periodization is essential to making the most of your daily workouts and obtaining maximal gains season after season. With this understanding you will be empowered to craft a highly effective training program, according to your current ability level—this chapter provides detailed guidance for designing a beginner-, intermediate-, and elite-level program. The chapter then concludes with some unique training considerations for youth, female, and over-fifty climbers.

Keys to an Effective Training Program

The premise of this book is that a well-informed, motivated, and mature individual can grow to climb at an exceedingly high level in just a few years. The preceding chapters provided a comprehensive look at the fundamental elements of climbing perform-

Figure 8.1 Training Goals

An ideal training program will optimize conditioning in these five areas.

ance—mental, technical, and physical—and you've also been armed with the knowledge of an introspective self-assessment test. You are now in a position to execute an uncommonly effective training program—one that will help you outperform the masses! To do so, the program must be designed to optimize your body composition, improve flexibility, increase antagonist-muscle conditioning, enhance stamina and recovery ability, and increase climbing-specific strength, power, and endurance (see figure 8.1).

Premeditate Your Training

The mass of people who engage in some form of conditioning program do so in a haphazard, ad-lib manner. There is little or no method to their madness other than to "climb a lot" and "get pumped." This unsystematic approach will produce mediocre results and can often end in injury.

Conversely, savvy climbers are proactive in designing and modifying their training program for maximum effectiveness. Wisely, the program targets their weaknesses, is modified regularly to stave off mental or physical stagnation, and is crafted in a way

to produce a peaking effect for an upcoming road trip or competition.

TARGET YOUR WEAKNESSES

Several times throughout this book, I've highlighted the importance of training the weakest link. For many climbers this weakest link involves poor technique, tactics, and mental control. While the unintelligent climber trains only for more physical strength, you know that it's paramount to train your weaknesses in all aspects of the performance triad. The amount of time you dedicate to training technique, the mind, and physical strength depends on both the results of your self-assessment and your current ability level.

As a rough rule of thumb, beginner and intermediate climbers should focus about 70 percent of their training time on improving technique, tactics, and the mental game. For these climbers, only 30 percent of their training time should be invested in general and sport-specific conditioning. Conversely, elite climbers (who possess highly honed technical skills) would be wise to invest much more training time in the pursuit of maximizing strength, power, and anaerobic endurance.

MANIPULATE THE WORKOUT TO "CONFUSE" THE BODY AND INCREASE MOTIVATION

Chapter 5 explained the importance of regularly modifying your training for climbing. Sadly, many individuals go through the same basic workout ritual week after week and get frustrated with their lack of progress. Furthermore, engaging in the same weekday training or weekend at the crags will slowly quell your motivation to work hard and push beyond your current limits.

Clearly, an intelligently designed program must regularly vary the focus of your training and climbing. In the gym it's vital to vary the fundamental details of workout intensity, volume, length, and the amount of rest between sets (or climbs). On the rock motivation and achievement often come in proportion to your willingness to try new types of climbing, visit new areas, and test the limits of what is possible (given your current ability). Later in this chapter you will learn how to use a ten-week mesocycle and fifty-two-week macrocycle to optimize the effectiveness of your training-for-climbing program.

PRODUCE A PEAKING EFFECT FOR A ROAD TRIP OR COMPETITION

Olympic and professional athletes design their training schedules to produce a peaking phase around the time of a major event or competition. No doubt some of the best competition climbers also use peaking strategies; I sense, however, that the majority of climbers do not deliberately plan their training in order to produce a peaking effect.

Really, it's not that difficult to structure your workout schedule to elevate yourself to peak form for a personal-best (hardest-ever) route or annual road trip. If you currently train and climb a few days per week, you're already doing the hardest part. All that's required now is to manipulate the intensity, volume, and rest frequency according to certain guidelines, and then track your progress in a training notebook. Details on all of the above are forthcoming.

Structuring Your Workout Schedule

In this section you will learn to manipulate your workout schedule over the time frame of several days, a few weeks or months, and a full year in order to gain optimal results. In the lexicon of sports scientists, these crucial time frames are known as the microcycle, mesocycle, and macrocycle, respectively.

MICROCYCLE

A microcycle relates to the structure, content, and volume of your training over the course of a given week. Since it is in the microcycle where you choose what to train and how much to train (or whether to rest) on a given day, it is the most important factor in determining the effectiveness of your program. Many climbers' programs are flawed from the get-go, because they incorrectly prioritize their training during the course of a single workout or week. Maximizing effectiveness requires training the right things in the right way and the right order. Hopefully, you gained a sense of the optimal workout

hierarchy in reading the previous chapters. After a complete warm-up, the best order of training and exercise is:

1. Actual climbing to learn skill and strategy, and improve technique.
2. Climbing and exercises that target maximum strength and power.
3. Climbing and exercises that target anaerobic endurance.
4. Antagonist-muscle, core, and other general conditioning exercises.
5. Aerobic training activities to improve stamina.

Certainly you can't effectively train all five of these areas every day. Instead, you must develop a list of short-term goals and an overall mission that narrows the focus of your actions in the microcycle. Whether you plan to train in two, three, or four of these areas, it's vital that you execute the training in accordance to this hierarchy. For instance, a beginner who plans to work on skill and strategy training as well as perform some general conditioning exercises would do so in that order. Similarly, an advanced climber might boulder to train skill and the mind, then proceed to training maximum strength and power, and conclude with some antagonist-muscle training. Working out in conflict with this hierarchy will severely compromise the quality of your training and results.

Planning Adequate Rest: There are two crucial rest phases within the microcycle: rest between exercises (or climbs) and rest between workouts. For the enthusiastic climber, it's quite easy to fall into the trap of under-resting—between climbs and between workouts. Therefore, it would be prudent to rest more than you want or think you need.

The length of rest taken between individual exercises and sets plays a primary role in the training stimulus. Rest periods of less than a minute or two (between climbs or exercises) result in high blood lactate concentrations and thus train anaerobic endurance (that is, muscular endurance). This mode is the hallmark of the highly effective interval-training strategy covered in chapter 7. Conversely, resting three minutes or more between sets allows for greater recovery and, therefore, higher quality and intensity of training. Longer rests are best used when training technique (new skills), maximum strength, and power.

The optimal amount of rest between workouts is more difficult to gauge. Depending on the intensity of training, it could take anywhere from twenty-four to seventy-two hours (or more) to fully recover and benefit from the training stimulus. Low-intensity general exercise or easy climbing that produces little muscle soreness can be done up to five or six days per week. The highest-intensity training (complex and hypergravity training), however, might require up to ninety-six hours for full supercompensation, limiting workouts to twice per week. Chances are, you will be training somewhere in between these extremes, so three or four days of training/climbing may be ideal for you.

MESOCYCLE

The Principle of Variation states that you must regularly vary your workouts in order to avoid long-term training plateaus, and it's in the mesocycle that you can best manipulate your schedule toward this end. You can leverage the proven strategy of periodization by changing your training focus, intensity, and volume every few days or weeks. Described below are two powerful mesocycles for climbers.

The 4-3-2-1 Training Cycle: This is the training cycle that I advocate for most non-novice and non-elite climbers (the so-called average climber). The phases of this cycle are: four weeks of climbing skill and stamina training, three weeks of maximum-strength and power training, two weeks of anaerobic endurance training, and one week of rest (see figure 8.2).

The four-week climbing skill and stamina phase involves, well, climbing a lot! This climbing can be done indoors, outdoors, or as a combination of both. You must, however, faithfully obey an important distinction of this phase—that is, to avoid maximal climbing and "projecting," and instead log lots of mileage on a wide variety of routes that are one-half to two number grades below your maximum ability.

Figure 8.2 The 4-3-2-1 Training Cycle

The result of this four-week phase will be improved technique and tactics, acquisition of new motor programs (climbing skills), and the development of local endurance and general stamina. Climbing four days a week is ideal as long as you are not climbing at your limit or to extreme levels of fatigue. You can also engage in general conditioning exercises and stamina-building activities (aerobic training) during this phase.

Three weeks of maximum-strength and power training is the next stop in the cycle, and chapters 5 and 7 detail numerous methods and exercises you can employ; hard bouldering, hypergravity training, and reactive training are ideal choices since powerful movements and maximum effort are hallmarks of this phase. Given the high intensity and physical stress of such training, it's important to take plenty of rest between boulder problems, exercises, and workout days. Moreover, you should avoid training on consecutive days. One day on, one day off, or one day on, two days off, is optimal protocol during this training phase. Therefore, your total commitment to climbing-specific training and actual climbing will be just two or three days per week, although you would also perform some antagonist training twice per week and perhaps engage in some modest aerobic training on nonclimbing days.

The two-week anaerobic endurance phase is the most fatiguing and grueling portion of the cycle. Training at moderately high intensity and with reduced rest between exercise and climbing sets will test your mettle as a growing muscular pump and the telltale "burn" of increasing blood lactate adversely affect your physical and mental state. Interval training is the cornerstone method of developing anaerobic endurance (A-E), although there are many other exercises to employ as detailed in chapter 7. The common practice of climbing as many hard routes as possible in, say, a ninety-minute gym workout (essentially, ninety minutes of interval training!) is the most popular application of interval training. Unfortunately, many climbers overuse this method—and some use it exclusively!—and thus fall victim to overtraining and the resultant plateau or drop in performance, perhaps even injury. The A-E training stimulus during this two-week phase should be applied in a one-day-on, two-days-off (accomplished climbers) or two-days-on, two-days-off (elite climbers) stratagem.

The final phase of the ten-week cycle is simply seven days away from climbing and climbing-specific training. Begin with two or three days of complete rest, and then add in light general conditioning activities (jogging, biking, hiking, and such) for the remainder of the week, if you like. This week off is as important as any other week in the cycle, because it allows both your physical strength and motivation to regenerate. Moreover, your "feel" for effective movement and climbing technique will peak after a week off thanks to the phenomenon of reminiscence.

The Reminiscence Effect involves a phenomenon common among skill-sport athletes: Their intuitive feel and technical execution peak after a period away from training or competition. A week or two off every few months is all it takes to benefit from this "less is more" effect. Upon returning to the rock, you will feel more relaxed, automatic, and natural as your body remembers (reminisces) the well-learned motor skills. Of course, you will also be more physically and mentally fresh after a week off from training, making this the perfect time to commence a road trip or work a hardest-ever project.

The 3-2-1 Training Cycle: Since the elite climber possesses highly refined technical skills and a voluminous library of schemas, there is much less to be gained during the four-week volume-climbing phase

Figure 8.3   The 3-2-1 Training Cycle

of the 4-3-2-1 Cycle. For these 5.12-and-above climbers, acquiring a higher absolute level of maximum strength, power, and anaerobic endurance is central to achieving the next level of performance. Consequently, it would be best to skip the four weeks of skill and stamina training, and instead engage in a more focused 3-2-1 training mesocycle (figure 8.3). The resultant program would commence with three weeks of maximum strength and power training, followed by two weeks of anaerobic endurance training, ending with four to seven days of rest from climbing-specific training and climbing.

Given this intense focus on strength training, however, it's important to never forget that when you're climbing at your limit, any tiny technical flaws or lapse in focus or confidence can bring you down in a nanosecond. The bottom line: No climber should ever take on the closed-minded attitude that more strength is the end-all answer to climbing harder—the *real* answer is to train your limiting constraints (whatever they are), which of course includes factors such as raw strength and power.

MACROCYCLE

The macrocycle is your annual game plan of off-season training, on-season training and climbing, and off-season breaks away from climbing. In traditional sports the macrocycle is planned around the competitive calendar, with the goal of peaking for a major

Figure 8.4 Sample Macrocycle

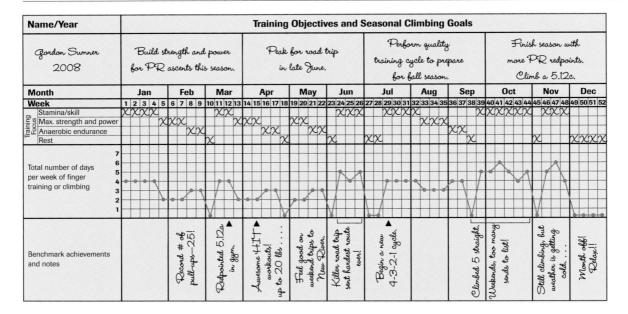

competition. In our sport, however, the idea is to structure a training program to produce a peaking effect for a major road trip, a competition, or the best climbing season in your region.

You can loosely map the macrocycle on a calendar by identifying the months of your on-season road trips or competitions, the months you expect to perform off-season training, and any downtime you plan to take during the year. Note that downtime is vital for recharging your motivation and healing any known (or unknown) injuries that have likely developed during the course of a long climbing season. For many climbers, taking the month of December off makes the most sense and offers the nice reward of holiday parties after a year of dedicated training and tight dietary surveillance.

Figure 8.4 depicts a typical macrocycle. Note that a couple 4-3-2-1 Training Cycles are fit into the off-season training period, along with another during the midseason. The fall months are targeted as the peaking period, followed by a month off to conclude the year. A blank fifty-two-week macrocycle is contained in appendix B for your use.

Targeting Training on Your Preferred Subdiscipline

In chapter 1 you learned the importance of obeying the SAID Principle (specific adaptation to imposed demands) in optimizing your training for your favorite subdiscipline of climbing. Figure 1.7 depicts how the demands of these subdisciplines vary over a continuum from bouldering to alpine climbing. Maximizing the effectiveness of your training requires targeting your workouts accordingly.

The vast majority of climbers reading this book participate in the three subdisciplines of bouldering, sport climbing, and multipitch climbing, and this text is obviously focused on helping these climbers improve their performance. Still, big-wall and alpine climbers should be able to glean plenty of useful information. For instance, in accordance with the SAID Principle, a serious alpine climber would benefit much more from high-volume endurance Stair-Master training and trail running than from bouldering on a home wall or hanging on a fingerboard. Of course, the most specific and effective training for big-wall and alpine climbers is simply doing lots of submaximum climbing.

Conversely, building a home wall or joining an indoor gym is the single biggest advantage that boulder, sport, or multipitch climbers could give themselves. Beyond this investment, the time these climbers spend training or on the rock should mimic the performance demands of their preferred focus. Boulderers should dedicate more of their mesocycle to maximum-strength and power training, while multipitch and big-wall climbers would want to spend many more weeks of the mesocycle on training anaerobic endurance and stamina. Sport climbers possessing a high degree of technical skill, however, would do best to cycle their focus back and forth between maximum strength/power and anaerobic endurance. As they become more advanced, the 3-2-1 Training Cycle described earlier would be ideal.

Clearly, the best training program for you will change over time as your technical ability and your physical strengths and weaknesses change. For this reason, active self-coaching, with regular self-assessments and course correction, is critical in maintaining a successful training program. The time invested in plotting your program intelligently and striving to stay on course over the long term will pay huge dividends in how far and how fast you progress in this sport. You might also consider hiring a personal climbing coach (visit USAclimbing.org for a list of coaches by region) to help guide your training—the objective analysis and expert guidance can be a real wild card in obtaining the most rapid gains in ability possible.

IMPORTANCE OF A HOME WALL OR GYM MEMBERSHIP

Regardless of your ability, nothing beats indoor climbing for sport-specific, time-efficient training, any time of the day or year. Hopefully, there is a good commercial facility within a reasonable distance of your home or workplace. If so, join the gym and use it at least twice per week—this is the number one thing you can do to improve climbing ability and fitness. Many of us are less fortunate (the nearest climbing gym to my home is about an hour away), however, so it's vital to invest in a home wall in place of that gym membership.

If your space is tight, simply build an 8-foot by 8-foot fifty-degree overhanging wall with a small section of ceiling climbing atop it. While this setup has obvious limitations (physical and mental), it will enable you to get an excellent upper-body workout as well as help improve some aspects of climbing movement and body position. If a larger space is available, it would be wise to construct three additional sections of wall: a less overhung wall (twenty to thirty degrees past vertical), a supersteep, sixty-five-degree overhanging wall, and a slightly overhanging (about five degrees past vert) traverse wall. A garage with a high ceiling offers a good location for your home wall, especially if there is a way to control the climate in the summer and winter; however many homeowners feel it's more practical to build their home gym in the basement.

Another excellent strategy is organizing a community wall. Recruit five or ten energetic climbers to pitch in a couple hundred dollars each. Rent a garage or some similar structure that has room to build several hundred square feet of climbing surface with a variety of angles, and then complete your facility with a campus board, HIT System, and fingerboard.

Designing an Effective Personal Training Program

Obviously, there is a limit to how precisely I can prescribe an optimal training program for you via the static format of a book. On the pages that follow, however, I lay out the basic, fundamentally important guidelines that you should follow in developing your training program. Do so, and you will be far better off than the typical climber who trains in a haphazard, trial-and-error manner.

Most important, you must adopt the appropriate training template for your current ability level. Over time you can tweak this program according to the results you experience and in line with the good training sense you've developed from reading this book. As long as you act in ways consistent with the principles and concepts described throughout this text, you will remain on course toward your goals.

One of the most basic and powerful concepts in this book states that you must train in the manner

Table 8.1 Climber Classifications for Training Programs

Beginner	Accomplished	Elite
• Less than one year climbing	• Actively climbing more than one year	• At least three years active climbing
• Toprope ability less than 5.9	• Toprope at or above 5.9	• On-sight lead ability at 5.11 trad and/or 5.12 sport
• Little or no lead-climbing experience	• Lead climbing up to 5.10+ trad or 5.11+ sport	• Boulder harder than V7
• Boulder less than V3	• Boulder V3 to V7	

best suited to you and not do as others do. Remember, to outperform the masses, you must do things they aren't doing! Toward this end, this section provides training guidelines for three basic groups of climbers—beginner, accomplished, and elite. These categories are defined in table 8.1.

Beginner-Level Workout

PRIMARY MISSION

Learn climbing skills and technique, optimize body composition, and improve general conditioning. Engage in mental training to improve thought and emotional control before, during, and after a climb or workout.

WORKOUT GUIDELINES

Climb up to four days per week (ideally climbing outdoors two of the days) and visit at least one new climbing area per month. Reduce body fat with improved dietary surveillance and up to four days of aerobic training per week. Train the antagonist muscles twice per week using the exercises described in chapter 6. If you cannot climb during the workweek, you should instead engage in some of the entry-level pull-muscle exercises in chapter 7. Time spent training and climbing should break down according to figure 8.5.

SAMPLE WORKOUTS

Table 8.2 outlines two beginner-level workouts, one for days when you visit a climbing gym or the other

for days when you want to train for climbing but no gym is available. You may need to modify the volume and exercise selection based on your current level of fitness. Furthermore, overweight individuals should engage in additional aerobic training several days per week—see chapter 6 for details on general training.

Figure 8.5 Workout Time—Beginner

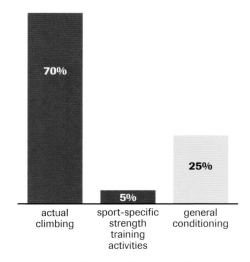

Beginners should invest the majority of the training time in actual climbing. Any fitness training should mostly focus on general conditioning.

Table 8.2 Beginner Workouts

Beginner's Workout with Climbing

- 5–15 minutes general warm-up activity followed by 5–10 minutes mild stretching.

- 30–60 minutes submaximal practice climbing; focus on learning new skills, efficient movement, and mental skills.

- 15–30 minutes strenuous bouldering or climbing at your limit.

- 3–5 sets pull-muscle exercises (see table 7.1).

- 2 sets each push-ups, Shoulder Presses, and Reverse Wrist Curls (or perform this antagonist training on a rest day from climbing).

- 5–15 minutes cool-down activity and stretching.

Beginner's Workout with No Climbing

- 5–15 minutes general warm-up activity followed by 5–10 minutes mild stretching.

- 3–8 sets pull-muscle exercises (see table 7.1).

- 5 sets core exercises (Knee Lifts, Crunches, Aquaman, and such).

- 2–5 sets Straight-Arm Hangs.

- 2 sets each Bench Presses (or push-ups), Shoulder Presses, Dips, Pronators, and Reverse Wrist Curls.

- 5–15 minutes cool-down activity and stretching.

SAMPLE MICROCYCLES

Two slightly different microcycles are shown in table 8.3—one for those able to climb during the work-week (home or commercial gym, or outdoors) and the other for those unable to climb except on weekends.

Table 8.3 Beginner Sample Microcycles

Four-Day-per-Week Climbing Schedule

Monday	Tuesday	Wednesday	Thursday	Friday	Saturday	Sunday
Rest day or aerobic training	Climb and general conditioning (see chapters 6 and 7)	Rest day or aerobic training	Climb and general conditioning	Rest day	All-day climbing	Climb or general conditioning and aerobic training

Weekend-Only Climbing Schedule

Monday	Tuesday	Wednesday	Thursday	Friday	Saturday	Sunday
Rest day or aerobic training	Aerobic training and general conditioning (see chapters 6 and 7)	Rest day or aerobic training	Aerobic training and general conditioning	Rest day	All-day climbing	All-day climbing

Summary of Training for a Beginning Climber

- Climb up to four days per week and at as many areas as possible. Climb for volume over difficulty—maximum learning of a wide range of skills and tactics is far more important than the grade of routes ascended.
- Engage in conditioning exercises that focus on optimizing body composition, improving flexibility, and toning the antagonist muscles. Improved dietary surveillance is crucial for improving body composition.
- Sport-specific strength training should be limited to the beginner exercises, and actual climbing should be given preference over doing these exercises.
- Strive for awareness of your thoughts and emotions throughout the day and while climbing. Practice the mental exercises described in chapter 3, and begin using them as part of your preclimb preparations and while on the rock.

SAMPLE MESOCYCLE

I do not advise the use of a formal strength-training mesocycle (such as the 4-3-2-1 Cycle) for a true novice; nor do I suggest you attempt to climb at maximum difficulty or push excessively hard on the rock. Instead, your medium-term goals should be to increase your volume of climbing as well as the diversity of techniques used. If you climb regularly, it's prudent to take a week off from climbing every few weeks to allow for systemic consolidation of skills and strengthening of tendons (which take much longer than muscles to strengthen). I propose roughly a 4-1 Cycle in which the above microcycles are executed for four weeks, followed by a week off from climbing and training (except for general conditioning and aerobic activity).

SAMPLE MACROCYCLE

Executing a "perfect" macrocycle is less important for beginners than it is for accomplished and elite climbers, though you can still benefit from some long-term planning relating to possible road trips and when you might take your annual month off. You might simply repeat the 4-1 Cycle throughout the year, except for those times when you're on an extended climbing trip or taking a month off. Use the blank macrocycle in appendix B to plot your training.

Accomplished Climber Workout

PRIMARY MISSION

Maximize economy of climbing movement with constant focus on refining mental and technical skills. Expand motor skills and schema-rules by gaining experience on many different rock types and by avoiding specialization as long as possible. Reduce time spent on general conditioning and increase the

Figure 8.6 Workout Time—Accomplished

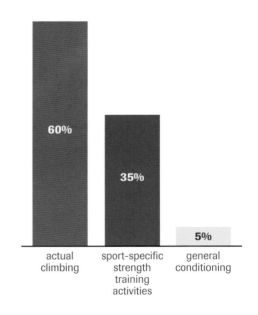

Accomplished climbers need to spend about one-third of total training time on sport-specific strength training activities.

volume of sport-specific strength training that targets improving maximum grip strength, lock-off ability, pulling power, and anaerobic endurance.

WORKOUT GUIDELINES

Climbing three to four days per week (indoors and/or outdoors) is the backbone of this program. For most people, this will require joining a climbing gym or building a home training wall to help facilitate weekday climbing. Strive to climb outside as often as possible—every weekend if possible!—to enable learning of the diverse skills and techniques not represented by human-made walls. Serious strength training should be executed according to the 4-3-2-1 Cycle with a strong focus on the intermediate-level exercises described in chapter 7. Any climbing should be done before your strength training, and never climb or do climbing exercises more than a total of four days per week. Train the antagonist and core muscles twice per week, on either climbing or non-climbing days. Maintain close dietary surveillance during the latter portion of off-season training and during on-season training/climbing. Err on the side of over-resting—the harder you train, the more you need to rest in order to fully recover and avoid overuse injuries! Your time spent training and climbing should break down in the proportions shown in figure 8.6.

SAMPLE WORKOUTS

Every intermediate-level climber has a different "perfect" training program depending on his or her unique physical, technical, and mental weaknesses, as well as time available and climbing goals. Still, actual climbing is the most essential part of this workout program for *all* accomplished climbers. Targeted physical training is also important, both for the pull muscles and for the antagonist push muscles. Use the three workouts in table 8.4 as templates from which you can build the optimal workout for you. Modify and vary the program over the mesocycle and macrocycle and also in accordance with the principles of training detailed in chapter 5. In the context of the 4-3-2-1 Training Cycle, use the stamina and skill template for four weeks, the maximum-

strength and power for three weeks, and the anaerobic endurance workout for two weeks.

SAMPLE MICROCYCLES

Your discipline at planning and executing quality workouts over a seven-day microcycle is a primary factor in determining the results you obtain. Integrating climbing days, hard training days, and sufficient rest days is the crux of the matter. Train too little or rest too little, and you will shortchange yourself. Table 8.5 provides four microcycles to help guide your scheduling. Depending on your access to a climbing wall or rock, select either the weekend-only climbing microcycle or the four-days-climbing microcycle. Use the microcycle as a template for planning your weekly schedule, but recognize that you may need to adjust or deviate from the schedule depending on travel or the need for additional rest. If you're using the 4-3-2-1 mesocycle, you will similarly need to adjust the structure of the microcycle to accommodate the correct number of weekly workouts prescribed by the 4-3-2-1 program.

SAMPLE MESOCYCLE

Dedicated periods of serious strength training for gains are best scheduled according to the 4-3-2-1 Cycle. Figure 8.2 shows a highly effective ten-week program that allows for adequate rest and thus produces maximum strength gains without the risk of overtraining or injury. High-end accomplished climbers may benefit more by using the 3-2-1 mesocycle as shown in figure 8.3.

Peak climbing season (when you climb for performance and travel the most) will make it difficult to follow a strict ten-week mesocycle. At these times you may deviate from the schedule by taking two full rest days before a weekend climbing trip and at least a full rest day after the weekend climbing. Often the best in-season training strategy is to develop a seven-day microcycle that best accommodates your weekly climbing while still allowing for at least one "maintenance" training day. When you find a weekly schedule that works, stick with it for several weeks or until you can commit to a more structured 4-3-2-1 regimen.

Table 8.4 Accomplished Climber Workouts

Stamina and Skills Workout (2–4 hours)

- 5–15 minutes general warm-up activity (or easy climbing) followed by 5–10 minutes of mild stretching.

- 90–180 minutes practice climbing and lapping moderate (submaximal, no-falls) routes. Build up to 1,500 feet of climbing; if the gym's routes average 30 feet in length, you'll need to climb a total of 50 routes (or up and down 25).

- 2 sets each Dips, Bench Presses (or Push-Ups), Shoulder Presses, Pronators, and Reverse Wrist Curls. (Ideally, perform this antagonist training on a rest day from climbing.)

- 5–15 minutes cool-down activity and stretching.

Maximum-Strength/Power Workout (1.5–2.5 hours)

- 5–15 minutes general warm-up activity (or easy climbing) followed by 5–10 minutes mild stretching.

- 30–60 minutes maximal bouldering and hypergravity bouldering.

- 30–60 minutes maximum-strength and power-training exercises. Select appropriate forearm exercises (3–7 total sets) and pull-muscle exercises (3–7 total sets) from figures 7.1 and 7.5, respectively. Always train grip strength before the larger pulling muscles. Gradually introduce some complex training—couple exercises according to table 7.6. Conclude with 3–5 sets of core training.

- 2 sets each Dips, Bench Presses (or push-ups), Shoulder Presses, Pronators, and Reverse Wrist Curls. (Ideally, perform this antagonist training on a rest day from climbing.)

- 5–15 minutes cool-down activity and stretching.

Anaerobic Endurance Workout (1.5–2.5 hours)

- 5–15 minutes general warm-up activity (or easy climbing) followed by 5–10 minutes of mild stretching.

- 30–60 minutes interval training. Alternate climbing boulder problems (or lapping sport climbs) with roughly equal periods of rest. Select climbs that are strenuous but nontechnical. You should get pumped but not pump out; as fatigue accumulates you will need to climb progressively easier routes or increase rest periods to avoid muscular failure.

- 30–60 minutes anaerobic endurance exercises. Select appropriate forearm exercises (5–10 total sets) and pull-muscle exercises (5–10 total sets) from figures 7.1 and 7.5, respectively. Always train forearm endurance before the larger pulling muscles. Conclude with 3–5 sets core training.

- 2 sets each Dips, Bench Presses (or push-ups), Shoulder Presses, Pronators, and Reverse Wrist Curls. (Ideally, perform this antagonist training on a rest day from climbing.)

- 5–15 minutes cool-down activity and stretching.

Table 8.5 Accomplished Climber Sample Microcycles

Four-Day-per-Week Climbing Schedule 1

Monday	Tuesday	Wednesday	Thursday	Friday	Saturday	Sunday
Rest day or aerobic training	Climb and pull-muscle and antagonist training (see chapters 6 and 7)	Rest day or aerobic training	Climb and pull-muscle and antagonist training (see chapters 6 and 7)	Rest day	All-day climbing	All-day climbing, or aerobic training, or pull-muscle and antagonist training

Four-Day-per-Week Climbing Schedule 2

Monday	Tuesday	Wednesday	Thursday	Friday	Saturday	Sunday
Rest day or aerobic training	Climb and pull-muscle and antagonist training (see chapters 6 and 7)	Climb and pull-muscle training (see chapters 6 and 7)	Aerobic and antagonist training	Rest day	All-day climbing	All-day climbing, or aerobic training, or pull-muscle and antagonist training

Weekend-Only Climbing Schedule 1

Monday	Tuesday	Wednesday	Thursday	Friday	Saturday	Sunday
Rest day or aerobic training	Pull-muscle, finger, and antagonist training (see chapters 6 and 7)	Rest day or aerobic training	Pull-muscle and antagonist training (see chapters 6 and 7)	Rest day	All-day climbing	All-day climbing, or aerobic training, or pull-muscle and antagonist training

Weekend-Only Climbing Schedule 2

Monday	Tuesday	Wednesday	Thursday	Friday	Saturday	Sunday
Rest day or aerobic training	Pull-muscle, finger, and antagonist training (see chapters 6 and 7)	Pull-muscle and finger training (see chapters 6 and 7	Antagonist and aerobic training	Rest day	All-day climbing	All-day climbing, or aerobic training, or pull-muscle and antagonist training

Summary of Training
for an Accomplished Climber

- Climb up to four days per week and gain exposure to as many different types and styles of climbing as possible. Refine mental and technical skills to maximize economy of movement—the fastest way to becoming a better, stronger climber.
- Engage in regular, scheduled sport-specific strength training to increase maximum grip strength, upper-body power, and anaerobic endurance. Focus primarily on the intermediate exercises listed in figures 7.1 and 7.5. During a particular workout, always perform actual climbing before engaging in strength-training exercises.
- Commit to training the antagonist muscles twice per week. These are critical for maintaining muscle balance and preventing injury.
- Work on becoming a more mental climber. Practice mental-training strategies throughout the week, and strive to leverage all your mental tools when you step onto the rock.

SAMPLE MACROCYCLE

The average accomplished climber gets outdoors twenty or more weekends per year and may go on as many as two to four extended road trips per year. Therefore, careful macrocycle planning is vital to maximize conditioning for these trips and to help produce peaking for an extreme project or personal-best ascent. Use the blank macrocycle in appendix B to structure an effective long-term training plan that accounts for your travel plans, the best outdoor climbing season, and when you choose to take your month off from climbing.

Elite Climber Workout

PRIMARY MISSION

Identify and correct any technical weak spots or energy leaks (no matter how small) that compromise climbing performance. Constantly evaluate and refine mental skills—you can always improve more in this area! Work to eliminate subtle forms of self-sabotage by narrowing your focus onto the process of climbing and letting go of any outcome-oriented thinking. Fitness-training workouts must be highly specific to your preferred climbing subdiscipline (bouldering, sport climbing, multipitch, or big walls), and they must stretch the limits of what you are currently capable of doing. Sound performance nutrition is critical for accelerating recovery from severe workouts and to ensure maximum supercompensation.

Figure 8.7 Workout Time—Elite

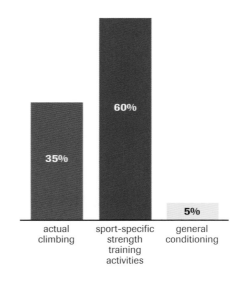

Only elite climbers need to focus extensively on sport-specific strength training activities—up to 60 percent. Design workouts to target a preferred subdiscipline or simulate a current project route.

WORKOUT GUIDELINES

Unlike the mass of climbers, the elite performer needs to spend a disproportionate amount of training time on strength training (see figure 8.7). For boulderers and sport climbers, several weeks or even a month or two at a time may be dedicated to strength/power training and hard bouldering with little or no actual roped climbing. Multipitch and wall climbers must invest a large amount of time into actual climbing—climbing for volume, exercising to build muscular endurance, and stamina-training

activities are what it's all about. Frequent training with the elite-level exercises in chapter 7 is essential to achieving further physical gains.

Access to an indoor climbing wall, boulders, or crags is absolutely necessary for elite-level training. Use of the 3-2-1 Cycle can be highly effective for both on- and off-season training, although many elite climbers will train intuitively. With many years of climbing and training under his or her belt, a mature elite climber can often intuit the right amount of training stimulus and rest. Still, the microcycles, mesocycles, and macrocycle described herein offer

---

Table 8.6   Elite Climber Workout

Maximum-Strength/Power Workout (1.5–2.5 hours)

- 5–15 minutes general warm-up activity or easy climbing followed by 5–10 minutes mild stretching.

- 30–60 minutes maximal bouldering and hypergravity bouldering.

- 20–30 minutes complex training (coupled hypergravity and reactive training). See table 7.6.

- 3–7 sets advanced pull-muscle maximum-strength exercises. Select from figure 7.5.

- Conclude with 4–6 sets core training, including at least 2 sets of front levers.

- 2 sets each Dips, Bench Presses (or push-ups), Shoulder Presses, Pronators, and Reverse Wrist Curls. (Ideally, perform this antagonist training on a rest day from climbing.)

- 5–15 minutes cool-down activity and stretching.

Anaerobic Endurance Workout (1.5–2.5 hours)

- 5–15 minutes general warm-up activity or easy climbing followed by 5–10 minutes mild stretching.

- 45–75 minutes interval training. Alternate climbing boulder problems (or lapping routes) with roughly equal periods of rest. Select climbs that are strenuous but nontechnical. You should get pumped but not pump out; as fatigue accumulates, you will need to climb progressively easier routes to avoid muscular failure.

- 30–60 minutes anaerobic endurance exercises. Select appropriate forearm exercises (5–10 total sets) and pull-muscle exercises (5–10 total sets) from figures 7.1 and 7.5, respectively. Always train forearm endurance before the larger pulling muscles. Conclude with 3–6 sets core training.

- 2 sets each Dips, Bench Presses (or push-ups), Shoulder Presses, Pronators, and Reverse Wrist Curls. (Ideally, perform this antagonist training on a rest day from climbing.)

- 5–15 minutes cool-down activity and stretching.

Summary of Training an Elite Climber

- Plan and execute an optimal—not maximum—strength-training program that targets your personal weakest link. The goal is to maximize grip strength, upper-body power, and anaerobic endurance.

- Constantly evaluate your technique and mental performance to identify subtle flaws that are preventing further gains. Economy of climbing movement is paramount, and it's your mental, technical, and tactical skills that determine your fuel efficiency. Make the mental strategies described in chapter 3 into life skills that you employ 24/7.

- Err on the side of over-resting instead of overtraining. Use performance nutrition and generous amounts of sleep and rest to enhance recovery and maximize gains from training.

- Be a compulsive planner of training, travel, and rest. Try to leave nothing to chance, and avoid trial-and-error training or getting drawn into some else's (flawed) training routine.

- Evaluate all you do in your daily life with this question: Is it helping me reach my goals or holding me back in some way?

useful guidance for such intuitive training. Finally, brief but regular bouts of antagonist-muscle training, copious rest, and proactive performance nutrition are vital to accelerate recovery and help stave off injury and overtraining.

SAMPLE WORKOUTS

Table 8.6 provides two highly focused workout templates, one for training maximum strength and power and the other for building anaerobic endurance. You will need to modify the volume of training as well as exercise selection based on your capabilities, time available to train, and your climbing preference. Design and vary your workouts according to the training principles outlined in chapter 5.

SAMPLE MICROCYCLES

The appropriate amount of training stimulus (workout length, frequency, and intensity) will vary greatly among elite climbers based on climbing preference, quality of nutrition, genetic factors, and age, among other things. Some individuals may do best by training hard just twice per week, while others do better by training and climbing a total of four days per week. Given the tendency of elite climbers to push their limits, however, it is often necessary to take forced rest days instead of training or projecting while sore. As a guiding principle, elite climbers should "train hard when training, and rest completely when resting." While many elites will choose to train intuitively, it would be best to roughly follow one of the accomplished climber microcycles shown in table 8.5.

SAMPLE MESOCYCLE

As in planning weekly training and climbing, many elites will intuit their multiweek mesocycle. Even so, it's critical that you consider your outdoor climbing and travel plans, then build a workout schedule around these dates. One planning strategy is to schedule rest and workout days backward from your climbing days—for example, allow for at least forty-eight hours of rest before a weekend of climbing and then plan a workout day or two prior to these rest days. On a calendar, mark in your climbing days and trips, then mark the preceding rest days, then fill in your training days. Elite climbers preferring a more structured schedule will do best by planning their workouts according to the 3-2-1 mesocycle shown in figure 8.3.

SAMPLE MACROCYCLE

Elite climbers tend to be very goal-oriented and compulsive long-term planners. It's in the macrocycle that you need to book long road trips, competitions, and an annual month off from climbing, so you can plan the most effective training schedule to produce a physical peaking for key events. You can plot your own macrocycle using the blank chart found in appendix B.

Training Considerations for Female, Over-Fifty, and Junior Climbers

This final section takes a look at special considerations for female climbers, those over age fifty, and juniors. I've intentionally kept this section brief, because I feel that these groups are particularly gifted for climbing; there are only a few things they need to consider or do differently compared with others.

Unique Issues for Female Climbers

Female climbers differ from males both physiologically and psychologically. While the psychological differences are more difficult to measure, there are clear physiological differences that may be an asset or liability in terms of climbing performance. The average female is about 5 inches shorter, thirty-five pounds lighter in total body mass, and forty-five pounds lighter in lean body mass (due to a higher percentage of body fat) than the average male. This large difference in lean body mass (muscle) is largely attributed to greater levels of the hormone testosterone in males (Bloomfield 1994).

Consequently, the average female possesses approximately 40 percent of the upper-body strength and 70 percent of the lower-body strength when compared with men. In terms of strength-to-lean-body-mass, however, the ratio is notably less— females possess about 55 percent of the upper-body strength and about the same in lower-body strength as men (Wilmore 1974). Thus, it's clear that the greater level of adipose tissue in females has a negative effective on physical performance, especially in sports requiring a high strength-to-weight ratio. The female climber, therefore, will benefit much more from regular aerobic training (to lower her percentage of body fat) than her male counterpart— running for twenty to forty minutes several days per week will effectively increase strength-to-weight ratio in many females (due to changes in body composition).

Though females are naturally weaker than males (less testosterone and lean mass), they do respond to strength training in the same ways as men. Consequently, the serious female climber should not hesitate to engage in the sport-specific strength-training exercises described in chapters 6 and 7. In particular, the focus should be on increasing maximum strength in the pull muscles and the general condition of the core and antagonist push muscles.

The first few weeks or months of training will produce marked improvement thanks to neural adaptations. Beyond that, strength gains will come more slowly as hypertrophy (muscle growth) becomes a more significant player in producing strength gains. For this reason it's vital that strength training for the female climber be just as focused as for the male. The typical health club workout is no more appropriate for female climbers than for males, and in the long run could have a negative effect on climbing performance.

Technically and mentally, the beginning female climber is often a better performer than her male counterpart, and this is something that every female climber should recognize and leverage to the greatest possible extent. More flexibility, a lower center of gravity, less body weight, shorter fingers, and a more measured approach to climbing can all help a female climber outperform her male counterpart despite possessing less strength. So while sport-specific strength training is a must for any serious female climber, she should not overlook her gifts of style, strategy, creativity, and finesse.

As a final note, it's a common misconception that physical performance tends to be worse during menstruation. While the menstrual cycle's effect on performance varies widely among individuals and from sport to sport, at least one study has shown that grip strength was greater during the actual menstrual phase (Davis 1991). Ultimately, you need to develop an awareness of just when is your best performance time of the month. You can then plan your training and climbing to exploit this period, whether it's for a few high-intensity workouts or making a personal-best ascent!

Conditioning for Over-Fifty Climbers

As adult climbers age, numerous physiological changes combine to form an increasing constraint on performance, especially beyond the age of fifty. A few of the unfortunate changes include reduced VO_2 max (aerobic capacity), decreased muscle mass, a lower proportion of fast-twitch muscle fibers, and reduced recovery. Despite these inevitable life changes, you can still climb at a very high level given a renewed focus on the mental and technical aspects of climbing and a steady dose of strength training. I know of more than a few fifty- and sixty-somethings who climb 5.12, ascend big walls, and trek in the mountains. You can, too, given a three-pronged approach of injury avoidance, physical conditioning, and mastery of skills.

INJURY AVOIDANCE

Unlike teenagers with their resilient bodies, older climbers are susceptible to injury during every single workout and climb. Common issues range from muscle pulls to dislocated shoulders, torn tendons, and a variety of other joint and spinal problems. Fortunately, you can significantly reduce your risk by engaging in a comprehensive warm-up before every training and climbing session. Younger climbers might rush through a warm-up in just a few minutes, but older climbers would be wise to complete a full thirty-minute warm-up of general aerobic activity, light exercise, stretching, and easy climbing. Such a progressive warm-up will markedly decrease injury risk by warming and lengthening the muscles and spreading synovial fluid to lubricate the joints. While thirty minutes of nonclimbing exercise might not be your idea of a good time, it will enhance the quality of your climbing and reduce the risk of muscle or joint injury that might lay you up for months or even knock you out of climbing completely.

Another way the mature, disciplined climber can avoid injuries is simply by avoiding potentially injurious moves while climbing. The goal is to foster a level of kinesthetic awareness at which you can assess—or often intuit—the risk potential of a given move. Whether it is an awkward-feeling drop-knee, a tweaky-feeling pocket, or an improbable-feeling lunge, your discipline to heed the sensory feedback and rapidly evaluate the situation before forging onward can save you. Ultimately, you will need to make a quick decision as to whether you should retreat from the risky-feeling move, test the move once to see how it feels, or just push onward in the belief that you will succeed without incident. As a rule, the older you get, the more you should view such a risky-feeling move as stop sign instead of a caution sign.

PHYSICAL CONDITIONING

Physical conditioning for over-fifty climbers is not all that different from the program I prescribe for the mass of climbers. You can safely employ most of the exercises contained in this book. Most of your limitations relate to dynamic, forceful training exercises, which become increasingly dangerous with advancing age. Climbers over fifty years of age would be wise to not engage in the most dynamic forms of campus training, One-Arm Lock-Offs or One-Arm Pull-Ups, frequent lunging, and steep V-hard bouldering. Of course, every climber possesses different generic encoding, experience, and physical capabilities, so there are surely a few senior climbers who prevail through the most stressful endeavors. But for the vast majority of older climbers, dynamic training is dangerous training. Otherwise, your fitness-training goals are similar to those of every other climber: optimize body composition, improve aerobic capacity and stamina, and increase muscular strength and endurance.

Preplanning workout and rest days is of great importance for the older climber. Too many back-to-back workout (or climbing) days, too little rest, and poor nutrition over just a few consecutive days will crack open the door to possible injury or illness. Compound this over several weeks and it will fling the door wide. Once an older climber is injured and sick, reduced immune efficiency and changing hormone levels mean slower recovery and a faster drop-off of physical conditioning than for a younger climber. The bottom line for over-fifty climbers: Train, rest, and eat on a calculated schedule that will reduce injury risk, and do nothing to tempt injury.

A climber for life, the master of rock John Gill still enjoys pulling down at age seventy. ERIC J. HÖRST

TECHNICAL AND MENTAL MASTERY

The best older climbers are usually Zen masters who leverage the fact that climbing performance is two-thirds technical and mental and only one-third physical. By exploiting superior skill and wisdom, and bringing many years of experience to the table, older climbers can become true masters of rock by climbing very near their maximum capacity. Whether that top capability is 5.8 or 5.13, you can spot these elder masters by their measured approach, smooth sailing through scary terrain, and even the occasional calculated lunge or grunt that shows they are still willing to pull out all the stops to send.

Developing such mastery takes many years; in fact, in a complex sport such as climbing you can still acquire and refine mental and technical skills even after ten or twenty years' experience. So while your physical capacities may be steady or waning, you can often compensate by improving mentally and technically. Consequently, you should strive to strike a balance between fitness training—still an important part of the equation—and going climbing at one of the myriad wonderful crags around the world. And, after all, isn't that the bottom line? Simply by moving over stone, you tap into the life force that climbing provides, which transcends ability, gender, and age. That's the power of climbing!

Training for Junior Climbers

Kids can unquestionably learn complex sports skills more rapidly than adults, and in recent years we've seen numerous "wonder kids" take the sport-climbing world by storm. Clearly these young, generally pre-pubescent climbers possess the slight physique ideal for difficult climbing. There are numerous other physiological traits that work in their favor to enhance function and rate of recovery. Unfortunately these young climbers often lack the maturity, self-awareness, and life experience to transfer their sport-climbing prowess to a wide range of climbing pursuits. They are also not prepared for the rigors of serious sport-specific training as outlined in this text. Let's take a look at the appropriate type of activity and training for youth climbers of different ages.

TRAINING FOR YOUTH CLIMBERS (UNDER AGE THIRTEEN)

Preteens are much better off simply climbing for fun over performance. Climbing indoors or outdoors up to four days per week will allow their natural ability and strength to surface. The coaching emphasis should be on skill training and the fundamental aspects of the mental game. No strength training is advised other than basic body weight exercises such as pull-ups, push-ups, dips, abdominal crunches, and basic free-weight training with very light dumbbells. Special attention should be given to performing antagonist training (push-muscle exercises twice per week) to maintain body balance, since the pulling muscles naturally grow stronger from regular climbing.

Despite this conservative approach to training, most preteens will progress rapidly in bouldering, indoor climbing, and sport climbing, developing the foundation for becoming successful all-around climbers in the future if they choose to do so. Some preteens—most likely those with the best coaching or natural ability—will experience a meteoric rise in ability and apparent strength, all without any training outside of climbing.

TRAINING FOR JUNIOR CLIMBERS (AGES THIRTEEN TO SEVENTEEN)

The greatest gains in strength and power come during the period of the adolescent growth spurt—around thirteen for girls and fourteen for boys (Bloomfield 1994). Still, anthropometric changes may have a positive or negative impact on performance. Teenagers lacking strength and power can begin some climbing-specific training, including some of the finger and pull-muscle exercises covered in chapter 7. They should not engage in the most stressful forms of training (campus training, hyper-gravity, HIT), however, until age sixteen or seventeen, at the earliest.

Still, the training emphasis should remain focused on developing good technical and mental skills. Teenage climbers would benefit tremendously from exposure to an expanding range of climbing activities such as traditional and alpine climbing. Some individuals may naturally gravitate toward competition climbing, though this should be the youth's choice, not that of an overbearing parent.

As teenage climbers transition into young adulthood (age seventeen or eighteen), they can begin a more serious and formal training program for climbing. Many of these late-teen climbers will already be accomplished or elite, and they can now engage in the elite training program as outlined earlier in the chapter.

The most common setbacks for teenage climbers are overuse injuries in the tendons, joints, and bones of the fingers, including stress fractures and damage to the growth plates. Juniors experiencing chronic pain in the fingers (or elsewhere) should cease climbing for a few weeks and consult a doctor if the pain continues. As a hard-and-fast rule, climbing and training must be limited to an aggregate of four days per week. The guidance of an adult climber or coach is extremely beneficial both in helping structure workouts and in monitoring rest and nutritional habits.

Youth climbers should focus on developing technique and skills while doing only a modest amount of strength training. Here thirteen-year old Alyssa Sullivan sails up 5.10 terrain at Mount Lemmon, Arizona.
ERIC J. HÖRST

Performance Nutrition

Judge your success by what you had to give up in order to get it.

—*The Dalai Lama*

The foods and beverages you consume play a primary role in determining your mental acuity, physical performance output, and ability to recover from vigorous training or climbing. Therefore, a thoughtfully designed diet will provide a noticeable edge in performance, whereas engaging in a "see-food diet"—you see food and you eat it!—will continue to hamper your performance in a covert way that you may never recognize.

While it's impossible to say exactly how big a part diet plays in climbing performance, I estimate that most climbers can realize a 10 to 20 percent improvement in their training, recovery, concentration, energy, and overall climbing performance if they dedicate themselves to improved dietary surveillance.

As a serious athlete and performance coach, I follow the changing trends in nutrition with great interest. In the late 1980s high-carbohydrate, low-fat diets were the rage; in the mid-1990s high-protein diets were in vogue; and in the early 2000s the high-fat, low-carbohydrate diets are what sold the most books and got the greatest hype. Interestingly, all

Jasmine Caton jamming up the "enduro corner" on **Astroman** *(5.11c), Yosemite, California.*
RICH WHEATER

these diets are backed by scientific studies showing that they worked (in producing weight loss) to some degree given that you execute them exactly and presuming you are faced with one or more of the health issues common to obese Americans. For a reasonably fit athlete, however, there is no need to engage in one of the fad diet regimens—nor any benefit. Proper performance nutrition is not that complex a subject; in the pages that follow, I will provide you with basic guidelines that will make eating right easy.

I was fortunate to realize the causal connection between nutrition and performance many years ago. Though I occasionally fall from the wagon, I credit sound nutrition—about forty-eight weeks per year—for my ability to train exceedingly hard, avoid injury, recover quickly, and still climb at a high level in my forties and despite over thirty years of climbing abuse to my joints, tendons, and muscles. I hope I can help you do the same, too!

Macronutrients

There is no single perfect diet for climbers, just as there is no single perfect training program. To some extent, the amount and best type of foods for you depend on your climbing preference. For instance, alpine climbers have significantly different nutritional needs and energy requirements than those of folks who partake in cragging or bouldering.

Our study of performance nutrition begins with a look at the three macronutrients: protein, fat, and carbohydrate. As in the prior chapters, the focus will remain on the best strategies for rock climbers, with only general information for alpine climbers.

Protein

Protein has many functions in the body, including building and repairing of tissue, acting as a major component of the immune system, and making up enzymes, which facilitate every reaction that goes on in the body.

According to registered dietitian and nutritionist Barb Branda Turner, growing individuals need more protein than adults do simply because they are actually laying down large amounts of new tissue. Healthy adults have a fairly extensive protein pool to draw on; that is, the proteins we consume are recycled several times for different functions in the body. For this reason daily protein requirements for adults are modest, even if they are training to increase muscle mass. Successful training is much less a factor of consuming a lot of protein than of using the appropriate training strategy and eating enough carbohydrates to fuel your training.

DAILY REQUIREMENTS

Between 1.2 and 1.5 grams of protein per kilogram of body weight per day is adequate for most climbers. For a seventy-two-kilogram (160-pound) individual, this translates to 86 to 108 grams per day. This is higher than the 0.8 to 1.0 gram per kilogram recommended for sedentary individuals by the FDA. Some studies have shown a slightly higher need in athletes, not just to increase muscle mass but also to facilitate recovery from exercise and compensate for the catabolic (tissue-consuming) effects of long, intense exercise. Still, I (and most nutritionists) do not buy in to the massive protein-intake guidelines (as much as 2.0 to 3.0 grams per kilogram per day) prescribed in some fitness magazines.

BEST PROTEIN SOURCES

Low-fat dairy products such as skim milk and yogurt, plus grilled chicken and fish, and lean red meats provide you with the best protein value for your calorie. For example, a 3-ounce piece of lean red meat such as tenderloin contains only 180 calories and 25 grams of high-quality, complete protein. A glass of skim milk contains about 10 grams of complete protein and almost zero fat. If you prefer not to

Table 9.1 Caloric Content of Macronutrients

Macronutrient	Calories/gram
Carbohydrate	4
Protein	4
Fat	9

eat much meat (like me) or dairy products, whey protein powder mixed into skim milk, 100 percent pure fruit juice, or water is an excellent source of high-quality protein. Incomplete proteins—these sources that do not contain all twenty amino acids—are also useful when eaten in combination. This is of particular importance to vegetarian athletes, who, by the way, are more likely to be protein-deficient.

Fat

It's true that most Americans eat far too much fat, which contributes to our high incidence of heart disease, cancer, hypertension, and obesity. Still, getting too little fat has serious implications as well. Dietary fat is necessary as a source of essential fatty acids, which are involved in critical physiological processes such as the functions of the immune system and hormone production. Furthermore, our cell membranes consist largely of phospholipids (fatty acid derivatives), without which we would not be able to make healthy new cells, including muscle cells. A dietary fat deficiency in female athletes has been shown to cause amenorrhea (menstrual cycle irregularities), which may affect the development and maintenance of bone tissue.

DAILY REQUIREMENTS

On average the body's minimum fat requirement is 15 to 25 grams per day. Usually fat-intake recommendations are expressed in terms of percentage of total calories consumed daily. For climbers, 15 to 30 percent of total calories should come from fat, depending on your climbing preference.

For cragging and bouldering, where a low percentage of body fat is desirable and the energy demands are largely anaerobic, fat intake should be restricted to 15 to 20 percent of total calories consumed. Alpine climbers, however, may be better off consuming up to 30 percent of daily calories from fat. These endurance climbers place great demands on the larger muscles of the body (especially the legs) and expend much more energy per day than, say, sport climbers. Fat is more calorie-dense than carbohydrate and protein (see table 9.1), and it's a good fuel for long, slow aerobic activities. Both these attributes make foods with a higher fat content more advantageous for alpine climbers than for crag climbers.

FOUR TYPES OF FATS

In consuming your daily requirement of fat, it's important to know which of the four types of fat—saturated, monounsaturated, polyunsaturated, and trans fatty acids—are "good" and "bad." Although each contains the same nine calories per gram consumed, they are not all created equal in terms of their role in performance nutrition. Consequently, it's important not only to eat the optimal amount of fat but also to have the best ratio among the different types of fatty acids.

- **Saturated fats** are most common in animal products such as milk and dairy, meats, and poultry. They are also present in significant amounts in some nuts, including Brazil and macadamia. Although excessive saturated fat intake does increase serum cholesterol, in particular the LDL or "bad" cholesterol, a certain amount is needed by our bodies to be made into fatty-acid-containing compounds such as hormones and phospholipids.
- **Monounsaturated fatty acids** are found in vegetables and oils including canola, olive, peanut, and avocado. These "monos" are thought to be the most beneficial in protecting against heart disease because of their ability to lower LDL without reducing HDL (the "good" cholesterol).
- **Polyunsaturated fatty acids** are common in fish, especially tuna, mackerel, salmon, and trout, and in corn, sunflower, and soybean oils. The omega-3 "polys" found mainly in fish and flaxseeds are currently being investigated for their

roles in fighting inflammatory diseases such as arthritis and other illnesses, including migraine headaches and heart disease.
- **Trans fatty acids** are found in trace amounts in almost all sources of natural fats, but most of those in our diet come from hydrogenated oils. During the process of hydrogenation, liquid vegetable oils are converted into solids by bombardment with hydrogen atoms (as in the making of margarine and shortening). Hydrogenation in effect converts unsaturated fatty acids into saturated fatty acids largely through the formation of trans bonds. Recent studies have raised concerns about these bonds, because they produce effects similar to those of saturated fats and may, in fact, be cancer causing.

While most well-trained athletes have a very healthy cholesterol profile (unless they smoke or have a genetic predisposition to problems), it would be wise to limit your intake of trans fatty acids. Unfortunately, hydrogenated oils and partially hydrogenated oils are found in such a wide range of foods that they are hard to avoid. For instance, many of the breads, cookies, and snack foods you buy off the shelf at the grocery store contain high amounts of these harmful oils. (Read the labels—you'll be surprised how many foods you eat daily contain them!) Most commercial fried foods are cooked in oils that contain trans fatty acids. Surprisingly, even some health foods and energy bars contain partially hydrogenated oils.

In terms of fat consumption, the best approach is to consume about equal amounts of saturated, monounsaturated, and polyunsaturated fatty acids and minimize intake of trans fatty acids. Try to eliminate hydrogenated oils from your diet, and in doing so you will reduce your consumption of these unhealthy fats to acceptable levels. (Unfortunately, it's very difficult to escape them completely in this world of highly processed and prepackaged foods.)

Examine the labels of the foods you eat most regularly and determine which items are doing you the most nutritional damage. Chances are you can make huge strides by eliminating just a handful of killer items like french fries, fried meats, snack cakes and muffins, salty snacks (buy baked chips and crackers instead), and any highly processed food designed for maximum shelf life (no doubt, high in hydrogenated oils).

Carbohydrates

Although fat and protein can be used to provide energy, carbohydrate is the most efficient and effective source of energy for the muscles and brain. A high-carbohydrate diet is also important for athletes due to its protein-sparing effect. If you do not consume enough carbohydrates to meet your energy needs, muscle protein will be broken down for energy—the last thing any strength or power athlete would ever want! Consequently, the popular low-carbohydrate diets (Atkins, Zone, Ketogenic, and so forth) are inappropriate for most active climbers.

Carbohydrates come in two forms: sugars and starches. The sugar foods include fruit, sugar, soda pop, jam, honey, and molasses, while common starches are breads, rice, cereals, and pasta. Because these are the best sources of energy for high-intensity training and climbing, I'm sure you are already consuming plentiful amounts of these foods. Not all carbohydrates are created equal, however: Different carbohydrates release sugar into the bloodstream at different rates. The very best athletes know how to leverage this information to maintain stable energy throughout the day and to significantly increase the rate of recovery after a hard workout or day of climbing. If you are serious about climbing better, this subject should be of great interest to you. Enter the glycemic index.

GLYCEMIC INDEX

Historically, nutritionists classified carbohydrates only into the two basic groups of simple carbohydrates (sugars) and complex carbohydrates (starches). Simple sugars were said to produce a rapid rise in blood sugar and quick energy, while complex carbohydrates were said to provide slow, steady energy. Although this concept holds true in general, recent studies have found that there is a large variability in the rise in blood sugar following the ingestion of various foods from both the sugar and starch groups.

To investigate and more accurately classify the metabolism of carbohydrates, researchers developed the glycemic index (GI)—a powerful nutritional tool I first introduced to climbers in my 1994 book *Flash Training*. This index determines how the ingestion of a particular food affects blood sugar levels in comparison with the ingestion of straight glucose. Consumption of high-GI foods causes a rapid increase in blood sugar and a large insulin response. Low-GI foods produce more subtle changes. Climbers can use knowledge of the glycemic index to control energy levels and to speed recovery after a workout. Here's how.

Stable insulin levels are optimal for long-duration stop-and-go activities such as all-day climbing and long training sessions. Experts also agree that a steady insulin curve promotes muscle growth and discourages fat storage. This makes low- to medium-GI foods preferable for climbers in most situations. High-GI foods produce large swings in blood sugar and an insulin spike. One minute you are jonesing to crank another hard route and the next you're yawning and feeling strangely weak.

Figuring the glycemic index of certain foods is more difficult than it might seem at first. For instance, most foods classified as simple carbohydrates (cereal, candy, some fruit juices) are high-GI foods. However, so are potatoes, white rice, bread, and bagels—all considered complex carbohydrates. Low-GI foods include vegetables, whole grains, brown rice, and milk (see table 9.2).

As a general rule, the more processed and easily digestible a food, the higher its glycemic index (for instance, liquids have a higher index than similar food solids). High-fiber foods tend to elicit a slow insulin response and have a relatively low GI. Finally, foods containing some protein and fat along with carbohydrates come in lower on the scale.

This last piece of information is useful if you don't have the gumption to memorize and use this index. Consuming some protein and fat during each of your carbohydrate feedings serves to moderate the overall glycemic response of the meal. So for a long day at the crags, select a sports drink that contains some protein and pack mainly balanced-type energy bars (those containing nearly equal amounts of calories from protein, carbohydrate, and fat).

The one good time to consume high-GI foods such as juice, soda pop, and most sports drinks (like Gatorade) is at the end of your workout or day of climbing. Intense exercise primes the muscles to immediately reload energy reserves in the form of glycogen. High blood sugar and the insulin spike help drive this repletion process. The optimal window for these high-GI foods is the first two hours following exercise. After that, favor low- to medium-index foods for slow, steady refueling. See chapter 10 for more information on this and other recovery strategies.

DAILY REQUIREMENTS

Carbohydrates should account for nearly two-thirds of your daily caloric intake. This means that roughly two-thirds of your plate should be covered with pasta, rice, potatoes, and vegetables, with the other third comprising lean, protein-rich foods. Be sure to apply the same rules when snacking. Try to pair up carbos such as a bagel or fruit with some protein like skim milk, yogurt, or a small amount of peanut butter. The protein helps slow down the digestion of carbohydrates and results in longer-lasting energy.

You can also calculate your approximate need for carbohydrates according to your body weight. Training for two hours per day, you would need roughly

Table 9.2 Glycemic Index of Common Foods

High (> 70)		Medium (50–70)		Low (< 50)	
Sports drinks	70–85	Banana	55	Balance Bar	30
Clif Bar	70+	PowerBar	65	Peanuts	14
Bagel	72	Raisins	64	Apple	38
Carrots	71	Granola bars	61	Orange	43
Corn chips	73	Macaroni	64	Pear	36
Cornflakes	77	Shredded wheat	58	Grapefruit	23
Doughnut	76	Sweet potato	54	Yogurt (w/ fruit)	30
Honey	73	Bran muffin	60	All-Bran	42
Jelly beans	80	Oatmeal	61	Whole wheat	37
Potatoes	83	Wheat crackers	67	Spaghetti	41
Rice (instant)	91	Cookies	60	Beans	48
Rice cakes	82	Orange juice	57	Lentils	28
Cracker (soda/water)	76	Soft drinks	68	Milk (skim)	32
Glucose	100	Sucrose	65	Fructose	23

seven grams of carbohydrate per kilogram of body weight. For example, if you weigh seventy-two kilograms (160 pounds), the requirement would be for approximately 500 grams of carbohydrates; at four calories per gram of carbohydrate, this would equal 2,000 calories. Engaging in a full day of strenuous climbing, however—compared with two hours of training—may demand as much as ten to fourteen grams per kilogram of body weight.

Water

Water may be the most important nutrient to get right when you are climbing, yet I sense that many climbers are chronically dehydrated. Dr. Kristine Clark, director of sports nutrition at Penn State's Center for Sports Medicine, says that "even a 1 to 2 percent drop in water will cause problems in performance." The earliest symptoms of mild dehydration are a loss of concentration and enhanced fatigue. Clark adds that "a 3 percent drop in water

level can create headaches, cramping, dizziness." Furthermore, a recent study has shown that dehydration leading to just a 1.5 percent drop in body weight resulted in a statistically significant drop in maximum strength (Schoffstall 2001).

In a sport as stressful as climbing, dehydration also increases your chance of a joint or tendon injury. Consider that proper hydration facilitates transport of nutrients to the cells, helps protect tissues from injury, and maintains joint lubrication. Therefore, for the purpose of injury prevention, maintaining proper hydration as you train or climb is as important as a proper warm-up.

RECOMMENDATIONS FOR PREVENTING DEHYDRATION

As a rule of thumb, it's a good idea to prehydrate ("camel up," as it's called) before you go to the gym or head out climbing by drinking two to four glasses of water. Follow this with a minimum of an eight-

Table 9.3   Estimated Nutrient and Calorie Needs

Climber	Macronutrient	Grams Needed	Calories	Total
Male (160 lbs./72kg), active day	carbohydrate	520g	2,080	
	protein	115g	460	3,170
	fat	70g	630	
Male (160 lbs./72kg), rest day	carbohydrate	360g	1,140	
	protein	85g	340	2,230
	fat	50g	450	
Female (110 lbs./50kg), active day	carbohydrate	350g	1,400	
	protein	80g	320	2,170
	fat	50g	450	
Female (110 lbs./50kg), rest day	carbohydrate	250g	1,000	
	protein	60g	240	1,582
	fat	38g	342	

ounce serving every hour throughout the day. This would total two quarts of water consumed over an eight-hour period on the rocks. This is a bare minimum amount—what you might drink, say, on a cold day when you perspire very little. Climbing on a humid, eighty-degree day, however, would roughly double this requirement. That means carrying four quarts of water with you for an eight-hour day of climbing. Of course, I doubt you know of very many, if any, climbers who carry three or four quarts of liquid to the crags—thus, the mass of climbers are unknowingly detracting from their ability and increasing injury risk due to mild dehydration.

Optimal Macronutrient Ratio

As you may have gleaned from the previous sections, the optimal macronutrient ratio for a climber depends on the type of climbing activity. High-intensity, stop-and-go climbing like bouldering or cragging is best fueled with a 65:15:20 ratio of carbohydrates, protein, and fat, respectively. The long, slow distance training and climbing of an alpine climber would demand a higher total calorie count per day than the typical rock climber, and this need would be more easily met with a higher-fat diet (though adequate carbohydrates are still necessary). Consequently, a macronutrient ratio of 55:15:30 would be more suitable. See table 9.3 for sample calorie counts for a typical male and female rock climber, though you personally could have significantly different requirements.

Micronutrients and Sports Supplements

The subject of micronutrients and sports supplements is so broad that it's impossible to discuss in a comprehensive manner in an instructional text like this. Still, the use of vitamin supplements and functional foods is so common in sports that the subject is worthy of at least a primer.

Sales of vitamin and sports supplements is a multibillion-dollar industry that bombards us with multilateral, never-ending advertising. Some of the weight-loss and strength-gain claims are truly remarkable, but very few of these claims are backed by reliable scientific studies. Many products are promoted with strong anecdotal claims and well-paid pitchmen, but very few actually do what the advertisers claim.

It's my belief that up to 90 percent of the sports supplements on the market are nothing other than modern-day snake oil, yet a serious athlete looking to maximize performance must be careful not to throw the baby out with the bathwater. On the pages that follow, we'll sort out the handful of products that could potentially enhance your training response and climbing performance.

Micronutrients

Vitamins and minerals are the essential dietary micronutrients. Although the body needs only very small amounts of these nutrients (compared with the macronutrients), they do play a vital role in almost every bodily function—from muscular growth and energy metabolism to neural conduction and memory. Consequently, your health and athletic performance can suffer in a number of ways if you are not consuming enough of these micronutrients.

Studies have shown that as much as two-thirds of self-selected diets contain less than the recommended daily allowances (RDA) of certain vital vitamins and minerals. Furthermore, despite being updated in recent years, RDAs are still believed by many experts to represent low-end requirements for a serious athlete.

VITAL VITAMINS

High-intensity and high-volume exercise (as in bouldering and alpine climbing, respectively) both place great metabolic demands on the body and generate elevated levels of free radicals, which may slow recovery and increase your chance of illness. The antioxidants that combat these free radicals, like vitamin C and vitamin E, are crucial micronutrients you would be wise to consume in greater than the RDA-suggested amounts.

One study showed that supplementing with 1,200 IUs of vitamin E modulated free-radical production and reduced the amount of muscle damage following heavy weight training, in comparison with a placebo group (McBride 1998). Vitamin C has also been shown to help reduce muscle damage, in addition to being necessary for the formation of collagen (the substance that forms connective tissue in the skin and muscles) and supporting the immune system. Therefore, it would be wise to consume extra vitamin C and vitamin E, above and beyond what you can acquire through your diet or from a daily multivitamin. Consider taking one gram of vitamin C and 400 IUs of vitamin E daily, split into two doses (morning and evening).

Certainly there are a host of other vitamins that you might benefit from consuming in amounts higher than the RDA guidelines. Still, eating a decent well-rounded diet and taking a generic daily multivitamin supplement should adequately meet your needs for these other vitamins.

PRECIOUS MINERALS

Magnesium and zinc are two minerals shown to be consumed in less than recommended amounts by a majority of the population. For athletes, a deficiency in these minerals could mean you're getting short-changed on training response. Several recent studies have shown a statistically significant increase in muscular strength in a group of athletes taking supplemental magnesium and zinc (in the form of a patented supplement known as ZMA) versus a control group of athletes taking a placebo (Brilla 1998). Clearly, any climber engaging in serious strength training could benefit from taking this ZMA supplement (available from several different companies).

Another important mineral is selenium, known primarily for its function as an antioxidant. If you are consuming extra vitamin C and vitamin E, you might want to add 100 to 200 micrograms of selenium (taken in split doses with meals) to your supplement regimen.

Calcium and iron are two other minerals that some climbers may be lacking. Vegetarians often fall short on iron consumption, and some women may not get enough iron and calcium in their diets. A multivitamin is the best way to obtain extra iron, especially since its absorption is enhanced in the presence of vitamin C (also in a multivitamin). Females wanting to get extra calcium in their diets could take a calcium supplement (Tums are cheap and taste good!) or simply drink a few glasses of skim milk each day.

Sports Supplements

The most effective way to increase climbing performance is through a long-term, dedicated effort to improve your technique, mental control, and upper-body strength. Unless you are working to dial in on each of these areas, the few sports supplements that do work are probably a waste of money. If you are actively honing your technical skills and training to increase your physical and mental fitness, however, you may be able to further improve your performance through use of a handful of ergogenic (performance-enhancing) supplements.

PROTEIN POWDERS

As discussed earlier, athletes have a greater daily protein requirement than sedentary people, since strenuous exercise results in a higher protein turnover. While mega amounts are not necessary (as some supplement companies and fitness magazines suggest), a 160-pound climber does need to consume between 86 and 108 grams of protein per day. This modest amount can be met through a well-rounded diet; it may be tough to consume adequate protein, however, if you do not eat meat such as chicken, fish, and lean red meats. There is also the limiting factor relating to the biological value of the protein source consumed. Not all protein sources are equal when it comes to providing your body with the necessary building blocks.

Consequently, scientists have developed a number of ways to measure the quality of protein sources. The biological value (BV) is one of the most commonly used; it's based on how much of the protein consumed is actually absorbed and utilized by the body. The higher the BV, the greater the amount of protein that is actually available to be used by the body to strengthen muscles and connective tissues, and to support enzyme formation, among other things.

When the BV scale was originally developed, the egg was considered the perfect protein source (remember Rocky?) and sat alone atop the chart with a value of one hundred. Since then new technologies have enabled the creation of superproteins that are equally valuable to the body but without the fat found in many high-protein foods. Whey is the current superstar of proteins, with a BV of one hundred (though for some reason a few companies inflate this number). Therefore, whey protein could be viewed as superior to the lower-BV foods such as fish, beef, chicken, or soy in helping meet the protein needs of an athlete.

While whey protein costs approximately $0.40 to $0.70 per twenty-gram serving, the investment is a good one considering its ease of use and high BV. Many brands are available from health food stores, supplement catalogs, and online merchants, so shop around for the best deal. Designer Whey Protein by Next Proteins is one excellent brand with several good flavors that mix easily in milk, juice, or water. Such liquid protein is ideal first thing in the morning, and it can increase your rate of recovery when consumed immediately following your workout or a day of climbing (more on this in the next chapter).

Table 9.4 Biological Values of Protein Sources

Food	BV
Whey	100
Whole egg	100
Milk	91
Egg white	88
Fish	83
Beef	80
Chicken	79
Soy	74
Beans	49
Peanuts	43

Not all protein sources are equal when it comes to providing your body with the necessary building blocks. Select mostly high-BV foods from the top half of the list.

One of the highest-quality and most affordable protein sources is skim milk (see table 9.4). Since each glass contains ten grams of protein, consuming a quart of milk per day would provide forty grams toward your total protein requirement. As someone who only occasionally eats meat, I have relied on skim milk as my primary source of protein for the last thirty years (since I first read that John Gill slammed back milk protein after climbing). At 2.5 gallons of milk per week for more than thirty years, I've somehow consumed nearly 4,000 gallons of skim milk since I started climbing. All I can say is, "Got milk?"

Even those who are lactose-intolerant can consume milk without any nasty side effects by purchasing acidophilus milk. Regardless, be sure to always select 1 percent or skim milk, since whole milk contains a significant amount of saturated fat.

SPORTS DRINKS

Since the invention of Gatorade in the early 1970s, sports drinks have grown into a massive industry. It's now hard to find a serious athlete who does not consume sports drinks to help replenish energy. Dozens of different sports drinks are available in bottled form, including Gatorade and Powerade, the two most popular drinks on the market right now. Many others are sold in a bulk powdered form ideal for mixing up at home before a workout or day at the crags.

As you might expect, not all sports drinks are the same. Some are merely glorified sugar water, while others include electrolytes or any number of vitamins, minerals, herbs, or other nutrients said to increase athletic performance. Clearly, many of the claims are unsubstantiated—and at two bucks a bottle, some are just a big rip-off.

The active ingredients in these products fall into two main categories: electrolytes and fuel replacements. A simple understanding of both will help you understand how these drinks might be of benefit to you.

Electrolytes such as potassium, magnesium, calcium, sodium, and chloride are critical for concentration, energy production, nerve transmission, and muscle contraction. Fortunately, electrolyte loss during exercise is quite slow, so even a full day of climbing won't cause significant depletion. A reasonable diet and multivitamin provide you with all the electrolytes you need for ordinary training or a day of climbing. Still, a sports drink with electrolytes may be beneficial if your food supply will be limited for a few days, as in big-wall or alpine climbing.

Fuel sources in the sports drinks are mainly carbohydrates, including glucose, sucrose, fructose, maltodextrin, and lactates. Glucose and sucrose (table sugar) are the fuel sources in the original sports drink Gatorade and have since been adopted

Snack and rehydrate every hour or two. You'll climb better all day long and top out on long routes with energy to spare! ERIC J. HÖRST

by many other companies. Ironically, some athletes now shun drinks with large amounts of glucose and sucrose to avoid a blood sugar spike. Unless you are engaged in an activity that continues steadily for a couple of hours (such as long-distance biking, running, or hiking), this quick increase in blood sugar may be followed by an energy crash as insulin kicks in to reduce the elevated blood sugar level. In a stop-and-go sport like climbing, this pullback on blood sugar can leave you feeling more fatigued and tired than before you consumed the drink!

Consequently, you should avoid any drink whose first ingredient (after water) is glucose or high-fructose corn syrup—both are signs that the drink has a high glycemic index and will release sugar rapidly into the blood. Instead, shop around for powdered sports drink mixes that list fructose (not the same as high-fructose corn syrup) or a protein source such as whey as the first or second ingredient. These have a lower glycemic index and hence provide a slower, more sustained release of carbohydrate ideal for climbers. Accelerade by Pacific Health Labs or PowerBar's Performance Recovery are two good choices.

Carbohydrate (glycogen) depletion in the muscles and liver is a primary cause of fatigue when performing long-duration activities of more than ninety minutes. The traditional use of sports drinks is for situations when additional fuel is needed for prolonged activity lasting more than ninety minutes. Therefore, consuming a fructose-based or protein-containing sports drink during the course of a day at the crags will help maintain energy levels throughout the day, though consuming some food would be beneficial as well. Conversely, an hour or two of bouldering or a short gym workout will not benefit from the added fuel of a sports drink.

While a slow-release, fructose-based or protein-containing sports drink is ideal for when you are climbing, it might be better to consume a high-GI drink upon completion of your workout or day of climbing. Numerous studies have shown that elevating blood sugar as soon as possible after exercise provides the substrate for synthesis of muscle glycogen (Robergs 1991). This is especially important if you plan to climb the very next day—replenishing glyco-gen stores takes up to twenty-four hours, so you need to get the process started immediately and at high speed (see chapter 10 for more recovery tips).

ENERGY BARS

Energy bars have been a dietary mainstay of many climbers since PowerBar hit the scene back in the late 1980s. Originally intended for endurance athletes like bikers and runners, many of the energy bars are designed to deliver a rapid release of sugar into the bloodstream. Therefore, many energy bars possess a high glycemic index (greater than seventy); these are easily identified by their first ingredient, high-fructose corn syrup. Climbers in search of sustained energy are better off sticking to foods with a GI of less than seventy, since they provide more sustained energy and less of an insulin response.

The numerous balanced-style bars that have entered the market in recent years typically possess a glycemic index in the forty-to-sixty range. The higher amount of protein and fat contained in these bars helps slow the release of sugar into the bloodstream. The balanced 40:30:30 macronutrient ratio also helps conserve glycogen and may even help spare muscle protein from being used for energy during a long day of climbing. Consequently, consuming a couple of Balance Bars (Fig Newtons are also good) and drinking lots of water may be the single best combination to maintain energy, spare muscle protein, and prevent dehydration.

CREATINE

Dozens of sports supplements claim to help build muscle and increase strength. While most are, in fact, worthless, creatine has been proven to increase explosive strength (Toler 1997; Kreider 1998). But is creatine a good supplement for climbers?

First, creatine is by far the most noticeably effective sports supplement on the market. When it is consumed daily in doses of 10 to 25 grams, users actually see their muscles get larger and harder—the results can be quite amazing—as they gain lean muscle mass (that is, the users' body weight increases). Consequently, creatine-containing products have become the biggest-selling sports supplements in the country, and they are widely used by football and baseball players, weight lifters, bodybuilders, and millions of fitness buffs. But are these effects beneficial for climbers? Let's take a look at how creatine works.

Creatine is a compound that's natural to the body, and it's used in the muscles to help create ATP (the energy source for brief, explosive movements). Creatine is also present in animal foods such as red meat, but the amount consumed in a normal diet is quite small (a couple of grams per day). Studies have shown that taking twenty grams per day of supplemental creatine for five or six days will enhance performance in short-duration, high-intensity exercise such as sprinting or weight lifting. This creatine-loading protocol is the method used by most athletes—but it's the wrong protocol for climbers!

Two side effects of creatine loading are weight gain and what's known as cell volumizing. Both these effects occur because creatine associates with water as it is stored in the muscles. Over the six-day loading phase, more and more creatine is stored and an increasing amount of water is drawn into the muscle cell. This gives muscles a fuller, "pumped" feel and look—just what bodybuilders and fitness buffs want. This loading process, therefore, results in a water weight gain of several pounds or more in most individuals. This is a good thing for athletes in sports where increased weight and speed (inertia) can be used to your advantage (tackling, swinging a bat, or swinging your fist). In a sport that requires a high strength-to-weight ratio, however, it can have a negative impact on performance.

Some climbers have argued that stronger muscles (due to creatine loading) can easily lift the extra weight gained in the growing process. The problem, however, is that creatine loads in all muscles of the body, not just the climbing muscles, and will load proportionately more in the largest muscles of the body—the legs! Of course, increasing leg muscle size and weight is a bad thing for climbers, since they are never the limiting factor. There's just no way around it: Creatine loading is not a good thing for climbers.

If you are still not convinced, let's consider the cell-volumizing effect of creatine loading. Body-builders love the fact that their muscles pump up more easily when they are loaded with creatine. I quickly noticed this same effect when I experimented with creatine after it first appeared on the market in 1993. It seemed strange at the time, but I pumped out faster when I was on creatine—this despite the fact that I felt like I had a little more zip in my muscles. What I quickly concluded was that the cell-volumizing effect of creatine leads to more rapid occlusion of the capillaries that innervate the muscle, thus slowing blood flow and causing the rapid pump. In climbing, the goal is obviously to postpone full-on pump as long as possible.

That said, I do believe that well-timed, small doses of creatine can help climbers recover more quickly and without the nasty side effects of loading. The protocol I've developed and used for many years now is to add just five grams of creatine to a quart of sports drink that I sip throughout the day when

Vitamin and Sports Supplement Tips

1. Take a daily multivitamin each morning with breakfast.
2. On training or climbing days, take an additional 500 to 1,000mg of vitamin C, 400 to 800IU of vitamin E, and 100 to 200mcg of selenium, split into a morning and evening dose.
3. Consider consuming extra protein (especially if you eat little meat or dairy products) by drinking a whey protein shake each morning and evening.
4. When climbing, snack on fruits, balanced-style energy bars, sports drinks (choose those possessing some fructose and/or protein), and other low-GI foods. Consider adding five grams of creatine (no more) to your bottle of sports drink to further enhance recovery.
5. Avoid mass-marketed sports supplements, especially those with the wildest claims—most are frauds.

climbing. This provides a slow trickle of creatine into the blood and muscles to aid recovery between routes. For training, I wait until the end of the workout; then I initiate the recovery cycle by consuming five grams of creatine mixed into a sports drink.

The bottom line: Use creatine in small doses and it may enhance your recovery with no noticeable weight gain or other negative side effects. If you decide to supplement with creatine, follow the above guidelines closely and never consume more than five grams per day.

SPORTS SUPPLEMENTS THAT DON'T WORK

The list of sports supplements that don't work is too long to completely cover in this text. I can, however, list a few of the most popular, most hyped supplements that have little or no reliable research to back up the big claims, or—worse yet—pose health dangers.

First and foremost is androstenedione (aka andro), along with other testosterone boosters. The research on these substances is largely contradictory and somewhat scary. One study showed that andro increased testosterone in women, while another showed it increased estrogen in men! Several other studies showed absolutely no effect to taking these supplements. Stay away from this stuff.

Without getting long-winded, here's a list of other supplements that will only piss your money away (no proven ergogenic effect): NO_2, vanadyl sulfate, pyruvate, OKG, gamma oryzanol, inosine, chitosan (and other "fat whackers"), algae (of all colors), GHB, MCTs, shark cartilage, and many homeopathic supplements.

10

Accelerating Recovery

Knowing is not enough; we must apply. Willing is not enough; we must do.

—*Johann Wolfgang von Goethe*

If you are serious about climbing performance, then you must be serious about accelerating recovery. Knowing how to limit fatigue and speed recovery is as important as knowing how to perform a drop-knee, lock a finger jam, or float a deadpoint. The bottom line: If you are not playing a proactive role in the recovery process, then you are definitely not training optimally or climbing up to your capability.

We all know, firsthand, that physical fatigue is a primary limiting factor whether pulling down at the crags or training in the gym. Therefore, it stands to reason that being able to accelerate recovery means you will get more back during a midclimb shakeout and while resting between climbs and days of climbing. As a result, you will perform better on the rocks today, tomorrow, and on all your future outings. Similarly, more rapid recovery between training sessions can translate into more long-term strength gains, since you can work out more often while still getting adequate rest and without risk of overtraining.

While many of today's enthusiastic climbers are keen on staying current on the latest climbing and training techniques, surprisingly few individuals are

*Persevering high up on the classic **Arizona Flyways (5.11c), Mount Lemmon, Arizona***
ERIC J. HÖRST

aware of the numerous strategies for accelerating recovery. Recovery from exercise has been the subject of dozens of recent research studies, and any serious climber would be wise to heed the findings of these sports scientists. On the pages that follow, I will present the leading-edge recovery strategies used in these studies, as well as provide instruction on specific techniques that will help you slow fatigue and speed recovery while on the rock.

Clearly, recovery ability is a function of several factors, including age, sex, and level of conditioning. Regardless of these factors, however, I guarantee that you can recover more quickly by playing a proactive role in the recovery process—instead of just letting it happen, as many climbers do. By placing the same importance on optimal recovery as you do on training optimally, you will enhance your training response as well as your overall climbing performance!

The Basics of Fatigue and Recovery

Proactively managing fatigue and taking the steps to accelerate recovery require an understanding of the basic physiological processes involved in energy production, fatigue, and recovery. We'll begin our primer on this subject with a look at what causes fatigue, and then look at three recovery time frames.

Causes of Fatigue

Several factors contribute to the fatigue you experience while training or climbing. These factors include the depletion of muscle fuels, the accumulation of metabolic by-products, low blood glucose, muscular cramps and microtraumas, and finally central fatigue.

207

DEPLETION OF ATP-CP

Adenosine triphosphate (ATP) and creatine phosphate (CP) are energy-rich phosphate compounds stored within the muscle cells in small amounts. Brief, maximum-intensity activities (such as a short, vicious boulder problem, a one-arm pull-up, or a 100-meter sprint) are fueled by ATP and CP; the supply of these fuels, however, limits this action to between five and fifteen seconds.

This limitation on maximum energy output explains why it's next to impossible to perform Double Dyno campus training for more than fifteen seconds, or why you have less than fifteen seconds to pull a maximal move (for you) on a route before your muscles give out. Continued exercise beyond this time threshold is only possible by lowering the intensity of the activity, so that the lactic acid energy system can contribute to energy production.

Fortunately, ATP is continually synthesized within the muscles (by little ATP factories called mitochondria), and ATP stores become fully replenished in just three to five minutes of complete rest (Bloomfield 1994).

ACCUMULATION OF METABOLIC BY-PRODUCTS

Sustained moderately high-intensity activity lasting between fifteen seconds and three minutes is fueled primary by anaerobic metabolism of glycogen fuel (see figure 5.4). Unfortunately, metabolic by-products of this energy production—chiefly, lactic acid—result in muscular discomfort and, eventually, muscular failure. How long you can exercise during periods of rising lactic acid concentration depends on your lactate threshold—that is, how high in intensity can you exercise before blood lactate levels grow greater than your body's ability to metabolize it.

Anaerobic endurance training will increase your tolerance to lactic acid as well as elevate your anaerobic threshold. Furthermore, anything you do to enhance blood flow through the working muscles will help disperse lactic acid to your liver and non-working muscles, where it's converted back to glucose. Continued high-intensity exercise (with no rest), however, will cause lactic acid levels to sky-rocket and muscular failure to occur in less than three minutes. This explains why the "pump clock" runs out in less than three minutes on long, near-maximum (for you) crux sequences. You must get to a rest in less than three minutes or you'll end up taking a lactic acid bath!

During rest periods, the clearance time of lactic acid can be anywhere from ten to thirty minutes, depending on the initial level of the lactic acid accumulation and whether the rest is active or passive (more on this later).

DEPLETION OF GLYCOGEN

Steady, long-term exercise typically depletes glycogen stores in ninety minutes to two hours. Running out of glycogen causes the infamous hitting-the-wall phenomenon in marathon running, and it is a contributing factor to your inability to climb hard toward the end of a long day on the rock.

Fortunately, climbing is a stop-and-go activity, so a full two-hour supply of glycogen can be stretched out to last nearly all day. You can also spare your glycogen supplies through regular consumption of additional fuel (sports drinks and foodstuffs) throughout the day. Research implies that carbohydrate feeding during exercise can help extend your glycogen supply by 25 to 50 percent (Coyle 1984).

Your starting level of glycogen is also a crucial factor in determining how long and hard you will be able to climb. If you are climbing for a second or third straight day, you will certainly have less than the full ninety-minute to two-hour supply of glycogen. This is because complete replenishment of glycogen stores takes twenty-four hours—a good dinner and a full night's sleep are not enough to restock the supply completely. When climbing on successive days, it's therefore vital to consume more calories throughout the day (to spare glycogen)—and even so, you will likely hit the wall sooner on day two than you did on day one.

LOW BLOOD GLUCOSE

Blood glucose (sugar) is but one of the possible fuel sources for working muscles, but it's the only fuel source available to the brain and nervous system. As

Figure 10.1 Recovery Curve

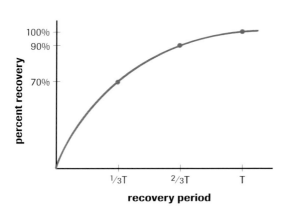

Recovery to 90 percent of baseline levels occurs in about two-thirds of the time needed for complete recovery.

glycogen supplies dwindle during long-duration activity, the working muscles become increasingly reliant on blood glucose for fuel. As a result, blood glucose levels drop and increasing levels of exhaustion and mental fatigue set in.

As mentioned above, ingestion of carbohydrates will help delay this fatigue by helping to maintain an adequate level of blood glucose.

MUSCLE CRAMPS AND MICROTRAUMAS

Muscle cramps and microtraumas can contribute to the sense of muscular fatigue, though in somewhat different time frames. Muscle cramps typically occur near the end of an exhausting period of muscle action—for instance, when some of the muscles in your back or arms lock up after a long, strenuous section of jamming or upon reaching complete exhaustion in the midst of a long sport climb. In such an instance, twenty to thirty minutes of rest, gentle stretching, and massage, as well as consuming some fluids, will help alleviate the cramping and restore normal muscular function.

Microtraumas are a primary cause of the all-too-common delayed-onset muscle soreness (DOMS). This muscle soreness, which becomes evident from twenty-four to forty-eight hours after strenuous exercise, is a result of microscopic muscle tissue tears and the accompanying tightness and swelling (edema). Strength will be diminished for as long as pain persists, possibly as long as two to five days.

CENTRAL FATIGUE

In addition to muscular fatigue, strenuous exercise can have adverse effects on the central nervous system (CNS). This so-called central fatigue can impair coordination, concentration, and your ability to perform difficult motor skills. Repeated high-intensity movements such as lunging and campus training are the hardest on the CNS. However, excessive amounts of any specific training stimulus—fingerboard, Hypergravity Isolation Training, campus training, and such—or performing the same type of bouldering movement over and over can also produce central fatigue.

Unfortunately, severe central fatigue can take longer to recover from than that due to any of the other causes. Consider that recovery of a nerve cell takes up to seven times longer than a muscle cell (Bompa 1983). Of course, this level of fatigue may never be experienced by the typical recreational climber; whereas elite climbers, who push the envelope both in the gym and on the rock, are likely to experience central fatigue. If you still feel physically "off" even after a few successive rest days, you may be experiencing central fatigue. It may take another two to ten days away from training and climbing to recuperate completely, but you will find yourself performing better than ever after this break away from climbing (per the Reminiscence Effect described in chapter 8).

Three Recovery Periods

Recovery is not linear, but instead exponential (see figure 10.1). For example, recovery from an exhaustive crux sequence, climb, workout, or day of climbing will initially be rapid, with about 70 percent of complete recovery taking place in the first one-third of the recovery period (Bompa 1983). Recovery improves to 90 percent after two-thirds of the time needed for complete recovery.

Knowing that recovery is an exponential process is powerful information that can be applied to the three crucial recovery periods that I've defined as recharge, refuel, and rebuild.

RECHARGE (SHORT-TERM RECOVERY)

This first recovery period takes place from ten seconds to thirty minutes following the completion of muscular action. The recharge period includes the ten-second shakeout you take in the midst of a crux sequence as well as the midclimb rest you milk for five, ten, or even twenty minutes, if possible.

The two metabolic processes at work during this recovery period are resynthesis of ATP and the removal of lactic acid from the working muscles. As stated earlier, ATP resynthesis takes less than five minutes, and complete lactic acid removal occurs in less than thirty minutes. As depicted in figure 10.1, however, recovery to 90 percent of baseline levels occurs in about two-thirds of the time needed for complete recovery. Therefore, you can assume that the majority of ATP resynthesis has occurred in just over three minutes and about 90 percent of the lactic acid has been removed in about twenty minutes. Strategies to further hasten recovery during the recharge period will be detailed later in this chapter.

It should be noted that nothing you consume during this initial recovery period has any impact on exercise resumed immediately after this brief rest. Water takes at least fifteen minutes to empty from the stomach, and sports drinks or foodstuffs take even longer. If you have concluded your climbing or training for the day, however, this initial thirty-minute period is vital for enhancing long-term recovery (more on this in a bit).

REFUEL (MEDIUM-TERM RECOVERY)

The refuel recovery period occurs from thirty minutes to twenty-four hours following cessation of exercise. Therefore, this phase of recovery takes place during the two-hour break between climbs that you might take during the hottest part of the day and, of course, during the overnight period following a training or climbing day.

With ATP resynthesis and lactic acid removal completed in the first thirty minutes, the refuel stage is defined by the replenishment of blood glucose and glycogen stores (in muscles and the liver), and some minor repair of tissue microtraumas. Since refueling is the hallmark of this period, consuming a large amount of the right type of carbohydrates is necessary to facilitate the process.

Numerous strategies for enhancing this replenishment process will be described later in the chapter, but—as mentioned earlier—you can assume that about 90 percent of this refueling has taken place in about sixteen hours (two-thirds of the total recovery period). Thus, the typical twelve-hour break between consecutive days of climbing will result only in approximately 80 percent replenishment of glycogen stores (assuming you begin refueling immediately upon finishing up the first day on the rocks).

REBUILD (LONG-TERM RECOVERY)

Muscle growth and neuromuscular adaptation typically take place from one to four days following strenuous exercise. The degree of delayed-onset muscle soreness experienced is proportionate to the amount of microscopic damage inflicted on muscle fibers during exercise. Minor DOMS may subside in forty-eight hours, while severe soreness signals a greater degree of damage that may take four or more days to rebuild.

You can now see that a single rest day is enough to allow the muscles to recharge and refuel, yet complete supercompensation—that is, rebuilding the muscle to a stronger level than before the exercise stimulus—requires additional rest for the neuromuscular system to recuperate. Therefore, while you may be able to perform at a reasonably high level after just one day of rest, truncating the rebuilding process negates the supercompensation period (per chapter 5) and will inhibit gains in strength. In the long term, chronic under-resting can result in decreased performance, injury, and even risk of illness.

Whether you are training indoors or climbing a personal-best route outside, the ability to accelerate recovery is tantamount to elevating your absolute level of performance. In the gym faster recovery between exercises or climbs translates to higher-intensity stimuli or faster learning, respectively. On the rock hastened recovery at a marginal rest may make the difference between a brilliant on-sight or hardest-ever flash and dangling on the rope in frustration.

On the pages that follow, you will learn fourteen powerful techniques for accelerating recovery and, thus, improving the quality of your training and climbing. But knowing is not enough—you must apply these strategies with the same dedication and resolve as when pursuing your endeavors in the gym or at the crag.

Accelerating Short-Term or Intraclimb Recovery

Your capacity to perform difficult moves or exercises repeatedly, with only short rest breaks, is directly proportionate to your recovery ability in the short term. Described as the recharge period above, only certain recovery mechanisms come into play during the first ten seconds to thirty minutes following strenuous activity. The goal during this time is to help expedite the recharge process. This is done by minimizing the magnitude of fatigue (in the first place), enhancing forearm recovery with the G-Tox and active rest, and engaging in pre-exercise hydration.

Limit Fatigue by Climbing More Efficiently

Let's start off with the most simple, yet powerful method to enhance short-term recovery—limit the magnitude of fatigue, as much as possible, through economy of movement and optimal climbing technique. Obviously, you will use less ATP and CP, as well as produce less lactic acid, if you can lower the intensity of muscular contraction and the total time under load. In this way you immediately reduce the magnitude of the fatigue you must recover from, and you will return to baseline strength more quickly.

It's in this area that the average climber can realize a windfall of unknown capability. The fact is, most climbers move too slowly, possess less-than-ideal technique, and stop to place gear or think when they should be pushing on to the next rest. While lack of experience and technical ability are the

real limiting factors here, slow climbing and hesitation will lead you to believe that a lack of strength is the primary problem.

If any of this sounds familiar, then some dedicated technique-training practice will go a long way toward elevating your game (see chapter 4). By learning to move swiftly and accurately through hard moves, and by relaxing your grip and lowering tension in the antagonist muscles, you will use less ATP and CP on difficult sequences and produce less lactic acid. In this way you immediately reduce the magnitude of the fatigue you must recover from at a midclimb rest position, and you will return to baseline strength more quickly between attempts or sends.

Enhance Forearm Recovery with the G-Tox

The dangling-arm shakeout is the technique traditionally used to aid recovery in the commonly fatigued forearm muscles. A few seconds or, hopefully, a few minutes of shaking out provides some recovery, but often not enough. The effects of a full-on pump can take frustratingly long to subside, and when hanging out at a marginal rest, it's possible to expend as much energy hanging on with one arm as is being recouped in the other. Such a zero-net gain in recovery does nothing to enhance performance—in such a situation you would likely have fared better by blowing off the so-called rest and climbing onward.

Luckily there is the G-Tox, a shakeout technique that I developed, to accelerate recovery of finger strength while hanging out at a midclimb rest. For more than fifteen years, I have been promoting the benefits of alternating the position of your resting arm between the normal dangling position and an above-your-head raised-hand position. This simple practice provides a noticeable increase in recovery rate. I named this recovery technique the G-Tox, because it uses gravity (as an ally, for once) to help detoxify the fatigued muscle and speed recovery.

The discomfort and pump that develop in your forearms while climbing are largely the result of accumulating lactic acid (LA) and restricted blood flow. As described in chapter 5, LA is a by-product of the anaerobic metabolism of glycogen, an energy pathway that comes into use during extended contractions of greater than about 50 percent of maximum intensity. Worse yet, contractions of as little as 20 percent of maximum intensity begin to hamper capillary blood flow, and at 50 percent of maximum contraction blood flow may be completely occluded (closed off). As a result, LA concentrations skyrocket until blood flow can resume during periods of low-intensity contraction or complete rest.

What's more, when dangling your arm in the traditional shakeout technique, it's common to experience an initial increase in the sensation of being pumped. This is because, as the muscle relaxes, blood flow into it resumes—but the venous return of the "old blood" out of the muscle is more sluggish. This traffic jam perpetuates the pump and slows recovery, yet many climbers continue to dangle their arms and complain about how sickening of a pump they have.

The G-Tox technique puts gravity to work by aiding venous return of blood toward the heart. By helping get blood out of the arm more quickly, this practice enhances the removal of lactic acid and, therefore, returns you to a baseline level of blood lactate more quickly. The effects of this technique are unmistakable—you will literally see the pump drain from the elevated arm due to the interesting fact that arterial flow into the arm is less affected by gravity than is venous return flow.

So why not just use the raised-arm position for the full duration of the rest instead of using the alternating technique as described above? Since the raised-arm position requires some muscular contraction in the upper arm, shoulder, and chest, these muscles would fatigue and possibly hamper climbing performance if you held the raised-arm position for a long time. Consequently, the best protocol for recovery is alternating between the two arm positions every five to ten seconds. Do so, and you will definitely feel the difference the G-Tox makes!

Engage in Active Rest

Along with the G-Tox, active rest is another underused yet highly effective strategy for accelerating recovery. While the G-Tox shines in its effectiveness to enhance recovery at a midclimb shakeout, use of active rest between climbs is an equally effective strategy for increasing the rate of lactic acid removal from the working muscles and bloodstream.

Several recent studies, including one excellent study on climbers (Watts 2000), have shown that active rest significantly reduces blood lactate compared with the more common practice of passive rest. In the Watts study fifteen expert climbers attempted to redpoint a 20-meter, 5.12b gym route, with eight of them engaging in active rest (recumbent cycling) and the others assigned to passive rest immediately following completion of the route. Periodic measurements of blood lactate revealed that the active-rest group returned to preclimb levels within twenty minutes, while the passive group took thirty minutes to return to baseline levels. Therefore, low-intensity active rest accelerated the clearing of lactic acid from the blood by almost 35 percent.

Applying this research finding at the crag is simple. Upon completing a pumpy route or redpoint attempt, instead of sitting down and resting passively (or worse yet, having a smoke), grab your water bottle and go for a casual twenty-minute hike. This will help clear lactic acid more quickly as well as provide a mental break from the action. Both these factors will enhance your performance on the next route!

Another study compared recovery after maximum exercise in four groups: passive rest, active rest, massage, and combined massage and active rest (Monedero 2000). After fifteen minutes of rest, blood lactate removal was greatest in the group performing combined active rest and massage. Therefore, you may be able to further improve the Watts strategy of active rest by performing some self-massage on your most fatigued muscles (usually the forearms, upper arms, and shoulders).

A more recent study has shown that shorter periods of active recovery provide similarly positive effects on lowering blood lactate concentrations compared with equal periods of passive rest. The study tested ten climbers engaging in five, two-minute climbing trials, followed by two minutes of either active or passive recovery. The active-recovery group started the next trial with lower arterial lactate concentration than the passive-recovery group, and they recorded lower perceived exertion scores at the end of each climb (Draper 2006). The bottom line on this study is that in bouldering, it's better to walk around between ascents or attempts and sustain a higher heart rate to speed recovery.

Prehydrate Within Two Hours of Exercise

Muscles are more than 70 percent water, and it plays a vital role in cellular function and the transport of nutrients and metabolic waste. If you are dehydrated, it will hurt your performance and slow recovery. Therefore, it's prudent to prehydrate by consuming a quart of water in the two hours preceding a workout or climbing. Continue sipping water throughout the duration of activity at a minimum rate of eight ounces every hour (twice this, if it's hot).

Accelerating Medium-Term or Intraday Recovery

Intraday recovery is the medium-term recuperation that occurs throughout the day and up to twenty-four hours following exercise. What you do (or don't do) during this recovery period plays a direct role in how much energy you will have during the latter part of a long day of climbing; it's also the primary factor in how much recovery you acquire in a single night of rest. Of course, this is of big-time importance if you are in the midst of a long, all-day route or when you plan to climb two days in a row.

Earlier I referred to this medium-term recovery phase as the refuel period, since restoring a normal blood glucose level and replenishing glycogen is the basis for most recovery gained from thirty minutes to twenty-four hours following exercise. Consequently, consuming the right carbohydrates at the right time is the single most vital action to accelerate recovery. Still, stretching, massage, and the use of relaxation exercises will also increase your rate of recuperation. Let's delve deeper into each of these areas.

Refuel Early and Often

The single biggest error in recovery strategy by most climbers is delayed consumption of calories during and after a day of climbing. The natural tendency is to become so engaged in the activity of climbing that you forget to eat and drink. This is compounded by the fact that strenuous exercise naturally suppresses hunger.

REFUELING WHILE YOU CLIMB

Earlier it was explained that consuming calories throughout the day helps maintain blood glucose and, thus, helps slow the use of your limited supply of glycogen. Toward this end, you should take in your first dose of calories between one to two hours after beginning your climb. If you are cragging, this might mean consuming a piece of fruit, a Balance Bar, or eight ounces of sports drink after completing the first strenuous climb of the day. Continue eating a small serving of food every two hours throughout the day. In the case of all-day climbing, this means a total of four snacks—for example, two pieces of fruit and two energy bars.

This may seem like an awful lot of food, and it is if you are only climbing for half a day or going bouldering (halve these amounts in these situations). To keep climbing hard throughout the day and to speed recovery for a second day of climbing, however, you should consume a minimum of 600 to 800 calories during the course of the day.

Selecting the right kinds of food at the right time is a matter of the glycemic index (GI). As introduced in chapter 9, high-GI foods elicit a rapid rise (then drop) in blood sugar, while medium- and low-GI foods release fuel into the bloodstream more slowly. In a stop-and-go sport like climbing, steady blood sugar is vital for maintaining steady concentration and steady energy. Therefore, consume only low- and medium-GI foods while you are still engaged in physical activity (see table 9.2). Upon completing your day on the rocks or reaching the end of your workout, however, it's best to consume higher-GI foods and beverages. This latter distinction is powerful—there is a growing body of research indicating that what you eat in the first thirty minutes after exercise is the single largest determining factor in how fast you recover.

KICK-STARTING GLYCOGEN REPLENISHMENT AFTER CLIMBING OR TRAINING

As incredible as it may seem, recent research has shown that waiting two hours after exercise to consume carbohydrates will reduce your glycogen replenishment by 50 percent compared with eating immediately upon cessation of the activity (Burke 1999). Therefore, when planning to climb a second day, you significantly handicap tomorrow's performance by delaying refueling. Similarly, delayed refueling after training slows the recovery and rebuilding processes and, possibly, delays complete recovery by as much as a full day.

Let's take a closer look at the best refueling strategies in the hours following climbing or a vigorous workout.

First thirty minutes after climbing: Ingestion of high-GI foods immediately after exercise substan-

tially increases the rate of muscle glycogen replacement (Richter 1984). More recent studies have shown that glycogen synthesis may take place another 40 percent faster if protein and carbohydrate are consumed together, due to a greater insulin response (Niles 1997). Consequently, the best protocol for accelerating glycogen replenishment appears to be a 4:1 ratio of carbohydrate to protein consumption (Burke 1999).

Since solid foods enter the bloodstream more slowly than liquids, it's best to drink this carbohydrate–protein blend post-exercise. For example, a 160-pound climber would want to consume approximately one hundred grams of carbohydrate and twenty-five grams of protein. Drinking a quart of Gatorade, juice, or another glucose- or high-fructose-corn-syrup-based sports drink would provide nearly a hundred grams of high-GI carbohydrate. Consuming a high-protein energy bar or a whey protein shake would provide roughly twenty-five grams of protein. Another highly practical option is to drink a 4:1 (carbohydrate-to-protein ratio) sports drink such as Accelerade. Take these actions immediately after your workout or climbing and you will jump-start recovery, big time!

Two hours after climbing: Assuming you consumed the initial feeding of carbohydrates and protein within the thirty-minute time frame, you can wait until about two hours post-activity to eat a complete meal. Ideally, the meal should comprise foods providing a macronutrient ratio of about 65:15:20 (calories from carbohydrate:protein:fat), as explained in chapter 9. Such a meal might include a large serving of pasta, a piece of lean meat, and a salad or some vegetables. Whereas high-GI foods are best eaten immediately after exercise, medium- and low-GI foods are more advantageous in the two to twenty-four hours after exercise. They will provide a slower, longer-lasting trickle of glucose into the bloodstream that will support steady glycogen resynthesis.

Before going to sleep: A small meal of carbohydrate and protein within thirty minutes of going to sleep will further support glycogen resynthesis and

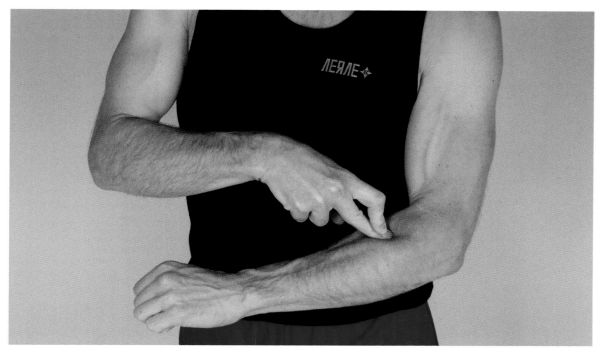

Cross-fiber friction (with braced finger) self-massage is an excellent way to increase blood flow and warm up the forearm muscles prior to training.

tissue rebuilding overnight. Skim milk may be the perfect before-bedtime food—it possesses low-GI carbohydrate, high-quality protein, and the amino acid tryptophan, a precursor to serotonin, which slows down brain activity. Drink a tall glass of skim milk (consider mixing in some whey protein powder) or have some milk on a small bowl of whole-grain cereal before bedtime. It'll do your body good!

Stretch and Massage the Hardest-Working Muscles

Earlier, you learned about an impressive research study showing that combining active rest and massage accelerated recovery by enhancing the removal of lactic acid from the blood. Deep-fiber-spreading sports massage is also an effective practice to enhance medium- and long-term recovery.

The guy who literally wrote the book on the subject is Jack Meagher. In his text *Sports Massage*, he explains how the use of a specific form of sports massage can provide up to a 20 percent increase in performance, in addition to reducing the risk of injury and accelerating recovery.

HOW IT WORKS

Traditional massage has long been used to increase blood flow and oxygen transport in the muscles. The benefits of this superficial "rubbing" are brief, however, and have little residual effect on performance.

Sports massage utilizes a deep-fiber-spreading technique that produces hyperemia (a dilation of the blood vessels) through the full depth of the muscle. Furthermore, the state of hyperemia lasts long after the procedure has ended, so the enhanced blood flow can accelerate recovery and aid healing after strenuous exercise.

Sports massage also helps reduce the number of small and often unfelt spasms that regularly occur in the muscle. These spasms may go unchallenged by conventional stretching and warm-up exercises and, left unchecked, can rob you of coordination and induce mechanical resistance and premature fatigue.

HOW TO DO IT

There are several strokes you may want to learn, but the most effective is called cross-fiber friction. This stroke is best executed with a braced finger (see the photo). The motion is a simple push in followed by a short push back and forth across the muscle fiber. Keep the stroke short and rhythmic; only gradually increase the pressure to penetrate deeper into the muscle.

Although sports massage can be used on all muscles, focus your efforts on the upper body and, in particular, the finger flexors and extensors, and the pronator teres and brachioradialis (upper forearm muscles), the biceps and triceps (muscles of the upper arm), and the large muscles of the shoulders and back. Incorporate five to ten minutes of massage into your regular warm-up routine. This, along with the warm-up activities and stretches detailed in chapter 6, will better prepare you for an excellent workout or day on the rocks.

SPORTS MASSAGE TO ACCELERATE RECOVERY

Your body has inherent mechanical weaknesses where sport-specific movements can trigger stress overload. In climbing, the muscle most overloaded are the forearms, upper arms, and back. These muscles are the first to tire, and they are typically the slowest to recover. Fortunately, you can modulate fatigue and hasten recovery through application of sport massage to the specific stress points—often called trigger points—inherent to climbing movements.

To become familiar with these stress points, it's best to have some understanding of how a muscle works. First, voluntary muscles have two ends, each of which is attached to a bone via a tendon. One end is a fixed attachment called the origin, and the other is a movable attachment called the insertion. For example, the origin of the bicep muscle is at the shoulder, and the insertion is just below the elbow. The motor nerve enters the muscle in the thick muscle belly between the origin and insertion. It is here that all contractions begin, and they spread toward the ends of the muscle as more forceful contractions are needed. Consequently, only a maximum effort will recruit the high-threshold fibers situated near the ends of the muscle.

For this reason a proper (submaximum) warm-up does not work the whole muscle. The end fibers (near the origin and insertion) largely miss out on the warm-up process, and thus they are more likely to underperform when called into action for high-intensity movements. Fortunately, sports massage applied to these points before a workout or climb helps warm even the least used fibers, and enables maximum efforts with minimal resistance and risk of injury.

These trigger points are also more likely to harbor stress and become cramped post-exercise. Use of sports massage and trigger point therapy will help relieve these stress points and speed recovery. You can best address these trigger points with what is called the direct-pressure stroke. Apply firm, constant straight-in pressure with a braced finger, a wooden Bodo or shepherd's crook (available from www.bonnie prudden.com), or a friend's elbow, and hold for fifteen to thirty seconds. Direct pressure is especially useful when applied to the trigger points near the base of the muscles. This will help relieve any known or unknown spasms, increase local circulation, and aid healing. (Be sure never to apply sports massage tactics to tendons, joints, or injured tissues, however.) Conclude your massage with some mild stretching.

Use Relaxation Techniques

Chapter 3 described an excellent relaxation technique called the Progressive Relaxation Sequence. Though commonly used before going to sleep, progressive relaxation is also highly effective for relaxing the muscles and quieting the mind during a midday break from climbing. When resting between climbs or taking a break before returning to work on a project, find a quiet spot, lie down, and spend ten to twenty minutes performing progressive relaxation. Upon completing this process, sit up for a few minutes and enjoy the day before proceeding to the next climb.

Make a midday relaxation break a regular part of your climbing ritual and you'll find yourself climbing better, and with less fatigue, late into the day.

Accelerating Long-Term or Interday Recovery

The interday recovery period involves the long-term recuperation from a severe workout or a couple of hard days of climbing. Depending on the intensity and volume of the activity, full recovery could take anywhere from one to four days (or more).

When you wake up in the morning with sore muscles (delayed-onset muscle soreness), it's a sign that you incurred microtraumas and that a recovery period of at least another twenty-four hours is needed. Of course, you have two choices in this situation. The first is to go climbing (or work out) for a second straight day, despite the soreness, realizing that your performance will be less than ideal and your risk of injury is increased. Or you could take a day or two off and allow your neuromuscular system to recuperate to a level of capability higher than before the workout (supercompensation).

Certainly, there are times when you will select the first option of climbing a second day straight, but there should be an equal number of instances when you decide that "less will be more." Weekend climbing trips are the classic situation in which you'd want to climb two days in a row, regardless of sore muscles. Given proper nutrition, a good warm-up, and a prudent approach to pushing yourself on the second day, you will usually get away with climbing sore.

Choosing to take a day or two of rest, however, is clearly the intelligent decision when climbing indoors or during an off-season training cycle. Hopefully, you gleaned from chapter 5 that proper rest is as important as training stimulus in becoming a stronger climber, and that under-resting is a primary cause of injury. Enthusiastic indoor and sport climbers are most commonly guilty of under-resting, but regardless of your preference, it's important that you distinguish yourself from the mass of climbers who overtrain. If you find yourself drawn to overtraining with the crowd, remember that in order to outperform the masses, you cannot do what they are doing!

Eat Frequent, Small Meals

Instead of eating the typical three meals per day, you can accelerate recovery by consuming six smaller meals or snacks spaced evenly throughout the day. Avoid high-GI foods; they are less effective for recovery after the first two hours post-exercise. Instead select low- and medium-GI foods for all your meals and drink at least ten glasses of water throughout the day.

At least three of your meals should contain a significant portion of protein. For instance, breakfast could include a couple of eggs, skim milk, or whey protein; lunch might include some low-fat yogurt, skim milk, or a can of tuna; and for dinner it might be good to eat a piece of lean red meat, chicken, or fish. Each of these meals should also include some carbohydrate, and at all costs avoid fat-laden fried foods and any snack foods containing hydrogenated oils. Strive for a macronutrient profile of roughly 65:15:20 (carbohydrate:protein:fat) for each major meal.

While the other three feedings need be only a couple hundred calories, they are vital for maintaining steady blood glucose and continuing the recovery processes throughout the day. Low- and medium-GI foods are the best choice, with a piece of fruit or a balanced-type energy bar being ideal selections.

Take a Multivitamin and Antioxidants

In today's world of highly processed foods, it's often difficult to consume enough of the vitamins and minerals that athletes need by simply eating a well-rounded diet. Chapter 9 set forth a basic supplement program that I feel all serious climbers should abide by. It's most important to consume extra vitamin C, vitamin E, and selenium; taking a daily multivitamin would also be wise.

Stretch and Massage Sore Muscles

Gentle stretching and sports massage are widely accepted as effective means to lengthen the muscles and enhance recovery following strenuous exercise. Professional athletes have full-time trainers who help with post-exercise stretching and rest-day massage (must be nice!). Though I won't pay for you to add a masseur to your climbing-support staff, I do suggest that you stretch for ten to fifteen minutes per day and partake in some sports massage of sore muscles. Follow the stretching procedures outlined in chapter 6 and, of course, the primer on sports massage provided earlier in this chapter.

Long-Term Recovery Tips

1. Eat small frequent meals—consume six smaller meals and snacks comprising low- to mid-GI foods and protein sources.
2. Drink eight ounces of water every one to two hours to rehydrate and flush toxins from your body.
3. Take a daily multivitamin and other antioxidants as detailed in chapter 9.
4. Avoid excessive consumption of alcoholic beverages, since these provide little quality nutrition, lead to dehydration, and suppress growth hormone response following exercise.
5. Engage in daily stretching, massage, and active-recovery activities such as hiking, biking, and easy running.
6. Apply a heating pad to sore muscles and tendons, twice daily for ten to fifteen minutes, to increase blood flow and accelerate recovery and healing. Note that you should never place a heating pad on a swollen or acutely injured body part.
7. Get at least seven to eight hours of sleep per night; nine to ten hours (or more) after mega-long day climbs or multiday big-wall or alpine ascents.
8. Strive for a calm, relaxed, easygoing disposition—this will help lower cortisol levels and foster more rapid recovery.

Get Plenty of Sleep

Here's an important recovery technique that this full-time working, four-day-a-week-training, weekend-climbing, book-writing, thirty-year veteran of the rocks wishes he could get more of! Although most neuromuscular regeneration occurs during sleep, I always fall back on the fact that nothing is produced or achieved during sleep.

Seriously, sleep is vital for any climber serious about training and passionate about maximizing ability. The bare minimum amount of sleep per night is seven to eight hours, though nine to ten hours is ideal following an extremely strenuous workout or a long day of climbing. No doubt, it's a busy world—and sleep may seem like the only activity that's expendable. If you closely evaluate a typical day, however, you will likely be able to identify some low-value activities like surfing the Net, watching TV, and certain social events that can be reduced or eliminated to allow for more sleep. It can take great discipline to give up some of these activities—visualize your climbing goals!—but the long-term payoffs will dwarf the hollow pleasure of these low-value pastimes.

Engage in Light Activities

Earlier you learned of a couple of great research studies that showed the value of active rest in accelerating recovery from strenuous exercise (by enhancing removal of lactic acid). In the context of long-term recovery, active rest is also beneficial because it enhances circulation to the damaged muscles and produces a general loosening effect on stiff muscles.

The best active-rest activities for climbers are hiking, jogging, light mountain biking, and even some limited less-than-vertical or big-hold climbing Still, it's crucial that each of these activities be performed at a low enough intensity that you don't get heavily winded or pumped and only break a light sweat. Limit yourself to thirty to sixty minutes of active-recovery exercise, and remain disciplined in not letting the activity escalate into anything more than active rest.

Possess a Positive, Calm Personality 24/7

This last recovery tip is subtle yet very powerful. Possessing a positive, relaxed, and easygoing attitude not only puts you in a better performance state, but has been proven to increase recovery and maybe even encourage muscular growth.

Strenuous exercise and stressful situations cause a drugstore's worth of chemicals and hormones to be released into the bloodstream. Some of these hormones have long-term positive effects, such as growth hormone, which is anabolic. The fight-or-flight hormones like epinephrine and cortisol, however, can have a long-term negative effect when released chronically. In particular, cortisol has been shown to be catabolic, meaning that it results in breakdown of muscle.

In light of the above factors, elite athletes have long been interested in enhancing the release of growth hormone and preventing high levels of cortisol. This is the very reason some athletes take anabolic steroids.

Fortunately, you can modulate levels of growth hormone and cortisol with proper training, quality nutrition, and adequate rest, as well as through adjustments in your lifestyle. For instance, individuals with Type A, aggressive behavior naturally exhibit higher levels of cortisol (Williams 1982) and reduced levels of growth hormone. It's also been shown, however, that behavior modification and reduction of the stressors in life can reverse this effect and provide more beneficial training (Dinan 1994). Therefore, possessing a relaxed approach to climbing and a humorous attitude about life in general will play an underlying but beneficial role by enhancing the quality of your training adaptations, accelerating recovery, and boosting climbing performance.

It's important to recognize that training (climbing) and recovery are opposite sides of the same coin. You must place equal importance on doing both optimally and to the best of your ability. Clearly, it requires a shift in perspective to actually plan and engage in the process of recovery in the same way you plan and engage in the process of training. But in doing so, you will distinguish yourself from the masses by producing uncommonly good results, and by avoiding downtime due to injury and illness.

Injury Treatment and Prevention

Our greatest glory is not in never failing, but in rising up every time we fail.

—*Ralph Waldo Emerson*

This last chapter might not be necessary if this were a book on training for bowling or training for badminton. Despite what we tell our parents, however, climbing is a sport with an unusually high incidence of injury. Several studies report that up to three-quarters of all recreational and elite climbers have suffered a climbing injury. Fortunately only a small number of injuries are severe traumas produced by falls—the rest are overuse and minor acute injuries that most commonly occur in the fingers, elbows, and shoulders. These insidious "nuisance injuries," while far from life threatening, can become chronic and debilitating, and they are extremely frustrating for an otherwise healthy individual passionate about climbing.

The goal of this chapter is to increase your awareness of the causes and symptoms of the most common overuse injuries. Early identification is the best way to mitigate an overuse injury, whereas ignoring the early pangs and hoping that it will go away is almost always a recipe for a chronic injury that could sideline you for months. Ultimately, learning to recognize at-risk situations both when you're training and when you're climbing, and

Daniel Woods crushing Armed Response (V13), South Africa. KEITH LADZINSKI

embracing a prudent approach to these activities that errs on the side of caution, is the best medicine for preventing injury.

Over the last decade numerous relevant studies have been presented by British, French, German, and American researchers, and several excellent articles were published in climbing magazines by physicians experienced in treating injured climbers. Based on this growing body of knowledge, I will present what seems to be the current treatment protocol for the most prevalent injuries; still, I urge you to seek professional treatment from a physician familiar with sports injuries (call around and ask this question straight out). Countless climbers have fallen into the trap of self-treatment and trying to climb through an injury—these approaches often make matters worse and can lead to unnecessarily long-term downtime. The bottom line: Read this chapter as an injury primer that encourages proactive, professional treatment of all injuries, and not as an absolute guide to the subject.

Overview of Climbing Injuries

A wide variety of injuries can result from climbing and sport-specific training activities, and a survey of available literature yields a broad range of pathologies from tendinitis to broken bones. While acute trauma resulting from falls is a very real issue, this overview of climbing injuries focuses on the chronic overuse injuries that typically result from the process of climbing and training, instead of falling. For more comprehensive coverage of both acute and overuse climbing injuries I strongly recommend that you read the excellent book *One Move Too Many* (Hochholzer 2003).

221

Types of Injuries

Injury surveillance data from several recent studies confirms that the majority of climbing injuries are not the result of falls. A well-designed British study revealed that three-quarters of climbing injuries were of the chronic overuse variety (Doran 1999). In this study 111 active climbers of all ages and abilities were questioned with regard to injuries incurred over the two previous years. One hundred forty overuse injuries from forty-nine climbers were reported—obviously some climbers in this sample experienced multiple or recurrent injuries during the twenty-four months of the study.

A breakdown of these overuse injuries confirms what experienced climbers have known anecdotally for years: The fingers, shoulders, and elbows are the three most common sites of nonfall injuries (see figure 11.1). Of all the injuries revealed in the British study, 40 percent occurred in the fingers, 16 percent in the shoulders, and 12 percent in the elbows. Other common sites for injury, though much less prevalent, were the knees (5 percent), back (5 percent), and wrists (4 percent). These findings agree surprisingly well with a German study (Stelzle 2000) of 314 climbers of both sexes and all degrees of climbing ability, which identified the most common injuries as finger tendon (39 percent), elbow (11 percent), and knee (about 5 percent).

Contributing Factors

An almost unanimous conclusion of the many injury studies is that occurrence of overuse injuries is directly proportionate to climbing ability and the perceived importance of climbing to the individual. Other cofactors include use of indoor climbing walls and use of campus boards and fingerboards in training for climbing.

The British study depicts a dramatic increase in injury rates among 5.11 climbers versus 5.10 climbers (see figure 11.2). At the 5.12 level, nearly 88 percent of climbers surveyed had experienced overuse injuries in the prior two years. By comparison, only 20 percent of individuals climbing at levels below 5.9 incurred overuse injuries, the lowest relative frequency of all categories (Doran 1999).

Figure 11.1 Sites of Nonfall Injuries

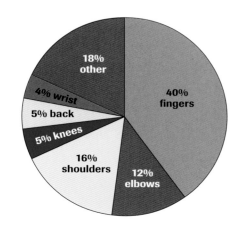

Figure 11.2 Overuse Injuries

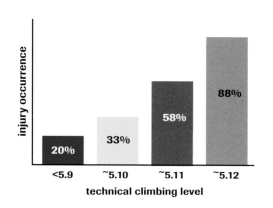

Occurrence of overuse injuries is directly proportional to climbing ability.

At least two studies show a statistically significant relationship between perceived importance of climbing and incidence of injury. Doran (1999) says, "The frequency of injury occurrence was signifi-

222

cantly higher in those who perceived climbing to be very important to those who rated it as not so important." An important corollary to this relationship is that enthusiastic climbers are more likely to return to climbing before full rehabilitation has occurred, thus leading to a pattern of recurrence.

Another British study of 295 climbers at a recent World Cup event found that those most at risk for overuse injuries were climbers with "the most ability and dedication to climbing." The analysis showed a linear relation between lead-climbing grade and overuse injuries (Wright 2001).

A number of other variables have been identified as cofactors in contributing to overuse injuries, including climbing preference and training practices.

Consensus among experts in the field is that incidence of overuse injuries has increased since the advent of indoor walls and sport-climbing tactics. An article in *Sports Medicine* proposes that the preponderance of overhanging terrain at indoor climbing facilities is a contributing factor to the increase in upper-body injuries (Rooks 1997). At the least, indoor walls do enable year-round climbing and make it oh-so-easy to test your absolute limit, thanks to toprope belays and well-bolted leads. Clearly, this is an environment that can lend itself to overtraining and a general lack of rest time away from the stresses and strains of climbing. I know of a few individuals who climbed indoors five or six days per week—and all, sooner or later, suffered significant finger, elbow, or shoulder injuries.

Training practices have also been implicated as a contributing factor in overuse injuries of climbers at all ability levels. One study found that 37 percent of individuals engaging in sport-specific training used a fingerboard or some other similar setup to perform one- and two-finger pull-ups. Of this group of low- and high-end climbers, 72 percent reported at least one injury of the hands or arms (Bannister 1986).

Doran (1996) reports that most of the climbers in his study performed some form of supplementary training; in particular, fingerboards and dynamic double-handed campus training were popular among the injured climbers. The obvious implication is that these high-stress, ultraspecific forms of training may be injurious or at least exacerbate low-grade preexisting injuries. These conclusions all make good sense and, therefore, underscore the importance of a prudent, mature approach to sport-specific training that knows when to say enough and errs on the side of over-resting rather than overtraining.

One puzzling part of the Doran (1996) study is the finding that climbers who conducted a regular warm-up had an increased frequency of injury in comparison with those who did not warm up. Not only is this idea counterintuitive, but it is contradictory to a large body of literature claiming that a proper warm-up is vital for preventing injury. Toward this end, another British researcher had previously found that increased frequency of injury was partially attributable to an absence of (or too brief) a warm-up regimen (Bollen 1988).

It's my sense that it would not be best to abandon your warm-up activities based on a single study. There are several possible explanations for the unlikely findings of the Doran study. First, one of the hallmark findings of this study was that ability level was proportionate to frequency of overuse injury. Therefore, high-end climbers were far more likely to experience overuse injuries than low-end climbers. I wonder, however, if high-end climbers are more likely to engage in warm-up activities (since they take climbing and training so seriously), while low-end climbers are more likely to "just go climbing" and skip the warm-up regimen. Could this explain the unusual findings that warm-up activities increase the risk of injury?

Another possible explanation of this finding could be that climbers who regularly warm up before training and climbing do so too quickly, severely, or excessively. For instance, it's widely accepted that stretching cold can injure connective tissues and muscles. Furthermore, excessive amounts of stretching can lead to loose joints and aggravate existing injuries. In the final analysis, I suspect we will find that a slow, incremental warm-up (comprising general activity and mild stretching) does not increase injury risk and is, in fact, a worthwhile and beneficial process prior to hard training or climbing.

Figure 11.3 Finger Anatomy

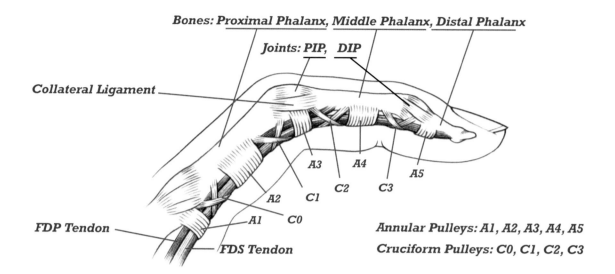

Bones: Proximal Phalanx, Middle Phalanx, Distal Phalanx

Joints: PIP, DIP

Collateral Ligament

A3 A4 A5

C2 C3

A2 C1

FDP Tendon

A1 C0

FDS Tendon

Annular Pulleys: A1, A2, A3, A4, A5
Cruciform Pulleys: C0, C1, C2, C3

Common Injuries and Treatment

Based on the research outlined above, we know that about 75 percent of all climbers have had or will experience an overuse injury. Furthermore, it's well documented that the four most common sites of injury are the fingers, elbows, shoulders, and knees. In this section we'll take a closer look at each of these problem spots. Hopefully, this information will empower you to recognize symptoms early on and thus modify your activity or seek medical attention before the injury becomes more severe or chronic. One caveat that all climbers should recognize straight up is that you must seek medical attention for any condition that gets worse after withdrawal from climbing and training. This could indicate a tumor, infection, or other disease that needs immediate medical attention.

Finger Injuries

Considering the incredible mechanical loading we place on our fingers when climbing, it's no surprise that they are the most common site of injury. Unfortunately, these pesky finger injuries are often hard to

diagnose precisely and, worse yet, in the early stages tend to be ignored. Many climbers rationalize that they can climb through one injured finger, since they have nine healthy fingers and can still manage to crank at a near-maximum level. Continued climbing on an injured finger may increase the severity of the injury, however, and thus double or triple (or more) the downtime needed to recover.

Understanding the most common injuries requires some knowledge of hand anatomy (see figure 11.3). To begin with, there are no muscles in the fingers. Flexion of the fingers and wrist is produced by the muscles of the forearm that originate from the medial (inside) elbow and terminate via long tendons that attach to the middle phalanx (MP) and distal phalanx (DP) of each finger. The flexor digitorum superficialis (FDS) muscle inserts into the palm side of the MP and produces flexion of the proximal interphalangeal (PIP) joint. The long tendon of the flexor digitorum profundus (FDP) muscle passes through a split in the FDS and then inserts on the palm side of the DP. The FDP controls flexion of the distal interphalangeal joint (DIP).

Figure 11.4 Annular Pulley Injuries

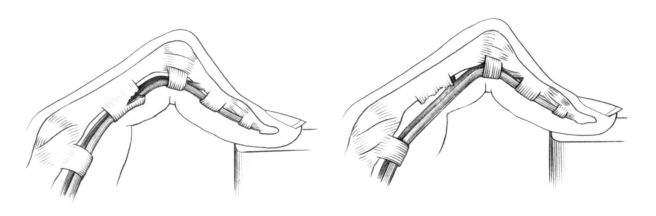

A2 pulley injury—partial tear (left) versus complete tear (right).

Both flexor tendons (FDS and FDP) pass through a tunnel-like, synovia-lined tendon sheath that provides nourishment and lubrication. The flexor tendon and sheath are held close to the bone by five annular pulleys (A1, A2, and so forth) and three (sometimes four) cruciform pulleys that prevent tendon "bowstringing" during flexion. Biomechanical studies have shown that the A2 and A4 pulleys are the most important (Lin 1989). As a conceptual model, visualize the whole system of the flexor tendon, sheath, and annular pulley as functioning like a brake cable on a bike.

TENDON PULLEY INJURIES

The most common finger injuries experienced by climbers involve partial tears or complete ruptures of one or more of the flexor tendon annular pulleys. In many cases only a partial tear of a single pulley occurs; in more serious incidences, however, one or more pulleys may rupture entirely, resulting in palpable or visible bowstringing, respectively. The exact nature and extent of the injury is difficult to diagnose without use of magnetic resonance imaging (Gabl 1996), though a recent Austrian study has

shown Dynamic Ultrasonography to be highly effective at depicting finger pulley injuries in rock climbers as well (Klauser 2002).

The A2 pulley is the most commonly injured of the five annular pulleys, and you can blame the common crimp grip as the main culprit. In using the crimp grip, near-ninety-degree flexion of the PIP joint produces tremendous force load on the A2 pulley, in addition to forceful hyperextension of the DIP joint. Injuries to the A2 pulley can range from microscopic to partial tears and, in the worst case, a complete rupture (see figure 11.4). Small partial tears are generally insidious, because they develop over the course of a few climbs, a few days of climbing, or even gradually during the course of a climbing season. Less frequent are acute ruptures that result during a maximum move on a tiny crimp hold or one-finger pocket. Some climbers report feeling or hearing a *pop*—a likely sign of a significant partial tear or complete rupture—though other injuries could also produce this effect.

Depending on the severity of an A2 pulley injury, pain and swelling at the base of the finger can range from slight to so debilitating that you can't perform everyday tasks like picking up a jug of milk. Swelling may limit the range of motion during flexion, and bowstringing may be felt or seen (Marco 1998) if one or two additional pulleys (usually A3 and A4) are ruptured, respectively. Slight tears may be asymptomatic when the finger is at rest, but become painful during isometric contraction (as in gripping a hold) or when pressing on the base of the finger near the top of the palm.

Treatment of an A2 pulley injury must begin with completed cessation of climbing and discontinuation of any other activity that requires forceful flexion of the injured finger. Doing anything that causes pain will slow healing of the injured tissue and may even make the injury worse. Therefore, the intelligent climber will cease climbing at the very moment of the injury so that the healing process may begin and the time frame for healing is most brief. By contrast, the immature climber may try to climb through the injury, which all but guarantees a worse tear and an even longer, eventually forced, exit from climbing.

The goal during the first few days following injury is to control inflammation (if present) with ice and non-steroidal anti-inflammatory (NSAID) medicines like ibuprofen or Naprosyn. Cease use of NSAIDs within three to five days (or less), since long-term use has been shown to impede the healing process and may even weaken tendons (see "Vitamin I" later in this chapter). "Buddy taping" (to an adjacent finger) or splinting of the injured finger can be beneficial during the first few days following injury, especially if you find it hard to limit use of your injured finger.

Depending on the severity of the tear, pain typically subsides in two to ten weeks. Becoming pain-free, however is not the go-ahead to resume climbing! This is where many climbers go wrong—they return to climbing too soon and reinjure the partially healed tissue. As a general rule, wait an additional two weeks beyond becoming pain-free, then slowly return to climbing. In the case of a modest A2 pulley injury, this may mean a total of about forty-five days of climbing downtime.

A French study of twelve elite climbers with A2 pulley injuries found that eight subjects were able to successfully return to climbing after forty-five days of rest (Moutet 1993). More severe pulley tears, however, may require as much as two or three months of rest before you can progressively return to climbing. The bottom line on these frustrating pulley injuries is to nip them in the bud by immediately initiating a rest and healing period away from climbing. Each successive day you continue to climb on the injured finger may effectively multiply the length of the healing process (and your eventual time away from climbing).

In the case of a complete or multiple annular pulley rupture (Grade IV injury), surgical reconstruction is necessary. Hand surgeons have long performed reconstruction of annular pulleys in nonclimbing cases where a deep laceration had damaged the flexor tendon and tendon pulleys. Free tendon grafts are the most common method of pulley reconstruction (Seiler 2000). The grafts are most often harvested from the dorsal wrist extensor retinaculum or the palmaris longus, and loops of the tendon are sewn in place of the damaged pulley (Moutet 2003; Seiler 1995; Lister 1979). It has been shown that reconstruction with three loops can withstand as much force load to failure as a normal annular pulley (Lin 1989).

An Austrian study reveals that annular pulley reconstruction has produced good functional and subjective results in climbers after eighteen to forty-three months of recovery time (Gabl 1998). Still, American physician Joel Rohrbough has examined numerous climbers who exhibit chronic bowstringing and continue to climb hard without disability. Based on this, he recommends against surgery, though he does encourage individuals to make an educated choice after discussion with a qualified surgeon (Rohrbough 2000).

So how can you protect injured fingers from further damage? Reinforcing flexor tendon pulleys with cloth athletic tape is a popular method—but is this practice really effective? Several physicians are on record as stating that firm circumferential taping is beneficial. Rohrbough (2000) notes that "tape is a tremendous help, giving support to a weak or healing pulley, helping to hold the tendon against the bone." Robinson (1988) says, "Use of tape around the fingers between joints is helpful," because it acts to reinforce the flexor tendon pulleys, protect the joint from extreme positions by limiting range of motion, and helps protect the skin. Jebson (1997) advises using protective taping for two to three months upon returning to climbing after an A2 pulley injury.

Despite these endorsements of prophylactic taping, I've seen one magazine article stating that taping "doesn't make the tendon any stronger—in fact, it may restrict blood flow to the repairing tendon and weaken it" (Crouch 1998). Furthermore, a study done in Texas found "no statistically significant difference in load to A2 pulley failure between taped and untaped fingers" and concluded that "we do not support taping the base of fingers as a prophylactic measure" (Warme 2000). Let's sort things out.

Based on an objective analysis of all available studies, it seems that the above statements about the ineffectiveness or even harmful effects of taping are flawed. First, the statement about taping "restricting blood and weakening the tendon" might be true if tape was worn all day and night. It's hard to imagine that taping for a few hours while training or climbing could have such a negative effect; after all, athletes in a wide range of sports tape everything from feet and ankles to wrists and fingers while in training or competing. Why would climbers' intermittent use of supportive taping be uniquely dangerous?

What about the recent study that found no difference in A2 pulley strength between taped and untaped fingers? Well, that study was done using frozen cadaveric hands that were rigidly mounted in a specialized jig to maintain a crimp-grip position. One has to wonder if the warm hands of a living climber might exhibit different properties with regard to tendon strength and might even use a subtly different grip than our "climbing cadaver."

Interestingly, a Swiss researcher has apparently answered this question for us (Schweizer 2000). He built a device to measure tendon and tendon pulley forces in vivo—that is, live climbers' hands—and determined the force of bowstringing as well as the

Treating A2 Pulley Injury

1. Immediately cease climbing and any other activity that requires forceful flexion of the injured finger. Consult a doctor if there is noticeable bowstringing on the flexor tendon.
2. Use ice and consume NSAID medications only if the injury produces palpable or visible swelling. Cease use of ice and NSAIDs as soon as swelling diminishes— further use will slow healing!
3. In especially painful cases, consider buddy taping or splinting the injured finger to limit use for a few days following injury.
4. As pain decreases—and only when all swelling is gone—begin light daily finger activity such as finger flexions, squeezing a rubber doughnut, mild stretching, and massage. This light exercise is important to ensure proper healing.
5. Use a heating pad for ten to fifteen minutes, three times a day, to increase blood flow and accelerate healing. Smokers should consider breaking the habit, since smoking has been shown to slow healing of tendons and ligaments.
6. Use the therapy described in steps 4 and 5 for at least two to four weeks before beginning a gradual return to climbing. Use prophylactic taping every time you climb, and spend the first week or two climbing relatively easy routes with big holds and good footholds.
7. Return to maximal climbing if easy climbing yields no pain. Continue taping and avoid tweaky holds for several months, since complete tendon healing can take a hundred days or more. Climb smart!

force applied to the pulley tape. Two slightly different taping methods were used—over the A2 pulley at the base of the finger, and over the distal end of proximal phalanx near the PIP joint—as he tested

Prophylactic Taping Methods

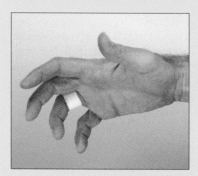

The A2 ring is the more common method of prophylactic finger taping. Using the widest piece of tape possible without interfering with PIP flexion (anywhere from 0.5 to 1.0 inch, depending on the length of your fingers), wrap three firm turns of tape around the base of the finger, directly supporting the A2 pulley. Apply the tape as tightly as possible without restricting blood flow. This may take a bit of experimentation, but remember that loose taping serves no function other than protecting the skin. Retape your fingers every few hours to maintain the necessary tightness throughout a full day of climbing.

The Swiss method (as used in the Swiss study mentioned below) involves firm circumferential taping at the distal end of the proximal phalanx—that is, just above the A2 pulley and immediately below the PIP joint. Use a narrower strip of tape, approximately 0.33 inch wide, and wrap as tightly and as close to the PIP joint as possible without restricting blood flow or flexion.

The X method may provide additional tendon support to the A3, A4, and cruciform pulleys, and it's very effective at preventing skin wear (and pain) when you're climbing on sharp pockets or rough indoor holds. Tear a long strip of tape, approximately 16 inches in length by 0.75 inch wide. With a slight bend in the finger, begin with two turns of tape over the proximal phalanx (on top of the A2 pulley), and then cross under the PIP joint and take two turns around the middle phalanx. Cross back under the PIP joint and conclude with another turn or two around the base of the finger.

sixteen fingers in the typical crimp-grip position. This study revealed that taping over the A2 pulley decreased bowstringing by 2.8 percent and absorbed 11 percent of the force, while taping just below the PIP joint (just beyond the A2 pulley) decreased bowstringing by 22 percent and absorbed 12 percent of total force. The obvious conclusion is that circumferential taping does provide a small reduction in total force on the tendon pulley system, though the author does not feel it would be enough to prevent a pulley rupture.

Therefore, it seems that taping should have a small positive effect in reinforcing the A2 pulley, and you should consider this practice for providing some protection of a previously injured tendon. Three different taping techniques are shown in the "Prophylactic Taping Methods" box above.

FLEXOR TENDINOSIS, AND TENDON RUPTURE AND AVULSION

Several other injuries can produce pain and diminished function in ways similar to an injured annular pulley. (As stated earlier, diagnosis can be difficult—see a physician to be completely sure what you are dealing with.) Tendinosis can develop in the FDS or FDP tendon as a result of repetitive stress. In this case pain may be limited to the palm side of the finger or extend into the palm or forearm (Jebson 1997). Extended rest is the primary treatment, followed by a gradual return to climbing a few weeks after cessation of pain (as described for tendon pulley injuries).

In rare cases a flexor tendon may rupture or avulse (pull out at the point of insertion). Jebson (1997) states that an FDS tendon rupture may occur with the crimp grip, while an FDP tendon rupture is more likely with a pocket grip. Either rupture or avulsion would occur acutely with immediate onset of pain. Jebson states that symptoms include pain at the FDS or FDP tendon insertion, finger swelling, and an absence of active flexion of the PIP joint (FDS rupture) or DIP joint (FDP rupture). Surgical reattachment may be required.

You may be surprised to learn that flexor tendon ruptures, avulsions, and to a lesser extent annular pulley injuries occur occasionally among football players. These acute injuries, commonly called "jersey finger," occur when a tackler with an outstretched arm catches a finger on the jersey of the ball carrier sprinting past him. It is interesting to observe that many linemen and linebackers use prophylactic taping to support the flexor tendon and the A2 and A4 pulleys—it would seem that professional football players have also concluded that prophylactic taping works!

COLLATERAL LIGAMENT INJURIES

Ligaments connect bone to bone across a joint, providing stability (see figure 11.3). Collateral ligament sprains and avulsions at the PIP joint are known to occur in climbers, particularly as a result of a powerful lunge or awkward torque off a "fixed" finger (as in a jam or tight pocket). A sprain manifests with mild to moderate pain and swelling around the PIP joint, but with no loss of stability (Jebson 1997). A rupture or avulsion will produce significant pain and swelling as well as loss of stability, medially or laterally.

Treatment of incomplete collateral ligament injuries typically involves splinting of the PIP joint for ten to fourteen days, after which buddy taping can be used and range-of-motion exercises started (Bach 1999). Climbing can gradually be reintroduced despite persistent low-grade pain and swelling, which may take months to resolve (Jebson 1997).

Complete collateral ligament injuries at the PIP joint are usually treated operatively. If the collateral ligament is completely avulsed from the bone, non-operative treatment may result in chronic swelling and long-term instability (Bach 1999). Surgical repair can improve this, and full function is often restored in approximately three months.

Other Finger and Hand Injuries

A wide variety of other finger and hand injuries are possible in a sport that requires fingers to crimp, pinch, and jam under high passive and dynamic force loads. No doubt, you will experience your share of household injuries like torn tips, palm flappers, or back-of-hand gobies. There are a few more subtle injuries that can affect climbers, however, including carpal tunnel syndrome, swollen or arthritic PIP and DIP joints, and growth plate injury among youth climbers.

CARPAL TUNNEL SYNDROME

Carpal tunnel syndrome (CTS) is a condition in which a nerve passing through the wrist, with the flexor tendons, is exposed chronically to too much pressure. This syndrome affects a small number of climbers, but its occurrence does not appear to be disproportionately common in climbers (Robinson 1993). Therefore, it's difficult to conclude whether a climber with this syndrome incurred it from the repetitive gripping of rock holds or from some other source. Regardless, the symptoms include numbness, burning, and tingling of the fingers; these symptoms may become worse at night or during activity or elevation (Lewis 1993). Treatment involves cessation or lowering intensity of climbing, anti-inflammatory medicines, and splinting of the wrist in a neutral position at night for three to six weeks. Surgical decompression of the carpal tunnel may be required if this conservative treatment fails and symptoms are severe enough to be disabling.

ARTHRITIS

For years I have heard speculation that active "rock climbers will someday become severe arthritis sufferers." Fortunately, anecdotal evidence of many twenty- and thirty-year veterans, as well as recent studies of longtime climbers, indicates that these predictions are not quite panning out. In this study, radiographs of the hands of veteran elite climbers were compared with an age-matched control group. An increased rate of osteoarthritis for several joints was found in the climber group, though no significant difference in the overall prevalence of osteoarthritis was found between the two groups (Rohrbough 1998). A more recent study compared recreational climbers to nonclimbers by measuring bone strength and dimensions and occurrence of osteoarthritis. The study concluded that climbers are not at an increased risk for developing osteoarthritis; it also discovered that climbers' finger and hand bones are wider (indicating that additional bone is deposited subperiosteally) and stronger (Sylvester 2006). These studies are really good news for those of us entering middle age with many years of climbing under our belts!

Still, it's possible that individuals who predominantly use the crimp grip may experience some mild swelling and arthritis in the PIP and DIP joints. As shown in figure 11.4, use of the crimp grip produces hyperextension of the DIP joint under large passive force, while the PIP joint is sharply flexed under great force. Therefore, both the DIP and PIP joints are possible sites of mild swelling and arthritis (Robinson 1993).

If you are an aging climber who experiences some swelling, pain, or stiffness of the DIP and PIP joints, you will find some relief through use of non-steroidal anti-inflammatory medications. A growing body of research also points to a supplement called glucosamine sulfate as an effective treatment for mild osteoarthritis. Daily supplementation of 1,500 milligrams of glucosamine sulfate has been shown to reduce pain and stiffness, and—more important—to slow the degradation of affected joints (Reginster 2001). Acquiring these benefits requires a long-term commitment to taking glucosamine sulfate, because the effects are cumulative, not immediate as in taking anti-inflammatory medicines. But the promise of slowing or halting joint degradation is a huge benefit for individuals—climbers and nonclimbers—over forty years of age who take glucosamine sulfate daily.

Many supplement manufacturers are now adding two other compounds, chondroitin and MSM, to their glucosamine sulfate supplements. Chondroitin is believed to produce benefits similar to glucosamine sulfate, and one study showed positive results in patients with joint problems from four to eight weeks of taking both supplements together (McAlindon 2000). However, a more recent meta-analysis of the best-designed studies showed no positive effects in taking chondroitin alone (Juni 2007). MSM shows more promise based on a recent pilot study. Participants who received 3 grams of MSM, twice per day, for twelve weeks experienced a significant reduction in pain and improved physical function compared with a placebo group (Kim 2006). In summary, all relevant studies showed these compounds to be safe, and with almost no side effects; however, only glucosamine sulfate and MSM, taken in long-term daily doses of 1.5 to 3.0 grams each, produced statistically significant beneficial results.

GROWTH PLATE INJURY IN JUNIOR CLIMBERS

Junior climbers make up one of the fastest-growing demographics, with hundreds—perhaps thousands—of young climbers now entering competitions and beginning structured training programs. Correlating to the rising popularity of junior competitions and the intensive training used by many participants is an increase in nontraumatic growth plate

"Vitamin I" Use: The Good, the Bad, and the Alternatives

Pain is a common companion of climbers. For some it's the benign pain of muscular soreness after a hard day of climbing or a severe workout. Many others, however, unfortunately experience the pain of acute or overuse injury. Given the ubiquity of injured and sore climbers, use of NSAID medications to treat inflammation and mask pain is widespread. In fact, some climbers joking refer to ibuprofen as "vitamin I," since they take it as if it were a daily vitamin.

Daily use of NSAIDs, such as ibuprofen (Advil and Motrin), naproxen (Aleve and Naprosyn), and aspirin, does have its drawbacks, including risk of ulceration of the stomach, impaired kidney function, and anti-blood-clotting effects. Furthermore, regular NSAID use may actually slow muscle cell regeneration and hamper healing of muscles, ligaments, tendons, and cartilage (Almekinders 1999, 2003). Even more alarming is a study that found a marked decrease in the breaking strength of tendons after four and six weeks in ibuprofen-treated animals (Kulick 1986). In aggregate, these risks and side effects make a compelling case against regular NSAID use—and, the latter study may perhaps help explain why so many ibuprofen-using climbers experience tendon injuries.

So what are the alternatives for treating the pain and inflammation of an acute injury, delayed onset muscle soreness (DOMS) after climbing or training, and the persistent pangs of an overuse injury? Let's first examine the immediate response to acute injury, which is best treated with the RICE method (rest, ice, compression, and elevation). Icing the injured area for twenty minutes, three to six times a day, is highly effective for controlling swelling and reducing pain in the hours following acute injury. Continued use of RICE beyond the first few days following injury, however, will inhibit the healing process. (Get professional medical care if you have any sense that your injury might be serious or if it does not begin to improve given several days of rest.)

What about the most common cause of pain among climbers—delayed onset muscular soreness? Some climbers use topical rubs containing methyl salicylate, menthol, camphor, or various herbs such as arnica for spot treatment. While the stimulation of massage and the warming or numbing effect of some preparations may reduce the sensation of pain, there is little evidence that these concoctions promote healing beyond the effect of massage itself. It seems that any measure or activity that increases circulation will promote healing; thus engaging in low-intensity general exercise or use of a whirlpool or heating pad are effective treatments for DOMS.

Finally, there are those frustrating, slow-to-heal overuse injuries such as annular pulley strain, elbow tendinosis, shoulder impingement, and such. As outlined in this chapter, rest and rehabilitative exercise are the primary methods of treatment. NSAID use should be avoided, since these anti-inflammatory agents will slow healing and may even reduce tendon strength (as does smoking). Conversely, regular massage, heat therapy, and gentle stretching will encourage blood flow to the injured tissues and, thus, seem to be the best method to encourage healing once acute pain and inflammation have subsided.

Perhaps the best anti-NSAID alternatives, for vitamin I addicts, are the omega-3 essential fatty acids found in fish. You may be familiar with omega-3 EFA for its well-promoted preventive effects on coronary artery disease. Interestingly, daily consumption of fish, or fish oil supplements, also has been shown effective for treating musculoskeletal injuries and discogenic diseases (Maroon 2006). The effective dose to be heart-healthy is just 1 gram of omega-3 EFA per day; however, an everyday dose of 2 to 4 grams (more than you could likely consume from eating fish) is needed to provide the natural anti-inflammatory effects that would benefit climbers.

In conclusion, you should just say no to regular
(continued)

fractures, known as epiphyseal fractures. The common symptoms are slow onset of pain and swelling of the middle finger joint, and in some cases the inability to crimp grip on holds. The condition is easily diagnosed via X-ray.

A recent German study (Hochholzer 2005) evaluated twenty-four junior climbers with nontraumatic epiphyseal fractures. Interestingly, only one of the injured climbers was a girl—so boys seem to be at greater risk—and all were between the ages of thirteen and sixteen. Injury to growth plates can cause permanent damage, so a temporary withdrawal from climbing is essential for adolescents experiencing finger joint pain. Parents and coaches must enforce a rest period of at least a few months or more away from climbing until the youth climber is asymptomatic. In terms of prevention, parents and coaches should limit climbing activity to three days per week during the adolescent growth spurt, and disallow use of advanced training exercises such as campus training, hypergravity training, and intensive fingerboard training until at least age sixteen or the end of puberty (achievement of maximum adult height).

Elbow Tendinopathy

Pain near the bony medial (inside) or lateral (outside) epicondyles of the elbow is an exceedingly common ailment among serious climbers. In most cases the onset of pain is very gradual: A schedule of frequent climbing produces microscopic injury that fails to repair before the tendon is subjected to additional strain. A tendinosis cycle develops and amplifies as breakdown exceeds repair and the microtraumas accumulate over many weeks and months. In the early stage of tendinosis, pain is dull and may be felt only after a day of climbing; however, pain experienced in the course of everyday activities such as opening a door or washing your hair is a sign of advanced tendinosis. The hallmark of tendinosis is its gradual onset and lack of inflammation and visible swelling.

A similar yet less common and often misdiagnosed injury is tendinitis. The suffix *itis* means "inflammation," and the term *tendinitis* should be reserved for acute tendon injury accompanied by inflammation and palpable swelling. In climbing, tendinitis occurs most often near the medial epicondyle as the tendon is injured during a maximal one-arm pull on a small hold or in performing advance training exercises without adequate warm-up or training experience.

A third, more subtle class of tendon injury is paratenonitis (formerly termed tenosynovitis and tenovaginitis), an inflammation and degeneration of the outer layers of the tendon and the synovia-lined tendon sheath. Paratenonitis can develop in the tendons of the arms and fingers and in concert with either tendinosis or tendinitis.

Regardless of which tendon ailment you possess, the one commonality is the extremely slow rate of healing. While muscles possess abundant blood flow and a relatively rapid rate of healing, blood flow to the ropelike collagenous tendons is poor, and laying down new collagen make take a hundred days or more (Khan 1999). Exacerbating these slow-healing injuries is the tendency of enthusiastic climbers to rush back into training and climbing prematurely.

Worse yet, researchers have discovered that an enduring tendinosis cycle often leads to collagen repair with an abnormal structure and composition, thus making the repaired tendon less able to withstand tensile stress and more vulnerable to further injury. Following acute injury, the strength of a repaired tendon can remain as much as 30 percent lower than normal for months or even years (Leadbetter 1992; Liu 1995).

In severe, chronic cases of elbow tendinitis or tendinosis, surgery may offer the only lasting remedy. The most popular procedure is to simply excise the diseased tissue from the tendon, then reattach healthy tendon to the bone. Eighty-five to 90 percent of patients recuperate in three months, 10 to 12 percent have improvement but some pain during exercise, and only 2 to 3 percent have no improvement (Auerback 2000).

Following is a closer look at the two most common elbow injuries and their treatments.

MEDIAL TENDINOSIS AND TENDINITIS

Pain near the medial epicondyle is commonly called golfer's elbow or climber's elbow. Pain develops in the tendons connecting the pronator teres muscle and/or the many forearm flexor muscles (responsible for finger flexion) to the knobby, medial epicondyle of the inside elbow.

In many cases medial tendinosis is caused by muscular imbalances of the forearm and an accumulation of microtraumas to the tendons that result from climbing too often, too hard, and, most important, with too little rest. Consider that all the muscles that produce finger flexion are anchored to the medial epicondyle. Furthermore, the muscles that produce hand pronation (that turn the palm outward to face the rock) originate from the medial epicondyle. This subtle fact plays a key role in causing this injury: Biceps contraction produces supination (turning of the palm upward), but in gripping the rock you generally need to maintain a pronated, palms-out position. This battle, between the supinating action of the biceps pulling and the necessity to maintain a pronated hand position (to maintain grip with the rock), strains the typically undertrained

teres pronator muscle and its attachment at the medial epicondyle.

Given the above factors, it's easy to see why the tendons attaching to the medial epicondyle are subjected to sustained stress and, inevitably, develop microtraumas. Just as muscular microtraumas are repaired to new level of capability, the tendons increase in strength and can withstand higher stress loads given adequate rest. Unfortunately, the repair and strengthening process occurs more slowly in tendons than in muscles. Eventually the muscles are able to create more force than the tendons can adapt to—the result is injury.

Tendinosis will reveal itself gradually through increasing incidence of painful twinges or soreness during or after climbing. Tendinitis, however, is evidenced by acute onset of pain in the midst of a single hard move, and is usually followed by inflammation and palpable swelling. Even in these cases cumulative microtrauma may be involved in making the tissue vulnerable to acute trauma.

As in treating other injuries, you can more easily manage tendinopathy (any tendon injury) and speed your return to climbing by early recognition of the symptoms and proactive treatment. The mature and prudent approach of attending to the injury early on versus trying to "climbing through it" could mean the difference between six weeks and six months (or more) of climbing downtime.

Treatment of tendinosis and tendinitis has two phases: Phase I involves steps to relieve pain and reduce of inflammation (in the case of tendinitis); Phase II is engaging in rehabilitative and stretching exercises to promote correct alignment of collagen tissue and prevent recurrence.

Phase I demands withdrawal from climbing (and all sport-specific training) and commencement of pain-reducing and anti-inflammatory measures. Icing the elbow for twenty minutes, three to six times a day, and use of NSAIDs will help reduce inflammation and pain following injury; cease use within a few days to a week. A cortisone injection may be helpful in chronic or severe cases, though this practice is somewhat controversial among physicians and, in fact, may be detrimental to the healing process (Nirschl 1996). Depending on the severity of the injury, successful completion of Phase I could require anywhere from two weeks to two months.

The goal of Phase II is to retrain and rehabilitate the injured tissues through use of mild stretching and strength-training exercises. Since forearm-muscle imbalance plays a primary role in many elbow injuries, it's vital to perform exercises that strengthen the weaker aspects of the forearm—hand pronation for medial tendinosis and hand/wrist extension for lateral tendinosis (more on this in a bit).

Always perform some general warm-up activity and consider warming the elbow directly with a heating pad before beginning the stretching and strengthening exercises. Stretch twice daily the forearm flexor, extensor, and pronator muscles as described in chapter 6. Once the stretching exercises have successfully restored normal range of motion with no pain, you can introduce strength training with the Forearm Pronator exercise shown on page 121. It's important to progress slowly with training exercises and to cut back at the first sign of pain. Begin with just a couple of pounds of resistance and

gradually increase the weight over the course of a few weeks. Use the stretching exercises daily, but do the weight-training exercises only three days per week.

After three to four weeks of pain-free training, begin a gradual return to climbing. Start with low-angle and easy vertical routes, and take a month or two to return to your original level of climbing. Continue with the stretching and strength-training exercises indefinitely—as long as you are a climber, you must engage in these preventive measures. Failed rehabilitation and relapse into chronic pain may eventually lead to a need for surgical intervention.

Finally, let's take a look at the use of counterforce bracing, or circumferential taping of the upper forearm, as a curative (or preventive) measure for elbow tendinosis. A counterforce brace designed specifically for elbow tendinosis can provide some comfort by dispersing forces away from the underlying tissues (Nirschl 1996). These braces are not a substitute for proper rehabilitation, however; they instead act only to help prevent recurrence after full rehabilitation. There is little evidence that supportive

Treating Elbow Tendinosis and Tendinitis

1. Cease climbing and sport-specific training.
2. Apply ice to the injured area and take NSAID medications only if the injury produces visible or palpable swelling (most elbow tendinopathy does not). Cease use of ice and NSAIDs as soon as swelling diminishes—further use will slow healing.
3. Never use NSAIDs to mask pain in order to continue climbing while injured. Regular use of NSAIDS (and smoking) may actually weaken tendons!
4. If no swelling is present, begin mild stretching, light massage, and use of a heating pad (ten to fifteen minutes) three times per day. Most important is twice-daily use of the forearm stretches shown in chapter 6.

5. If no swelling is present and if pain is minor, engage in rehabilitative exercises on an every-other-day basis. Perform some warm-up activities such as arm circles, finger flexions, massage, or use of a heating pad. Use Reverse Wrist Curls for lateral tendinosis and Forearm Pronators for medial tendinosis.
6. Cautiously return to climbing when your elbow is pain-free and no sooner then after two to four weeks of strength-training exercise. Begin with easy, foot-oriented climbing for the first few weeks and limit use of the crimp grip. Cease climbing if you experience pain while climbing and immediately return to step 2.

taping of the forearm provides the same benefit as use of a counterforce brace.

LATERAL TENDINOSIS

Lateral tendinosis, commonly called tennis elbow or lateral epicondylitis, is an irritation of the tendons that attach the forearm extensor muscles to the lateral epicondyle on the outside of the elbow. The forearm extensor muscles are antagonists to the forearm flexor muscles used so prominently in gripping the rock and, therefore, the extensors are often disproportionately weak compared with the flexors. Furthermore, grip strength is greatest when your hand is in the extended position—this explains why your arm "chicken wings" out from the rock when you struggle to grip small crimp holds. It's the extensor muscles that facilitate this chicken wing position and, thus, constant straining to stick crimp holds can lead to tendon injury where the extensor muscles attach to the lateral epicondyle. (Note reducing your use of the crimp grip will lower your risk of tendinosis.)

Onset of pain is typically gradual, and will first appear after a hard day of climbing. Without rest and treatment, the condition will progressively worsen to the point that climbing becomes prohibitively painful and even everyday tasks are hampered. Since such a severe case often requires a six-month (or longer) rehabilitation period away from climbing, it's paramount that you take the necessary steps to mitigate this injury early on.

The treatment protocol for lateral tendinosis is similar to that described above for medial tendinopathy. Time away from climbing is mandatory—very few people successfully climb through elbow tendinosis of either kind. Frequent icing and limited use of anti-inflammatory medication is helpful during the initial period of pain, but these treatments should never be used to allow continuation of climbing. As pain and swelling subside, daily use of the stretching exercises is absolutely necessary as the first step in the rehabilitation process. Gradually introduce Reverse Wrist Curls (page 120) to strengthen the forearm extensor muscles; add weight incrementally over the course of a few weeks. Use a heating pad for a few minutes before stretching—daily use of a heating pad may also speed rate of healing. In mild cases of tendinosis, you may be able to complete the rehabilitation process and begin a slow return to climbing in six to eight weeks. A counterforce brace worn just below the elbow may be beneficial upon beginning a slow return to climbing.

Remember, recurrence or severe episodes may take six months or longer to overcome—let this knowledge compel you to cease climbing and engage in the rehab protocol described below at the first signs of pain.

Shoulder Injuries

The shoulder joint takes lot of punishment from climbing, especially in those obsessed with V-hard bouldering, steep terrain, and sport-specific training. A variety of injuries can occur, ranging from impingement or tendinitis to a partial dislocation or tear of the rotator cuff. Given the complexity of the shoulder joint, however, a diagnosis can be difficult; expert consultation or an MRI will likely be required to detect small tears of the rotator cuff and other subtle injuries.

IMPINGEMENT SYNDROME, BURSITIS, AND TENDINITIS

These conditions are closely related, and they are a common source of shoulder pain among athletes in sports that demand consistent, forceful overhead arm movements. Pain and inflammation often develop under the acromion, the bony top portion of the shoulder where the shoulder blade and collarbone meet, as a result of tendinitis and swelling of the bursa (a fluid-filled sac that provides cushion between the bone and surrounding tissues). Onset of pain is gradual over weeks and months, and may eventually lead to pain in the upper arm and difficulty sleeping on the arm or shoulder.

Diagnosis begins with a physical examination, including movement and strength testing to evaluate pain and weakness throughout the range of motion. X-rays and an MRI may be performed to rule out other causes of shoulder pain, such as arthritis, bone disease, and tears in the rotator cuff. Impingement syndrome may be confirmed if injection of a small amount of anaesthetic under the acromion relieves pain.

Treatment of these conditions begins with steps to reduce pain and inflammation: icing for twenty minutes, three to six times per day; limited use of NSAIDS (such as ibuprofen and Naprosyn); and cessation of climbing and overhead hand movements. As pain subsides, gentle stretching and strengthening exercises can be introduced gradually—these rehabilitative exercises are essential to lower risk of injury relapse upon returning to climbing (see the "Shoulder Rehab Exercises" box). In minor cases followed up by dedicated rehabilitation, a return to climbing may be possible in one to two months. More serious cases may require six months or more away from climbing, and perhaps even steroid injections or surgery.

SHOULDER INSTABILITY

Shoulder instability is a condition that's become increasingly common among high-end climbers with a taste for overhanging routes as well as individuals who engage in excessive fingerboard training. The condition develops gradually from long-term, repeated exposure to straight-arm hangs, Gaston moves, and severe lock-offs, as well as from overzealous stretching or climbing on overhanging routes day after day or hard boulder problems without adequate rest and training of the stabilizing antagonist muscles. No matter the mechanism, constant stretching of the ligaments and a growing imbalance of the muscles that surround and stabilize the shoulder joint can lead to instability and risk of injury.

Dr. Joel Rohrbough has worked with many climbers and believes that a partial dislocation known as subluxation is the most common shoulder injury among climbers. This injury produces instability of the shoulder joint and manifests with pain from deep within or in back of the shoulder (Rohrbough 2001). In most cases the ball portion of the shoulder joint is levered forward during extreme movements with the elbow located behind the plane of the body. Furthermore, the force of the levering motion on the shoulder joint increases when the arm is extended with the elbow pointing outward (and extending behind the plane of the body), as in grabbing a high Gaston hold or making a long reach on overhanging rock.

Fresh shoulder injuries should be treated with the two-phase process of resting until pain diminishes and then use of rehabilitative exercises to strengthen the rotator cuff muscle group. Climbing activity must be markedly reduced or eliminated while you engage in the rehabilitative process, and you should also avoid any overhead motion or other activity that causes pain in the shoulder. Anti-inflammatory medicine and ice applied twice daily are useful in reducing initial pain and swelling.

The common course of therapy begins with gentle stretching and strengthening of the shoulder, but with no exercises above the level of the shoulder. Perform the four exercises from the "Shoulder Rehab Exercises" box every other day, and gradually increase the weight from one pound to five pounds over about a five-week period. Gradually, you can introduce some basic push-muscle exercises (see chapter 6) that strengthen the antagonist muscles. Decrease resistance on or eliminate completely any exercise that is too painful. Of course, rehabilitation is best guided by a professional physical therapist, and you may need anywhere from two to six months before you can reintroduce climbing activities.

Unfortunately, a significant number of people with shoulder injuries ultimately require a surgical solution. The procedure may include removal of damaged tissue, repair of minor rotator cuff tears, or surgical tightening of affected ligaments and tendons. Surgery will be followed with long-term physical therapy; given a successful outcome, climbing activity may resume in six to twelve months.

Shoulder Rehab Exercises

Reduce or cease climbing upon onset of shoulder pain. Apply ice (several times a day) and take NSAID medications to reduce pain and swelling for up to one week. See a doctor if you experience severe pain or if your condition does not improve with rest.

As pain declines, begin using the following rehabilitation exercises three or four days per week. Be sure to perform each exercise on both sides of the body (with both arms). The weight used should be light: Begin with a dumbbell that seems too light, and gradually increase in one-pound increments over the course of a few weeks. There is no need to use heavy weights; in fact, performing these exercises with more than five to fifteen pounds will unfavorably stress the smaller muscles of the rotator cuff. Supplement your rehab with the antagonist push-muscle exercises detailed in chapter 6 when you become pain-free.

Dumbbell Internal Rotation

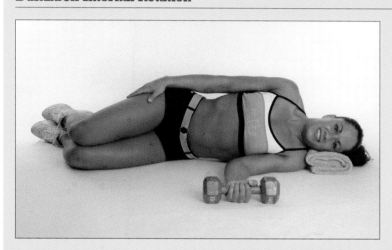

1. Dumbbell Internal Rotation

Lie on your side with your bottom arm in front of your waist; place a rolled-up towel under your head to support your neck. Rest your other arm along your hip and upper thigh. Hold a two- to five-pound dumbbell in the hand of your bottom arm, positioning this forearm perpendicular to your body. Lift the weight up to your body and hold for a moment before lowering it back to the floor. The upper portion of your arm should remain in contact with the floor throughout the range of motion—think of your upper arm and shoulder as a door hinge that allows your forearm to swing "open and closed." Continue in a slow but steady motion for a total of fifteen repetitions. Do two sets on each side, with a three-minute rest between sets. Increase weight in one- or two-pound increments, but do not exceed ten pounds. Using heavy weight is not necessary and may even result in injury. *(continued)*

2. Dumbbell External Rotation

Lie on your side with your bottom arm in front of your waist and a rolled-up towel under your head to support your neck. Alternatively, you can bend your bottom arm and use it as a headrest. Hold a two- to five-pound dumbbell in the hand of your top arm. Rest the upper arm and elbow on the top side of your body, and then bend at the elbow so that the forearm hangs down over your belly and the weight rests on the floor. Now raise the weight upward toward the ceiling until your forearm passes a parallel position with the floor. Pause at this top position for a moment, and then lower the weight to the floor. Your upper arm should remain in contact with the side of your torso and act only as a hinge that allows your forearm to swing up and down. Continue in a slow but steady motion for a total of fifteen repetitions. Do two sets on each side, with a three-minute rest between each set. Increase weight in one or two-pound increments, but do not exceed ten pounds. Use of heavy resistance is not necessary or desirable.

Dumbbell External Rotation

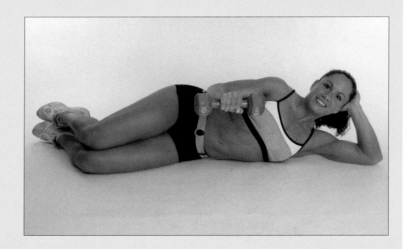

Bent-Over Arm Raise

3. Bent-Over Arm Raise

Standing with one leg slightly ahead of the other, assume a bent-over position with your free arm braced on your knee or hip. Holding a five-pound dumbbell in the opposite hand, lift your arm up to your side until it's parallel to the floor. Hold for a moment and lower slowly to the starting position. Keep your elbow straight throughout the range of motion. Do three sets of ten to fifteen repetitions. Increase the weight as strength gains allow, but do not exceed fifteen pounds. *(continued)*

Bent-Over Arm Kickback

4. Bent-Over Arm Kickback

Assume the same bent-over position as in the previous exercise, but this time lift the five-pound dumbbell behind you until it's parallel to the floor and in a position next to your hip. Hold here for a moment, then return to the starting position. Maintain a straight arm throughout the range of motion. Do three sets of ten to fifteen repetitions. Increase the weight as strength gains allow, but do not exceed fifteen pounds.

Knee Injuries

Injury to the knee is a relatively new phenomenon in climbing that correlates directly to the proliferation of indoor and sport climbing. New climbing techniques like the drop-knee weren't popularized until the 1990s, but this is now a staple move of the steep indoor and outdoor climbs that are so prominent today. Repeated use of the drop-knee, especially under high force load, can tear the specialized cartilage in the knee called the meniscus (Stelzle 2000), as can high-stepping in a full-hip-turnout position. A meniscus tear—or, worse, a tear of a knee ligament—can also occur during a forceful, uneven landing when jumping off a boulder problem.

MENISCUS TEAR

Meniscus is a tough, fibrous type of cartilage that sits between the ends of the femur and tibia (see figure 11.5). The menisci serve primarily as shock absorbers between the ends of the bones to protect the articulating surfaces (McFarland 2000). There are two separate C-shaped meniscal cartilages in the knee, one on the inner half of the knee (the medial meniscus) and the other on the outer half (the lateral meniscus). A partial or total tear of a meniscus can occur during forced rotation of the knee while the foot remains in a fixed position. In climbing, these tears most often occur in severe drop-knee positions, which produce inside rotation of the knee under pressure.

A small meniscus tear can develop gradually from repeated use of these climbing moves, or a tear may occur suddenly. Some tears involve only a small portion of the meniscus, while others produce a bucket handle, or complete separation of a piece of cartilage. Symptoms can range from mild pain and no visible swelling to severe pain and swelling and reduced mobility (McFarland 2000). Many meniscal tears cause popping, clicking, and locking of the knee in certain positions.

Not all meniscus tears cause big problems. A minor tear in the thick outer portion of the meniscus may be able to repair itself given fairly good blood supply. Also, use of the supplement glucosamine sulfate is believed to support the formation of new car-

Figure 11.5 Meniscus Tear

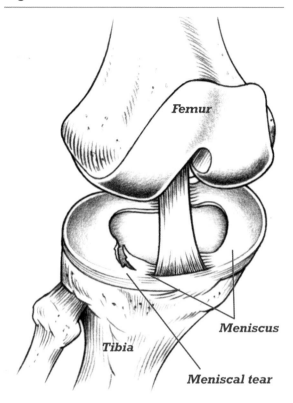

The meniscus can tear when the knee is forced to rotate while the foot remains in a fixed position. A severe drop-knee move or a twisting jump off a boulder problem can cause this injury.

tilage and may enhance the healing process. In minor cases, symptoms will disappear on their own; persistent pain that affects daily activities or produces significant pain in certain climbing positions may require surgery, however.

Arthroscopic surgery is very successful in relieving pain and restoring full function to the injured knee. The goal of arthroscopic surgery is to preserve as much of the meniscus as possible so as to decrease the chance of future arthritis (McFarland 2000). Tears on the outer margin of the meniscus are more amenable to repair, since they have greater blood flow compared with the thin, inner margin of the meniscus. Tears in the thin portion of the meniscus are typically excised; entirely detached pieces of cartilage are removed.

Recovery from arthroscopic surgery is rapid. The procedure is generally performed as outpatient surgery, followed by three to seven days of rest, ice packs, and elevating the limb. Crutches are often used during the first postoperative week, though weight can be placed on the injured leg as can be tolerated. Most patients return to work in less than a week, and other normal activities can be added during the second and third week after surgery.

Physical therapy may be beneficial but is not required for fit individuals who can begin a gradual return to physical activity after two or three weeks. A full return to training activities and climbing typically takes two to three months.

Preventing Injuries

This chapter began by quoting studies that place your odds—as an avid rock climber—of getting injured as at least three to one. Therefore, it seems appropriate that we conclude this tome with an attempt at lowering those odds!

First, abstinence is the only preventive measure that is absolute. Climbing is a stressful sport, and injury may be unavoidable. Still, I estimate that you can lower the risk by at least 50 percent if you follow all the preventive measures outlined below. Undoubtedly, some of these guidelines fly in opposition to the modus operandi of many climbers. By now, however, you are familiar with the thread weaving throughout this book: "To outperform the masses, you must do things that they do not do."

Ten Rules for Preventing Overuse Injuries

Detailed below are ten strategies for lowering your exposure to overuse injuries. Clearly, there will be situations that demand breaking one or more of these rules. By climbing and training in accordance with these guidelines most of the time, however, you will likely decrease your risk of injury and never, or only rarely, join the injured mass of climbers.

1. FOCUS ON TECHNIQUE TRAINING OVER STRENGTH TRAINING.

Many overuse injuries result from too much of a focus on strength training too early in an individual's climbing career. As advised throughout this book, it's fundamental to develop a high level of technical competence before jumping full-bore into sport-specific training. Not only does good technique help you reduce stress on your fingers and shoulders, but it also helps maximize economy of movement and, thus, increases apparent strength on the rock.

Remember that two to four days per week of climbing will naturally produce rapid gains in sport-specific strength in beginners. Because tendons strengthen at a slower rate than muscles, novice climbers are not exempt from injury risk. With little experience, these new climbers have not yet developed the keen sense needed to distinguish "good pain" from "bad pain." The number of climbers who become injured during their first year or two in the sport—as they quickly progress from, say, 5.5 to 5.10 (or higher)—is alarming. Therefore, awareness, maturity, and a prudent approach to training are vital traits that must be fostered in all enthusiastic climbers.

Finally, it's important to avoid the added stress of using highly specific training tools, like a fingerboard or campus board, during the first year or two of climbing. After that, these activities can be added gradually as part of an intelligent, well-planned training-for-climbing program.

2. REGULARLY VARY THE TYPE OF CLIMBING.

Varying the type and magnitude of climbing stressors on the body is a highly effective way of lowering your exposure to injury. For instance, alternating consecutive weekends of climbing between sport and traditional routes naturally varies the type of specific strains placed on the body. Likewise, regularly changing the focus of weekday climbing and training activities—for example, alternating among bouldering, roped gym climbing, and general training—prevents any single system from being overly stressed. This practice of constantly mixing things up is the essence of cross-training applied to climbing.

3. USE PROPHYLACTIC FINGER TAPING IN THE MOST STRESSFUL SITUATIONS AND AFTER INJURY.

This subject was covered in length earlier in the chapter, but it's worth underscoring here—supportive taping of the finger tendon pulleys helps lower the force load placed on the tendons and may help prevent injury. Still, prophylactic taping is not something you should use every day and on every climb. Subjecting the finger tendons and annular pulleys to gradually increasing levels of stress is what will make them stronger and able to function under higher and higher loads in the future. The use of taping all the time could have a negative impact on the long-term strength of this system.

Reserve use of prophylactic taping techniques for workouts or climbs that you expect will push the envelope of what your tendons have previously experienced. For instance, taping would be a wise measure for attempting a hardest-ever route, any climb known to possess injurious hold types (one-finger pockets, extreme crimps, and the like), or high-intensity training techniques such as campus or hypergravity training. Of course, individuals recovering from recent finger injuries should tape their fingers during the early stages of returning to climbing.

4. PROCEED CAUTIOUSLY THROUGH DANGEROUS MOVES.

An important sense to develop is that of knowing and managing movement through inherently dangerous moves or sequences. In recognizing that you are entering a dangerous sequence (say, a one-finger lock with poor feet) and in sensing that you are near injury on a move, you are empowered to either disengage from the move or cautiously navigate the sequence as expeditiously as possible. Clearly you need experience in such situations in order to develop this sense, but you can foster this important skill by knowing your body and the sensations you feel on various types of movements.

As a final note, a climber will often escape injury on the first attempt or pass through some heinous move, then get injured by attempting or rehearsing the painful move repeatedly. This is obviously a very unintelligent approach—no single route is worth getting injured and, possibly, laid up for months over. The bottom line: If you find yourself climbing into a move that feels overly painful or injury-scary, simply lower off and find a better route to enjoy.

5. DON'T CLIMB TO EXHAUSTION.

There is nothing I enjoy more than occasionally maximizing a day of climbing fun by pulling down right into the evening twilight. As a regular practice, however, this is a prescription for injury. This chapter covered a range of overuse injuries that are largely caused by accumulated stress beyond what the body is capable of handling—that's why they call them overuse injuries!

Knowing when to say when is one of the subtle climbing skills that you can't learn from a book or video, but only through experience. Obviously, the best strategy is to err on the side of ending climbing early in the day versus right after you feel that finger tweak. The chapter on strength training hammered home the idea that quality training stimulus is far more important that the quantity of training. In strength training, less is often more.

When climbing, the right decision on when to call it a day is much less clear, since you want to maximize climbing fun and achievement without getting injured. In this situation only you can decide what's right for you. Don't be swayed into another burn on a strenuous route if you are approaching exhaustion and think your climbing technique will not be up to snuff. Keep in mind that many injuries occur late in the day, when you are tired and climbing sloppily.

One rule of thumb you might adopt is to call it quits early when planning to climb again the very next day or if you are already on your second day of climbing. In this way, you will limit undue accumulation of stress. Conversely, when sandwiching a single day of climbing between two rest days, you can feel better about packing in as many climbs as possible before dark.

6. DON'T CLIMB OR TRAIN MORE THAN FOUR DAYS PER WEEK.

In most cases it's counterproductive to climb and train for climbing more than a total of four days per week. Consequently, if you are climbing four days a week on the rock, in the gym, or both combined, you should do no other sport-specific training during the three remaining days of the week. Even with three days' rest out of seven, your body will struggle to repair the microtraumas incurred to the tendons and muscles during your four climbing days. For this reason, it is wise to incorporate a training cycle that provides a complete week off every month or two. This is valuable catch-up time for your biological climbing machine!

In a pure strength- and power-training program (such as in focused off-season training), you may only be able to train two or three days per week while resting four or five. Earlier in this chapter I presented several studies that indict overtraining (or under-resting) as one of the most common causes of overuse injury. Don't set yourself up for failure by succeeding at overtraining. Listen to your body and, when in doubt, favor over-resting.

7. ALWAYS WARM UP AND COOL DOWN.

Anyone with experience in traditional sports knows firsthand the importance of a proper warm-up and cool-down. Unfortunately, I have observed more than a few climbers who just tie in and start climbing without any preparatory warm-up activity, stretching, or submaximum climbing.

All that's needed for a good warm-up is to break a light sweat by jogging, hiking, or riding a bike for five to fifteen minutes. Follow this with some light stretching exercises, as described in chapter 6. Start your climbing for the day by doing a series of easy boulder problems or a route or two that is much easier than you might want to get on. This minor inconvenience is a worthy investment in avoiding injury and maximizing your performance later in the day.

A brief cool-down is also beneficial, since it will loosen up tight muscle groups and enhance the recovery process. In particular, stretching and a few minutes of light aerobic activity help maintain increased blood flow and speed dispersion of lactic acid accumulated in the most fatigued muscles.

8. MAINTAIN MUSCLE BALANCE BY TRAINING ANTAGONIST-MUSCLE GROUPS.

Training the antagonist muscles is one of the most overlooked—and most vital—parts of training for climbing. Muscle imbalances in the forearms, shoulders, and torso are primary factors in many of the overuse injuries covered in this chapter. If you are serious about climbing your best and preventing injury, then you must commit to training the antagonist muscles twice per week.

The time and equipment involved is minimal. All of the antagonist-muscle exercises described in chapter 6 can be performed at home with nothing more than a couple of dumbbells. As for the time commitment, it's less than twenty minutes, twice per week. I advise doing these exercises at the end of your weekday climbing or sport-specific workout. Keep the weights light, and do every single exercise outlined for the antagonist muscles of the upper body and forearms, as well as the handful of exercises for the core muscles of the torso.

9. USE PERIODIZATION TO VARY YOUR TRAINING SCHEDULE.

Many sports scientists consider periodization to be the gold standard for interweek planning of an effective and optimal strength-training program. As described in chapter 5, periodization involves a premeditated variation in workout focus, intensity, and volume, which in the long term produces a maximum training response. Periodization may also reduce the risk of overuse injury, since the training focus and intensity change every few days or weeks.

In a highly stressful sport like climbing, the most valuable aspect of periodization may be the intermittent rest phases or breaks away from all sport-specific activity. Chapter 8 advised use of the 4-3-2-1 and 3-2-1 cycles for most intermediate and elite climbers. Use of this training cycle provides one full week of rest out at the end of the training cycle, for systemic recovery and to blunt long-term accumulation of overuse stress. In the yearlong macrocycle it is advised to take one full month off from climbing-related stresses. These breaks away from climbing go a long way toward allowing the slow-to-adapt tendons and ligaments to catch up to the gains in muscular strength. It's also a healthy break for your mental muscle!

10. MAKE GETTING PROPER REST AND NUTRITION TOP PRIORITIES.

Getting proper rest and nutrition seems like an obvious rule for a serious athlete, but I'm often surprised by the bad dietary and sleep habits possessed by some very serious climbers. Fortunately, I have noticed improvement and increased awareness about rest and nutrition issues in recent years. No doubt the better-informed and more disciplined climbers are performing closer to their ultimate potential and with fewer injuries.

Chapter 9 on "Performance Nutrition" and chapter 10 on "Accelerating Recovery" provide many useful strategies to employ as you increase the priority placed on these subjects. If you use most of these strategies, most of the time, I am confident that you will outperform the masses and reduce your risk of overuse injuries.

Certainly an occasional late night out or free day of eating whatever you like won't hurt (in fact, it's a great reward after sending a major project!). Still, consistent lack of sleep and poor nutrition slow recovery between workouts and days of climbing, and undoubtedly make you more vulnerable to injury. Most important is good nutrition and a solid eight to nine hours of sleep in the day or two following an especially hard workout or day(s) of climbing. Remember that training and recovery are opposite sides of the same coin—if you put the effort into training optimally, then it would be a waste not to do everything in your power to recover optimally as well.

Jeff Batzer showing no handicap as he tops out on Upper Refuse, Cathedral Ledge, New Hampshire ERIC J. HÖRST

AFTERWORD

The power of climbing is awesome. The simple act of moving over stone can change your day, and it can change your life. Climbing takes you to places you have never been before—breathtaking vistas that few humans ever see and deep into the very core of your being. In this way climbing helps us discover who we are and gives us the gift of insight into our true potential and what really is possible in our lives. Many "flatlanders" never gain this insight, and, worse yet, far too many people around the world will never have the opportunity to experience the wonder of climbing (or any other pleasure-seeking activity) because they spend each day of their lives just trying to get by. From this perspective, I trust you will agree that in simply being able to go climbing and pursue self-actualization, we are better off than the majority of people on this planet. Regardless of your current disposition, vow to live each day with an attitude of gratitude. Look for ways to brighten the day of everyone you meet, and consider contributing some time or money to aid those who are less fortunate. I invite you to check out some of my favorite charities listed below. Share some of your climbing power with the world!

- MakeAWish.org
- RedCross.org
- WorldVision.org
- WoundedWarriors.org

Muscular Anatomy

Finger/wrist flexors

Pronator teres

Biceps

Anterior deltoid

Teres major

Latissimus dorsi

Serratus anterior

Trapezius (upper)

Deltoids

Pectoralis major

Triceps group

Brachioradialis

Fingers/wrist extensors

Obliques group

Rectus abdominis
(abdominals)

Psoas group
(hip flexors)

Adductors

Quadriceps group

Rectus femoris

Vastus lateralis

Vastus intermedius

Vastus medialis

Gastrocnemius
(medial)

Soleus

Calf muscles

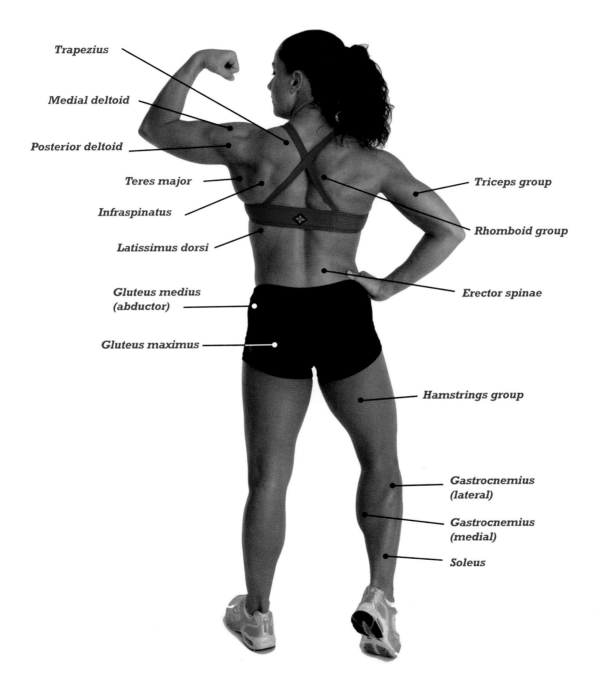

Trapezius

Medial deltoid

Posterior deltoid

Teres major

Infraspinatus

Latissimus dorsi

Gluteus medius
(abductor)

Gluteus maximus

Triceps group

Rhomboid group

Erector spinae

Hamstrings group

Gastrocnemius
(lateral)

Gastrocnemius
(medial)

Soleus

A P P E N D I X   B

Training Charts

Use the two blank training charts on the following pages to track your training progress. The "Training and Climbing Macrocycle" will enable you to set annual training objectives and seasonal climbing goals as well as record your actual progress. You can use the chart to plan your training for the four seasons, target specific types of training, track the number of days you train, and record your achievements throughout the year.

Use the "Energy–Emotion Levels" chart to track your physical energy and emotional mind-set hour by hour throughout the day. You can use this chart to observe patterns, identify negative triggers, modify your emotional state, and better manage your energy and emotions for optimal performance.

Training and Climbing Macrocycle

Name/Year		Training Objectives and Seasonal Climbing Goals										
Month		Jan	Feb	Mar	Apr	May	Jun	Jul	Aug	Sep	Oct	Nov	Dec
Week		1 2 3 4 5	6 7 8 9	10 11 12 13	14 15 16 17 18	19 20 21 22	23 24 25 26	27 28 29 30 31	32 33 34 35 36	37 38 39	40 41 42 43 44	45 46 47 48 49	50 51 52
Training Focus	Skills/stamina												
	Max. strength and power												
	Anaerobic endurance												
	Rest												
Total number of days per week of finger training or climbing	7												
	6												
	5												
	4												
	3												
	2												
	1												
Benchmark achievements and notes													

Energy–Emotion Levels

Name: _____

Date: _____

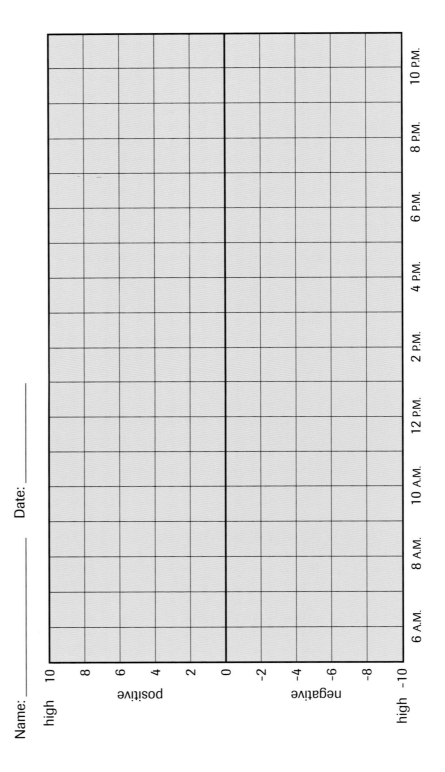

252

The Self-Assessment Test in chapter 2 covers physical strength, mental focus, and techniques and tactics. Taking the test should help you to gauge your overall strengths and weaknesses and pinpoint some specific areas for improvement. If you gave yourself a score of 3 or lower on any of the questions, you've identified weak spots that should be targeted for training. Here is a brief comment on each of these common problems as well as some specific tips for improving your climbing performance. For more in-depth information on any of these topics, see the chapters referenced below.

1. If your footwork deteriorates during the hardest part of the climb, you might be focusing on the lack of good handholds instead of zeroing in on crucial footholds (often the key to unlocking hard sequences).

   TIP: When the going gets tough, focus on your feet! (See chapter 3.)

2. If your forearms balloon and your grip begins to fail, you are probably overgripping the holds and/or climbing too slowly.

   TIP: On near-vertical walls, relax your grip and place maximum weight over your feet. When the wall angle is overhanging, the number one rule is to climb fast from one rest to the next. (See chapter 4.)

3. If you have difficulty stepping onto critical footholds during hard sequences, lack of flexibility or weak hip flexor muscles is the likely problem.

   TIP: Begin daily stretching for a minimum of ten minutes and practice high steps in a gym setting. (See chapter 6.)

4. If you find you get anxious and tight as you head into crux sequences, normalized breathing is the key to reducing tension and anxiety.

   TIP: Before starting up a climb, close your eyes and take five slow, deep breaths (each breath should take at least ten seconds). Try to maintain steady breathing as you climb. Take three more slow, deep breaths at each rest position and before you begin the crux sequence. (See chapter 3.)

5. If your biceps pump out before your forearms, it usually means you're hanging out with bent arms. Straight-arm positions are fundamental to good climbing technique.

   TIP: Whenever possible, hang "by the bone" and not with flexed arm muscle. Straight-arm positions are especially important when placing gear, shaking out, or pausing to decipher the next sequence (see chapter 4).

6. Do you have difficulty hanging on to small, necessary holds? Although poor body positioning can make small holds even harder to use, it's likely that your contact strength (grip) needs work.

   TIP: Spend more time training on steep walls and gym cave areas, and go bouldering more often. Some limited fingerboard and hypergravity training is also recommended for intermediate and advanced climbers. (See chapter 7.)

7. If you fail on sequences you know by heart, you might be making the common mistake of trying or inventing new sequences during a redpoint attempt.

   TIP: When you find a sequence that works, it's usually best to stick with it. Counter any midclimb thoughts of trying a new sequence with the definitive belief that you already know (and can do) the best sequence.

8. If you stall at the start of crux sequences, you might be suffering from paralysis by analysis.

   TIP: When faced with a crux sequence, visualize two possible sequences, and then immediately try the one that looks more promising. Once you commit to a sequence, go for it! Only one thing should be on your mind—getting to the next good hold (or rest) as fast as possible.

9. Do you climb three or four days in a row? Unless you are one of those genetically gifted extreme outliers, climbing or training on three or four consecutive days is a practice that will lead to overtraining, injury, and a drop in performance.

   TIP: In this case, less is more. Switch to a two-day-on, one-day-off (or one-day-on, one-day-off) schedule and you will be training smarter and climbing harder!

10. Sewing-machine leg is common in the tight, anxious climber.

    TIP: Lengthen your warm-up and begin working some of the relaxation exercises described in this text. (See chapter 3.)

11. If you pump out on overhanging climbs, you should be aware that the pump clock starts running when you leave the ground. You might not be too weak to climb the route—just too slow!

    TIP: Practice climbing more quickly on known (wired) routes and when redpointing. Foster a watchful eye that's on the lookout for creative rests that might stop the clock for a few moments. (See chapters 3 and 4.)

12. Do you get out of breath when you climb? Rapid breathing while climbing results from excess tension, irregular breathing, or poor aerobic fitness.

    TIP: Concentrate on maintaining relaxed, normal breathing while you climb. Also, consider engaging in some aerobic training (preferably running) three to four days per week. Build up to a maximum of four, twenty-minute runs per week. (See chapter 6.)

13. If you begin thinking about how you might fail on a route before you even start, you should know that belief gives birth to reality. If the thought of failing crosses your mind, you likely will.

    TIP: Before you start up a climb, always visualize yourself successfully climbing the route from bottom to top. (See chapter 3.)

14. Do you miss hidden holds on routes? Tunnel vision is a common cause of failure, especially during on-sight climbing.

    TIP: Scope the route from a few different vantage points before leaving the ground. As you climb, keep an open mind for hidden holds—the key hold always seems to take a little extra effort to locate. If a route feels really hard for its grade, chances are there's a good handhold or foothold escaping your view. (See chapters 3 and 4.)

15. If you have difficulty hanging on to small holds or pockets, keep in mind that open-hand grip strength is crucial. Expert climbers favor it, while beginner climbers avoid it.

    TIP: While training and bouldering, force yourself to use the open-hand grip at least 50 percent of the time. Most intermediate and advanced climbers can significantly improve open-hand grip strength through use of HIT workouts. (See chapter 7.)

16. It's common to grab onto gear rather than risk a fall trying a hard move. Assuming the potential fall is safe, always go for the move instead of grabbing gear or hanging on the rope. The bad habit of grabbing gear is easy to develop and very hard to break. Plus, you'll never learn where your true limit is if you give up in this way.

    TIP: Counter any thought of grabbing gear with the belief that there is absolutely a good

hold just a few moves above you (there probably is!).

17. If much of your body weight is hanging on your arms, you might not be placing your weight (center of gravity) over your feet.

    TIP: Invest more time practicing technique and body positioning. Focus on keeping your crotch and hips in near the wall (except on slabs) and experiment with moves where you turn one hip or the other to the wall. Some flexibility training may be beneficial, too (see chapter 4).

18. Intense soreness after only one day of cragging means that your training volume and intensity are not congruent with your outdoor climbing goals.

    TIP: Step up your indoor training and always try for two solid training days during the workweek.

19. Do you have difficulty visualizing yourself successfully climbing the route? All peak performers acknowledge the importance of visualization.

    TIP: Get into the habit of climbing each route in your mind's eye at least twice before giving it a real go. (See chapter 3.)

20. If you think you cannot reach key holds on difficult routes, you should be aware that this is the oldest excuse in this sport. Funny thing is, some great short climbers never use this excuse! The reason—there is almost always a technical solution or intermediate hold to be discovered that will solve apparent reach problems.

    TIP: Try a move five, ten, or even twenty different ways and you'll almost always find one that works!

21. If your feet cut loose and swing out on overhanging routes and roofs, it's possible that poor footwork and body positioning are responsible. More often, however, it results from weak core muscles (torso).

    TIP: Perform the core-muscle exercises, described in chapter 6, at least twice weekly.

Also, spend more time in a bouldering cave working on your steep-wall footwork and body position.

22. If you get distracted by activity on the ground, remember that while climbing your focus must be locked onto the moves at hand, not directed downward. If less than 95 percent of your focus/attention is targeted on the climb, you don't have much of a chance of success.

    TIP: Clear your mind of what's happening on the ground. If you need confirmation that your belayer is paying attention, a simple "watch me" will do; then refocus on the move at hand. (See chapter 3.)

23. It's common for beginning climbers to have difficulty reading sequences. Reading sequences comes from experience—each time you go climbing is money in the bank!

    TIP: Climb up to four days a week to increase your rate of deposit. Always try to figure sequences from the ground and minimize use of beta (a real handicap to learning), except when climbing for performance.

24. Do you experience a deep flash pump on the first climb of the day? A flash pump results when you push your muscles too hard, too soon.

    TIP: Lengthen your warm-up period, add more stretching and some sports massage, and always do a few increasingly difficult routes before attempting your project.

25. If you have more difficulty climbing when people are watching, remember that the pressure of needing to perform is entirely self-imposed. Therefore, it can be turned off as easily as you turn it on.

    TIP: Commit to climb for yourself—for the challenge, adventure, and fun of it (all the reasons you got into climbing in the first place). Forget about the rest of the world, engage the process of climbing, and let the outcome take care of itself. (See chapter 3.)

26. If your feet unexpectedly pop off footholds, take heart that this is a common problem, even among some advanced climbers.

TIP: Refocus your attention on your feet for a few weeks. Evaluate whether you carefully place your feet on the best part of a hold or simply drop them onto the biggest-looking part. Also, do you hold your foot position stationary as you stand up or does your shoe move on the hold? These are things you need to practice in a nonperformance setting. (See chapter 4.)

27. Do you experience frequent elbow pain? There are two types of elbow tendinosis common to climbers. If you climb enough years, chances are you'll experience at least one of them.

TIP: Reverse Wrist Curls and forearm rotation exercises as well as regular forearm stretching will help prevent these problems. Perform three sets of Reverse Wrist Curls (twenty-five reps with a five- to fifteen-pound dumbbell) and two sets of Forearm Pronators, three days per week, year-round. Stretch both sides of your forearms each day. (See chapter 6.)

28. If you have trouble pushing yourself to the limit on a safe lead climb, your problem is more likely mental than physical. Keep in mind that mental fortitude is as important as brawn.

TIP: On safe routes consciously push yourself into the mental discomfort zone. At first this will feel like bitter medicine, but in time it will redefine your mental limits. (See chapter 3.)

29. If you have difficulty finding midroute rest positions, you are missing one of the keys to sending routes near your limit.

TIP: Creative practice (in a nonperformance setting) at finding funky rest positions, modeling the rest positions of other climbers, and climbing experience at a wide range of crags will, in time, make finding "thank God" rests instinctual!

30. If your first attempt on a hard route is usually better than second or third attempts that day, lack of muscular endurance and stamina are likely a contributing factor.

TIP: Climbing laps on training routes or boulder problems is a great way to improve endurance. Use the interval-climbing strategies detailed in chapter 7.

A P P E N D I X   D

Fitness Evaluation

This ten-part evaluation is strenuous. Perform a complete warm-up before proceeding, and rest extensively between tests. Take this fitness test annually to gauge your changes in conditioning for climbing. Submit your results at TrainingForClimbing.com.

Test 1: One set maximum number of pull-ups. Do this test on a standard pull-up bar (or bucket hold on a fingerboard) with your palms away and hands shoulder width apart. Do not bounce, and be sure to go up and down the whole way.

Evaluation: Total number of pull-ups in a single set to failure.

Results: _____

Test 2: One repetition maximum pull-up. Do a single pull-up with a ten-pound weight clipped to your harness. Rest three minutes, then add ten more pounds and repeat. (If you are very strong, begin with a twenty-pound weight and increase at ten- to twenty-pound increments.) Continue in this fashion until you have added more weight than you can pull up.

Evaluation: The maximum amount of added weight successfully lifted for a single pull-up divided by your body weight.

Results: _____

Test 3: One-arm lock-off. Start with a standard chin-up (palms facing) then lock off at the top on one arm and let go with the other.

Evaluation: Length of time in the lock-off before your chin drops below the bar.

Results:
Right arm _____   Left arm _____

Test 4: One set maximum number of Frenchies. Perform the exercise as described on page 166. Remember, each cycle consists of three pull-ups separated by the three different lock-off positions, which are held for five seconds. Have a partner time your lock-offs.

Evaluation: The number of cycles (or part of) completed in a single set.

Results: _____

Test 5: One set maximum number of fingertip pull-ups on a 0.75-inch (19 millimeter) edge. Perform this exercise as in test 1 except on a fingerboard edge or doorjamb of approximately the stated size.

Evaluation: The number of fingertip pull-ups done in a single go.

Results: _____

Test 6: Lock off in the top position of a fingertip pull-up (0.75-inch or 19-millimeter edge) for as long as possible.

Evaluation: Length of time in the lock-off until your chin drops below the edge.

Results: _____

Test 7: Straight-arm hang from a standard pull-up bar. Place your hands shoulder width apart with palms facing away.

Evaluation: Length of time you can hang on the bar before muscle failure.

Results: _____

Test 8: One set maximum number of abdominal crunches. Perform these on a pad or carpeted floor with your knees bent at approximately ninety degrees, your feet flat on the floor with nothing anchoring them. Cross your arms over your upper chest and perform each crunch until your shoulder blades rise off the floor.

Evaluation: Number of crunches you can perform without stopping. Do them in a controlled manner—no bouncing off the floor.

Results: _____

Test 9: Wall split as described on page 108. Be sure that your rear end is no more than 6 inches from the wall.

Evaluation: Position your legs so they are equidistant from the floor and measure the distance from your heels to the floor.

Results: _____

Test 10: High-step stretch. Stand facing a wall with one foot flat on the floor with toes touching the wall. Lift the other leg up to the side as high as possible without any aid from your hands.

Evaluation: Measure the height of your step off the floor and divide it by your height.

Results: _____

GLOSSARY

The following is a compilation of some of the technical terms and climbing jargon used throughout this book.

active recovery—The restoration of homeostasis following vigorous exercise that involves continued light-intensity movement; facilitates faster recovery by enhancing lactate removal from the blood.

acute—Having rapid onset and severe symptoms.

adaptive response—Physiological changes in structure or function particularly related to response to a training overload.

adipose tissue—Body fat.

aerobic(s)—Any physical activity deriving energy from the breakdown of glycogen in the presence of oxygen, thus producing little or no lactic acid, enabling an athlete to continue exercise much longer.

agonist—A muscle directly engaged in a muscular contraction.

anaerobic—Energy production in the muscles involving the breakdown of glycogen in the absence of oxygen; a by-product called lactic acid is formed, resulting in rapid fatigue and cessation of physical activity.

anaerobic endurance—The ability to continue moderate- to high-intensity activity over a period of time; commonly called power endurance or power stamina by climbers, though these terms are scientifically incorrect.

anaerobic threshold—The workload or level of oxygen consumption where lactate production by the working muscles exceeds the rate of lactate removal by the liver; typically at 50 percent to 80 percent of maximum intensity of exercise, and in proportion to one's level of anaerobic endurance conditioning.

antagonist—A muscle providing an opposing force to the primary muscles of action (agonist).

antioxidants—Substances (vitamins and minerals) proven to oppose oxidation and inhibit or neutralize free radicals.

ape-index—Fingertip-to-fingertip distance (across your chest with arms out to each side) minus your height; a positive ape-index is associated with above-average reach for a given height.

artery—A vessel that carries oxygenated blood away from the heart to the tissues of the body.

arthritis—A disease that causes inflammation, swelling, and pain in the joints.

arousal—An internal state of alertness or excitement.

ATP—Adenosine triphosphate; a high-energy molecule that is stored in the muscles in very small amounts. The body's ultimate fuel source.

atrophy—Gradual shrinking and deconditioning of muscle tissue from disuse.

backstepping—Outside edging on a foothold that is behind you while climbing a move with your side to the wall.

barndoor—Sideways swinging or uncontrolled turning of the body resulting from poor balance or body positioning.

basal metabolic rate—The minimum level of energy required to sustain the body's vital functions.

beta—Any prior information about a route, including sequence, rests, gear, clips, and so on.

biological value (BV)—A method for evaluating protein sources; a high BV protein source has a high percentage of nutrients actually absorbed from the human intestine as opposed to excreted.

blocked practice—A practice routine in which a specific task is practiced repeatedly, as in working a crux move or sequence.

bouldering—Variable practice of climbing skills performed without a belay rope at the base of a cliff or on small boulders.

campus (or campusing)—Climbing an overhanging section of rock or artificial wall with no feet, usually in a dynamic left-hand, right-hand, left-hand (and so forth) sequence.

campus training—A sport-specific form of plyometric exercise, developed by Wolfgang Güllich at the Campus Center, a weight-lifting facility at the University of Nürnberg, Germany.

capillary—The tiny blood vessels that receive blood flow from the arteries, interchange substances between the blood and the tissues, and return the blood to the veins.

capillary density—The number of capillaries per unit area of muscle tissue. Capillary density increases, mainly in slow-twitch fibers, in response to aerobic training.

catabolic—A breaking-down process in the body, as in muscle breakdown during intense exercise.

center of gravity—The theoretical point on which the total effect of gravity acts on the body.

chronic—Continuing over time.

concentric contraction—Any movement involving a shortening of muscles fibers while developing tension, as in the biceps muscle during a pull-up.

contact strength—Initial grip strength upon touching a handhold; directly related to the speed at which the muscular motor units are called into play.

cortisol—A hormone, released in response to emotional or exercise stress, that promotes fat utilization, inhibits inflammatory response, and facilitates breakdown of muscle proteins for energy.

cortisone—A synthetic form of cortisol used (injected) as an anti-inflammatory.

creatine phosphate (CP)—A high-energy phosphate compound stored in skeletal muscle and used to supply energy for brief, high-intensity muscle action.

crimp grip—The most natural (and stressful) way to grip a rock hold, characterized by hyperexten-

sion of the first joint in the fingers and nearly full flexion of the second joint.

crux—The hardest move, or sequence of moves, on a route.

deadpoint—The high position in a dynamic movement where, for a moment, all motion stops.

detox—To shake out, rest, and recover from pumped forearm muscles.

detraining—Reversal of positive adaptations to chronic exercise upon cessation of an exercise program.

drop-knee—An exaggerated backstep, commonly used on overhanging rock, where the inside knee is dropped toward the ground, resulting in a stable chimneylike position.

dynamic move—An explosive leap for a hold otherwise out of reach.

dyno—Short for "dynamic."

eccentric contraction—A muscle action in which the muscle resists as it is forced to lengthen, as in the biceps during the lowering phase of a pull-up.

electrolyte—A substance that, in solution, is capable of conducting electricity. Certain electrolytes are essential to the electrochemical functioning of the body.

endurance—The ability to perform physical work for an extended period of time. Cardiovascular endurance is directly related to VO_2 max, whereas muscular endurance is influenced by circulation and available oxygen.

enzyme—A protein molecule that aids chemical reactions.

epicondylitis—Inflammation of the tendon origins of the forearm flexors (medial) or extensors (lateral) near the elbow.

ergogenic—Performance enhancing.

estrogen—The sex hormone that predominates in females, but also has some functions in males.

extension—A movement that moves the two ends of a jointed body part away from each other, as in straightening the arm.

fast-twitch fibers—The muscle fiber type that contracts quickly and is used mostly during intense, powerful movements.

flagging—A climbing technique in which one foot is crossed behind the other to avoid barndooring and to improve balance.

flash—To climb a route first try without ever having touched it, but with the aid of beta.

flash pump—A rapid, often vicious, muscular pump resulting from strenuous training or climbing without first performing a proper, gradual warm-up.

flexion—A movement that brings the ends of a body part closer together, as in bending the arm.

G-Tox—A technique that uses gravity to help speed recovery from a forearm pump. It involves alternating, every five to ten seconds, the position of the resting arm between the normal hanging-at-your-side position and a raised-hand position above your shoulder.

glycogen—Compound chains of glucose stored in the muscle and liver for use during aerobic or anaerobic exercise.

glycemic index (GI)—A scale that classifies how the ingestion of various foods affects blood sugar levels in comparison with the ingestion of straight glucose.

Golgi tendon organ—Sensory receptors located between the muscle and its tendon that are sensitive to the stretch of the muscle tendon produced during muscular contraction.

gripped—Extremely scared.

hangdogging—Climbing a route, usually bolt-to-bolt, with the aid of a rope to hang and rest while practicing the sequence.

heel hook—Use of the heel on a hold, usually near chest level, to aid in pulling and balance.

homeostasis—The body's tendency to maintain a steady state despite external changes.

honed—In extremely good shape; with low body fat.

hormone—A chemical secreted into the bloodstream to regulate the function of a certain organ.

hyperemia—Increased blood flow in the working muscles during exercise or as a result of deep sports massage.

Hypergravity Isolation Training (HIT)—A highly refined and specific method of training maximum finger strength and upper-body power by climbing on identical finger holds (isolation) with greater than body weight (hypergravity). Also known as Hörst Isolation Training.

hypertrophy—Enlargement in size (for example, muscular hypertrophy).

insertion—The point of attachment of a muscle to a distal or relatively more movable bone.

insulin—A hormone that decreases blood glucose level by driving glucose from the blood into muscle and fat cells.

interval training—A method of anaerobic endurance training that involves brief periods of intense training interspaced with periods of rest or low-intensity training.

isometric—A muscular contraction resulting in no shortening movement of the muscle.

kinesiology—The scientific study of human movement.

kinesthetic—The sense derived from muscular contractions and limb movements.

killer—Extraordinarily good, as in a killer route.

lactic acid—An acid by-product of the anaerobic metabolism of glucose during intense muscular exercise.

lactic acid system—The energy pathway used in high-intensity activity over a short duration.

lean body weight—The weight of the body, less the weight of its fat.

ligament—Fibrous tissue that connects bone to bone, or bone to cartilage, to hold together and support the joints.

lunge—An out-of-control dynamic move; an explosive jump for a far-off hold.

macronutrients—Basic nutrients needed for energy, cell growth, and organ function (carbohydrates, fat, and protein).

manky—Of poor quality, as in a manky finger jam or a manky protection placement.

maximum strength—The peak force of a muscular contraction, irrespective of the time element.

micronutrients—Noncaloric nutrients needed in very small amounts, as in vitamins and minerals.

modeling—A learning technique where an individual watches, then attempts, a skill as performed properly by another person.

motor learning—A set of internal processes associated with practice or experience leading to a relatively permanent gain in performance capability.

motor skill—A skill where the primary determinant of success is the movement component itself.

motor unit—A motor neuron, together with a group of muscle cells, stimulated in an all-or-nothing response.

muscular endurance—The length of time a given level of power can be maintained.

NSAID—Non-steroidal anti-inflammatory drugs, usually available over the counter, that reduce pain, fever, and inflammation.

on-sight—When a route is climbed first try and with absolutely no prior information of any kind.

open-hand grip—The less-stressful finger grip involving only slight flexion of the finger joints.

osteoarthritis—A joint disease of older persons in which cartilage in the joints wears down and there is bone growth at the edges of the joint.

overload—Subjecting a part of the body to greater efforts (intensity or volume) than it is accustomed to in order to elicit a training response.

overtraining—Constant severe training that does not provide adequate time for recovery; symptoms include increased frequency of injury, decreased performance, irritability, and apathy.

overuse—Excessive repeated exertion or shock that results in injuries such as inflammation of the muscles and tendons.

plyometric—An exercise that suddenly preloads and forces the stretching of a muscle an instant prior to its concentric contraction, as in dynamic up-and-down campus training. Also known as reactive or shock training.

power—A measure of both force and speed (speed = distance x time) of a muscular contraction through a given range of motion. Power is the explosive aspect of strength. (Technically the

term *finger power* is meaningless, since the fingers normally don't move when gripping the rock.)

pronation—The inward turning of a body part, as in turning the forearm inward and the palm facedown.

proprioceptive neuromuscular facilitation (PNF)—A stretching technique that couples contraction and relaxations to enhance stretching gains. Most commonly, a five- to ten-second muscle contraction (against resistance from a partner) is followed by a relaxation period during which the partner slowly applies pressure to increase the range of the stretch.

proprioceptors—Sensory receptors found in muscles, tendons, joints, and the inner ear, that detect the motion or position of the limbs and body, thus providing kinesthetic awareness.

psyched—Raring to go or very happy.

pumped—When the muscles become engorged with blood due to extended physical exertion.

random practice—A practice sequence in which tasks from several classes are experienced in random order over consecutive trails.

reactive training—A power-building exercise that couples, in rapid succession, a forceful eccentric contraction with an explosive concentric contraction.

recommended dietary allowances (RDA)—Quantities of specific vitamins, minerals, and other nutrients needed daily that have been judged adequate for maintenance of good nutrition. Developed by the Food and Nutrition Board of the National Academy of Science.

recruitment—The systematic increase in the number of active motor units called upon during muscular contraction.

redpoint—Lead climbing a route bottom-to-top in one push.

Reminiscence Effect—The phenomenon of enhanced motor skill and performance after an extended time-off period from climbing and training.

schema—A set of rules, usually developed and applied unconsciously by the motor system in the brain and spinal cord, relating how to move and adjust muscle forces, body positions, and so forth, given the parameters at hand, such as steepness of the rock, friction qualities, holds being used, and type of terrain.

sharp end—The lead climber's end of the rope.

skill—The capability to bring about an end result with maximum certainty, minimum energy, and minimum time.

slow-twitch fibers—The muscle fiber type that contracts slowly and is used most in moderate-intensity endurance activities such as easy to moderate climbing or running.

sport climbing—Usually refers to any indoor or outdoor climbing on bolt-protected routes.

spotter—A person designated to slow the fall of a boulderer, with the main goal of keeping the boulderer's head from hitting the ground.

stabilizer muscle—A muscle that is stimulated to help anchor or stabilize the position of a bone.

strength—The amount of muscle force that can be exerted; speed and distance are not factors of strength.

strength endurance—See anaerobic endurance.

supination—Rotation of the forearm outward and palm-upward.

synovial fluid—A viscid fluid secreted by the membrane lining joints, tendon sheaths, and bursae to lubricate and cushion them during movement.

Tabata—A grueling interval-training protocol involving twenty seconds of maximum-intensity exercise followed by ten seconds of rest; usually repeated up to eight times. Named after its developer, Izumi Tabata.

tendinitis—An acute disorder involving the inflammation of a tendon and synovial membrane at a joint.

tendinopathy—A general term that just refers to tendon injury, without specifying a particular type of injury such as tendinitis (inflammation) or tendinosis (failed healing).

tendinosis—Chronic tendon pain due to an accumulation of microscopic injuries that don't heal properly; the main problem, then, is failed healing, not inflammation.

tendon—A white fibrous cord of dense connective tissue that attaches muscle to bone.

trad—Short for a traditional climb (or climber) that requires natural protection placements.

training effect—A basic principle of exercise science that states that adaptation occurs from an exercise only in those parts or systems of the body that are stressed by the exercise.

transfer of learning—The gain or loss in proficiency on one task as a result of practice or experience on another task.

trigger point—A long-lasting muscle spasm or contracture often associated with local muscular fatigue or injury.

tweak—To injure, as in a tweaked finger tendon.

variable practice—Practice in which many variations on a class of actions are performed; opposite of blocked practice.

vein—A vessel that returns blood from the various parts of the body to the heart.

visualization—Controlled and directed imagery that can be used for awareness building, monitoring and self-regulation, healing, and, most important, as mental programming for good performances.

VO$_2$ max—Maximal oxygen uptake, as in the measurement of maximum aerobic power.

wired—Known well, as in a wired route.

working—Practicing the moves on a difficult route via toprope or hangdogging.

SUGGESTED READING

Ament, Pat. *Master of Rock*. Mechanicsburg, Pa.: Stackpole Books, 1977, 1998.

Armstrong, Lawrence E. *Performing in Extreme Environments*. Champaign, Ill.: Human Kinetics, 2000.

Benardot, Dan. *Advanced Sports Nutrition*. Champaign, Ill.: Human Kinetics, 2006.

Brand-Miller, Jennie, et al. *The Glucose Revolution: The Authoritative Guide to the Glycemic Index*. New York: Marlowe and Company, 1999.

Brukner, Peter, and Karim Khan. *Clinical Sports Medicine*. New York: McGraw-Hill, 2006.

Burke, Edmund R. *Optimal Muscle Recovery*. Garden City Park, N.Y.: Avery Publishing Group, 1999.

Csikszentmihalyi, Mihaly. *Flow: The Psychology of Optimal Experience*. New York: Harper Perennial, 1990.

Garfield, Charles A. *Peak Performance: Mental Training Techniques of the World's Greatest Athletes*. New York: Warner Books, 1984.

Goddard, Dale, and Udo, Neumann. *Performance Rock Climbing*. Mechanicsburg, Pa.: Stackpole Books, 1993.

Guten, Gary. *Injuries in Outdoor Recreation*. Guilford, Conn.: Globe Pequot Press/Falcon Publishing, 2005.

Hochholzer, Thomas, et al. *One Move Too Many*. Ebenhausen, Germany: Lochner-Verlag, 2003.

Hörst, Eric J. *How to Climb 5.12*. Guilford, Conn.: Globe Pequot Press/FalconGuides, 2003.

————. *Mental Wings: A Seven-Step, Life-Elevating Program for Uncommon Success*. www.MentalWings.com, 2003.

————. *Learning to Climb Indoors*. Guilford, Conn.: Globe Pequot Press/FalconGuides, 2006.

————. *Conditioning for Climbers*. Guilford, Conn.: Globe Pequot Press/FalconGuides, 2007.

Long, John. *How to Rock Climb!* Guilford, Conn.: Globe Pequot Press/Falcon Publishing, 1993.

Meagher, Jack. *Sports Massage*. New York: Station Hill, 1990.

Prudden, Bonnie. *Pain Eraser: Discover the Wonders of Trigger Point Therapy*. New York: Evans and Company, 1980.

Schmidt, R. A., and C. A. Wrisberg. *Motor Learning and Performance: A Problem-Based Learning Approach*. Champaign, Ill.: Human Kinetics, 2004.

Stricker, Lauri. *Pilates for the Outdoor Athlete*. Conifer, Colo.: Fulcrum, 2007.

REFERENCES

Chapter 1

Ament, Pat. (1977, 1992) *Master of Rock*. Lincoln, Neb.: Adventure's Meaning Press.

Barss, Stephanie J. (1997) "Physiological attributes of recreational rock climbers." A master's thesis presented to the faculty of Western Washington University.

Bloomfield, J., Ackland, T. R., Elliot, B. C. (1994) *Applied Anatomy and Biomechanics in Sport*. Carlton, Victoria, Australia: Blackwell Scientific Publications.

Ericsson, K. A., Krampe, R. T., Tech-Rsmer, C. (1993) "The role of deliberate practice in the acquisition of expert performance." *Psych Rev* 100(3): 363–406.

Fox, P. W., Hershberger, S. L., Bouchard, T. J. (1996) "Genetic and environmental contributions to the acquisition of a motor skill." *Nature* 384: 356–358.

Goddard, Dale, Neumann, Udo. (1993) *Performance Rock Climbing*. Mechanicsburg, Pa.: Stackpole Books.

Güllich, W., Kubin, A. (1986) *Sportklettern Heute: Technik, Taktik, Training*. München, Germany: Bruckmann.

Hörst, Eric J. (1994) *Flash Training*. Evergreen, Colo.: Chockstone Press.

———. (1997) *How to Climb 5.12*. Helena, Mont.: Falcon Press/Globe Pequot.

Mermier, C. M., Janot, J. M., Parker, D. L., Swan, J. G. (2000) "Physiological and anthropometric determinants of sport climbing performance." *Brit J Sports Med* 34(5) (Oct): 359–365.

Seiler, S. (2000) "Limits to performance." *Sportscience* 4(2).

Watts, P. B., Martin, D. T., Durtschi, S. (1993) "Anthropometric profiles of elite male and female competitive sport rock climbers." *J Sport Sci* 11(2) (Apr): 113–117.

Chapter 3

Covey, Stephen. (1989) *The Seven Habits of Highly Effective People*. New York: Simon and Schuster.

Feltz, D., Landers, D. (1983) "The effects of mental practice on motor skill learning and performance." *Sport Psych* 5.

Garfield, C. (1984) *Peak Performance*. New York: Warner Books.

Knudson, D. V., Morrison, C. S. (1997) *Qualitative Analysis of Human Movement*. Champaign, Ill.: Human Kinetics.

Kubistant, T. (1986) *Performing Your Best*. Champaign, Ill.: Leisure Press.

Levinson, W. (1994) *The Way of Strategy*. Milwaukee: ASQC Quality Press.

Chapter 4

Schmidt, R. A. (1991) *Motor Learning and Performance: From Principles to Practice*. Champaign, Ill.: Human Kinetics.

Schmidt, R. A., Wrisberg, C. A. (2004) *Motor Learning and Performance: A Problem-Based Learning Approach*. Champaign, Ill.: Human Kinetics.

Chapter 5

Adams, K., O'Shea, J., O'Shea, K., Climstein, M. (1992) "The effect of six weeks of squat, plyometric, and squat-plyometric training on power production." *Appl Sport Sci Res* 6.

Bloomfield, J., Ackland, T. R., Elliot, B. C. (1994) *Applied Anatomy and Biomechanics in Sport.* Carlton, Victoria, Australia: Blackwell Scientific Publications.

Bloomfield, J., Fricker, P., Fitch, K. (1992) *Textbook of Science and Medicine in Sport.* Carlton, Victoria, Australia: Blackwell Scientific Publications.

Chu, Donald A. (1996) *Explosive Power and Strength.* Champaign, Ill.: Human Kinetics.

Kaneko, M., Fuchimoto, T., Toji, H., Suei, K. (1983) "Training effect of differing loads on the force–velocity relationship and mechanical power output in human muscle." *Scand J Sport Sci* 5.

O'Shea, K., O'Shea, J. (1989) "Functional isometric weight training: Its effect on dynamic and static strength." *J Appl Sport Sci Res* 3.

Tabata, I., Nishimura, K., Kouzaki, M., Hirai, Y., Ogita, F., Miyachi, M., Yamamoto, K. (1997) "Effects of moderate-intensity endurance and high-intensity intermittent training on anaerobic capacity and VO_2 max." *Med Sci Sports Exercise* 28: 1327–1330.

Tidow, G. (1990) "Aspects of strength training in athletes." *New Studies in Athletics* 1.

Watts, P., Newbury, V., Sulentic, J. (1996) "Acute changes in handgrip strength, endurance, and blood lactate with sustained sport rock climbing." *J Sports Med Physical Fitness* (Dec).

Chapter 6

Bell, G., Peterson, S., Quinney, A., Wenger, H. (1989) "The effect of velocity-specific strength training on peak torque and anaerobic rowing power." *J Sports Sci* 7.

King, J., et al. (2001) "A comparison of high intensity vs. low intensity exercise on body composition in overweight women." American College of Sports Medicine Annual Meeting.

Shrier, I. (1999) "Stretching before exercise does not reduce the risk of local muscle injury: A critical review of the clinical and basic science literature." *Clinical J Sport Med* 9: 221-227.

——— (2000) "Stretching before exercise: An evidence based approach." *Brit J Sports Med* 34(10): 324–325.

Watts, P. B., Martin, D. T., Durtschi, S. (1993) "Anthropometric profiles of elite male and female competitive sport rock climbers." *J Sport Sci* 11(2) (Apr): 113–117.

Wilmore, J. (1983) "Body composition in sport and exercise: Directions for future research." *Med Sci Sports Exercise* 15.

Chapter 7

Tabata, I., Nishimura, K., Kouzaki, M., Hirai, Y., Ogita, F., Miyachi, M., Yamamoto, K. (1997) "Effects of moderate-intensity endurance and high-intensity intermittent training on anaerobic capacity and VO_2 max." *Med Sci Sports Exercise* 28: 1327–1330.

Chapter 8

Bloomfield, J., Ackland, T. R., Elliot, B. C. (1994) *Applied Anatomy and Biomechanics in Sport.* Carlton, Victoria, Australia: Blackwell Scientific Publications.

Davis, B., Elford, J., Jamieson, K. (1991) "Variation in performance in simple muscle tests at different phases of the menstrual cycle." *J Sports Med Physical Fitness* 31.

Wilmore, J. (1974) "Alterations in strength, body composition and anthropometric measurements consequent to a ten-week weight training program." *Med Sci Sports* 5.

Chapter 9

Brilla, L. R., Conte, V. (1999) "A novel zinc and magnesium formulation (ZMA) increases anabolic hormones and strength in athletes." *Sports Med Training Rehab J* (Nov).

Duchaine, Daniel. (1996) *Bodyopus*. Carson City, Nev.: Xipe Press.

Graham, T. E., et al. (1998) "Metabolic and exercise endurance effects of coffee and caffeine ingestion." *J Appl Physiol* 85: 883–889.

Horswill, C. A. (1995) "Effects of bicarbonate, citrate, and phosphate loading on performance." *Int J Sport Nutrition* 5: S111–119.

Kelly, G. S. (1997) "Sports nutrition: A review of selected nutritional supplements for endurance athletes." *Alt Med Rev*.

Linderman, J. K., Gosselink, K. L. (1994) "The effects of sodium bicarbonate ingestion on exercise performance." *Sports Med* 18: 75–80.

McBride, J. B., et al. (1998) "Effect of resistance exercise on free radical production." *Med Sci Sports Exercise* 30(1).

Nissen, S., Panton, L., et al. (1996) "Effect of HMB supplementation on strength and body composition of trained and untrained males undergoing intense strength training." *FASEB J* 10A: A287.

Nissen, S., Sharp, R., et al. (1996) "Effect of leucine metabolite HMB on muscle metabolism during resistive exercise training." *J Appl Physiol* 81: 2095–2104.

Pasman, W. J., et al. (1995) "The effect of different dosages of caffeine on endurance performance time." *Int J Sports Med* 16: 225–230.

Robergs, R. A. (1991) "Nutrition and exercise determinants of post-exercise glycogen synthesis." *Int J Sport Nutrition*.

Schoffstall, J., et al. (2001) "Effects of dehydration and rehydration on the one-rep maximum bench press of weight-trained males." *J Strength Cond Res* 15.

Spriet, L. (1995) "Caffeine and performance." *Int J Sport Nutrition* 5: S84–99.

Toubro, et al. (1993) "Safety and efficacy of long-term treatment with ephedrine, caffeine and an ephedrine/caffeine mixture." *Int J Obes* 17 (1): S69–72.

Vukovich, M., et al. (1997) "Effect of HBM on VO_2 peak and maximal lactate in endurance-trained cyclists." *Med Sci Sports Exercise*.

Williams, Melvin H. (1989) *Beyond Training*. Champaign, Ill.: Leisure Press/Human Kinetics Publishing.

Chapter 10

Bloomfield, J., T. R. Ackland, B. C. Elliot (1994) *Applied Anatomy and Biomechanics in Sport*. Carlton, Victoria, Australia: Blackwell Scientific Publications.

Bompa, Tudor O. (1983) *Theory and Methodology of Training*. Dubuque, Iowa: Kendall/Hunt Publishing Co.

Burke, Edmund R. (1999) *Optimal Muscle Recovery*. Garden City Park, N.Y.: Avery Publishing Group.

Coyle, E. F., Coggan, A. R. (1984) "Effectiveness of carbohydrate feeding in delaying fatigue during prolonged exercise." *Sports Med* 5.

Dinan, T. G., et al. (1994) "Lowering cortisol enhances growth hormone response in healthy individuals." *Acta Physiol Scand* 151(3) (Jul).

Draper, Nick, et al. (2006) "Effects of active recovery on lactate concentration, heart rate and RPE in climbing." *J Sports Sci Med* 5: 97–105.

Meagher, Jack. (1990) *Sports Massage*. New York: Station Hill Press.

Monedero, J., Donne, B. (2000) "Effect of recovery interventions on lactate removal and subsequent performance." *Int J Sports Med* (Nov).

Niles, T. S., et al. (1997) "The effects of carbohydrate-protein drink on muscle glycogen resynthesis after endurance exercise." *Med Sci Sports Exercise* 29 Suppl 5.

Richter, E. A., et al. (1984) "Enhanced muscle glycogen metabolism after exercise." *Amer J Physiol* 246.

Watts, P. B., M. Daggett, P. Gallagher, B. Wilkens. (2000) "Metabolic response during sport rock climbing and the effects of active versus passive recovery." *Int J Sports Med* (Apr).

Williams, R. B., et al. (1982) "Type A behavior and elevated physiological and neuroendocrine responses to cognitive tasks." *Science* 29 (Oct): 218.

Chapter 11

Almekinders, L. (1999) "Anti-inflammatory treatment of muscular injuries in sport." *Sports Med* 28: 383–388.

———(2003) "An in vitro investigation into the effects of repetitive motion and nonsteroidal anti-inflammatory medication on human tendon fibroblasts." *Am J Sports Med* 23:119–123.

Auerback, David, M. (2000) Tennis Elbow/Lateral Epicondylitis. Southern California Orthopedic Institute. www.scoi.com.

Bach, Allan W. (1999) "Finger joint injuries in active patients." *Physician Sportsmedicine* 27(3).

Bannister, P., Foster, P. (1986) "Upper limb injuries associated with rock climbing." *Brit J Sports Med* 20.

Bollen, S. R. (1988) "Soft tissue injuries in extreme rock climbers." *Brit J Sports Med* 22.

Crouch, D. M. (1998) "Finger tips: The key to treating finger injuries is knowing what ails you." *Rock and Ice* 84.

Doran, D. A., Reay, M. (2000) "Injuries and associated training and performance characteristics in recreational rock climbers." In *The Science of Rock Climbing and Mountaineering*. Champaign, Ill.: Human Kinetics Publishing.

Gabl, M., Lener, M., Pechlaner, S., Lutz, M., Rudisch, A. (1996) "Rupture or stress injury of the flexor tendon pulleys? Early diagnosis with MRI." *Handchir Mikrochir Plast Chir* 28 (Nov).

Gabl, M., Rangger, C., Lutz, M., Fink, C., Rudisch, A., Pechlaner, S. (1998) "Disruption of the finger flexor pulley system in elite rock climbers." *Am J Sports Med* 26(5) (Sep–Oct).

Hochholzer T., Schoffl VR., Lightner S. (2003) *One Move Too Many*. Ebenhausen, Germany: Lochner-Verlag.

Hochholzer T., Schoffl VR. (2005) "Epiphyseal fractures of the finger middle joints in young sport climbers." *Wilderness Environ Med* 16(3) (fall): 139–142.

Jebson, Peter, Steyers, J. L., Curtis, M. (1997) "Hand injuries in rock climbing: Reaching the right treatment." *Physician Sportsmedicine* 25(5).

Jüni, P. (2007) "Meta-analysis: Chondroitin for osteoarthritis of the knee or hip." *Ann Intern Med.* 146 (8): 580–90.

Khan, K. M. (1999) "Histopathology of common tendinopathies. Update and implications for clinical management." *Sports Med* 27(6) (June): 393–408.

Kim, L.S. (2006) "Efficacy of methylsulfonyl-methane (MSM) in osteoarthritis pain of the knee: A pilot clinical trial." *Osteoarthritis Cartilage* 14(3): 286–294.

Klauser A., et al. (2002) "Finger pulley injuries in extreme rock climbers: Depiction with Dynamic Ultrasonography." *Radiology* 222(3): 755–61.

Kulick, M. (1986) "Oral ibuprofen: Evaluation of its effect on peritendinous adhesions and the breaking strength of a tenorrhaphy." *J Hand Surg* 11A: 100–119.

Leadbetter, W. B. (1992) "Cell matrix response in tendon injury." *Clin Sports Med* 2(3): 533–577.

Lewis, R. A., Shea, O. F., Shea, K. G. (1993) "Acute carpal tunnel syndrome: Wrist stress during a major climb." *Physician Sportsmedicine* 21(7).

Lin, G. T., et al. (1989) "Functional anatomy of the human digital flexor pulley system." *J Hand Surg Am* 14.

Lin, G. T., et al. (1998) "Biomechanical analysis of flexor pulley reconstruction." *J Hand Surg Brit* 14.

Lister, G. D. (1979) "Reconstruction of pulleys employing extensor retinaculum." *J Hand Surg Am.*

Liu, S. H. (1995) "Collagen in tendon, ligament, and bone healing." *Clin Orth Related Res Num* 318: 265–278.

Marco, R. A., Sharkey, N. A., Smith, T. S., Zissimos, A. G. (1998) "Pathomechanics of closed rupture of the flexor tendon pulleys in rock climbers." *J Bone Joint Surg Am* 80(7) (Jul).

Maroon, J.C. (2006) "Omega-3 fatty acids (fish oil) as an anti-inflammatory: An alternative to non-steroidal anti-inflammatory drugs for discogenic pain." *Surg Neurol* 65(4) (Apr): 325.

McAlindon, T., et al. (2000) "Glucosamine and chondroitin for treatment of osteoarthritis." *JAMA* 283: 1469–1475.

McFarland, Edward G., et al. (2000) Patient Guide to Knee Arthroscopy. Johns Hopkins Department of Orthopaedic Surgery. www.hopkins medicine.org.

Moutet, F., Guinard, D., Gerard, P., Mugnier, C. (1993) "Subcutaneous rupture of long finger flexor pulleys in rock climbers." *Ann Chir Main Memb Super* 12(3).

Moutet, F. (2003) Flexor tendon pulley system: Anatomy, pathology, treatment. *Chirurgie de la Main* 22(1).

Nirschl, Robert P., Kraushaar, Barry S. (1996) "Assessment and treatment guidelines for elbow injuries." *Physician Sportsmedicine* 25(4).

Reginster, J. Y., et al. (2001) "Long-term effects of glucosamine sulfate on osteoarthritis progres-

sion: A randomized, placebo-controlled clinical trial." *Lancet* 357(9252) (Jan 27).

Robinson, Mark. (1988) "Fingers: Get a grip on injury prevention and treatment." *Climbing* (Aug).

———. (1993) "Snap, crackle, pop: Climbing injuries to fingers and forearms." *Climbing* (Jun–Jul).

———. (1993) "The elbow: Understanding a common sore subject." *Climbing* (Apr).

Rohrbough, Joel. (2000) "'Pop' goes your climbing season." *Climbing* (Nov).

Rooks, M. D. (1997) "Rock climbing injuries." *Sports Med* 23.

Schweizer, A. (2000) "Biomechanical effectiveness of taping the A2 pulley in rock climbers." *J. Hand Surg.* 25: 102–107.

Seiler, J. G., Leversedge, F. J. (2000) "Digital flexor sheath: Repair and reconstruction of the annular pulleys and membranous sheath." *J S Orth Assn* 9(2).

Seiler, J. G., et al. (1995) "The flexor digitorum longus: An anatomic and microscopic study for use as a tendon graft." *J Hand Surg Am* 20.

Stelzle, F. D., Gaulrapp, H., Pforringer, W. (2000) "Injuries and overuse syndromes due to rock climbing on artificial walls." *Sportverletz Sportschaden* 14(4) (Dec).

Sylvester, A. D., Christensen, A. M., Kramer, P. A. (2006) "Factors influencing osteological changes in the hands and fingers of rock climbers." *J Anatomy* 209(5).

Warme, W. J., Brooks, D. (2000) "The effect of circumferential taping on flexor tendon pulley failure in rock climbers." *Am J Sports Med* 28 (Sep–Oct).

Wright, D. M., Royle, T. J., Marshall, T. (2001) "Indoor rock climbing: Who gets injured?" *Brit J Sports Med* 35(3) (Jun).

INDEX

Italicized page numbers indicate photographs.

Figures and tables are indicated with "f" and "t" respectively, following the page number.

A

abdominals
  exercises, *112,* 113
  stretches, 109–10, *111*
Accelerade, 203
accomplished (intermediate) climbers
  classification requirements, 178t
  complex training, 96
  finger and forearm training exercises, 137t
  pull-muscle exercises, 158t
  reactive training, 92, 93, 147
  training focus and weakness targets, 172
  workout schedules for, 180–84, 180f, 182t, 183t
achievement curves, 12
Action Directe, 11, *11*
active rest, 212–13, 219
adductor stretches, 108, *108*
adenosine triphosphate. *See* ATP (adenosine triphosphate)
advanced climbers. *See* elite (advanced) climbers
aerobic capacity, 95, 128, 187, 188
aerobic energy production, 84, 84f
aerobic training
  for body composition, 100–101
  female climbers and, 187
  high-volume, for stamina, 129
  running intervals, 128
  stamina and, 95–96, 127
A-E training. *See* anaerobic endurance (A-E) training
agonist muscles, 80
Aided Pull-Ups, 158–59
alcoholic consumption, 216, 218
alpine climbing
  nutritional needs, 193, 195, 199
  SAID Principle and, 15, 15f

sleep requirements, 218
training for, 86, 95, 100, 126, 129, 176
Ament, Pat, 3, *3,* 4–5
anabolic steroids, 219
anaerobic endurance (A-E) training. *See also* endurance training; stamina training
  climbing intervals for, 128
  lactic acid tolerance, 208
  overview, 93–95
  rest, importance of, 173
  sample workouts for accomplished (intermediate) climbers, 182t
  sample workouts for elite (advanced) climbers, 185t
anaerobic threshold, 83–84, 84f
androstenedione (andro), 205
ANSWER Sequence, 38, 40–41
antagonist muscles, 80, 120–26, 136, 244
anti-inflammatory medications, 226, 230, 231–32, 234
antioxidants, 200
anxiety, 41, 64
Aquaman, 113–14, *116*
arm positions and movements
  mantling, 66–67, *135,* 136
  reverse side pull (Gaston), 64, 66, 134, *135,* 136
  side pulls, 66, 134, *135*
  underclings, 65–66, *66,* 134, *135*
arms. *See also* arm positions and movements; forearms
  climbing techniques, 61–62, *62,* 64–66, *66*
  flexibility training/stretches for, 102, *105,* 105–6, *106*
arnica, 231
arthritis, 230
associated visualization, 42
ATP (adenosine triphosphate)
  creatine and, 204
  as energy production component, 83, 84, 84f, 93
  fatigue and, 208, 211

MLP (motor learning and performance), 52–53, 74–77, 81–82, 96

modeling, 57

monounsaturated fatty acids, 195

Moors, Caves, and Crags (Baker), 1–2

motivation, 128, 168, 171, 172–73, 175

motor learning and performance (MLP), 52–53, 74–77, 81–82, 96

Motor Learning and Performance (Schmidt), 52

MSM (methylsulfonylmethane), 230

multipitch climbing, 126, 127–28, 176–77

multisensory learning, 48

muscle cramps, 209

muscle failure, 90, 91, 94, 137–38

muscles
    creatine supplementing and, 203–5
    delayed-onset muscle soreness (DOMS), 209, 210, 217, 231
    endurance training tips, 94
    energy production and, 83–84, 84f
    fatigue and, 208, 209
    fiber types, 80–81
    maximum strength training tips, 91
    motor units of, 81
    movement and roles of, 80
    overdevelopment and growth of, 82–83, 100, 101
    physiological training adaptations, 89f
    sport massage affect on, *215*, 215–17
    strength training adaptations of, 81–83, 83f
    strength *vs.* power, 88–89
    stress affecting, 219

N

National Academy of Sports Medicine, 92

nature-*versus*-nurture, 8

negative visualizations, 43

negativity, 30, 32, 33, 38

neural system adaptation, 81–82

Nicole, François, 9

Nicole, Frederic, 9

novice climbers. *See* beginner (novice) climbers

NSAIDs (non-steroidal anti-inflammatories), 226, 230, 231–32, 234

nutrition
    caloric needs, 194t, 197t
    crash dieting, 101
    injury prevention and, 245
    macronutrients, 193–98, 194t, 197t, 198t, 199, 201t
    for optimizing body composition, 100–101
    performance and, overview, 193
    recovery acceleration and, 217–18
    refueling strategies during/after climb, 213–15
    strength gains and, 86
    supplements, 199–205
    tips, overview, 199
    water, 198–99

O

Olympics, 11

omega-3 fatty acids, 195, 231, 232

One-Arm, One-Leg Bridge, 114, *117, 118*

One-Arm Lock-Offs, 161

One-Arm Lunging, 93, 96, 147–48, *148*

One-Arm Pull-Ups, 160

One-Arm Traversing, 147

100-meter dashes, 8, 8f

One Move Too Many (Hochholzer, Schoffl, and Lightner), 221

on-sight ascents, 44

open hand, 132, *133*

opposing forces, 64–66

osteoarthritis, 230

over-fifty climbers, 188–90

overgripping, 61

overload, progressive, 86, 88, 90–91

overtraining, 87, 223

P

pace, 64

pain. *See also* injuries
    anti-inflammatory medications, 226, 230, 231–32
    fear of, 37
    muscle soreness, 209, 210, 217, 231

Papert, Ines, *50*

paratenonitis, 232

partners, 26, 124, 128, 156

passive rest, 213

medium-term/intraday (refuel), 210, 213–17
microcycle training and, 174
muscular and energy systems and, 83–84, 84f
nutrition for, 213–15, 217–18
periods of, overview, 210–11
rest and, 86–87, 86f, 87f, 212–13, 219
shakeouts, 211–12
short-term/intraclimb (recharge), 210, 211–13
sleep, 218–19
visualization exercises during, 44–45
water intake, 212, 213
Red Cross Boulder, 3
redpoint ascents, 44
refuel recovery, 210, 213–17
rehabilitation exercises, shoulder, *237*, 237–40, *238*, *239*, *240*
relaxation, 38–41, 217
Reminiscence Effect, 175
rest. *See also* recovery (supercompensation)
accelerated recovery with, 212–13, 217, 219
climbing visualizations during, 44–45
finger/forearm training and, 136
injury prevention and, 245
lactic acid clearance time, 208
microcycle training programs and importance of, 173–74
as training principle, 86–87, 86f, 87f, 88, 91
rest positions, 64
reverse side pulls, 65, 134, *135*, 136
Reverse Wrist Curls, *120*, 121–22, 235
rhomboids and trapezius stretches, 105–6, *106*
rhythm, 63
RICE (rest, ice, compression, and elevation), 231, 232
risk management, 30, 38, 43–44, 45
rituals
focus, 46–47
preclimb, 31
worry, 43
Robbins, Royal, 4
Robinson, Mark, 52
rock climbing, overview. *See also related topics*
genetics and performance, 8–10
history of, 1–7, *2*, *3*, 171
mental, physical and technical demands of, 8, 8f, 10

Rohrbough, Joel, 226–27, 236
rope climbing (Bachar Ladders), 2, 6, 92, 163–64, *164*
rubber bands, 122
running, 101, 208
running intervals, 128
ruptures, tendon, 229

S

Sacherer, Frank, 4
SAID (Specific Adaptation to Imposed Demands) Principle, 14–15, 15f, 95
saturated fats, 195
schema theory, 54–55, 54f
Schmidt, Richard, 52
selenium, 200, 218
self-assessments
Cycle of Improvement, 22–27, 22f
fear management, 36–38
objective evaluations, 18
technical abilities, 60t
tests for, 19–22
weakness targeting, 17–18, 74, 172
self-confidence, 31
self-image, 30
self-massage, *215*, 216
self-talk, 32, 49
Send Me, 76
serial skills, 53
shakeout techniques, 211–12
Sharma, Chris, 32
Sherrick, Mike, 2, 4
shoulders
conditioning exercises for, 122–23, *123*
flexibility stretches for, *105*, 105–6, *106*
injuries and treatments, 235–40
rehabilitation exercises for, *237*, *238*, *239*, *240*
side hip raises, 113, *115*
side pulls, 66, 134, *135*
side pulls, reverse, 65, 66, 134, *135*, 136
Single-Leg Squats, *119*, 119–20
skills
acquisition rates, 55–56, 56f
definition, 53
learning and practicing, as training subtype, 13, 51

motor learning theories and, 52–53
practice strategies for, 56–58
schemas, 54–55, 54f
strength/fitness *vs.*, relationship, 13–14, 14f
tips for development of, 59
training drills for, 74–77
transference of, 55
types of, 53–54
Skinner, Todd, *7*, 142
sledgehammers, *121*, 122
sleep habits, 214–15, 218–19, 245
slow twitch (ST) muscle fibers, 80–81, 81f, 96
smiling, 41
smoking, 212, 234
Specific Adaptation to Imposed Demands (SAID)
    Principle, 14–15, 15f, 95
specificity, 85, 88, 131
speed training, 77, 91
sport climbing
    SAID Principle and, 15, 15f
    training focus, 95, 126, 127, 149
    as training program subdiscipline target, 176–77
Sportklettern Heute (Güllich), 6
sport massage, 213, *215*, 215–17, 218, 231
sports drinks, 202–3
Sports Illustrated, 4
Sports Massage (Meagher), 215
Sports Medicine (journal), 223
sprains, 229
stability, 62–63, *65*, 66
stabilizer muscles, 80
stamina training. *See also* anaerobic endurance
    (A-E) training; endurance training
    for big-wall and alpine climbers, 129
    for boulder, sport and multipitch climbers,
        127–28
    overview, 126–27
    for strength training, 95–96
    tips for, 129
Steep-Wall Lock-Offs, *161*, 161–62
Steep-Wall Traversing, 118
steroids, 219
Stick Game, The, 76
Straight-Arm Fingerboard Hangs, 154–55

strength
    climbing ability correlation with, 10
    definition, 88
    skill *vs.*, relationship, 13–14
strength and fitness training
    anaerobic endurance (A-E) training for, 93–95
    bouldering as, 90
    climbing ability correlation with fitness, 10
    complex training for, 96–97
    concepts of, 88–91
    exercise physiology and, 80–84, 81f, 83f, 84f
    female climbers and, 187
    functional isometrics as, 90–91
    goals of, overview, 172f
    hypergravity training as, 90
    physiological adaptations to, 88, 89f
    power training for, 91–93, 92f
    principles of, 84–88
    skill *vs.* fitness relationship, 13–14, 14f
    stamina training and, 95–96
    as training subtype, overview, 13, 79–80
strength deficits, 82
strength gains, rates of, 89–90
stress, 31, 38–41, 216–17, 219
stretching. *See also* warm-ups
    abdominals, 109–10, *111*
    arms, 102, *105*, 105–6, *106*
    back, 107, *107*, 110–11, *111*
    buttocks and lower-back, 107, *107*
    fingers, 102–4, *103*, *104*
    groin, 108–9, *109*
    as injury treatment, 231
    legs, *108*, 108–10, *109*, *110*
    overview, 102
    to prevent injuries, 244
    for recovery acceleration, 218
    shoulders, *105*, 105–6, *106*
ST (slow twitch) muscle fibers, 80–81, 81f
subdiscipline targeting, 176–77
subluxation, 236
Sullivan, Alyssa, *191*
supercompensation. *See* recovery
supplements, 199–205, 218, 230, 231, 232
surgery, 226, 229, 236, 241
surgical tubing, 3

water intake, 198–99, 210, 212, 213, 218
weight
   center of gravity, 60, *61*
   hypergravity training with additional, 90, 139, 140, 146t
   rest positions and, 64
weight belts, 139, 159
weight control, 96
weight pull-ups, *5*
whey, 201
Williams, Dick, 3–4
women. *See* female climbers
Woods, Daniel, *220*
workout schedules
   for accomplished (intermediate) climbers, 180–84, 180f, 182t, 183t
   for beginner (novice) climbers, 178–80, 178f, 179t
   for elite (advanced) climbers, 184–86, 184f, 185t

   injury prevention and, 244–45
   macrocycles, 175–76, 176f
   mesocycles, 174–75, 174f, 175f
   microcycles, 173–74
worry rituals, 43
wrist curls, *120*, 121–22

X

X finger taping method, *228*

Y

Yaniro, Tony, 88
Yosemite's Camp 4, 4–5
youth climbers, 190–91, *191*, 230, 232

Z

zinc, 200
"zone, the," 30

ABOUT THE AUTHOR

An accomplished climber of more than thirty years, Eric J. Hörst (pronounced *hurst*) has climbed extensively across the United States and has established more than 450 first ascents. A student and teacher of climbing performance, Eric has personally helped train hundreds of climbers, and his training books and concepts have spread to climbers in more than fifty countries. He is widely recognized for his innovative practice methods and training techniques, and since 1994 he has served as a training products design consultant and online Training Center editor for Nicros, Inc., a leading manufacturer of climbing walls and handholds.

Eric is author of *Conditioning for Climbers, How to Climb 5.12,* and *Learning to Climb Indoors,* all of which have foreign translations. He regularly contributes to outdoor and fitness magazines such as *Climbing, Rock and Ice, Urban Climber, Outside, National Geographic Adventure, Men's Health, Muscle and Fitness, Experience Life,* and *Men's Journal,* and he has appeared on numerous TV broadcasts. Eric broadcasts twice-monthly *Training Tip* podcasts at PodClimber.com. Visit Eric's Web site, Training-ForClimbing.com, for training articles and information on all his books, or to schedule a training seminar, an editorial interview, or speaking engagement.

Eric currently lives in Lancaster, Pennsylvania, with his wife, Lisa Ann, and his sons, Cameron and Jonathan.

Conditioning for Climbers (FalconGuides, 2008) is the ultimate manual for climbers who are looking to improve their physical capabilities. Regardless of your age, ability, or sports background, this book will empower you to develop and engage in a supremely effective conditioning program. The book follows a logical progression of self-assessment, goal setting, general conditioning and weight loss, core conditioning, and climbing-specific training to develop strength, power, and endurance. The text concludes with guidance in developing a personalized conditioning program, complete with tips on preventing injury and improving nutrition for peak performance.

How to Climb 5.12 (FalconGuides, 2003) is a performance guidebook to attaining the most rapid gains in climbing ability possible. It provides streamlined instruction on vital topics such as accelerating learning of skills, training the mind and body, and becoming an effective on-sight and redpoint climber.

Learning to Climb Indoors (FalconGuides, 2006) is the most complete book available on indoor climbing. Topics covered include beginning and advanced climbing techniques, tactics, strategy, basic gear, safety techniques, self-assessment, and a primer on mental training and physical conditioning. This guide includes everything you need to know from day one as a climber through your first year or two in the sport.